THE SECRET O.
HAPPINESS

THE SECRET OF HAPPINESS

OR, SALVATION THROUGH GROWTH

EDMOND HOLMES

GYAN

Published by

Gyan Publishing House
5, Ansari Road
Daryaganj, New Delhi-110002
Phone: 011-47034999, 9811692060
E-mail: books@gyanbooks.com

Distribution Network
gyanbooks.com
India, USA, Canada, UK, Australia

ISBN: 978-93-7447-285-9 (PB)

First Published, 1919

2nd Impression 2026

Printed at: Gyan Press, Delhi.

THE SECRET OF HAPPINESS
Author: EDMOND HOLMES

THE SECRET OF HAPPINESS

OR, SALVATION THROUGH GROWTH

What in ill thoughts again. Men must endure
Their going hence even as their coming hither.
Ripeness is all. SHAKESPEARE—*King Lear.*

Whether we be young or old,
Our destiny, our being's heart and home,
Is with infinitude, and only there;
With hope it is, hope that can never die,
Effort and expectation and desire,
And something evermore about to be.

WORDSWORTH—*The Prelude.*

Unity itself divided by Zero will give Infinity.
Make thy claim of wages a zero, then;
thou hast the world under thy feet.

CARLYLE—*Sartor Resartus.*

THE SECRET OF HAPPINESS

OR

SALVATION THROUGH GROWTH

BY

EDMOND HOLMES

Author of "What Is and What Might Be"
"The Tragedy of Education," "In Defence of What Might Be," &c.

LONDON
CONSTABLE AND COMPANY LTD.
1919

INTRODUCTION

EVER since I began to read for "Greats" at Oxford I have been trying to think out the great problems that perplex us all. It did not take me long to discover that if I was to bring order into my thoughts I must try to write them down. The attempt to do this led to the further discovery that, unless I could combine sincerity with lucidity in writing, I could not hope to attain to sincerity and lucidity of thought. There seemed to be a close connection between sincerity and lucidity; but sincerity was my first concern. When I had written a passage I would read it over and ask myself: Is this what I am really trying to say? This question gave rise to another: Is this what I really think? Thus my attempt to give expression to my thoughts led me to scrutinize them continuously. Under the searchlight of my scrutiny new aspects of, new subtleties in, my thoughts began to disclose themselves, and these in their turn demanded, and were duly reacted upon by expression.

As time went on I made a third discovery—that the interaction of thought and expression was a process to which there were no limits, and therefore that there could be no finality in thinking. But it was not till middle life that this discovery came home to me as a conviction. When I was young I had the ardour and audacity of youth, and I thought myself quite competent to construct a complete system of thought. I did in fact construct such a system, a bulky work in three parts (each of which, if printed, would have filled a stout volume) which bore the portentous titles of (1) Method; (2) System; (3) Proof. When I had finished this work I found that I had begun to outgrow it, and I made no attempt to publish it. Undismayed by my failure, I set to work at another system; but when the end of it was in sight I found that the point of view from which I had approached my subject was ceasing to interest me, and I left the work unfinished.

Since then I have published many books, but I regard them all (with the doubtful exception of one or two volumes of verse) as by-products of my central effort to construct an adequate theory of things. For, though the direct results of that effort had been elaborate failures, the effort itself had not been wasted. It had helped me to evolve an unformulated creed, which, besides throwing light on the path of my own life, provided me with a base of operations from which to attempt the solution of some of the large problems that revolve, like satellites, round the largest of all. For example, when I had served as a School Inspector for more than thirty years, it suddenly dawned upon me that a man's theory of education ought to be governed by his theory of life; and straightway, guided by my own theory of life, I began to think and write about education. In my published books I have made free use of my two unpublished "systems of thought," having not only embodied in the former some of the ideas which I had elaborated in the latter, but having also treated the two derelict structures as quarries from which I could take at will the materials that I needed for my less ambitious ventures.

I now come to the main purpose of this bit of autobiography. In this, my third attempt to untie "the master knot of human fate," I have, not unnaturally, entered into partnership with my two former selves and made use, as I thought fit, of the fruits of their labours. It is therefore possible that there are passages in this work (apart from one or two which I have deliberately quoted) which have already appeared in print. If this is so, I must ask to be excused for having repeated myself (without a suitable apology), on two grounds. The first is that in order to make sure of avoiding those "undesigned coincidences" I should have had to read through all my published prose works, a task for which I had neither time nor inclination. The second is that if I have unwittingly repeated myself, the repeated passages belong more properly to this book, as the heir-at-law of its two unpublished predecessors, than to those in which they first saw the light. I may add that a booklet which I recently published, called *The Problem of the Soul,* has always belonged to this book, and now takes its place in it, slightly modified, as the second of its five parts.

Having said so much about myself I will ask leave to say a little more. I have no learning, and no head for metaphysics. Why, then, have I presumed to concern myself with these great matters? Because the choice of a creed rests, in the last resort, with the individual consciousness. Because one exercises the right of private judgment, even in the act of renouncing it. Because submission to dogmatic direction, though it may sterilize interest and capacity, cannot relieve one from responsibility for the ideas that dominate one's life. Because, if that responsibility is accepted, the demand which it makes upon one ought, as far as possible, to be met in full. Because, above all, the problems which I am trying to solve are of interest, not to experts only, but also, and more especially, to "plain average men," of whom I am one. If I have any advantage over other plain average men, it is that I have kept alive a strain of poetry (if I do not flatter myself unduly) which is, I believe, innate in most of us, but which many men, under the deadening pressure of education and other adverse forces, allow to die out of their lives. This strain of poetry, by vitalizing my intuition, has saved me from being enslaved to my own theories, and through its solvent influence has prevented my convictions from crystallizing into dogmas, and has kept them fluid and mobile. It is not by the exercise of reason alone that man works his way towards the truth of things, but by the maintenance of what I may call a progressive balance between reason and intuition, between conscious thought and subconscious "vision." This means, I suppose, that the dream of attaining to certitude or even to mental repose in this exalted region must be abandoned, and that the quest of ideal truth must be regarded as an end in itself. I, for one, am well content that this should be so. To find final satisfaction in mental unrest is to bid defiance to perplexity and doubt. This indeed is the lesson which I learned in middle life, when I discovered that there were no limits to the interaction of thought and expression.

But I could not then fathom its depth of meaning. To emphasize that lesson, to convince myself that high thinking (like real living) is in very truth an adventure into the infinite, and that as such it is the only solution which its own problem admits of, is one of the main purposes of this book. It will perhaps be objected that fluidity of belief is incompatible with fixity of purpose. But there is an obvious answer to this possible objection. It is with rigidity, not with fixity, of purpose that fluidity of belief is incompatible ; and rigidity of purpose—fixity of means, as well as of aim—is weakness, not strength. What fluidity of belief (if it is not allowed to degenerate into indifference) does to purpose, is to give it that elasticity of fibre which makes it both pliable and strong. It is, I admit, a difficult matter to keep belief fluid, to avoid the opposite extremes of dogmatic rigidity and agnostic indifference. But the attempt is worth making, even though it involve the labour of a lifetime ; for, with the higher agnosticism, with the faith which is so secure that it does not ask to be formulated, there will come into one's life a large tolerance, a wide sympathy, a far-reaching hope, and a deep peace.

CONTENTS

PART IV

The Process of Growth

PART V

The Fruits of Growth

THE SECRET OF HAPPINESS

PART I

THE FAILURE OF FEUDALISM

CHAPTER I

THE PRESENT DISCONTENT [1]

IF the secret of happiness was ever ours we have lost it for a while. For where there is happiness there is joy and there is peace. But to-day, instead of joy there is widespread discontent; and instead of peace there is a world-encompassing wave of unrest.

So true are these words that it is difficult to say anything in support of them which is not the statement of a truism. The resources of the material world are being developed with ever-increasing rapidity, and the wealth of what we call the "civilized world" is increasing by leaps and bounds. But the increase of wealth does not bring with it increase of happiness. The rich are not satisfied with their riches. For, if they were, they would not labour unceasingly to add to them. The middle classes are not satisfied with their bourgeois comforts. For the standard of comfort is continuously rising; so that what is luxury in one decade is mere comfort in the next, and may well become squalor in the third. The poor are not satisfied with their poverty; and it is among the more prosperous classes of "workers" that discontent is rifest and keenest. For the rise in the standard of comfort,

[1] This chapter was written before the Great War began. See the opening paragraph of the next chapter.

though the middle classes suffer most from it, affects all classes from highest to lowest; and the result of it is that the richer we grow and the more millionaires we breed, the poorer we become. It is to this practical paradox that the all-absorbing hunt for wealth, which makes our inequalities more and more oppressive and our contrasts more and more offensive, is gradually leading us.

When we look at things from the standpoint of social position—a standpoint which is ever tending to coincide with that of wealth—we see that similar influences are at work. The multiplication of social grades is one of the by-products of our growing wealth. It is said that even in an English village there are seven distinct grades, and that between grade and grade there is little or no social intercourse. When social gradation seems to have been fixed by "Providence," men are willing to acquiesce in it; but when it is in a state of incessant flux, discontent is at once the cause and the effect of its mobility. Each grade in turn is envious of the grade above it and strives to rise to its level. Yet the highest grade of all is perhaps the least contented; for the pleasure of effort and pursuit is withheld from it; and on its summit, to which all its inferiors aspire, instead of the sunshine of joy and love, there is a wet mist of boredom and ennui.

From East to West and from West to East the atmosphere of the world is impregnated with discontent and unrest. In this and other Western countries class hatred is one of the passions which the demagogue deliberately exploits. "Strikes" and "lock-outs" are more numerous and on a larger scale than they have ever been. A world-wide war between Labour and Capital seems to be imminent, if it has not actually begun. For both sides are organizing their armies; and some at least of the current strikes and lock-outs must be regarded as "reconnaissances in force."

Even the immobile East is in travail with enormous changes. In India there is much political unrest, which is not the less serious because its aim is uncertain and its scope undefined. China has recently expelled a dynasty which had ruled her for three centuries, and proclaimed herself a republic. Japan has gone through a series of transformation scenes and become one of the "Great Powers" of the world. And the end of her evolution is not yet; for the ideals of her growing industrialism are at war with those of Bushido, and her traditional reverence for and devotion to authority are being slowly sapped.

Look where we may, we see that authority is being called in question. Our religious creeds are dead or dying, and the churches and sects are being "modernized" with or without their consent. In the political world despotism is confronted by anarchism, while weaker governments think it prudent to legalize rioting and condone acts of *sabotage*. In literature there is a craze for individuality which sets all precedents and unwritten laws at defiance. In art the same tendency leads from paradox to paradox. Impressionism, post-impressionism, cubism, futurism, vorticism, and I know not what other "isms" succeed one another with breathless rapidity; and what was a rank heresy a decade ago is a stale orthodoxy to-day. In music, as in poetry, cacophony is a fashionable affectation and euphony is despised. In social life custom and tradition are openly rebelled against, and restraints of all kinds are systematically flouted. The marriage tie is losing its sanctity, and "the other woman" has become the recognized heroine of romance. Marital authority is an absurd anachronism. Parental authority is going by the board. Our daughters break away from the home and insist on carving out careers for themselves. Woman claims entire equality with man, and tries by methods of assault and battery to wring political enfranchisement from the Government of the day. If we no longer take all our pleasures sadly, the reason is that defiance of the authority of decorum adds a zest to some of them which they formerly lacked. The chaperon has long since vanished from the ball-room; and the liberty which came in with her departure is degenerating into open licence.

And side by side with the revolt against authority goes on that pursuit of external ends which (as we shall presently see) the régime of external authority imposed upon the world. As the belief in a "future life" and "another world" wanes, the desire to live with the whole energy of one's being in a materialized "this world" and a secularized "this life" grows apace. So strong and so widespread is the "mania for owning things," so large a part does it play in politics as well as economics, that the hunt for wealth has now become national as well as individual, and is even threatening to involve the Great Powers, through their competition for markets and sources of supply, in a series of world-convulsing wars.

But, swift and far-reaching as is the succession of changes through which human society, in its present state of feverish unrest, is passing, man's knowledge of the outward world and his mastery of its resources keep easily ahead of all other aspects of his progress. In science discovery follows discovery; in applied science invention follows invention; and some at least of these triumphs of human ingenuity are bidding fair to revolutionize the material conditions of life. The mysterious forces of electricity are being pressed, more and more, into the service of man. The waterfalls of the world transmit their power to great cities hundreds of miles away, where they light the streets and houses and work innumerable factories. The petrol-engine, having enabled us to traverse the high roads with the speed of an express train, is now beginning to open a new era in marine navigation, and is also giving man the long-sought mastery of the air. Telegraphs and telephones—wired and wireless—the gramophone, the cinematograph and the rest are helping us to annihilate time and space. And so on. Yet men are not a whit the happier for all these achievements. Nay, they add to the fever and unrest of the age. For new ends are perpetually set before us which our externalized desires are unable to resist. "Respectability" was once content with a "gig." Now it is content with nothing less than a motor-car. And it will not be long before it aspires to an aeroplane or an airship. And when its votary soars through the air he will be no happier than when he rushed along or even than when he jogged along a dusty road.

Matthew Arnold has described in familiar lines an age which had much in common with ours, though the sphere of its activities was far narrower, the resources at its command far smaller, and the fever of its unrest proportionately less :—

In his cool hall, with haggard eyes,
The Roman noble lay;
He drove abroad, in furious guise,
Along the Appian Way.

He made a feast, drank fierce and fast,
And crowned his hair with flowers;
No easier nor no quicker passed
The impracticable hours.

Our Appian Way is the Portsmouth Road, which we traverse on Sundays "in furious guise," racing down to Hindhead (where we lunch) and back to Ockham or Ripley (where we have tea) and on to London, in clouds of dust of our own upstirring. And we "make feasts" and "drink fierce and fast" at the Ritz, the Carlton, and the Savoy. But for us too the hours prove "impracticable"; and strive as we may to kill Time, we cannot speed its passing. Even the "working classes," as we call them, are infected with the microbe of *ennui*. They clamour for shorter hours of work; but when their playtime comes they find that it hangs heavy on their hands. The "dullness of the country" drives the sons and daughters of the peasantry, in quest of cheap amusement, into the slums of the great towns; and there, in the gin palaces, or on the football ground, or at the music-hall, or at the picture theatre, they labour assiduously to lighten the heavy burden of their scanty leisure.

It might be thought that this "incredible whirl and rush" was due to some widespread upwelling of originality and will-power. But this is not so. There are leaders of revolt as of all other movements; but the rank and file of men are as passively obedient as they ever were. In their reaction against authority as such, they do but substitute one authority for another,—the demagogue or the "boss" for the emperor or the king, the caucus for the junta, the "cartel" for the secret council, the "union" for the guild, syndicalism for feudalism, a negative for a positive dogmatism, fashion for custom, unstable opinion for unwritten law.

Our anxiety to keep abreast of all the changes of fashion (in conduct, as in dress) and to know what is the right thing to do (as well as to wear) is almost pathetic in its earnestness and singleness of heart; and our loyalty to the most inconstant of all mistresses outrivals the loyalty of a clan to its chief. For blindness of devotion, indeed, our anarchical loyalty has never been equalled. Authority in the past has always professed to be based—in part at least—on regard for and knowledge of such high abstractions as truth, goodness, justice, beauty. The churches have professed to be the exponents of divinely revealed truth. The moral codes, to be the exponents of divinely established law. Kings and parliaments have ruled in the name of justice and order. The canons of taste which have tyrannized over letters and art have been formulated in the name of beauty, the laws of which they were supposed to express. But we obey the fashion of the moment just because it is the fashion of the moment, and not because it is supposed to be right or just or beautiful or true. The ideal that sways us is in fact the negation of all ideals, just as the authority to which we are loyal is the negation of all authority. We may flatter ourselves, if we please, that ours is freer than most ages from hypocrisy and cant; but there is something of cant in our horror of all cant, and something of hypocrisy in the mask of moral earnestness which our cynicism wears when we denounce hypocrisy. The young cynic, fresh from Oxford or Cambridge, who professes to have emancipated himself from all conventions, is a conventionalist to his finger-tips. He repudiates the conventions of yesterday because it is the correct thing to do so—in other words, because he is unable to resist the pressure of a convention of to-day.

Nor need we flatter ourselves that, because our experiences are many and varied, we are living our lives more fully than we used to do. If anything, we are living them less fully, for change follows change so quickly that we never have time to settle down to the business of living—

> And never once possess our souls
> Before we die.

"A mad world" our forefathers would say if they could revisit it. But there is something of method in its madness. The very paradoxes in which we are doomed to entangle ourselves show that the master words of our speech are changing their values while we are using them, and therefore that an old order of things is passing away and a new order beginning to stir into life. Meanwhile the zeal with which we throw ourselves into the successive changes of fashion, and the rapidity with which change follows change show that, in spite of ourselves, we are seeking in deadly earnest for something which we have lost (if indeed it was ever ours) —seeking it in deadly earnest, yet with the aimlessness and inconsequence of one who, having lost a valued treasure, has not the least idea where to begin his search or how to conduct it. The treasure which we have lost is the secret of happiness. The very fever of our unrest, the very bitterness of our discontent tell us this. When, if ever, did we possess that greatest of all treasures, and where and how are we to begin to seek for it ? If we are to answer these questions, we must first ask ourselves what is the old order of things which is passing away, and what is the new order of things which is beginning to stir into life ?

CHAPTER II

THE GENESIS OF FEUDALISM

THE foregoing chapter was written before the Great War began. In the unrest which it describes there were two main currents.

The first was economic and social. The poor were restless with discontent and envy ; the rich were restless with still unsatisfied ambition, or with the Nemesis of satisfied ambition—ennui. With this movement we need not at present concern ourselves.[1] The cure for economic and social discontent will not be found until a larger problem has been solved.

The other was a deeper current—vaguer, obscurer, less self-conscious, more spiritual. It may perhaps be characterized as the unrest of revolt—revolt against the galling pressure of authority in general, and in particular of convention, custom, tradition, and dogma—a movement which was in some sort controlled and even directed by the very forces that were being resisted and defied, and which was therefore confused, chaotic, and uncertain of its meaning and its aim. When the War came, this movement, this blind revolutionary ferment, this undisciplined struggle for moral, social, and intellectual freedom changed its character. Germany stood forth as the champion and embodiment of autocratic authority ; and the Allied nations were therefore compelled, consciously or unconsciously, willingly or unwillingly, to take up the cause of freedom and make it their own. This meant that the forces of revolt were gradually directed into other and worthier channels than those which they had

[1] So far as the pre-war unrest was due to ennui, to boredom, to the eye not being satisfied with seeing, nor the ear filled with hearing, the War, with its absorbing interests and its insistent demands for strenuous service, provided an effective remedy for it.

been striving to cleave for themselves,—into the channels of patriotism, of self-devotion, of self-imposed discipline, of moral indignation, of hatred of cruelty and injustice, of pity, of tolerance, of brotherly love. And while this was happening, the follies, frivolities, and eccentricities of the pre-war movement were being gradually swamped by the rising tide of high purpose and stern resolve, and by a growing sense of the seriousness and profound significance of life, —a sense which was fostered in no small measure by unwonted familiarity with death.

With this change in the character of the revolt against authority has come a clearer perception of what was and is at stake. Prussia, the evil genius of Germany, is felt to be the last and most formidable stronghold of feudal tyranny; and the War is resolving itself, in the last resort, into a struggle between autocracy and democracy, between self-will and self-preservation, between the claim to dominate others and the right to live one's own life. We are beginning to realize that these are the forces which were blindly struggling for mastery before the War began, and which in the heat of their chaotic conflict, with all its cross-currents and cross-purposes, generated the ferment of lawlessness and unrest that was characteristic of those tumultuous but, as we now see, prophetic years.

Seen from another point of view, that struggle was and is the effort of a new order of things to free itself from bondage to the old. What the new order is we can but dimly discern, for it has yet to reveal itself; and though we believe that it will give us a fuller measure of freedom than we have hitherto enjoyed, we cannot say how it will do this or in what scheme of life it will ultimately express itself. But the features of the old order have long been familiar to us; and now that the Central Powers, under German leadership, have made themselves its champions and have put its principles into practice with German logic and thoroughness, we see its inner meaning and its ulterior purport more clearly than we had ever done before. This is a gain to those who are trying to understand the new order and prepare for its advent. For to know what the old order stands for is to know what the new is in revolt against; and as this revolt is an effort at self-expression, as it has living principles and spontaneous tendencies behind it, it is clear that the more carefully we study the old order, the better shall we be able to forecast the features of the new.

The old order of things is, in a word, *Feudalism.* As a formal system, feudalism passed away long ago, but as an informal system—social, political, economic, and ethical—as a principle of order, as an ideal of life, it is still with us; and though it seems to be dying, its power of rallying is almost inexhaustible; and if it is now *in extremis,* its death-bed struggles are of almost superhuman strength.

What was—and is—essential in feudalism is the exercise of irresponsible authority by those who rule. Mediæval feudalism had, in addition to this, two differential features which intensified the pressure of irresponsible authority on human life and gave a distinctive and lasting bias to its influence on character and conduct. In the first place, irresponsible authority was spiritual as well as secular. The period during which the "feudal system" prevailed was the period in which the power of the Catholic Church was greatest and its position most secure. In the second place, in the secular world irresponsible authority was exercised, largely if not wholly, by a ruling *caste.* The feudal system covered the land with a multitude of petty autocrats (the feudal lords). This led to the formation of an autocratic caste and, as the natural result of this, to the outgrowth of the feudal *spirit,*—a spirit which gained strength from its informal alliance with the spirit of ecclesiastical domination, and which is still in the ascendant in the upper classes of Western Society.

By irresponsible authority I mean authority which, professing to be based either on supernatural sanction or on superior force, does not feel called upon to justify itself to those whom it governs and has no sense of responsibility towards them. Those who exercise irresponsible authority are not necessarily indifferent to the welfare of their subjects. On the contrary, they usually profess to have their welfare at heart; but they claim that they alone are competent to provide for their welfare and that they alone have the right to do so. Where authority is irresponsible, we have the strange though familiar spectacle of a small minority, who are in no sense representative of those whom they govern and are but little in touch with them, professing to know what is best for the welfare of the community as a whole, and taking measures to impose well-being (as they interpret the word) on the rank and file of their fellow-citizens, without allowing them to have any say in the matter, and without realizing that well-being is not well-being (in the deeper sense of the word) unless men have helped to evolve it for themselves. The particular embodiment of irresponsible authority, of which we in the West have felt and still feel the pressure, is feudalism; and the passing of feudalism is therefore the passing of a tradition which for many centuries has socialized and moralized us and otherwise moulded our lives.

Feudalism is the child of Supernaturalism, the God of supernatural religion being the feudal Over-lord of the earth and all its races and nations. Supernaturalism is the child of Dualism, the "Yes *or* No" of popular thought finding its last and most comprehensive expression in the disruption of the Universe into Nature and the supernatural world. Dualism is generated, in part by the inadequacy of language—its inability to measure the range and subtlety of Nature—and by the reaction of its defects and limitations on human thought; in part by the spiritual indolence of the average man, by his reluctance to think out the great problems of existence, and by his readiness to accept the excuse for evading that responsibility, which the inadequacy of language provides. The task of measuring, or at least of making due allowance for, the infinite range and infinite subtlety of Nature is one of almost insuperable difficulty for even the most serious of thinkers; and it is no matter for wonder that popular thought, reluctant to grapple with so formidable a problem, should take refuge in dualism, in ignorance of the heavy price which it will have to pay for delivering itself into bondage to "the Opposites."

That price is the ascendency of supernaturalism, in religion, in morals, and at last, under a thin disguise, in social, political, and economic life. The transition from dualism to supernaturalism is easily traced. Consciously, the average man, who is in large measure sense-bound, regards the outward and visible world as intrinsically real. Unconsciously, or subconsciously, he feels that there is a higher reality in himself. But the fact that he consciously seeks for reality outside himself constrains him, as a thinker, to project the inward reality of which he is dimly aware into the outward world,—not into the outward and visible world which he calls Nature, but into an outward and invisible world which he calls supernatural. Had he been able to merge himself, with all his higher possibilities, in Nature, the need for a supernatural world would not have arisen. And if he were able to identify supernature with higher Nature, the fundamental fallacy of supernaturalism would correct itself. But, as a thinker, he comes under the control of his only available medium of expression—language; and the inherent dualism of language reflects itself in the dualism of his thought, the antithetical terms in which language abounds—*good* and *bad*, *high* and *low*, *light* and *darkness*, and the rest—finding their counterpart in his philosophy in a series of quasi-objective antitheses, among which the antithesis of Nature and the Supernatural is central and supreme. The consequence is that, far from identifying supernature with higher Nature, he interposes between Nature and the supernatural world a gulf of separation, an unfathomable and (in the order of Nature) impassable gulf, into which drains unceasingly the reality of both the dissevered worlds.

This separation of reality (or what passes for such) from the supreme source of reality (or what passes for such), this separation—to use familiar words—of Nature from God, must needs have serious consequences which will make themselves felt on every plane of man's being and in every sphere of his life. The glaring contrast between the presumed perfection of the supernatural God and the obvious imperfection of his handiwork—the natural world—necessitates the doctrine of the Fall, the doctrine of the corruption and degradation, first of human nature, and then of Nature as such, through a primal act of disobedience on the part of Man. The doctrine of the Fall necessitates the doctrine of a supernatural revelation, if the consequences of the Fall are not to be irremediable; of the communication of divine grace from Heaven to fallen man; of the selection, for this purpose, of special instruments—chosen prophets, a chosen people, a chosen church; of the delegation of spiritual authority to those recipients of the divine grace; of the achievement of "salvation" through blind and quasi-mechanical obedience to supernatural direction instead of through the vital processes of natural growth.

From supernaturalism to feudalism the path is open and straight. The supreme source of spiritual authority and the supreme source of secular authority are obviously one. In other words, the God of supernatural religion is the ultimate owner of the earth and all its material resources, and therefore the Overlord of all the rulers of the world; and the authority which he delegates to kings and princes is doled out by them to their vassal nobles and knights, and through these to a hierarchy of officers and officials, till its pressure is felt by all the rank and file of mankind.

The historical genesis of the Feudal System was, I need hardly say, a different thing from the logical genesis of feudalism. It was out of the social and political chaos which preceded and followed the downfall of the Roman Empire of the West that the feudal system arose. Its origin, in this sense of the word, was obscure and complex, and I will not attempt to trace it. But if we are able to take a wide and far-reaching view of things, we shall see that the logical genesis of feudalism controlled and even determined the historical. For feudalism, as an all-embracing scheme of life, may be said to have been generated by the confluence of two main streams of tendency,—Roman imperialism and Judæo-Christian ecclesiasticism, the latter being an expansion and modification of Jewish legalism; and in each of those streams of tendency the ruling principle was distrust of human nature, and faith in obedience to external authority as the only means of salvation, the only way to happiness, well-being, and life.

Republican Rome, by the force of her character and the might of her arms, gained the whole world—the whole Mediterranean world—and in doing so lost her own soul.

A republic might conquer an empire, but for obvious reasons could not govern it. It was only by concentrating all authority in the hands of one supreme ruler that chaos could be averted or rather that its advent could be delayed. The consequent transformation of the Republic into an Empire was, in the world of ideas, a revolution of the first magnitude. Instead of ascending from the base of the social pyramid, or from some intermediate level, and then descending from the apex, authority now entered the community from above, and, without attempting to justify itself to its subjects, demanded their implicit obedience.[1] "The State," says Treitschke, in words which might have been written eighteen centuries ago, "is in the first instance power. It is not the totality of the people itself. . . . On principle it does not ask how the people is disposed: it demands obedience." Whence the State derives its power Treitschke does not make clear; but in the days of Imperial Rome there was, in theory at least, no uncertainty on this point. The deification of the Emperors based itself on the assumption that the ultimate source of authority was not in human nature but in the supernatural world.

The triumph of Judæo-Christian ecclesiasticism pointed, more directly, to the same conclusion. The history of Rome is the history of the transition from clan to empire. The history of Israel is the history of an analogous movement in the religious world. For the multitude of tribal and civic "false gods" Israel substituted one omnipotent autocrat. This was his unique achievement. But just as Rome transformed political life by conquest, by successful self-assertion, so Israel transformed religion by placing his own national deity on the throne of the Universe. To obey the will of this deity, who combined the functions of ruling the Universe and directing with meticulous care the affairs of a petty nation, was to obey in all its details a minutely elaborated code of law. Under his rule

[1] In establishing Imperial rule at Rome, Augustus, the first of the Emperors, paid due regard to the *form* of the Republican Government; but, while thus "saving the face" of the old régime, he took good care to concentrate the reality of power in his own hands. His successors, abandoning the pretence of being constitutional rulers, played the autocrat without let or hindrance.

the distinction between the religious and the secular life became effaced, not through the secular life being transfigured by an inward and spiritual conception of duty and destiny, but through its being invaded and at last overrun by a casuistical ceremonialism which professed to expound to man the high purposes of God. This invading wave reached its high-water mark in Pharisaism, which, with a fearless and pitiless logic, carried out the first principles of legalism into all their consequences, however repugnant these might be to right reason, to conscience, and to common sense. That Pharisaical Judaism should ever become a universal religion was impossible, for no one code of law could pretend to regulate the lives of all the peoples of the earth; and the more the Jewish law was systematized and elaborated, the less adaptable it became and the less capable of being transplanted to other lands.

Yet it is to Judaism that the Western world owes the religion which it has professed for fifteen hundred years. The explanation of this seeming paradox is comparatively simple. The Jews, whatever may have been their failings, had one great quality. They took religion very seriously—so seriously indeed that, as we have seen, they tried to efface the distinction between the religious and the secular life. It is true that in making this attempt the formalists, who, after a prolonged struggle, were left in possession of the field of national life, inverted the real order of things, materializing the religious life instead of spiritualizing the secular. But the idea of effacing that deadly distinction was so grandly adventurous, that because they entertained it with whole-hearted earnestness—even though their own attempt to realize it ended in abysmal failure—the Jews were privileged to give religion to half the human race. For a serious people will be serious, not only in affirmation, but also, and perhaps more especially, in denial and revolt. It was therefore inevitable that Jewish legalism, by its excesses and abuses, should provoke a fierce reaction against itself. The exponents of this reactionary movement were the prophets of Israel. And the last and greatest of the prophets was the Founder of Christianity. As devotion to legalism reached its climax in the practices of the Pharisees, so the reaction against legalism reached its climax in the teaching of Christ. True to the tradition of his nation, he set himself to efface the distinction between the religious and the secular life. And he achieved his purpose. But he did so by reversing the procedure of the Pharisees, by providing for the spiritualization of man's daily life through the medium of a new and revolutionary conception of God. For whatever may be doubtful as to the character and ultimate purpose of Christ's self-imposed mission, it is certain that he was uncompromisingly hostile to Pharisaism, and that he opposed to its rigid externalism and formalism an inward conception of God—a conception which was spiritual, poetical, intuitive, undogmatic, and even agnostic, in the true sense of that much-abused word.

Could this inward conception of the universal God, could this vision of One who is the life of every life and the soul of every soul, become the animating principle of the new religion for which the Græco-Roman world seemed to be waiting? Alas! no: the times were not yet ripe for so radical a transformation of the religious consciousness. The Jews rejected as a blasphemy a conception of God which was as repugnant to their national egoism as to their theological prejudices. The followers of Christ, who were steeped in the Jewish tradition, who took over-seriously their Master's provisional acceptance—for purposes of argument and illustration—of the Jewish Scriptures, and who were for the most part unable to fathom the profundity of his ideas, subconsciously identified his all-loving "Father in Heaven" with the stern and vindictive God of the Jews, and tried to harmonize the inwardness of the Sermon on the Mount with the externalism of the Old Testament scheme of life. And when Christianity ceased to be the religion of a Jewish sect, its exponents, in their loyalty to its Jewish founder, accepted as divinely true the very conception of God and man which Christ had striven to transform beyond all recognition, and made it—as he found it, not as he left it—one of the corner-stones of their creed. They went further than this. Another corner-stone of their creed was devotion to the person of Christ—devotion which culminated, by a strange irony of fate, in the worship of the apostle of divine immanence as a supernatural God. When this cult was fully established, the tragic misunderstanding of Christ's teaching, on which the structure of orthodox Christianity may be said to have been based, was complete.

Yet the theology of Christianity has always kept open its communications with the theology of Christ. In the doctrine of the Incarnation Christianity has taught that very man is very God. In the doctrine of the Holy Spirit it has taught that the true self of each of us is, in the last resort, divine. But these emancipative doctrines have been either ignored or misunderstood by Christendom. For to obey the will of the immanent God is to obey the laws of man's own highest self. And as those laws must be discovered before they can be obeyed, and as they are to be discovered only by being obeyed, the cult of the immanent God makes demands on human nature—demands for lifelong self-devotion and lifelong self-illumination—to which few men are willing to respond. Hence the failure of Christendom to realize, to live up to, the sublime doctrines of the Incarnation and the Holy Spirit. Hence its tacit rejection of Christ's spiritual message, of his appeal to the inward life and the inward light. Hence its acceptance of the story of the Fall and the doctrine of Original Sin,—a story and a doctrine which shift the responsibility for man's salvation from man to his Maker, who must himself redeem from ruin what he has allowed to fall from grace. Hence the recrudescence of Judaism in Christianity. Hence the triumph of the supernatural over the immanent God, the baser currency, according to its wont, driving the purer out of circulation. Hence the desire of the "believer" to be saved by machinery, instead of by growth and life. Let God formulate his will for mankind, as he did of old for his chosen people, and men will obey it, and in doing so will save their souls alive. With this prayer at its heart, Christianity—inspired by the gracious and commanding personality of Christ, but unable to fathom the spiritual depths of his teaching—set forth to evangelize the Gentiles.

But before Christianity could embark on its career of conquest, one great departure from Judaism must be made. The Law must be left behind. Jewish legalism had long been tending to identify itself with its own Extreme Right, with the formalism, the literalism, and the casuistry of the Pharisees. These had been sternly denounced by Christ. But that was not the only reason why Christianity broke with legalism. The inherent rigidity of the Law, its lack of a supreme ethical principle by which to interpret its own rules, its inability to provide for new cases except by formulating new rules and sub-rules, unfitted it for the task of adapting itself to the various and ever-varying conditions of life which would be met with in other lands and other ages. What Cardinal Newman says of a formula holds good of a rigid system : it " either does not expand or is shattered in expanding." It was possession of the Law which had differentiated the Jew from the Gentile ; and it was only by renouncing the Law, that Jerusalem, or any wave of spiritual life and energy that emanated from Jerusalem, could hope to sweep away the barrier between Jew and Gentile and win the latter to the worship of Jehovah.

But if, on the one hand, Christianity was to free itself from the incubus of the Law, and, on the other hand, the principle of salvation through obedience to external authority was to be maintained, how was the will of the supernatural God to be communicated to man ? To this question there could be but one answer. A living organism must take the place of a lifeless system. The Church must take the place of the Law. The priest must take the place of the doctor and the scribe. In no other way could "authority" be conciliated with adaptability, and the oracles of God be interpreted to man by a voice which would never grow old. When these changes had been accomplished, Christianity would be ready to become the religion of the Mediterranean world, Judæo-Christian ecclesiasticism would be ready to take its place by the side of Roman imperialism, and the dawn of the new era would be at hand. That Roman imperialism was then in its decadence, and that the dawn of the new era was therefore bound to be stormy and protracted, is a matter of historical interest on which we need not dwell. It is with the spirit of the new era that we are now concerned.

The confluence of ecclesiasticism and imperialism was not

followed by their fusion. Like the Rhone and the Saône at Lyons, the two rivers flowed side by side in the same channel, but did not merge into a single stream. There was indeed a constant struggle for priority. Sometimes an Emperor deposed a Pope. Sometimes a Pope excommunicated an Emperor. At the beginning of the thirteenth century the Pope came near to being the Suzerain of Christendom as well as the ruler of the Church. A century later the Papacy had come under the domination of monarchical France. More often than not, the Church was the aggressor; and the resistance of King or Emperor to papal aggression was typical of what was going on in every grade and sphere of human life. So long as religion centres in the cult of a supernatural God, the opposition of the secular to the religious life will hold good, and whatever attempts either life may make to absorb the other will fail. For the priest, as the interpreter of the oracles of God, will put forward pretensions which the layman, obedient to the instinct of self-preservation, will strenuously resist. In the consequent struggle, after the first great surrender, the layman will more than hold his own. The vital forces which are making for the evolution of the human spirit will see to that. But he will have paid a heavy price for his victory. For he will have acquiesced in the fatal distinction between the secular and the religious life; and he will have abandoned the latter to the control of the priest, or some other exponent—personal or impersonal—of God's will.

There was another reason why ecclesiastical and secular feudalism, though they had much in common, were unable to blend. The Church was an organic whole. The Empire, in the feudal era, was not. "In theory," says Stubbs, "the feudal system originates in the conquest of a kingdom, which is parted out by the King or general among his followers, who held their shares of him by military service, and subdivided that share to their followers on similar or lower services." Under this system the ownership of land gave the landlord political authority over his tenants, and through these over his sub-tenants. In theory the ownership of all the lands in the realm was vested in the king, who was therefore in his own right the highest source of authority and the highest object of loyalty and devotion. But the king himself had an overlord. Strictly speaking, indeed, he had two. What the vassal lord was to the king, the king was to the Emperor of the West. In theory—but not in practice. Had the empire been genuinely elective, and had the electoral college been composed of all the sovereigns of Western Christendom, the secular overlordship of the Emperor might have been as real and as effective as the spiritual overlordship of the Pope. But the association of the empire with the German crown prevented the Emperor from enforcing, or even asserting, his theoretical ascendency over his fellow sovereigns, who naturally resisted the claim of one kingdom to supremacy over the rest. Though he was obviously needed to complete the symmetry of the feudal structure, such deference as was paid to him was purely sentimental; and, except in Italy, which, as the headquarters of the Papacy, was of special interest to him, he was at best *primus inter pares*. And even in Italy his claim to political supremacy was stoutly and, as a rule, successfully resisted. No: the real overlord of the feudal monarch (if indeed he acknowledged any overlord) was the supernatural God. If the monarch won new lands for himself by conquest, he did homage for them to the God of Battles. If he came into peaceable possession of his kingdom he did homage for it to the Prince of Peace. The divine right of kings—and sub-kings [1]—was of the essence of the philosophy of feudalism; and if it was in humility that the king deferred to the overlordship of the Almighty, it was in pride that he proclaimed himself the Lord's Anointed and accepted the crown from the spiritual representative of God.

In the feudal era, then, we have a two-fold descent of authority from God to man, a descent of spiritual authority

[1] By sub-kings I mean "the barons," the feudal lords. In feudal times the king (under God) was, in theory, the sole landowner. When fiefs became hereditary, tenancy changed, in effect if not in theory, to ownership, and the vassal lord became a more or less independent ruler. The degree of his independence varied inversely with the degree of his overlord's force of character—and wealth. Unless the king was himself a powerful feudal magnate, the owner *de facto* of large hereditary estates, he had not the means of enforcing his authority. With the passing of the feudal system, effective sovereignty was transferred in most countries from the barons to the king.

through the Pope, the bishops, and the priests, to the lay members of the Church, and a descent of secular authority through the kings of Christendom and their vassal lords to the rank and file of their subjects. The difference between the two movements was that in the descent of secular authority an all-important link was missing. The kings of Christendom had no human overlord. Each of them claimed to hold his kingdom direct from the Most High, just as if each Archbishop had claimed to be a Vicar of Christ on earth. The result of this was that, whereas in the Church the Pope has been the fountain-head of patronage as well as of authority, in secular Christendom the Emperor exercised neither patronage nor authority outside the fluctuating limits of the Empire, while even within those limits nomination by him to vacant thrones and sub-thrones gave way at an early date to the hereditary transmission of authority, till at last even the Imperial crown became hereditary—*de facto*—in the House of Habsburg, and Imperialism revealed itself as the hollow mockery which it had long been.

But the vital principle of feudalism—the superimposition of authority on the community, as opposed to the inherence of authority in the community—was in no way affected by these distinctions or these changes. The Pope, sitting in the chair of St. Peter, might be the undisputed head of the Catholic Church. The Emperor might be such a nonentity that even in Germany each king or duke or count or knight could claim to rule his subjects as the Anointed of God. In either case what was essential in feudalism was jealously preserved. The ruler, whoever he might be, was neither representative of nor responsible to the ruled. It was for him to command. It was for them to obey. The "State" was no organ of the people, or aspect of the people's life, but a power which had descended upon the community from "Heaven" or some other external source. "On principle" (to repeat Treitschke's words), "it did not ask how the people was disposed. It demanded obedience."

CHAPTER III

SECULAR FEUDALISM

HAPPINESS may be defined as the conscious (or subconscious) realization of well-being; or, more briefly, as the sense of well-being. If we knew what constituted well-being and how it was to be secured, we should have guessed the secret of happiness.

In feudal times a systematic attempt was made by irresponsible authority—authority which was not representative of the people and which gave account to them of none of its ways—to impose well-being on those whom it governed. Feudal authority was, as we have seen, of two kinds—secular and spiritual. Secular authority sought to impose political, social, and economic well-being on its subjects. Spiritual authority sought to impose on them mental, moral, and spiritual well-being.

How far did this two-fold attempt succeed? How did feudalism affect the character, the mentality, and the social life of those who came under its influence? Did it make for the well-being and, through the well-being, for the happiness of mankind? In our attempt to answer this question we shall find it convenient to respect the distinction between secular and ecclesiastical feudalism. For that will enable us to respect another distinction which we must recognize at the outset if we are to bring order into our thoughts. The man who governs his fellow-man without their consent brings pressure to bear on them—pressure which may easily become harmful—from two separate quarters. In the first place he does for them what they ought to learn to do for themselves. In doing this he atrophies certain mental and moral faculties by preventing them from being exercised; and as those mental and moral faculties have many implications and may even be said to cover the whole range of human life, in atrophying them he tends to arrest, or at least to retard, the whole mental and moral development of the subject people. In the second place, he sets them an example of arrogance and ostentation, which they will respond to either by imitating it or by abasing themselves before it, each of these attitudes being the counterpart and correlate of the other. In doing this he tends to externalize and materialize their lives. Under the feudal régime the baneful pressure which emanates from irresponsible authority was intensified in each of its typical aspects. The tendency to arrest development by atrophying faculty was intensified by the fact that the pressure of irresponsible authority was spiritual as well as political, that spiritual feudalism went hand in hand with secular feudalism, and that the influence of spiritual authority went deep into life and left no side of life untouched. And the tendency to externalize and materialize life was intensified by the fact that under the feudal system (the consequences of which have not yet passed away) political power was inherent in the ownership of property, the attractive force of material possessions being thereby raised to an abnormally high power.

Of these two tendencies, it will be found convenient to study the former when we are considering the effect of spiritual feudalism,—the latter, when we are considering the effect of secular feudalism, on the mental, moral, and social development of the Western world. That the two tendencies—and the two kinds of feudalism—interacted unceasingly goes without saying; and if I deal with them separately, it must be understood that I do so for the better ordering of my own thoughts rather than because the line of demarcation between them is clearly defined.

Let us first deal with the tendency of secular feudalism to externalize and materialize human life. History tells us that what might have been expected to happen in the secular world did happen. The fundamental dualism which, in the world of ideas, prepared the way for the feudal era, was bound to reproduce itself, and in point of fact did reproduce itself, in every feudal community. The wide and deep gulf between the supernatural God and Nature reappeared as a wide and deep gulf between those who ruled and those who obeyed. On one side of the gulf were the land-owning classes, a small minority who ruled their fellow-citizens, not as their elected leaders, but as their hereditary lords, their right to rule, though in theory derived from the favour of God, being actually inherent in their might, and their authority over the rank and file of the people being as absolute and irresponsible[1] as that of a flockmaster over his sheep. On the other side were the landless and therefore disfranchised masses, whose lives were ordered for them, so far as authority could order them, without their consent, and who changed masters as a matter of course, whenever a queenly bride brought a principality with her as her dowry, or two kingdoms were united by a royal marriage, just as sheep or cattle change owners when an estate is inherited or sold. The few who ruled had every advantage which power, position, and property could give them. The many who obeyed, being cut off from the higher life of the community, and being socially and economically, as well as politically, oppressed, were poor, helpless, ignorant, and rude. That the former should become proud to the verge of arrogance, that they should exalt themselves as a superior order of beings, that they should look down on their fellow-men as little better than brute beasts, may be said to have been pre-ordained. " In the eyes of the Polish *szlachta*," says the writer who calls himself " Rurik," " it was no greater crime to kill a peasant than a dog." In France the Revolution swept away legalized abuses which bore witness to a similar attitude on the part of the *Seigneur* towards the peasantry on his estates. And the *Jacquerie* in France, the Peasants' War in Germany, and the Peasant risings in this and other

[1] The serfs were the chattels of their lords. Their very bodies belonged to him. The villeins (or *roturiers*), whatever may have been their nominal status, were in effect entirely at his mercy. "There were no other guarantees," says Professor Vinogradoff, "to the maintenance of the rights of the superior rustic than the moral sense and the self-interest of their masters. Should the lords infringe the well-established rights of their subjects, the latter had no court to appeal to and only God could inflict punishment on the oppressors." "On the whole," says the same writer, "serfdom appears as a characteristic corollary of feudalism."

countries were the violent protests of an oppressed and disinherited class against a tyranny which was half contempt, half brutality—and all injustice. Their own theoretical dependence on the favour of Heaven ought perhaps to have taught the feudal magnates humility. In point of fact it was either forgotten or, if remembered, served to swell their pride. Their religion taught them that all men have immortal souls, and are therefore equal in the sight of God; but they paid scant heed to its teaching. The sense of power, the feeling of being able to dispose at will of the lives and destinies of their fellow-men, was too strong for them. The doctrine of human equality counted for little in the eyes of men who were in a position to treat their own fellow-citizens as the dirt beneath their feet. The gulf which separated the rulers from the ruled was impassable and unfathomable; and in its depths the infinitude of the human soul disappeared and was lost to thought.

This was no new departure in the history of mankind. The strong had oppressed the weak, the rich had exploited the poor, the upper classes had despised and held aloof from the lower long before the days of feudalism. In the Græco-Roman world the slave market was a recognized institution; and the slave was counted as a chattel, not as a human being. And even the free proletariat were regarded by their "betters" with aversion and contempt. When Horace said—

Odi profanum vulgus et arceo

he was the spokesman of his class. But feudalism (which came into the world after the abolition of the slave market) by disfranchising the landless and making each landlord an autocratic ruler in his own domain, went far towards enslaving the whole proletariat, including those who in the days of slavery would have been free. At any rate it tended to weaken the weak, to impoverish the poor, to reduce the degraded to a lower depth of degradation. And its general effect was, therefore, to intensify the ruthlessness of the strong, the rapacity of the rich, and the pride and aloofness of those who were highly placed.

These are sweeping statements which need to be freely

discounted; but, as statements of general tendency, they are, I think, correct. The feudal system has passed away, but feudalism survives; and in proportion to the strength of its hold on a country is the arrogance of the upper classes and their supercilious contempt for the lower. The brutality of the discipline in the German army is part of the aftermath of Prussian feudalism, the attitude of the officer towards his men being a faithful reproduction of the attitude of the Prussian landlord-officer of the eighteenth century towards the serfs whom he led to battle. In the Baltic Provinces of Russia, when a German baron gives audience to a tenant, he turns his back on the latter and looks out of a window; and when the tenant has said his say, the baron, with his back still towards him, holds out his hand to be kissed and so dismisses his visitor. In Austria, where there is less brutality than in North Germany, but not less feudal pride, the attitude of the nobility towards the rest of the community is aptly set forth in Prince Windischgraetz's epigram: "Mankind begins with the barons." These are extreme cases, but they help us to realize how the nobles and knights in feudal times bore themselves towards the rank and file of the people. Still more significant, however, because so much more widely spread, is the attitude which the upper classes, even in democratic countries like our own, instinctively adopt towards the lower. They assume that the lower orders are *by nature* rough, rude, brutal, boorish, coarse in their tastes and pleasures, inartistic, unintellectual, incapable of refinement or culture. They forget that for centuries feudalism gave the masses the worst environment that could possibly be devised, and that the conditions under which many of them live to-day, now that the feudal baron has been succeeded by the capitalist, are in some respects even worse than those which prevailed in the Middle Ages. If they could consider the matter without prejudice, they would realize that defects which offend them in the lower orders are probably due to the deadening pressure of an adverse environment rather than to base or tainted blood. But so strongly are they dominated by the tradition of their own inherent superiority, that they assume, almost as a matter of course, that the bulk of their fellow men are of an inferior breed to themselves.

This feeling is a legacy from feudal days. In itself offensive and even anti-human, it is but a faint reflection of the arrogance which the feudal lord drank in, one might almost say, with his mother's milk. Now *arrogance* may be defined as aggressive egoism. Or, as aggressive separatism. Or, as aggressive individualism. What is essential in it is the refusal of the individual to go out of himself into the larger life of sympathy and love, to realize his oneness with his kind. This refusal is whole-hearted and unreserved. The arrogant man holds himself aloof, deliberately and defiantly, from his fellow men. He may, indeed, identify himself with his own caste or order; but only because he prides himself on bearing the hallmark with which his order stamps its members. He may fight for the privileges and work for the aggrandizement of his order; but only because in so doing he will be fighting for his own privileges and working for his own aggrandizement. Even in his relations to his peers he will be ready, when the opportunity comes, to break away from them and play for his own hand. For the communal sentiment, the feeling of unselfish, uncalculating devotion to a common cause, is one which he does not understand. His very loyalty to his leader is too often rooted in self-interest. The Norman knights who fought at Senlac were loyal to their Duke, but their chief motive to loyalty was the promise of plunder. When a feudal monarch was indolent or weak, the selfishness of the vassal lords was free to assert itself, and the community was plunged into civil strife and social chaos. In fine and in brief, the arrogant man, whatever age he may belong to and whatever may be the source of his arrogance, is at heart a self-centred individualist. As such he is sick, though he does not know it, with a mortal malady. If moral goodness is resolvable, as in the last resort it surely is, into forgetfulness of self and sympathy with others, arrogance, which is the direct negation of those qualities, must be regarded as one of the deadliest of moral defects; and the social and political system which could infect a whole section of the community, and that the most exalted and conspicuous, with so anti-human an attitude towards life, must be held to have betrayed the cause of human progress.

If the feudal lord could have kept his arrogance to himself, the moral atmosphere of the community might not have been poisoned by his influence. But he could not keep it to himself. No man can keep his vices to himself. Moral evil is always infectious; and of all forms of moral evil the most infectious is the arrogance of those who are highly placed. If the feudal lord was there to rule and command, he was also there to be envied by those beneath him, perhaps to be admired, certainly to be imitated. The man who is in a position to order life for a multitude of lesser men must be presumed to have solved the problem of ordering life for himself. If such a man, with all the advantages which power, privilege, and property could give him, had not attained to well-being, who could hope to reach that goal? But if he had attained to well-being, and if arrogance was an effluence from that state of blessedness, were those who looked up to him to blame for making him their model and bearing themselves towards their underlings as he bore himself towards them? Just as children instinctively imitate their elders, believing them to be their betters, so do men instinctively imitate those who are, or who are supposed to be, on a higher level of life than themselves.

I have said that feudalism rent the community asunder and interposed an unfathomable gulf between the rulers and the ruled. The truth of this statement is not affected by the obvious fact that in every organized society, whether feudal or democratic, there are many social and administrative grades, and that each of these is at once subordinate to those above it and in a position to dominate those below it. For what happens in the case of one who both rules and is ruled is that the gulf of which I have spoken reappears, or tends to reappear, in his own person and his own life. If he belongs to a highly feudalized society, such as the Prussian State or the German Army, the chances are that he will be alternately servile and arrogant, that he will cringe to-day and make up for it by bullying to-morrow. At any rate, if arrogance is a prominent characteristic of those who are in high places, it is pretty sure to descend, owing to our tendency to imitate what we look up to, from level to level of the social pyramid, and to sink at last to the lowest level of all; for there is no one so lowly that he cannot sometimes, from some point of view, look down on others. We have seen that in an ordinary English village there are many distinct social grades, and that each of these looks down on those beneath it and keeps itself aloof from them "in society." It is probable that on the lower social levels the sense of superiority and aloofness seldom has the strength of undiluted arrogance. Nevertheless the distilled essence of arrogance, however diluted it may be, is always in it.

While arrogance is descending from level to level, a counter vice is ascending to meet and interpenetrate it—the vice of the weak and oppressed, *servility*. And not only does each of these characteristic vices interpenetrate its opposite, but it even ascends or descends, as the case may be, to the very source from which its opposite springs. Just as arrogance descends from level to level till it reaches the very base of the social pyramid, so does servility ascend from level to level till it rises at last to the very apex. The servility of courtiers is proverbial; and the servility of a court favourite to his royal master is only equalled by his arrogance towards the rest of the world.

It is in self-defence rather than from inclination that men become servile. The confession of inferiority which is implicit in the servile attitude is not congenial to the natural man. But if servility is more excusable than arrogance, because less gratuitous and more obligatory, its consequences are not less deadly. The ultimate basis of all right thinking and right doing is the conviction that things are what they are, not what they seem to be or are said to be. Servility abandons this fundamental conviction in favour of the assumption that things are whatever authority may affirm them to be. In other words, it abandons the belief in, and therefore the quest of, the intrinsically real. But the intrinsically real is the same as the ideal; and the ideal controls and finally determines all our moral standards and tests. The servile man externalizes his ideals, and in doing so externalizes his standards of worth and tests of right and wrong. His aim is to satisfy a master, not to satisfy his own higher self; and the approval of a master, not the "inward light" of the soul, is the sunshine of his life.

From externalism to materialism there is but a single step. I have said that the servile man externalizes his ideals. It would be more correct to say that he de-idealizes them. The ideal is nothing if it is not inward and spiritual. When it is externalized it becomes one of a crowd of competing and fluctuating ends. But the ideal is always the One behind the Many. Therefore, when it is externalized it ceases to be. And when idealism dies out of a man's life, materialism takes its place. The pursuit of outward ends becomes all-absorbing. Material possessions and the things that such possessions enable us to secure—position, power, privilege, pleasures, comforts, luxuries, and the rest—come to be regarded as the only prizes that are worth winning.

In feudal times materialism infected the whole community from its apex to its base. If servility was essentially selfish, the servile could at least plead that examples of selfishness were constantly set them in high places, that wherever they looked, self-seeking seemed to be the main business of life. For with feudal arrogance came rapacity, and with arrogance rapacity descended from social grade to grade. The feudal lord was arrogant, brutally and cruelly arrogant, because he had great possessions; and his desire for possessions was insatiable. Pride in possessions, pride in owning what others lack, is a poor kind of pride; but of all kinds it is the most common. Its presence is a proof of the growing externalization of life and the consequent debasement of our standards. The possession of inward goods—the "fruits of the spirit," the goods which are potentially common to all men—can never be a source of pride. Indeed the possession of such goods is incompatible with pride; for the infinitude of the inward ideal humbles a man even while it inspires and transfigures him, and the presence of pride is therefore a proof of spiritual destitution. The possession of outward goods is a source of pride because there are not enough of this world's goods to go round, and those who have more than their share are, in that respect and to that extent, superior to their fellow men.

Under the feudal system the ownership of land gave the owner political power over his tenants. No system could have been devised which would so greatly enhance the attractive force of property or so greatly stimulate rapacity.

And when the feudal system passed away, and political authority and responsibility ceased to be inherent in the ownership of land, the association of power, position, and privilege with property—not with landed property only, but with property of all kinds—remained. The consequence was that the economic changes which succeeded the decay of the feudal system, far from undermining the existing materialism, did but serve to strengthen and broaden its basis. And as from externalism to materialism, so from materialism to individualism there is but a single step. When I say that of this world's goods there can never be enough to go round, I mean that the desire for such goods grows with the possession of them, that the richer we become the higher our standard of luxury and even of comfort rises, and that therefore, for those who seek happiness in material prosperity, there can never be enough goods to go round. It follows that in a materialized society there will always be a scramble for possessions. But a scramble for possessions is of inner necessity an orgy of individualism. "Each for himself and the devil take the hindmost," must needs be the dominant motto. The individual may indeed co-operate with others. But his motive in co-operating will be fundamentally selfish. He will help to enrich others in order that he may enrich himself. In the general scramble for possessions the servile will play their humble parts. Servility is always dictated by self-interest. The poor man is not necessarily servile. A millionaire may, for purposes of his own, be more servile than the meanest of serfs. The end and aim of servility is to win the favour of the rich and powerful, and so secure material benefits at the cost of self-respect. Now what was most deadly in the feudal system was that, as it gave a great stimulus to arrogance, so it made servility almost compulsory. The serf was virtually dependent on his master for the bare means of subsistence. If he did not defer to him, if he did not show him all the outward signs of servility, he was in danger of starving. And when he emerged from serfdom, it was only by deferring to the rich and powerful, by trying—by whatever means—to win their favour and their patronage, that he could hope to rise, however slightly, in the scale of comfort. But in trying to win the favour of the rich and powerful he found himself competing with others, who, like himself, were in a more or less dependent position; and in order to meet their competition he had to fight vigorously and unscrupulously for his own hand. And it was not only for a rise in the scale of comfort, it was not only for an addition to his material possessions, that he competed so fiercely with all who crossed his path. It was also for admission to a higher social grade. In each grade in turn, the able and ambitious men, the men who might have done most for their fellows had they been content to identify their interests with those of the community, were tempted by the prevailing conditions to devote their talents to lifting themselves to a higher level—higher in respect of the three great essentials, property, position, and power—than that on which they had been born. To "rise in the world" on the shoulders of one's fellow men, to win the right to be arrogant, to be looked up to and envied, to look down on others with contempt and self-satisfaction,—this was the supreme prize which attracted ambition and stimulated effort, this was the end and aim of the "competitive selfishness" with which feudalism infected every grade of the community, from the king down to the serf.

It is true that counteracting influences have not been wanting. Wherever the feudal system was superimposed on tribal organization, the tribal sentiment of disinterested loyalty long survived; and the purer the tribalism and the less it had been modified by the reaction of Roman ideals and influences on the tribal invaders of the Empire, the stronger was the sentiment of loyalty and the longer the period of its survival. But from the beginning of the feudal era it was exposed to the undermining influence of that greed for property which is inherent in feudalism. And when the feudal system had passed away, when the capitalist had begun to take the place of the feudal baron, the ascendency of cupidity over loyalty had been securely, though of course not fully or finally, established. Thenceforth cupidity, materialistic individualism, the greed of the individual for property and its inherent advantages, swept through society like the infection of a plague. The rich strove—each for himself—to make themselves richer. The poor, when they were not struggling for the bare means of subsistence, strove—each for himself—to raise their standard of comfort. Out of the consequent state of social chaos there emerged at last a principle of order, which was also, as it happened, a principle of strife. With the advent of the capitalist had come another change which was destined to have disastrous and far-reaching consequences. In feudal times the ownership of property carried with it duties and responsibilities, political and social, as well as rights and privileges. With the passing of the feudal system, the duties and responsibilities ceased to be obligatory, but the rights and privileges remained. It is true that a sense of moral obligation, sustained by and partly based on custom, succeeded the sense of legal obligation; but that too gradually passed away. In the former part of the nineteenth century, the typical property-owner, whether the estate was personal or real, had no sense of moral obligation to his underlings, and no sense of responsibility to society for their welfare: whatever he did for them was pure charity. If he did nothing, and his conscience accused him, he sheltered himself behind the religious fatalism of the age, as set forth in the familiar lines—

> The rich man in his castle,
> The poor man at his gate,
> God made them, high or lowly,
> And ordered their estate,

and claimed the right to do whatever he pleased with his own. To dispute that right was radicalism, socialism, anarchism. The extension of the sphere of his *legal* obligation was the only remedy for his anti-social individualism; and that end was fought for by organized Labour and gradually won. How far was the limitation of the rights of property to be carried? This question is still in dispute. *L'appétit vient en mangeant.* The more Labour won, the more it demanded. As its pressure became stronger, Capital, alarmed for its own security, began to organize itself for purposes of defence and aggression; and trade unions, at one end of the economic scale, were met by trusts, cartels and other combinations at the other. In each case the individual co-operated with his fellows in order to protect his own interests, in order to aggrandize himself. The outcome of this dual movement was an organized war between Labour and Capital which had so far developed as to imperil the stability of the whole structure of Western civilization, when the Great War, provoked by the ambition and rapacity of the nation which is the last stronghold of mediæval feudalism, interrupted its progress and threatened civilization from another quarter.

We can now see what moral and social havoc has been wrought by feudalism. The arrogance with which it infected the landowning classes, and the servility with which it infected the landless, may seem at first sight to be mutually exclusive vices, the one being the vice of a "master," the other of "the herd." In reality they have everything that is vital in common, and are seldom disjoined, being in fact the face and reverse of the same tendency of human nature. That tendency is in the first place *externalism*, the tendency to seek for the real and the good outside oneself instead of in one's own soul. Then it appears as *materialism*, the tendency to ascribe intrinsic reality to outward things and therefore intrinsic value to material possessions, and to desire the latter accordingly. Then, as *individualism*, the tendency to take part in the general scramble for material possessions, and to play for one's own hand in doing so. Then, as *egoism*, the tendency to separate oneself from one's kind, to live for one's own aggrandizement, and to identify this separated, this self-centred personality with the true self. What we call arrogance is an effluence from the egoism of a "master." What we call servility is an effluence from the egoism of a "serf." But as there are few of us who are not at once masters and serfs, he who is arrogant to-day may well be servile to-morrow; and in respect of their ultimate origin and their inner meaning, the two vices are, I repeat, not two but one. By withdrawing from the people political power and political responsibility—which mean in the last resort power to order, and responsibility for the ordering of, one's own life—by associating these prerogatives with the possession of property, and concentrating them in the hands of autocratic rulers and their underlings, feudalism interposed an impassable gulf, first in the life of the community and then in each individual life, between the ruler and the ruled, between the will to power and the instinct to live. It thus destroyed the unity and inward harmony of the human spirit, and based its scheme of life on distrust of human nature and therefore on an appeal to man's selfishness, to the hopes and fears of his lower self.

We are trying to discover the secret of happiness. With this end in view, we are trying to get to the bottom of our "present discontent." The social system under which we are living is a survival from feudal times, and is still deeply infected with the spirit of feudalism. It is to the ascendency, then, of this spirit that our present discontent must be partly due. If feudalism has failed, as it certainly has, to make man happy (our own unhappiness being the aftermath of its failure), the reason is that by associating power, position, and privileges and opportunities of various kinds, not to speak of comfort, luxury, and pleasure, with the possession of property, it has taught us, as no other political system or social scheme of life has done, to lay up treasures for ourselves "where rust and moth doth corrupt and where thieves break through and steal." "For where our treasure is there will our heart be also"; and the heart of man cannot find permanent happiness in material possessions or even in those "good things of life" with which such possessions endow their possessor. A world in which nine men out of ten want what they cannot have, and the tenth man, who has what he wants, is dissatisfied with it, is not in a state of well-being; and where well-being is lacking, happiness, which is the sense of well-being, has not been won.[1]

But feudalism has done more than breed discontent among rich and poor. Obscurer and more subtle forces have been

[1] I have not forgotten that to-day we are supposed to be democratic, not feudal. In point of fact we are very far from having attained to democracy. The explanation of this is that we have tried to build a durable democratic structure on a feudal basis.

at work in it. By basing its scheme of life on distrust of human nature, by withdrawing from the masses powers and responsibilities which are the prerogatives of citizenship, by substituting dependence on embodied authority for reliance on a man's own energies and resources, by underrating and even despising knowledge and enlightenment, by acquiescing in the claim of the Church to dominate thought and conduct, secular feudalism went far towards paralyzing the higher activities of the human spirit and arresting the growth of the soul. And the sinister influences which it set in motion are still active. This is an aspect of the tragedy of feudalism on which I have as yet said little, but on which, as we shall now see, there is much to say.

CHAPTER IV

SPIRITUAL FEUDALISM

IN secular feudalism the pressure of authority on the individual was, directly, political and social; indirectly—and yet predominatingly—moral. For all the other aspects of man's life react upon his morals; and moral conduct makes or mars the man. In spiritual feudalism the direct pressure of authority on the individual was spiritual, mental, and moral; but its direct pressure on his morals, strong though it was, counted for less than the indirect pressure which it exercised through its ascendency over his spirit and his mind.

How did it gain this ascendency? As the first step towards answering this question, let us compare and contrast the religious with the secular world in the days when both were under feudal control. As in the secular world the feudal spirit generated arrogance in the higher social grades and servility in the lower, so in the religious world the same spirit—for at heart it was the same—generated dogmatism in the professional interpreters of the oracles of God, and docility, which easily became ultra-docility, in the rank and file of the faithful. And as in the secular world arrogance descended from the highest social grade to the lowest, while servility ascended from the lowest social grade to the highest, so in the religious world the faithful were dogmatic, from the head of the hierarchy down to the youngest catechumen, and docile, from the youngest catechumen up to the head of the hierarchy. But though the two worlds had so much in common, there was an important difference between them. In the secular world the serf was not taught or even expected to be arrogant. That was a lesson which he had to learn for himself. But in the religious world the docile were deliberately and systematically taught to be dogmatic. Indeed it may be said without exaggeration that dogmatism was the first and the last lesson which the docile catechumen had to learn. What the Church taught him was the truth of things as received from God ; and as it was his privilege to possess the truth, so it was his duty to proclaim it as the truth, and to maintain it, if necessary, against disbelief or doubt. So too in the secular world the feudal lord was arrogant from pride of place, and servile—if at all—reluctantly, and only from motives of self-interest. In the religious world, on the contrary, as the humblest of the faithful was a dogmatic defender of the faith, so the Sovereign Pontiff himself was the docile recipient of the truth as delivered to him by his Divine Overlord.

From this we can see that the relation between dogmatism and docility in the one world was far more intimate than that between arrogance and servility in the other. The two antitheses had much—almost everything—in common ; and in each of them the upward and downward movement which is of the essence of a true antithesis was controlled and limited by a fundamental unity. But whereas in the secular world arrogance could exist apart from servility, and servility apart from arrogance, in the religious world dogmatism was always and of inner necessity docile, and docility was always and of inner necessity dogmatic, each tendency in turn being actually, and not merely potentially, the other self of its opposite.

For this vital difference between the two authorities and the two worlds there were no doubt many reasons. But there was one which at once suggests itself. When Catholic Christianity was at the meridian of its power and glory, the religious world was, what the secular world was not, and had never been—an organic whole. In the secular world there were, as we have seen, many independent kingdoms and sub-kingdoms ; for the Holy Roman Empire was an idea which had never materialized, the so-called Emperor not being master even in his own domain ; and in the absence of a visible overlord to serve as the connecting link between earth and heaven, the feudal lord found it easy to persuade himself that the might of his arms was his right to rule, and easy to forget that he owed homage for his throne to the King of kings. But the Church, though it embraced all the secular states of Christendom, and though its children spoke a hundred different tongues, was a single community, owning one visible Head—the Pope, and one invisible Head—the Son of God. And though its constitution was typically feudal, authority descending upon it from above and being transmitted by a process of devolution from grade to grade, the Church was, in theory at least, a democratic community, in the sense that all who belonged to it, as the possessors of immortal souls, were equal in the sight of God. For these reasons, and also because the Church existed in order to secure salvation—the most precious of all boons—for each of its members, the loyal Churchman had a feeling of devotion to and identity with the society to which he belonged, which had no equivalent in the secular world, even in those communities in which the tribal tradition still lingered and the tribal sentiment of devotion to the community was still strong.

For though feudalism was in a sense the negation of tribalism, the combination of feudal organization with tribal sentiment was by no means rare in the Middle Ages, and still survives, as Europe knows to her cost, in Germany as a whole, and in particular in the Prussian State. But nowhere was the fusion of these opposites so complete as in the Catholic Church. If the organization of the Church was uncompromisingly feudal, if its theory of the soul was profoundly democratic, churchmanship itself, regarded as a sentiment, was the apotheosis of tribalism, transfiguring most of its virtues and exaggerating most of its defects. So completely, indeed, did the loyal churchman identify himself with the Church, that he made its very personality his own and accepted responsibility for all that it said and did and was. If the Church was dogmatic, each of its members was dogmatic. If the Church was ultra-docile, each of its members was ultra-docile. If the Church was intolerant, each of its members was intolerant. If the Church forbade the exercise of private judgment, if it persecuted heresy, if it virtually excommunicated the greater part of the human race, each of its members did the same.

We can now see why the pressure of authority on the individual in the religious world could be, and so often was, overwhelmingly strong. Sharing as he did in the corporate life of the Church, the churchman neither resisted nor resented the pressure of its authority, but on the contrary welcomed it, invited it, and surrendered himself to its influence. In fine, the pressure of the community on the individual was the pressure of the individual on himself. This meant that its influence on him, for good or for evil, was far stronger than it would have been if he had accepted it unwillingly and only under compulsion. What form did that influence take? The antithesis of dogmatism to docility, however much it may seem to efface itself, will always hold good. So let us think of the churchman as the willing victim of dogmatic pressure in spiritual things, and then ask ourselves how such pressure would be likely to affect his character and his life?

Let us first consider the general policy of the Church. While rejecting the Jewish Law as a scheme of conduct, the Christian Church remained unswervingly true to it as a philosophy of life. And what the Jewish Law had done to the human spirit, the Christian Church continued to do. It substituted guidance from without for guidance from within,—guidance into the paths of "Right Knowledge" and "Right Conduct." It explained the Universe to the believer; and, as difficulties arose, it interpreted to him its own explanation. It provided him with a scheme of life; and this too it interpreted, theoretically in its casuistry, practically through the confessional. In each case it did for him what he ought to have tried to do for himself. In explaining the Universe to him and requiring him to accept its explanation as final, it usurped the function of his *reason*. In providing him with a scheme of life and working that scheme out for him in detail, it usurped the function of his *conscience*. It might indeed have given guidance without usurping the function of either organ. But because it gave authoritative guidance—which, indeed, believing itself to be supernaturally guided, it was bound to do—and because its secret desire for domination was met and matched by the believer's secret desire for direction, it carried guidance so far as to arrest what it set out to foster—the growth of the soul.

When I say that the Church usurped the function, first of reason and then of conscience, I do not wish to suggest that its procedure was the same in both cases. Its proscription of conscience, though logically predestined, was indirect and unintentional. It was on reason, and, so far as it knew, on reason only, that it laid its ban. But if it imagined, as it seems to have done, that freedom of conscience was compatible with the suppression or enslavement of reason, its psychology was gravely at fault. We are apt to assume that reason is a dry, hard, impersonal, coldly logical faculty, which exists for the sole purpose of examining positive evidence and drawing logical conclusions. Reason is this, and no more than this, when its subject matter admits of such treatment. But as its true function is to throw light, by whatever means, on things in general, to understand them, to explain them, it must needs suit its procedure and even its character to its subject matter, if the sphere of its work is not to be unduly restricted. And in proportion as its subject matter gains in comprehensiveness and complexity; in proportion as our experience of it becomes individualistic and emotional; in proportion as it tends to make a direct and personal appeal to each of us and to take a fresh shade of colour from each percipient mind,—the coldly logical method of investigation becomes, for obvious reasons, less and less appropriate. Finally, when we exercise ourselves in the greatest of all matters, when we try to understand and explain the Universe, the impersonal, dispassionate treatment of a subject-matter which overwhelms with its infinitude and blinds with its excess of light becomes impossible. It follows that if reason is to deal with these august problems, it must ally itself with the intuitive faculties which culminate in creative imagination —insight, sympathy, taste, tact, conscience, faith, aspiration, and the like—ally itself with these, take them up into itself, assimilate them to itself, interpenetrate them and be interpenetrated by them. This means that, on the highest level of thought, the soul itself, in its unity and totality, is our only available instrument of research, reason being but a name for the soul when it is trying to understand and explain; and that therefore to forbid a man to use his reason for the quest of ultimate truth, is to paralyze his higher activities, to thwart his instinctive, though possibly latent, desire to live to his higher self.

The proof that on these exalted levels of thought reason is intuitive and emotional rather than coldly logical and dispassionately impartial lies in the fact that in banning reason the Church, wittingly or unwittingly (probably the latter), struck a deadly blow at the intuitional side of human nature. Had they not been unduly interfered with, the intuitional faculties would have continued to occupy themselves with great matters under the general supervision of reason,—supervision which in such matters is informal, sympathetic, penetrative, persuasive, and ready to adapt itself to each individual case. When the Church took over the duties and responsibilities of reason, it was probably quite willing that the intuitional faculties should continue their activities. But here a difficulty arose which proved to be insurmountable. It was against the claim of A, the individual churchman, to think out the great problems of life for himself that the Church had protested. In disallowing that claim, it made itself responsible for providing A with the true solution of his problems. And not A only. It had also to provide solutions for B, C, D, E, and all the other members of its community; and in defiance of the fact that no two of those members would, if left to themselves, have looked at the problem from precisely the same point of view, it had to provide one and the same solution or set of solutions for all of them. It thus found itself committed to the assumption that the innermost and ultimate truth of things could be set forth in human speech and taught as one teaches formulas in mathematics or chemistry. In accepting this assumption as a basic truth, the Church reduced within finite limits what is intrinsically infinite and unattainable, and therefore forbade by implication, not reason only, but all those human faculties—conscious, subconscious, unconscious or nearly unconscious—which reach out into the infinite, to occupy themselves with the greatest of all their appropriate problems; and in thus forbidding them to energize at their highest level, it atrophied their finer nerves and muscles, it arrested or, at best, retarded and stunted their growth.

The Church said to the people: "The truth of things is in my keeping. I will teach it to you, and you will disbelieve it at the peril of your souls." And to this demand for obedience in thought and word, as well as in deed, the people were for many centuries content to say "Amen." Now the man who believes whatever he is told to believe has both ceased to trust and ceased to use his intuition. And he has ceased to trust it and ceased to use it just where he has most need of it,—in dealing with the great problems and the great issues of life, matters with regard to which the impersonal methods of positive science are out of place. If his intuition were really at work, the chances are that he would find something to criticize and perhaps to dissent from in some at least of the doctrines which he is required to believe. For *quot homines, tot sententiæ.* Opinions vary from man to man. So do primary assumptions. So do outlooks on life. When a theory of things which professes to explain the fundamental mysteries of existence is accepted in its entirety by millions of so-called believers, we may be sure that it is accepted on its merits by very few of them. This means that for most of them intuition has ceased to work; and the reason why it has ceased to work is that it has been deprived of the co-ordinating, organizing, and therefore vivifying influence of reason, which is to the intuitional faculties what the General Staff is to an army in the field. This shows how vain it is to suppose that, when one of the vital organs of the soul has ceased to operate, the rest of them can continue to discharge their normal functions, and the soul in its totality continue to live a healthy life. As well might it be supposed that the action of the lungs can be stopped without deranging the other vital organs and without imperilling the well-being of the body as a whole.

And though the suppression of reason in the sphere of speculative thought interfered primarily with the higher intuitions, the mischief that it wrought did not end there. The whole intuitional side of man's being above the physical level was adversely affected by the dogmatic attitude of the

Church. If a man was not to trust his own nature when the supreme problems of life pressed for solution, for what purpose or purposes was he to trust it? In other words, for which, if any, of the problems of life could authoritative guidance be dispensed with? It was difficult in any case to delimit the respective spheres of obedience and initiative; and the growing ambition of the Church, its desire to dominate the life of the believer more and more completely, increased that difficulty by tending to lower the level at which the line of demarcation was to be drawn.[1] To disparage self-reliance where the need for it is greatest is to undermine it in greater or less degree on all the planes of man's activity. And the man who ceases to rely on himself when he is in difficulties will get out of the way of using his judgment and his insight, and will thus tend to atrophy through disuse those faculties and all the senses and sub-senses which they employ when they are at work.

What the Church did, then, when it forbade reason to attempt the solution of the greatest of all problems, was to deaden sensibility in general and spiritual sensibility in particular; to deaden the souls' capacity for evolving special senses in response to the pressure of special environments; to deaden the master faculty—half insight and half judgment—by means of which we steer our way through the difficulties, perplexities, and intricacies of life. The Church did not mean to do this—its quarrel was with reason only—but it did it none the less. Now of all the forms which spiritual sensibility takes, the most important is Conscience, partly because the sphere of its work environs all of us, partly because—as the result of this—it is a sense with which all men are endowed, but chiefly because according to the way in which it functions, and the use which is made of it, so does a man shape or misshape his character and direct or misdirect the growth of his soul. How, then, did conscience fare under the régime of ecclesiastical feudalism? How could it be expected to fare when its

[1] So aggressive indeed was the Church in its encroachments on the freedom of the human spirit, that, as we shall presently see, it was only by retiring into the world of physical nature and confining its activities to the problems of physical science, that reason was able—and even then only after a bitter struggle—to escape from ecclesiastical control.

theoretical problems were solved for it by the doctor of casuistry in his study, and its practical problems by the priest in the confessional box? The more a man's life is ordered for him, the less he will be able to order it for himself. If you fence a man in with commands and prohibitions, if you map out for him, not only the broad highways of his conduct, but also its byways and footpaths, you must not be surprised if he gets to rely on you for moral guidance and ceases to rely on his own sense of right and wrong.

But the Church did more than weaken conscience by relieving it of the necessity for exercising itself. It also sophisticated it: it obscured its vision and perverted its judgment. For, by making obedience to itself one of the first of virtues—obedience to external authority being intrinsically neither a virtue nor a vice—it upset and threw into confusion the whole of that natural scale of moral values which it is the function of conscience to discover and apply. By comparison with the supreme heinousness of the sin of disobedience, the difference, in respect of moral gravity, between this and that *act* of disobedience was always tending to efface itself.

The result was that, under the pressure of ecclesiastical authority, conscience tended to lose that sense of proportion which is of the essence of healthy intuition (in whatever sphere it may operate) and, in the absence of which, moral sensibility, losing touch with what is vital and essential, either dies out into moral callousness or degenerates into morbid conscientiousness. The man who could not see for himself that sins of anger, greed, and lust (for example) were more serious offences than (for example) neglect to fast on the prescribed fast days, had lost his insight into the facts and laws of the moral world.[1]

[1] I do not forget that the Catholic Church has always distinguished between *mortal* and *venial* sin. But such a distinction is difficult to draw, and, when drawn, is almost certain to mislead. To classify sins without regard to motives and circumstances is to externalize morality. And motives and circumstances differ so widely in different cases, that, if due regard is paid to them, classification becomes impossible, what is a mortal sin (for example) in the case of A being a venial sin in the case of B, who committed the same offence, but from a totally different motive and in totally different circumstances. In any case, if sins are to be classified, the classification must be personal and informal, and must be made by the individual conscience, not by a central authority.

And the chances are that the deterioration of his moral sense would carry him even further than this. He would find it easier to substitute fish for meat on fast days than to subdue the passions of anger, greed, and lust. And as the Church would lay special stress on the duty of submission to its own special ordinances (which it regarded as of quasi-divine authority) he would be exposed to a two-fold temptation to attach less importance to the commands which had a broadly human than to those which had a merely ecclesiastical sanction ; and, like the Pharisee who paid "tithe of mint and anise and cummin" and "omitted the weightier matters of the Law—judgment, mercy and faith," he would probably end by thinking more seriously of the ceremonial peccadillo than of the moral offence. Here, as elsewhere, the baser currency, when placed on a par with the sterling, would tend to drive the latter out of circulation.

Finally, and above all, when external authority pressed heavily on morals, correctness of outward action would necessarily tend to count for more than purity of inward motive. Indeed in extreme cases the former would count for everything and the latter would count for nothing. Where this was possible, the moral intuition had obviously ceased to work.

When we remind ourselves what are the constituent elements of a healthy conscience, how largely imagination and sympathy enter into it, as well as insight and judgment, we shall be able to realize how grave an injury was done to the intuitional side of human nature when the Church, having told men what they were to believe, and compelled them to believe it, obedient to the logic of the situation which it had created, went on to tell them in ever fuller detail what they were to do, and to insist on their doing it. Nor did the fact that, in thus tyrannizing over the human spirit, the Church was responding to the average man's secret demand for spiritual direction, lessen the mischievous influences that were unloosed by its actions. On the contrary, it doubled them. For the average man's demand for spiritual direction generated in the leaders of the Church a desire for spiritual domination ; and each of these tendencies—the one passively and the other actively harmful—unceasingly acted on and was reacted on by the other.

While intuition was thus degenerating under the sinister influence of dogmatic pressure, what had become of reason? Having been compulsorily divorced from intuition it had either taken service under the Church and devoted itself to "sciences," such as theology and casuistry, which are based, in no small measure, on a confusion between words and things; or it had retired to a sphere of work in which it might hope for freedom from ecclesiastical control,—the sphere of material Nature, the sphere of physical science. The evidence of the intuitional faculties, being largely personal and emotional, can never be conclusive, in the strict sense of that word. I mean by this that those to whom it does not appeal will always be free to reject it. But the evidence of the bodily senses, which, as Ruskin says, are "constant and common, shared by all and perpetual in all," and which are therefore organs of universal consent, is irresistible; and the reasoning which is based on that evidence, if its own procedure is correct, is not to be gainsaid. It might have been thought that in that sphere of work reason would not have been interfered with by "authority." But the appetite for domination grows by being indulged; and having subdued to its will the domains of belief and morals, the Church sought to extend its empire into the region of positive knowledge. Here however it met with effective resistance. The claim of external authority to deduce scientific truths from the text of sacred scriptures, and to set aside conclusions which were based on observation and experiment and had been verified by an appeal to experience, could not be permanently enforced. *E pur si muove* is an argument to which, in the last resort, there is no answer.

After a protracted struggle which, while it lasted, brought intellectual development almost to a standstill, reason won and made secure the freedom which it sought. But, by comparison with what it had left behind, the freedom that it won was the freedom of an exile, not of an enfranchised citizen. The spirit of man had to pay a heavy price for the partial emancipation of reason from the despotism of the Church. The intuitional faculties, abandoned by reason, had to bear unaided the deadening pressure of autocratic authority ; and reason, confining its activities for the most part to one plane or aspect of Nature, and surrendering, as an outlawed exile, the remaining planes to the theologian and the priest, lowered itself to the level of its subject-matter, and became unequal to the task of dealing with the master problems of life. And now that it is free to return to its forsaken home and take up again the high task of interpreting the Universe,—instead of allying itself with intuition and going forth with it on the greatest of all adventures, it either renounces its heritage in the name of agnosticism, or tries to no purpose to bring the inner mysteries of the Universe within the compass of scientific method. The word *rationalism,* as it is used to-day, connotes distrust of intuition not less than antipathy to supernaturalism ; and the rationalist is so far from understanding the meaning and purpose of intuition that he is apt to hold it responsible for the vagaries of religious belief. This divorce of reason from intuition has had calamitous consequences which have not yet worked themselves out. Which has been the greater of the two great evils that it has wrought, the despiritualizing of reason or the derationalizing of intuition—the degradation of reason to the level of inductive logic, or the degradation of intuition to the level of blind faith—it would be hard to say. What the future may have in store for us in the way of a reinterpretation of Christianity or a new treatment of the problems of philosophy, I cannot guess. But I am very sure that until reason and intuition have been reconciled and become fellow-workers in the quest of ideal truth, there will be no lasting happiness for the human spirit.

The theme of this chapter is one on which volumes might be written. I can do no more than touch on one or two of its more vital aspects. I have spoken of the influence of ecclesiastical feudalism on character and mentality. I will now consider its influence on conduct, on the bearing of man towards his fellow men. The aim of the Church was to control the head-springs of man's inner life. In this aim it succeeded only too well, chiefly because man shrank, as he still shrinks, with something akin to terror, from the mystery of his own inmost self; and, fearing lest its head-springs should send down the channel of his daily life a sudden and devastating flood which he would be unable to regulate, was more than willing that they should be placed under strict control. But to control the inner life from without is to externalize it; and to externalize it is to devitalize it. For in losing its inwardness it loses its identity; and therefore, as the life of man's life, it ceases to be. It is with the social consequences of this change in the centre of gravity of man's existence that I am now concerned. How well the Church did the work that it took in hand is proved by the fact that in the religious, as in the secular world, the pressure of feudal authority on the human spirit led, through externalism, to materialism, individualism, and egoism, and thus went far towards de-socializing and even de-humanizing man's life.

Let us trace the steps in this sinister process. If the Church was to secure obedience, it must be in a position to promise rewards to the faithful and to threaten pains and penalties to the rebellious. Such promises and such threats it made freely; and it was able to make them the more freely because both the rewards and the pains and penalties were to be in another world, and another life. Did this mean that they were spiritual, not material? Alas, no. External rewards and external punishments are necessarily material; and the desire for the former and the fear of the latter are necessarily materialistic. We cannot get away from this. We may etherealize our Heaven as much as we please. We may even try to etherealize our Hell. We may transplant them both to other and wholly mysterious parts of the Universe. We may project them into other and wholly mysterious cycles of time. But so long as we think of them as outside ourselves and outside our present lives, instead of as states of the soul, states which we may take with us into other worlds and other lives, but only because they are ours here and now; so long as we are virtuous for the sake of what we shall enjoy or from the fear of what we may suffer, instead of for the sake of virtue itself and its inevitable reaction on the soul,—we are materialists at heart: and though our lives may be correct, as measured by outward standards, our ideals are perverted and our outlook on life is wrong.

That the ethics of official Christianity are materialistic at heart is proved by the fact that the fear of Hell fire has always counted for more in the moral life of Christendom than the hope of Heaven. When the power of the Church was greatest, the fear of Hell fire, overhanging man's life like a lurid storm-cloud, was the motive by which the Christian was chiefly swayed. And it is a motive which still sways the faithful in all Catholic lands. If you will go into an Irish church during a mission service, or into a Jesuit seminary when the seminarists are receiving their last exhortation, you will probably find that fear of Hell is the motive to which the preacher makes his most impassioned appeal. The reason why the fear of Hell outweighs the hope of Heaven is that imagination, which is largely sensuous, can picture the fires of a Hell which resists our attempts to etherealize it, but cannot picture the joys of a highly etherealized Heaven. The flesh shrinks with terror from the prospect of intense, undying, quasi-physical torture; whereas the more we etherealize the joys of Heaven, the more monotonous and therefore the less desirable do they seem, so that for many minds the prospect of never-ending bliss does not materially differ from the prospect of never-ending ennui. Hence it is that escape from eternal punishment is the only aspect of eternal happiness which the ordinary mind can *realize*. Let Heaven be what it may. If only the menace of Hell can be averted, the believer will feel that he has saved his soul alive.

I have said that churchmanship, as a sentiment, was the apotheosis of tribalism. The statement is, I think, substantially true. But the tribesman's devotion to the tribe differed from the churchman's devotion to the Church in one important respect. The final end of the tribesman's action was the well-being of the tribe. The final end of the churchman's action was his own individual salvation. In his devotion to the tribe the tribesman forgot himself. It is true that the ruin of the tribe would have involved his own ruin. But that for him was a matter of secondary importance. The well-being of the tribe was his first and last concern. It was otherwise with the churchman. The Church, being under divine protection, could take care of itself. As the Church of Christ, and therefore the Church of God, it was in such good hands that its well-being was fully provided for. In this life it might be the Church Militant; but in the next life it would assuredly be the Church Triumphant. Being thus relieved from the necessity of working for the salvation of the Church, the churchman was free to work, with all his energy, for his own. His devotion to the Church, however strong it might be, was therefore fundamentally selfish. He might be fanatically loyal to the Church, he might be scrupulously obedient to its commands, he might toil for it, he might die for it on the field of battle; but the secret of his devotion was the conviction that it, and it alone, could open a way of escape for him from the fires, the quasi-material fires of Hell.

This was individualism—and individualism raised to a high power. In the secular world the individualist strove for earthly prizes. Whatever might be the attractions of these, they lacked two qualities which the prize of success in the religious world possessed—*finality* and *eternity*. Earthly prizes were, at best, incomplete and imperfect; and, if not actually perishable, they could not permanently satisfy. The prize for which the believer contended was perfect bliss, which would last, in its perfection, for ever. Perdition, on the other hand, meant an eternity of absolute pain. The addition of finality and eternity to the joys that the believer hoped for and the pains that he feared intensified his desire for salvation and also intensified the selfishness of his attitude towards his fellow men. Let him but escape the doom of Hell, and win the prize of Heaven, and the rest of the human race might perish. In entertaining this anti-human sentiment, in thus separating himself from his fellow men, he did but follow the example of the Church, with whose personality he had, as we have seen, in some sort identified his own. The Church, true to its Jewish ancestry, claimed exclusive rights in the favour and bounty of God, and exclusive possession of revealed truth. In making this claim it separated itself from the rest of mankind, whom it regarded (apart from the "uncovenanted mercies of God") as beyond the pale of salvation; and though it was always ready to preach the Gospel *in partibus infidelium*, its bearing towards those who rejected its message was hostile and intolerant. If the non-Christian peoples would not submit to its authority, they were *ipso facto* excommunicate; and it was well content that they should perish everlastingly. For its own rebellious children, for those who, having once belonged to its fold, rejected its teaching and disowned its authority, it had in reserve the dungeon, the torture-chamber, and the stake. When Christian kings thought to atone for lives of wickedness by the cruel persecution of heresy, when the burning of heretics in batches was a Court ceremony and was counted as an "act of faith," intolerance—the negation of sympathy, the transmutation of self-love into anger and hatred—had touched its limit. The story of the Inquisition is the darkest chapter in the history of mankind; but it was as much a predestined chapter in the history of the Catholic Church as were the Peasant Risings, with the horrors that attended their suppression, in the history of mediæval feudalism. And the attitude of intolerance which found logical expression in the atrocities of the Inquisition, when acquiesced in and reproduced by the loyal churchman, reacted on his desire for salvation and intensified its inherent selfishness and uncharitableness.

Individualism, raised to a high power, is egoism. The religious devotee who was so intent on achieving his own salvation as to be indifferent to the fate of others, whose hatred of dissent was due to his fear lest it should shake his own faith rather than to any interest in the welfare of the dissenter, was the most self-centred of egoists. That it was possible for him to think of himself as happy while the majority of his fellow-men were in hopeless misery, shows how destitute he was of the saving grace of sympathy, and how completely he had been drawn into the ever-narrowing vortex of his individual self. And his egoism was enhanced by the fact that he honestly believed it to be acceptable to God. A more hateful type of egoism it would be difficult to imagine. When a man dedicates his vices—cruelty, treachery, injustice, selfishness, or whatever they may be

—to God, their viciousness knows no limit. The scheme of life is self-condemned which allows and even tempts a man to do the work of the Devil, while professing to serve under the banner of God.

I do not wish to suggest that the pressure of ecclesiastical authority made individualists and egoists of all who yielded to its influence. Different persons reacted to it in different ways. Some did not feel the pressure. The Catholic Church has had its full share of saints (in the widest sense of the word); and the saint, being dead to self, can withstand all narrowing and hardening influences, and even turn them to good account. Others were consciously self-centred, but subconsciously sympathetic and unselfish. Others, again, were more self-centred in sentiment than in theory. But that a strong current was ever setting from the Vatican in the direction of individualism and egoism can scarcely be doubted. The merits and achievements of the Catholic Church were many and great; and it would be folly to underestimate them. But, looking at things from a social standpoint, I contend that, however much is to be placed to the credit of the Church, two things at least must be placed to its debit. As a community, it was essentially separatist and intolerant. In claiming universal dominion it broke away from the potential fellowship of the churches and the nations; it treated as rebels, or at best as outcasts, all who were not of its fold; it excommunicated the greater part of the human race, and in doing so excommunicated itself from the larger and diviner church of Humanity; and it waged war against freedom and mutual tolerance, and therefore in part thwarted and in part misdirected the spiritual development of the human family, which is a movement towards unity in diversity, not towards enforced uniformity. And its spirit of self-assertion and exclusiveness was caught by its children; and as it taught them that they were to achieve salvation by yielding obedience to itself rather than by realizing their oneness, through God, with all their kind, it became possible for the believer to promise himself an eternity of happiness in Heaven, which would be unalloyed and might even be enhanced by the knowledge that the bulk of his fellow men were doomed to everlasting perdition. It became possible, in other words, for a man to be fanatically loyal to the Church, and yet to be treasonably disloyal to the indwelling spirit of God.

For many centuries the Catholic Church—the Headquarters of spiritual feudalism—had things all its own way. What use did it make of its opportunities ? It set out to evangelize the nations. Has it done so ? It set out to impose moral and spiritual well-being on mankind. Has it done so ? Need I answer these questions ? To ask them at the time when Christendom seems intent on committing suicide is almost a mockery. The Church has always kept the teaching of religion in its own hands. Have men profited by its teaching ? Do they even believe what it has taught ? Complaints of the growing infidelity of the age, of the spread of agnosticism and atheism, of the gradual relapse of Christendom into paganism, come from many pulpits. And not from Catholic pulpits only. The High Church Anglican and the strict Calvinist take an equally gloomy view of the present state of the Christian world. The orthodox believer has everything to lose by admitting that Christianity has proved a failure. Yet these witnesses, who all regard themselves as orthodox, not only admit this but (by implication) insist upon it. If they may be believed—and their evidence derives weight from the fact that it tells against themselves—the Church, as the result of eighteen centuries of missionary activity, has paganized rather then evangelized the world. The Church will perhaps attribute its failure to the hardness of men's hearts. But this would be equivalent to saying that it had failed because it had failed. For its business was to soften men's hearts. And if, on its own showing, it has been unable to do so, it is surely self-condemned.

So far I have said nothing as to the interaction, in the feudal era, of the religious and the secular world. That the two worlds acted and reacted on one another continuously may be taken for granted. But I have found it convenient to think of their currents as flowing in separate, though parallel, channels. There is however one matter in which they have co-operated so effectively that they must be held jointly responsible for the consequences of their action. Feudal contempt for the mass of humanity, reinforced by the religious belief in original sin and the corruption of man's heart, has generated an immense underestimate of man's moral and mental capacity and also of what I may call his reserves of spiritual vitality. It was of course on such an underestimate that the whole fabric of feudalism was built. But it frequently happens that, when a tendency of thought expresses itself in action, it is reacted upon and profoundly modified by its practical results. And the distrust of human nature which led to the substitution of autocracy for democracy in both the religious and the secular worlds has now developed, in general into a cynical contempt for human nature, and in particular into a fixed belief on the part of the "refined and cultured" upper classes that the lower classes—the bulk of the human race—are congenitally vicious, stupid, coarse-fibred, and semi-brutal. This underestimate of man's capacity on all the higher planes of his being is paralyzing our vital energies and thwarting all our schemes of political, social, and ethical reform. Its bearing on the problem of human happiness is obvious. A life which is based on self-distrust, not merely as a theory, but also as a sentiment and a conviction, is a life of lowered vitality; and a life of lowered vitality is an unhealthy and unhappy life.

But it was not only by generating distrust of human nature that feudalism—secular and spiritual—lowered vitality. It was also, and above all, by doing what it set out to do—by trying to impose well-being (or what it was pleased to regard as well-being) on the rank and file of mankind; by socializing and moralizing them, with or without their consent; by coercing them into correctness of thought and sentiment and action; by subjecting them to the deadening pressure of irresponsible authority on all the planes of their being; by denying them freedom for self-development; by repressing their spontaneous activity; by arresting the growth of their souls.

CHAPTER V

THE MORAL OF FAILURE

THE history of feudalism is the history of a great experiment. What differentiated feudalism from other types of tyranny was that it was more openly and more directly based on supernatural sanction. It was in the name of the supernatural God that feudalism, whether spiritual or secular, denied to human nature the right to live its own life and order its own goings. And its machinery was so contrived as to transmit the pressure of supernatural authority to all parts of the body politic. The experiment had to be made. There have been many phases in man's development. Feudalism—I am using the word in its widest sense—was one of these. What happened was this. The spirit of man, dreaming of its own perfection and realizing how far it fell short of that ideal, smitten with a sense of its inadequacy and unworthiness, projected its dream into a world—partly real and partly imaginary—outside itself; personified it; found a fitting abode for it; invested it with supreme power and authority; humbled itself in the dust before it and its supposed instruments, lay and clerical; and tried to find salvation in submission to its will and obedience to its commands.

The experiment has lasted for many centuries; and though it is not yet over, we are in a position to say that it has failed. For we are at least as far from peace and joy as we were before we began it; and one of the sources of our unrest is our growing distrust of the very authority to which we had gone for help and guidance,—a feeling which is widening out into impatience of authority as such. The Nemesis of dogmatism is that in the fulness of time it provokes a reaction against itself, which calls the critical spirit into full activity, and that when those whose beliefs had been dictated and whose opinions had been moulded by authority begin to criticize, there is no doctrine, however sacred, which they will not call in question. The attempt to coerce men into correctness of thought and sentiment and action may succeed for a time ; but sooner or later it will lead to anarchy on every plane of man's life ; and the more thorough the coercive discipline, the more violent and revolutionary will be the anarchical reaction.

It is true that the proscription of reason by the Church, of which I have spoken, and its consequent retirement in exile into the world of physical phenomena, have enabled us, through the achievements of Science, to acquire a great and ever growing mastery over the material resources of Nature ; and it might be thought that this would have given us what we were seeking. But though commercialism and industrialism, following in the wake of scientific discovery and mechanical invention, have given us a great accession of wealth, a general rise in the standard of luxury and comfort, and many facilities and conveniences which had previously been beyond our reach, they have not given us happiness. We are still feverish with discontent ; nay, we are more than ever feverish with discontent ; for the higher our standard of comfort rises, the more exacting are our demands on life ; and when we try to diagnose our symptoms, we find that the very influences which were to have healed us have aggravated our malady.

We are unhappy because we will not trust our nature, the burden of responsibility which trust in it would lay on us being, as we think, too heavy for us to bear ; and because in all living creatures trust in nature is the only basis of a healthy life.

We are unhappy because in our self-distrust we go outside ourselves for guidance and motive power, and are therefore —since our natural tendencies continue to operate—the victims of an unending conflict between pressure from without and pressure from within.

We are unhappy because, instead of being content with the environment which Nature provides for us, which is large enough potentially for all our needs, and which, through our reaction on it, grows unceasingly with our growth, we create for ourselves a supernatural environment which, so far as it exists for us, our shallower selves re-act to but our deeper selves react against us.

We are unhappy (some of us) because we still worship a feudal autocrat who expects his subjects to pay court to him, and because no courtier can be permanently happy. His tenure of the royal favour is too precarious.

> A breath unmakes him as a breath has made.

We are unhappy (others of us) because, though our outlook on life is still feudal, we have renounced allegiance to our feudal Overlord, and have therefore no master principle of action, apart from self-interest and the right which is inherent in might.

We are unhappy because our expansive instincts and energies are continually thwarted and held back, the pressure of external authority on the human spirit, which was once consciously and systematically applied, though now less formally exerted, having all the force and persistence of a long-sustained tradition.

We are unhappy because, owing to the compulsory externalization of our lives, we are the victims of false ideals and false standards, which some of us are in secret revolt against, but which have so closely interwoven themselves with our normal environment and our daily lives that we cannot openly defy them without imperilling the stability of the whole social structure.

We are unhappy because, under the influence of our false ideals, life has become a general scramble for material possessions, and because the winners in that scramble, who are few, are never fully satisfied, while the losers, who are many, are seething with envy and discontent.

We are unhappy because the basis of modern society is still largely feudal, and because, as the result of this, there are powerful influences at work which tend to stultify, if they do not actually turn to base purposes, all our attempts at social and political reform.

We are unhappy because self-distrust leads to externalism, externalism to materialism, materialism to individualism, and individualism to egoism; and because egoism—the attempt of the soul to rest, for good and all, in its own unexpanded life, the refusal of the soul to go out of itself into a larger life, to find itself by losing itself—is the very negation of healthy and harmonious growth.

We are unhappy because our old first principles are becoming discredited and our old beliefs are dead or dying; and because reason and intuition—each suffering from its prolonged separation from the other, and each suspicious of and antipathetic to the other—refuse to co-operate to build up a new philosophy and a new faith.

In indicating the causes of our malady, I am suggesting the appropriate remedy.

We are unhappy because we seek for happiness outside ourselves, and because the only fountain of happiness, the only fountain of well-being, the only fountain of life, is within.

I will now summarize the contents of this section and draw the moral to which it seems to point. We want to discover the secret of happiness. We mean by happiness the sense of well-being. If all is well with me, and I feel—consciously or subconsciously—that all is well with me, I am happy. What we really want to discover, then, is the secret of well-being. How is well-being to be achieved? Under the feudal régime an elaborate attempt was made to impose it on man from without, to order his life for him on all the planes of his being, his contribution to his own salvation being limited to submitting himself to authority and obeying the word of command. This attempt is ending in disastrous failure, partly because the constant pressure of authority has proved hurtful to the growing soul, partly because the externalization of man's life has led him to seek happiness for himself in outward things,—a search which is warping his character and disorganizing his social life. Where, then, is the solution of our problem to be found? The failure of feudalism suggests the answer to this question. If well-being is not to be achieved by submission to pressure from without, it must be achieved by response to pressure from within—in a word, by *growth*.

PART II

THE MEANING OF GROWTH

CHAPTER I

THE LAW OF GROWTH

THE failure of feudalism has suggested to me that happiness is to be won, not by submission to pressure from without, whether coercive or attractive, but by response to pressure from within. By pressure from within I mean the pressure of those expansive, transformative forces which are making us whatever we have it in us to become. The due response to this pressure is what we call self-development or growth. When growth is healthy and harmonious, we have well-being. And when well-being is consciously or even sub-consciously realized, we have happiness.

The consentient voice of animate Nature ratifies these conclusions. On the physical plane of existence life is a process which has a dawn, a meridian, and a decline. When life is on the upward curve the organism is said to be growing. As it approaches its meridian—I am assuming that the conditions are favourable—it attains to the perfection of health; and if the resultant state of well-being could be consciously realized we should have the perfection of happiness. When a plant is growing under entirely favourable conditions, it has all the outward signs of well-being; and as we contemplate these with delight and admiration we begin to understand what the poet meant when he confessed his faith—

> that every flower
> Enjoys the air it breathes.

The merry gambols of young animals suggest that the rising

of the sap of life is a pleasurable process. And on the physical plane of human life, when growth is vigorous and bodily health is perfect, we have the physical equivalent of happiness,—high spirits.

But does human nature in its totality, does the life of man in all its length and breadth and depth, come under the law of growth? I must be allowed to assume that it does. I cannot by any mental effort think otherwise. Wherever there is life there is growth (or the opposite of growth—decay); and I find it impossible—I can use no weaker word—to separate in my thought the idea of life from that of growth. In the years of childhood and adolescence we see the gradual unfolding, not of physical powers and tendencies only, but also of those which are mental, moral, æsthetic, spiritual. If that process of unfolding is not to be called growth, I do not know what is the right name of it; nor do I know what growth means.

It does not follow that human life in its totality comes under the law of *physical* growth. When Professor Bateson says that "Shakespeare once existed as a speck of protoplasm not so big as a pin's head," he begs, as we shall presently see, a very large question. If we are to predicate growth of the whole human being, we must use the word in its widest and most comprehensive sense, we must have in mind only what is really essential in the process of growth. Now what is essential in the process of growth is the realization of potentiality, the transformation of a complex of possibilities into a fully developed organism, of what can be into what is. Such a transformation would not be possible if the organism, the ultimate product of growth, however large and complex it might be, were not present, in promise and potency, in the seed from which it grows. Each seed is fraught with its own destiny. It will grow, if it is allowed to grow, to what is in large measure a predetermined form. I mean by this that its expansive activities will move in a particular channel and arrive in the fulness of time—if all goes well—at a particular goal. The channel may not be accurately mapped out. The goal may be a matter for conjecture rather than for positive knowledge. But that the expanding life has a channel and a goal of its own, is certain. The oak tree is in the acorn, not in the beechnut. The banyan tree—

> With all its thousand downward-dropping stems
> Waiting to fall from all its thousand boughs,
> And all its lakhs and lakhs of lustrous leaves
> Waiting to push to sunlight—

is in the minute seed of the banyan fruit, which, though scarcely distinguishable from the seed of the ordinary fig, is fraught with an entirely different destiny. If, then, human nature in its totality comes under the law of growth, the question at once arises: What are the possibilities of human development? What is it that is to the human embryo what the oak tree is to the acorn or the banyan tree to the seed of the banyan fruit?

Before we attempt to answer this question we shall do well to ask ourselves what is to be our starting-point in this enterprise? In other words, how far back are we to go in quest of the human embryo? By human embryo I mean the embryo of the whole human being, not of the human body only. The acorn may be regarded as the embryo of the oak tree. But the acorn was once a mere speck on an oak twig, and had to go through a long process of growth before it was able to detach itself from the parent tree and start on an independent course of growth. This analogy, though we must not overwork it, is at least suggestive. It is as a new-born baby that the embryo of the human being starts on an independent course of growth. Let us, then, make the new-born baby our starting-point. If we go further back, if we go back to Professor Bateson's "speck of protoplasm," we shall make the grave mistake of resolving psychology into physiology just when we are attempting the solution of the greatest of all psychological problems.[1]

[1] It is of course possible that the incarnating, or reincarnating, soul (if there is such a thing) unites itself with the fertilized germ-cell and in doing so forms the human embryo. But when Professor Bateson says that Shakespeare once existed as a speck of protoplasm, he means that the soul of Shakespeare (if indeed he can be said to have had a soul) was *in* that speck. Such a thing as an incarnating, or reincarnating, soul is not dreamed of in his philosophy. The fertilized germ-cell which a "soul" has taken possession of is an entirely different thing from Professor Bateson's speck of protoplasm. We might, if we pleased, make the former our starting-point in our speculative enterprise, but we have nothing to gain by doing so, and in any case it is safer to start with the new-born baby.

What is it that is to the new-born baby what the oak tree is to the acorn ? With this question is bound up another. Is the growth of the human being strictly predetermined ? The plant and the animal are in the grip of physical necessity. Their destiny has been marked out for them by their breeding. They may fall far short of it. But they cannot possibly transcend it. It is the same, though possibly not to the same extent, with the body of man. But what of the higher planes of his being ? There he feels—and the feeling grows stronger as the dawning light of consciousness grows fuller and clearer—that it is open to him to help or hinder the process of his own growth. We cannot get behind this feeling of freedom. A profound philosophy of life is implicit in it. May we trust it ? This question is, I repeat, bound up with the question as to the possibilities of human development. To answer either question is to answer the other ; and it matters little which we start with. As however, if the sense of freedom is illusory, the enterprise on which I have embarked has neither purpose nor meaning and had better be abandoned at the outset, I will begin by asking whether man, though subject to the law of growth, is exempt from the necessity, which seems to bind all other living things, of growing to a predetermined form ; and if so, in what sense he is exempt and to what extent. The attempt to answer this question will necessarily widen out into a general survey of the problem of soul-growth.

CHAPTER II

HEREDITY AND ENVIRONMENT

A. The Physical Plane [1]

I HAVE now raised the vexed question of heredity and environment, and I must try to think it out. Growth is, in its essence, the realization of potentiality. As far as our experience goes, potentiality is always the product of generation, not of creation,—an inheritance, not a gift ; and the realization of potentiality is always effected through reaction to environment. It follows that there are two chief factors in growth—*heredity*, which gives us realizable potentiality, and *environment*, which makes the realization of potentiality possible. Why, then, is heredity so often opposed to environment ? Why is there a controversy as to the parts which environment and heredity, " nature " and " nurture," respectively play in human life ? Why does Professor Bateson tell us that " the long-standing controversy as to the relative importance of nature and nurture . . . is drawing to an end, and of the overwhelming greater significance of nature there is no longer any possibility of doubt " ? Why does Dr. Chalmers Mitchell say, on the contrary, that " with regard to mental, moral, and emotional qualities, which are of preponderating importance in man . . . nurture is incomparably more important than nature " ? How has this question arisen, and what is

[1] When I speak of the physical plane I am thinking of the physical side of physique and of that only. I do not forget that physique and spirituality (to use a comprehensive term), however much we may try to separate them in thought, will insist on overlapping and even interpenetrating one another,—that *expression*, for example, is a quasi-spiritual feature or aspect of the outer man, just as *temperament*, for example, is a quasi-physical feature or aspect of the inner man. But, having found it convenient, for the better ordering of my thoughts, to separate the physical from the higher planes, I must as far as possible exclude from the former whatever is not purely physical.

its real significance ? It has been said—and with some show of reason—that heredity and environment are the warp and woof of the tissue of life. But if these are the parts that they respectively play, there is no controversy between them. And perhaps if we could state correctly the question which, unknown to ourselves, we are trying to answer, we should find that our opposition of heredity to environment, of "nature" to "nurture," was based on a misconception, and that the question, as it was usually stated, was unreal. Meanwhile, however, we must face the fact that many practical problems perplex us which raise, or seem to raise, the question to which Professor Bateson and Dr. Chalmers Mitchell have given diametrically opposite answers. For example : the child of criminal parents, reared in a criminal slum, becomes a criminal. Is his criminality "in his blood," or is it the result of his unfortunate environment ? Or, if both causes have been at work, which has been the predominant influence ? Is the servility of the German people in the blood of the German race (if there is such a thing), or is it due to a tradition which has had an historical origin and which now permeates the environing atmosphere into which every German is born ? Is the apparent inferiority of the "lower orders" to the "upper middle classes" (let us say) in intellect, manners, and general culture vital or accidental ? Is it due to an inferior strain of blood or to a less favourable environment ? These are legitimate questions, and their practical significance is obvious.

But do they really commit us to a consideration of the parts which heredity and environment respectively play in human life ? I think not. I think that the question which is actually at issue has been obscured by a fog of confused thought, and that the ultimate source of that confusion has been our failure to distinguish between *racial* and *lineal* heredity, between the *common* and the *differential* elements in our inheritance. By the common elements I mean those which we inherit from the whole human race and which we therefore share with all our fellow-men. By the differential elements I mean those which we inherit from our own more recent line of ancestors and which are therefore in some special sense our own. The distinction between what we inherit from the whole human race (or perhaps from some remoter source of being) and what we inherit from our own lineal ancestors is a real one ; and it is a pity that it is so often ignored. Examples drawn from the physical side of human life will help me to make my meaning clear. Though no two men are exactly alike, yet all men have the same bodily structure, and each man inherits what is essential in his bodily structure from the whole human race. Thus every normal infant has so many bones arranged in such and such ways, such and such organs arranged in such and such ways, such and such limbs, such and such facial features and senses, an elaborate system of veins, nerves, and muscles, a series of skins, the beginnings of hair, nails, and teeth. These constitute the infant's racial inheritance. But infant differs from infant in respect of the size, form, colour, and proportions, both of its frame as a whole and of each of its constituent parts ; and these differential elements constitute its lineal inheritance, for it owes them—not wholly perhaps, but in large measure—to its more recent line of ancestors, to what we call, loosely and inaccurately, its "strain of blood."

Or put the matter thus. Racial heredity gives a man a human nose. Lineal heredity helps to determine the contour of his nose. Racial heredity gives a man a pair of human eyes. Lineal heredity helps to determine the colour and setting of his eyes. Racial heredity gives a man a human mouth. Lineal heredity helps to determine the size and shape of the mouth. And so on.

Now it is certain that when we oppose heredity to environment, we are thinking of lineal, not of racial heredity ; of the differential, not of the common elements in human nature. We take the common elements for granted. When we speak of the physique which the child inherits, we take for granted that he has so many bones, such and such organs, such and such a system of veins, nerves, muscles, and the rest. The child has these because he is a human being, not because he is the child of certain parents or the descendant of certain ancestors. We do not give a thought to the common elements in his bodily structure. What we are thinking of, when we speak of his physical resemblance to his parents or his ancestors, are the differential elements—the build of his skull, the contour of his nose, the colour and setting of his eyes, the size and shape of his mouth, the tint and texture of his hair, his height, weight, colouring, form, proportions, bodily vigour, and so forth.

It is also certain that, when we oppose heredity to environment, we are thinking of environment as coming in some sort and some measure under human control.

These reservations are all-important. To oppose heredity as such to environment as such, to ask which of the two influences plays the larger part in the process of growth, would be nonsense. As well might we ask (to revert to our borrowed simile) which counts for more in the weaving of a tissue, the warp or the woof. But when the reservations which I have indicated have been made, we begin to see a meaning in our much-debated problem. Does lineal heredity count for so much in human life as to commit us to a fatalistic, and therefore pessimistic, "theory of things"? If not, how are we to counteract its influence, when it happens to be harmful or unduly restrictive? By giving a favourable environment to its victim, is an obvious answer to this question. But environment can do no more than enable inherited potentiality to realize itself. How, then, can it remove, or even lessen, the disabilities which are inherent in one's "blood"? In one way—and one way only. By allying itself with racial heredity; in other words, by allowing the potentialities of our racial inheritance to realize themselves and play their several parts. The more the racial element in one's inheritance outweighs the lineal, the more the potentialities of one's racial inheritance outweigh the actualities, the greater will be the scope for the transforming influence of environment, and the less will heredity (in the conventional sense of the word) count in one's life.

This much we can see at the outset. Let us now consider a concrete case. A, the child of criminal parents, born and reared in a criminal slum, grows up a criminal. Does not this illustrate the force of "heredity"? Let us assume that it does. But B, another child of the same parents, born in the same slum, having been taken away from it early in life and brought up in respectable surroundings, grows up a respectable member of society. What has happened? Has "environment" triumphed over "heredity"? No, but racial heredity, having been given fair play, has proved stronger than lineal heredity. It is probable that B would not have been regenerated had he not been given a favourable environment. But it is certain that he would not have been regenerated had he not, as a human being, had in him certain social and ethical potentialities which were waiting to be realized. What environment did in his case, what it does in all similar cases, is to enable racial heredity, the nature of man as man, to bring its appropriate reserves of potentiality into action.

The question, then, which we have to consider is not what parts do environment and heredity respectively play in human life, but what parts do racial and lineal heredity respectively play in that great drama. Let us first consider this question in relation to the physical plane of life. Our starting-point is the body of the new-born baby. It is not until the baby is born, that its environment comes in any appreciable degree under human control. During its prenatal life its environment is under the control of "Nature"; and though the mother can do much to thwart the action of Nature, she can do nothing to aid it except in the sense of giving it fair play.

Now in the baby's physical inheritance the preponderant element is undoubtedly the racial. The possession of a nose is of much more importance than the shape of the nose. The possession of eyes, than the colour of the eyes. The possession of a mouth, than the size of the mouth. And so on. The pressure of lineal heredity on the individual is the pressure of a few centuries—at most perhaps, as in the case of the pure-bred Jew, of twenty or thirty. The pressure of racial heredity is the pressure of myriads of centuries—of all the ages, one might almost say, since life began. The pressure of lineal heredity is the pressure of a few scores of ancestors. The pressure of racial heredity is the pressure of unnumbered millions of men.

Yet it is on the physical plane that the directive, and therefore restrictive, influence of heredity is greatest, and the transforming influence of environment least. The explanation of this is simple. On the physical plane there are no great reserves of potentiality for environment to draw upon. Or, if there are, its power of drawing upon them is strictly limited. As far as it goes, the body of the new-born child is an actuality, an accomplished fact. Years of growth await it. But the process of growing will be carried on within narrow limits and, in the main, along predetermined lines. Environment can do much for the child. In a sense it can do everything. But it cannot work miracles. It cannot give him a third eye, or a sixth finger, or a thirty-third tooth. Nor can it add appreciably to his predestined strength or stature. If a child has it in him to grow, under perfectly favourable conditions, to the height of six feet, a bad environment may make him fall short of that limit, but no environment, however good, will enable him to transcend it. The influence of environment in what I may call the downward direction is limited only by death. In the upward direction it is limited by the physical constitution of man. From the point of view of physical development, the average environment of mankind, especially in what are called civilized countries, is very far from ideal. And because there is room in it for endless improvement, we are apt to overestimate the transforming influence of environment on physique. It is but right that we should labour incessantly to improve the material conditions under which men live. But even if we could give the growing child an ideal environment, we should do no more than enable him to fulfil his physical destiny. And that destiny is strictly limited. Or if there is an element of ideality, and therefore of infinity, in it, if even such physical perfection as man, whether collective or individual, has it in him to attain, is in a sense unattainable, the goal is near and cannot be transcended. Favourable physical conditions, if continued for some generations, might raise the average height of a nation by two or three inches; but even if they were continued for 10,000 years, they would not raise the average height of the nation to six and a half feet. The movement towards physical perfection is perhaps an infinite "series"; but if so, its infinity, like that of an arithmetical series which advances by ever-diminishing fractions, has finite limits.

The reason, then, why lineal heredity counts for so much on the physical plane is that racial heredity has fixed the typical form to which the individual is predestined to grow, and that the transforming influence of environment in what I have called the upward direction is therefore comparatively small.

It is true that A, whose physical inheritance is inferior to B's, may, under the influence of a better environment, become the stronger and healthier man. But the explanation of this is not that A has been transformed beyond recognition by his favourable surroundings, but that B, living under unfavourable conditions, has seriously deteriorated. It is because man as man cannot alter his physical frame or constitution, that the individual man cannot materially alter (except for the worse) the face or figure or constitution which he inherits from his forefathers. It is because man as man cannot alter the arrangement and general modelling of his facial features, that the individual man cannot materially alter (except for the worse) the build of his nose, or the colour of his eyes, or the shape of his mouth. It is because man as man cannot transcend the limits which racial heredity imposes on him, that the individual cannot appreciably transcend the limits which lineal heredity imposes on him. If "environment" is to triumph over "heredity"—in other words, if the influence of environment on the individual life is to outweigh that of lineal heredity, to the extent (for example) of removing or seriously lessening "inherited" disabilities—it must, as I have said, have large reserves of racial or common potentiality to draw upon. On the physical plane it has not such reserves, for the physical potentialities of the human animal have to a large extent been realized in the course of his evolution, and the margin in reserve is small.

In what relation, then, do lineal and racial heredity stand to one another on the physical plane? The latter is incomparably the larger and more important element; but from the point of view of the controversy between "environment" and "heredity" its preponderance scarcely counts. Under the influence of a good environment a child will make good growth. Under the influence of a bad environment he will make poor growth. But in either case he will grow towards a more or less precisely predetermined form. Predetermined, in the main and in the mass and also in systematized detail, by racial heredity; but in outline and in individuality of detail, by lineal heredity. And as it is the outline which first catches the eye, as we are naturally interested in what is differential in a man's face and figure, as we instinctively take a man's racial inheritance—the "constant and common" element in his physique—for granted, we say—and (in spite of the great preponderance of the racial element) we are on the whole justified in saying—that lineal heredity counts for much in the bodily life of man. And if we are asked what part it plays in his physical development, we answer that it transmits to him his racial inheritance and modifies it, puts the stamp of individuality on it, in the course of transmission; in other words, that it determines the particular lines along which, in response to the influence of environment—be that environment good or bad—the individual child will realize his racial inheritance and develop into an adult man.

CHAPTER III

HEREDITY AND ENVIRONMENT—*continued*

B. The Higher Planes

WHEN we leave the physical plane behind us, we pass into another world—a world of mysteries and infinities, a world of fathomless depths, of dark spaces, of unknown possibilities, a world of

> Far-folded mists and gleaming halls of morn.

The body of the new-born child is a concrete actuality. Its destiny—even its ideal destiny—is virtually fixed, partly by racial, partly by lineal heredity. The child may easily miss that destiny. The chances are that he will not fully realize it. It is certain that he will not transcend it. His "soul," on the other hand, is a complex of potentialities—mental, emotional, æsthetic, moral, spiritual—an undefinable, illimitable, inextricable tangle of latent tendencies, capacities, instincts, passions, desires. Some of these will soon press for realization. Others will wait their time in the background. Others, in the absence of a favourable environment, will remain shadowy possibilities to the end of the child's life. Others would remain for ever unknown and unguessed at, unless, like a flash of lightning at midnight, some supreme crisis should suddenly reveal their presence. Beyond these there is impenetrable darkness; but a wall of darkness is not necessarily a wall of limitation.

In this vast complex of potentialities how much does the child owe to racial, how much to lineal heredity? How much is his because he is a human being, how much because he is of such and such a "seed"? We cannot say. The question, as I have stated it, has not, I think, been fully considered; but by implication it has often been asked and answered, though no answer has yet been given which can be accepted as authoritative. For this is the point in which the controversy between heredity and environment really centres; and in that controversy even the experts take diametrically opposite sides, the Mendelians, for example, assuring us that "of the overwhelmingly greater significance of nature (heredity) there is no longer any possibility of doubt," while the Epigenesists (if that is their correct title) are equally confident that "nurture (environment) is inconceivably more important than nature."

When doctors disagree, when they flatly contradict one another, what can an amateur do but try to think the matter out for himself? This particular matter is, I need hardly say, by no means easy for anyone, whether expert or amateur, to think out. Indeed, it is the very magnitude of the task that confronts him which justifies the amateur in venturing to grapple with it. In the presence of what is infinite and ultimate the difference between expert and amateur becomes wholly negligible. The expert is one who has specialized in a particular field of inquiry. But who can specialize in the fundamental problems of life?

When we try to determine the limits (if any) of our racial inheritance, we are faced at the outset by one almost insuperable difficulty. To say with any approach to accuracy what potentialities other than physical are latent in a new-born baby, is for obvious reasons impossible. That the baby will in due season think, reason, plan, purpose, love, sympathize, imagine, and so forth may safely be predicted. But the range, the reach, the latent possibilities of these great tendencies—in this case and in that, and even in the average human being—are wholly unknown to us. Until potentiality has begun to realize itself we know as little about it as about the resources of an undiscovered land. As the baby becomes successively a child, an adolescent, and an adult man, his potentialities gradually realize themselves, and it becomes possible for us to study them. But, unhappily, while this is going on, education (in the widest and least technical sense of the word) is doing its deadly work—a work which is not the less deadly because, things being as they are, it is in large measure unavoidable—its work of cramping, warping, atrophying, devitalizing the growing soul. For, as a rule, only so much of our inherited potentiality is drawn upon in each case as will enable the child to play with decent success the part in life which circumstances—controlled in the main by the accident of his birth—are likely to assign to him. That amount varies greatly from case to case. If a child is predestined to enter one of the learned professions, an attempt will be made by those who educate him to realize potentialities which would remain dormant if he were predestined to become a peasant or a miner. But at best the amount which will be realized by the time the child arrives at maturity will be but an insignificant, and probably ill-selected and inharmoniously distributed, fraction of the mysterious whole. And the pity of it is that, as students of human nature, we are apt to assume that tendencies which have been left uncultivated—artistic, musical, literary, scientific, social, or whatever they may be—do not exist. The son of an agricultural labourer grows up an uncouth and uncultured boor; and we assume off-hand that he had no inherent capacity for refinement or culture; but it is possible, to say the least, that had he been brought up in a refined and cultured family he would have made as good a response to the stimulus of the environment as if he had been born a child of the house.

Things being as they are, then, the student of human nature has to choose between two alternatives. In the baby the higher nature of man has not yet begun to reveal itself. In the adult or even in the adolescent it has almost certainly been marred and mutilated by injudicious and inadequate "nurture." As it is better, on the whole, to grope in the dark than to follow a misleading sign-post, I propose to begin by exploring the unknown possibilities of the undeveloped child. This means that my adventures and experiments will be imaginative rather than practical, and that my appeals to experience will in the main be appeals to reason and common sense.

At a very early age the baby will begin to talk. In what language will he express himself? That will entirely depend on where and by whom he is reared. He has it in him to speak a hundred different languages. A friend of mine has brought up an Italian child who was rescued as a baby from the earthquake of Messina. That child speaks English like a native. Had there been no earthquake, she would now be speaking a Sicilian patois. Had she been adopted by a Russian, she would be speaking Russian ; by a Frenchman, French ; by a Chinaman, Chinese ; by a Negro, a Negro dialect. In brief, she had a capacity for learning any language or dialect that happened to be spoken by those who surrounded her. And so has every normal child. Her forefathers may have been of pure Sicilian blood (if there is such a thing) for countless generations ; but they transmitted to her no special aptitude for their own language. She may not have had a drop of English blood in her veins. But she learnt English in English surroundings as easily as she would have learnt her mother's tongue in Sicilian surroundings. What was transmitted to her—along what line or lines of descent I cannot say—was her racial inheritance, including a general capacity for learning to talk. And as every language and every sub-language—patois, dialect, or even prominent accent—has behind it a particular way of thinking and feeling, a particular outlook on life, we may safely conjecture that every child has it in him at birth to adapt himself to as many ways of thinking and feeling and to adopt as many outlooks on life as there are languages, and sub-languages, in this world of ours.

When the baby emerges from infancy, he will have to be educated. Now all systems of education, however much they may differ in other ways, have one thing in common. They take for granted that any child of normal ability can, if reasonably industrious, learn any subject that is suitable for his tender years. It does not follow, as some educationists seem to think, that every child ought to learn every conceivable subject. Nor does it follow that the common practice of forcing on children subjects for which they have no natural inclination is justified. Still the fact that children can, under compulsion, learn subjects in which they take no interest and can see but little meaning, shows that even the average child has in him large reserves of mental capacity, and that the assumption which underlies all our educational systems is to that extent well grounded. Nor does the fact that many children, when they leave school, have lost all their interest in mental work and much of their power of utilizing their latent capacity, prove anything except that a cramping and sterilizing environment can do much in the way of robbing a child of his birthright. To argue from what a child is when education has victimized him to what he was at birth is in all probability to go very far astray.

As the child grows up, the choice of a vocation will devolve upon his parents or guardians. What will they do? Will they examine his pedigree in order to see for what calling his inherited tendencies have specially fitted him? No, they will look to his environment, past and present, rather than to his lineage. They will look to their own means, to the way in which he has been educated, to the opportunities for continuing his education, to the possibilities of his being apprenticed to a trade, to the local demand for labour, and other such matters, and they will make their choice for him by reference to these considerations, unless indeed he has some strongly pronounced inclination of which they approve and which they are in a position to gratify. They will take for granted that if he is of average ability and is reasonably industrious, he will be able, sooner or later, to become proficient at any craft, or trade, or profession for which his circumstances, including his education, past and prospective, have fitted him. They will take for granted that he has it in him to make himself at home in a multitude of different callings, and that it must in the main be left to circumstances to determine which of these he is to adopt. It is true that aptitudes vary. We cannot all do all things equally well. There is no one who is not better fitted for some pursuits than for others. But there is no one who cannot, if he chooses, make himself tolerably proficient at any one of a large number of different pursuits. And if the average adolescent, in spite of the cramping pressure to which he has, almost inevitably, been subjected, has it in him to earn his livelihood in so many different ways, does it not follow that his inherent adaptability is practically unlimited—in other words, that he has boundless reserves of potentiality to draw upon? Since the present war began, our army has expanded to ten times its previous strength. How has this been done? By men going into it out of a hundred different callings, and learning what was a new trade for each of them the trade of war. And, though some of these apprentices were doubtless apter pupils than others, so well has the average Englishman, of whatever class or calling, learnt this new trade, that our vast army is now as efficient as it is resolute and brave. What better proof could be given of the inherent versatility of human nature, of the infinite resourcefulness of the soul?

Here, then, lineal heredity counts for very little, whereas racial heredity, controlled and guided by environment, counts for nearly everything and seems to have an unlimited range. But let us test the value of the conclusions which we have reached, by making an imaginative experiment. Let us arrange for a hundred babies—German, if you will—to be born and reared in ten foreign countries, ten in each—say in England, France, Russia, Spain, Italy, Holland, Sweden, the United States, the Argentine, and Canada.[1] Let us divide the inhabitants of each of these ten countries into ten social grades—landowners, peasants, merchants, shopkeepers, clerks, manufacturers, artisans, civil servants, professional men, ministers of religion. And let us arrange in each country for the babies to be brought up in these

[1] In each of these ten countries the population is preponderatingly, if not wholly, White. My reason for excluding other colours is that colour-prejudice would introduce a disturbing element into environment which would cause the proposed experiment to abort. If, for example, one of the German babies was brought up by Chinese or Hindoo foster-parents, the difference in colour and general appearance between him and his compatriots by adoption would tend to isolate him from his fellows and would make it difficult for him to share their social life. It must not, however, be supposed that I regard the White Race as *congenitally* superior to the rest of mankind. On the contrary, I am by no means sure that it is congenitally superior to even the most backward and "degraded" of the other races. The Australian aborigines are commonly regarded as one of the lowest of races in the scale of civilization; and we are apt to assume that they are of an altogether inferior and indeed barely human type. Yet a white teacher in an Australian school, writing of his aboriginal pupils in a Government Report, says that "age for age and opportunity for opportunity, the attainments and mental powers of these children are equal to those of the average white children." And one who has been Chief Protector of Aborigines in one of the Australian States writes that he has "every reason for believing that the aboriginal brain can grasp any modern idea or subject quite as readily as we."

ten social grades, one in each. Above all, let us arrange, in each case, for German influences to be excluded from the baby's life, if not from the day of its birth then from as near to that date as possible. Let us then look forward some twenty or thirty years. What will have happened? Can anyone doubt that a large majority of the German babies will have become loyal citizens of their adopted countries, and respectable members of their respective social grades? Some failures there will have been among them. But probably not a higher percentage than if they had belonged by birth to the various countries which I have specified, and been born into the social grades in which I have placed them. The chances are that each of them will have accepted the "Kultur" of his particular country [1] and (whether nominally or really) the religion of his particular foster-parents, and will have adopted the prejudices and general outlook on life of his particular social grade.

Consider what this means. Each of the babies had it in him to play a hundred different parts—the part of an English squire, of a French artisan, of a Russian peasant, of an American manufacturer, of a Dutch merchant, of an Italian priest, of a Swedish official, and so on. What vast potential resources he must have had at his disposal! Which particular part he had to play was decided by "chance." But potentially he was equal to all the parts and to as many more as we might choose to assign to him. His adaptability in fine reflected that of the whole human race, and the range of his latent capacity had no limits.

In this respect, if in no other, man stands apart from all other living things. Even his friend and companion, the dog, who probably comes next to him in mental and moral development, is separated from him as regards adaptability by an impassable abyss. It is true that the dog family can play a great variety of parts. But this has been made

[1] Were the career of one of these German babies to become the theme of a story by one of our "heredity" novelists, we should probably be told that when the baby became an adolescent he began to be tormented with apparently unaccountable cravings for *Sauerkraut* and lager beer. I do not think that those cravings would be felt. I think that from first to last the transplanted German, provided that he got enough to eat and drink, would be quite content with the food and drink of his adopted country.

possible, as anyone can see at a glance, only by very strict physical differentiation. Hence the supreme importance of breeding from the dog-fancier's point of view. Vocation, among dogs, is handed down from father to son, not as a tradition but as a tendency "in the blood." No amount of training could convert a Newfoundland puppy into a sheep-dog or enable a bulldog to course hares. With man it is entirely different. In spite of the distinctions of colour, with all that they imply, and in spite of a host of minor variations in face and figure, there is but one dominant human type. And that one type, besides being able to adapt itself to all climates and to a vast range of material conditions, can take up an unlimited number of different interests and pursuits. The average baby has it in him, as we have seen, to speak a hundred languages, to belong to a hundred nations, to learn a hundred trades and professions, to play a hundred parts in life.

And the infinitude of the racial inheritance which the average baby brings with him into the world is of many dimensions. The religious phenomenon known as "conversion," with the sudden transition which it sometimes effects from the very worst in a man to the very best; the winning of V.C.'s and other rewards of courage and self-sacrifice by criminals and other "detrimentals" on the field of battle; the upsurging, in moments of supreme crisis, of heroism and self-devotion from unsuspected abysses in some seemingly commonplace soul; the sudden melting of a hardened heart in the sunshine of sympathy and kindness; the transforming influence of the passion of personal love on a man's whole attitude towards life,—these and other phenomena of a kindred nature, which, though necessarily rare (for only exceptional combinations of circumstances can produce them), are not therefore to be regarded as abnormal, seem to show that the unfathomed depths of man's racial nature are as illimitable as its lateral range. "It is a wonder," writes one of our war correspondents, "that never palls but is always new: the spirit which these men of ours possess from no matter what corner of the Empire they may have come. One wonders where the grumblers, the cowards, the mean people whom one thought one met in ordinary life have gone. They are not here. Or, if they are, they are uplifted and transfigured. They doubtless, many of them, could not express it, but some wind has blown upon them, some sense of comradeship and brotherhood inspires them, something has made true soldiers and gallant men of them all." Such a transformation as is described in this passage is inexplicable except on the assumption that there are immense reserves of spiritual vitality in the soul of the "plain average man," and that though for the most part these forces lie dormant and undreamed of, they can awake and energize when some great crisis makes its mute appeal to the man's highest self.

What is the explanation of this fundamental paradox? Why is it that, whereas on the physical plane our racial inheritance seems to be strictly limited, on the higher levels of our being infinitude seems to be of its very essence? The answer to this question may be given in a single word: *Consciousness.* What consciousness is, how we have acquired it, into what factors it admits of being analyzed, we cannot say.[1] What we can say is, that though foreshadowings and "weak beginnings" of it are to be found below the level of human life, consciousness is a distinctively human endowment, or rather it is *the* distinctively human endowment, the feature which, more than any other, differentiates us from all other living things and is therefore characteristic of man as man. Now consciousness, by enabling man to look before and after, and also to look all round an ever-widening horizon, throws open to him all the resources of the universe, and in doing so reveals to him—*in posse,* if not *in esse*—corresponding resources in himself. In other words, it raises, or tends to raise, "to infinity" all his powers and tendencies which are not merely physical. Thus it transforms instinct into reason, blind purpose into self-determining will, feeling into fellow-feeling, perception into imagination, sensuous enjoyment into the quest of ideal beauty, carnal desire into spiritual

[1] We may, if we please, define consciousness as the self-awareness of the soul, or, again, as the self-awareness of life. But no definition can enable us to fathom its fundamental mystery. If we would know what consciousness is, we must turn for instruction to consciousness itself, and open our hearts and minds to its dawning light.

love, communal devotion into the "enthusiasm of humanity," the instinct of self-preservation into the thirst for "eternal life."

In the awakening of consciousness, life begins to be aware of its own limitless possibilities. Before consciousness awakes, the current of life flows, blindly and instinctively, in a narrow channel between containing walls which it may never overpass. As consciousness awakes, the channel begins to widen, and a tidal wave flows up it fraught with

> Murmurs and scents of the infinite sea.

That message from the sea is the revelation of life to life, of self to self. Can we wonder that the racial inheritancee of the human soul has no limit, when consciousness, which is its differential feature, is the very principle of infinitude in man's life?

In respect, then, of its racial inheritance the individual soul either is in itself a reservoir of unlimited potentialities, or else has such a reservoir at its command. What part does lineal heredity play in its development? We have seen that on the physical plane our racial heritage is far larger and far more significant than our lineal heritage, the possession of eyes, for example, being of far more consequence than the particular colour of the eyes, the possession of a mouth than the particular shape of the mouth, and so on. Will it not be the same on the higher levels of human life? Will not the ratio between the two heritages be at least maintained? So one instinctively argues. But we shall presently find it necessary to look at the matter from a different point of view. To speak of a ratio between two finite or quasi-finite quantities is permissible. But when one of the quantities is infinite and the other unknown, the relation between the two is scarcely one of ratio, in the accepted sense of that word.

But let us for the moment assume that the arithmetical or quasi-arithmetical point of view holds good. Let us assume that our lineal heritage is a more or less calculable quantity, and let us try to determine its dimensions. We shall find that, far from being the preponderant element in human nature which it is sometimes supposed to be, it is an elusive, a negligible, and even a vanishing quantity. We shall find that by far the larger part of what we attribute to lineal heredity may just as plausibly, and indeed with better reason, be attributed to environment,—in other words, to racial heredity being allowed to come into play.

Let us consider some concrete cases.

A, who is the child of disreputable parents, grows up a ne'er-do-well. B, who is the child of respectable parents, grows up a respectable citizen. Will it be seriously contended that A inherits his disreputableness and B his respectability from their respective parents ? Is it not more than probable that, had A and B exchanged homes at birth, B would have become the ne'er-do-well and A the respectable citizen ? From birth to maturity A has been exposed to the influence of a bad, B of a good environment. Considering how impressionable and imitative children are, one may surely argue that the vital difference in the respective environments of the two boys is sufficient to account for the divergence of their respective paths in life.

C, allowed from his earliest days to run wild in a disorderly slum, acquires the language of the gutter, and uses it with vigour and effect. Will it be seriously contended that he inherited a " foul mouth " from his parents ? Is it not practically certain that if a princeling had been exposed at the same tender age to the same influences he too would have become a master of oaths and obscenities ?

D, the son of drunken parents, takes to drink at an early age. Was he born into the world with a latent craving for alcohol ? He may have inherited from his parents some slight infirmity of will. But in the main his downfall must surely be attributed to his unfortunate environment. His parents, in their moments of maudlin affection, may well have initiated him into their own ways. In any case he spent the most impressionable years of his life in a demoralizing atmosphere ; and a bad example was habitually set him by those whom he was naturally prone to imitate.

E, having been persistently bullied by his parents and school-teachers, takes to bullying his younger brothers and smaller school-fellows. Is there a strain of bullying in his blood ? We cannot say. What we can say is that in all probability he, like D, succumbed to the influences of a demoralizing atmosphere, and imitated those whom he naturally made his models.

These are some of the failures in life. As it is with the failures so it is with the successes. The respectable son of respectable parents has been taught from his earliest days to idealize respectability. The prosperous son of prosperous parents has always been accustomed to regard prosperity as his birthright. The refined and cultivated son of refined and cultivated parents has grown up in an atmosphere of refinement and culture. The musical son of musical parents, the artistic son of artistic parents—each of these owes something to inherited temperament, but he owes at least as much—and probably more—to the subtly plastic influences, musical or artistic, which began to act upon him while he was still in his mother's arms.

I could add to such cases indefinitely. Whenever I hear it said that such and such a disposition or such and such a trait is inherited from parents or ancestors, I ask myself whether an alliance between racial heredity and environment will not adequately account for the given phenomenon, and I almost invariably find that it seems to do so. I ask the same question—let me say in passing—and am able to give the same answer when I am told by Mr. H. Chamberlain and others that national characteristics—the independence and reserve of the Englishman, the "canniness" of the Scot, the lawlessness of the Irishman, the pride of the Spaniard, the arrogance and servility of the German—are "in the blood" of the several peoples, for I find that in every case the explanation of the predominance of the given trait seems to be historical rather than racial (in the narrow sense of the word).

But if familiar causes suffice to account for a given phenomenon, why should we try to account for it on grounds which are at best dubious and insecure? We know what we are talking about when we say that children are impressionable and imitative. We do not know what we are talking about when we say that mental and moral qualities are "in the blood." Let us at least exhaust the possibilities of the known before we invoke the aid of the unknown.

How comes it, then, that the fantastic belief in lineal heredity as the predominant factor in the formation of mentality and character prevails so widely? Partly, I think, because the orthodox doctrine of the supernatural origin of the individual soul is falling into disrepute, and physiology seems to a certain type of mind to provide the only alternative to it. But chiefly, I think, for two reasons, each of which is based on an interpretation of facts which really point to a widely different conclusion. We believe in the constraining force of lineal heredity because the infinite variety of human development and the infinite diversity—or apparent diversity—of human gifts and endowments leads us to concentrate our attention on the differential elements in human nature and to lose sight of the common elements. And we believe in it because "pure breeding," whether in a family, a tribe, a people, or a class, does in each case undoubtedly tend to preserve a particular type of character and a particular outlook on life.

Let us first consider the former reason. The infinite variety of human life, as it manifests itself in history or as it unfolds itself, in all its length and breadth, before our eyes—the fact that there seem to be innumerable types of human beings, that in many cases each human being seems to be a type in himself—has led careless observers to conclude that lineal heredity dominates human nature on all its higher planes. Two men living in adjoining houses may have so little in common, except on the physical and mental planes, that they seem to belong to entirely different species. A has moral and spiritual qualities which are not merely lacking but are actually inverted in B. What then? Is there no such thing as human nature? If two trees, similar in many respects, bore edible and poisonous fruit respectively, we should say that they belonged to different species. Is it not the same with men? If B hates where A loves, if B lies where A speaks the truth, if B is self-centred where A is self-forgetful, if B is self-indulgent where A is self-restrained, do not A and B belong to different species of the genus Man? If this is so, how are we to account for the disruption of the human race into so many species? If it is not so, how are we to account for the facts?

"To those who chattered Rousseau," says Dr. Hayward, "Herbart flung the question, 'What is the nature of Man?'" The naturalists who interest themselves in psychology are divided, as we have seen, into two great schools, the school of "Nature" and the school of "Nurture." These schools have one doctrine in common—namely, that there is no such thing as human nature, in the Herbartian sense of the phrase, no such thing as the "true manhood" of which Froebel dreamed, no such thing as a central, magisterial, all-controlling, all-explaining stream of tendency in human nature, which is waiting to assert itself in every man and which is therefore characteristic of man as man. But their interpretations of the fact on which they base this negative conclusion—the bewildering diversity of human development—are diametrically opposed to, and may perhaps be held to cancel, one another. The "Nature" school attribute that diversity to the unscientific intermixture of the different "strains" of Humanity. The "Nurture" school attribute it to the infinite variety and complexity of man's environment, which causes a different inscription, so to speak, to be written by the "moving finger" of Fate on the "neutral clean sheet" of each individual soul. There is a third interpretation which is, I think, at once less fantastic and less fatalistic than either of these, and more in keeping with the relevant facts. That the variety of man's life reflects the variety of his environment may be freely admitted. But to predicate activity of man's environment and passivity of man himself, alone among living beings, is surely to invert the true order of things. The oak-tree is in the acorn; and in the absence of convincing proof to the contrary, I must believe that whatever a man may become, in response to the influences that are brought to bear on him, that he has it in him to be. If, then, the variety of man's life reflects the variety of his environment, the reason is that in response to the ever varying stimulus of his environment man develops himself in ten thousand different directions; and the reason why he is able to do this is that he has inexhaustible reserves of potentiality to draw upon—or, in other words, that his racial, as opposed to his lineal, inheritance has no limits.

But here we must distinguish between the individual and the race. For man as man the environment is world-wide and infinitely varied. For this or that man the immediately available environment is, as a rule, strictly limited and comparatively monotonous. It is true that beyond the immediately available environment there is room for indefinite advance and expansion. A farm labourer, for example, may also be a member of the Catholic Church, and a citizen of the United Kingdom ; and he may have it in him to react to the stimulus of each of these environing communities. But the pressure of what I have called the immediately available environment—the material conditions of a man's life, the restrictions imposed on him by his upbringing, the limiting influences inherent in his calling and his social grade, and the like—is at all times strong, and, as the years go by, may well acquire irresistible strength. Potentially, however, this man or that man and man as man may almost be said to coincide. The contrast between the greatness of the individual's ideal destiny and the littleness of his actual destiny is indeed the supreme tragedy of man's life.

Yet in that supreme tragedy man holds the title-deeds of his great inheritance. Because the environment of man as man is world-wide and infinitely varied, and the environment of this or that man is by comparison narrow and monotonous, there is room and to spare for each individual environment to have a distinctive character of its own which reflects itself in the character of the individual who responds to it. And the inference to be drawn from this fact is not that there are innumerable species of the genus Man, but that man as man has it in him to respond and adapt himself to any and every environment. In other words, if each individual in turn can surround himself with a little world of his own by reference to which his individuality is developed and defined, the reason is that, on the one hand, as A or B or C, he is strictly limited by material and quasi-material conditions, and, on the other hand, as a human being, he has the whole Universe at his command ; and the reason why, as a human being, he has the whole Universe at his command, is that its infinitude reflects itself in his, reflects itself in the limitless reserves of potentiality which constitute his racial inheritance, and which make it possible for him to respond to every pressure and react to every stimulus. Thus the bewildering diversity of human development, which has generated the belief in the omnipotence of lineal heredity, in reality bears witness to man's infinite adaptability; and infinite adaptability, being potentially common to all men, is inherited by a man, not from his lineal ancestors, but from the whole human race.

And this is not all. It is not merely because he is infinitely adaptable that man is able to develop himself in so many different directions, but because, as a conscious being, he can react upon and even control his environment, and through his control of it can bring an infinite variety of transforming influences to bear upon himself. We have seen that consciousness is the principle of infinitude in man's life, that it raises to infinity all his higher powers and faculties, changing, for example, instinct into reason, perception into imagination, blind purpose into self-determining will, and so on. By raising his powers and faculties to infinity, consciousness extends his environment, potentially if not actually, to the uttermost limits of the Universe. For we mean by a man's environment so much of the Universe as he is able to react to; and as man's perceptive, reflective, and volitional faculties expand, the sphere of his reactivity expands proportionately until he finds himself the centre of an almost illimitable world. Or we may, if we please, invert the order of causation and say that, by indefinitely expanding his environment, consciousness raises to infinity man's powers and faculties. For so greatly does the world in which he lives expand in the dawning light of consciousness, that he finds himself compelled in self-defence to study the laws of his ever-widening environment, to realize its latent possibilities, to make his choice, again and again, among its resources. In his attempt to study its laws, instinct gradually transforms itself into reason. In his attempt to realize its latent possibilities, perception transforms itself into imagination. In his attempt to choose among its resources, blind purpose transforms itself into self-determining will. As these characteristically human faculties unfold themselves, it becomes possible for a man not merely to react to his environment, but to react upon it, to master it in some measure, to make experiments with it, to modify it in many ways, to make it subservient to his needs, to mould it to his desires, to open his heart to some of its influences, to harden his heart against others, to expand it till it embraces all the stars of heaven, to narrow it till it shrinks to the dimensions of a miser's garret.[1]

In reacting on his environment, man reacts, through his environment, on his own development. And his capacity for so reacting is unlimited. The response of a plant or an animal to environment is blind, instinctive, and involuntary. The response of man, at any rate on the higher levels of his being, is, in varying degrees, conscious, intelligent, and deliberate. The difference between the two responses is the difference between what is finite and what is infinite. The communal devotion of ants or bees is mechanically perfect, and varies nothing from ant to ant or from bee to bee; but it is what it is—"finished and finite"—and cannot possibly become anything else. The communal devotion of human beings varies from man to man and never attains to perfection, which is an ideal, not an accomplished fact; but it is capable of soaring to the sublimest height of patriotism or widening out into the "enthusiasm of humanity." And it owes its range and its variety to the transforming influence of consciousness. This example is typical. Consciousness, the most distinctively human of all man's endowments, is the ultimate source of that bewildering diversity of human development which is apt to blind our eyes to the fundamental unity of our higher nature,—that diversity which the "Nurture" school of psychologists try to account for by reference to the tyranny

[1] With the power of modifying and even transforming one's own environment comes the power of affecting, in greater or less degree, the environment of others. Each of us, as he goes through life, is the centre of an ever-moving circle of disturbance. In some cases the circle is wide; in others—the majority—it is comparatively narrow; but it is always wide enough to involve many lives besides one's own. In a very real sense each of us *is* his brother's keeper. His own bearing in life inevitably reacts —for good or for evil—upon the lives of others, affecting some profoundly, others only slightly, but touching many lives and influencing in some degree all that it touches.

of environment, and the "Nature" school by reference to the tyranny of "blood." That bewildering diversity would not be possible if each of us, as his racial birthright, had not unlimited reserves of potentiality to draw upon. Still less would it be possible if the dawning light of consciousness did not reveal to us, little by little, our inward possibilities and outward resources, and so stimulate us, each in his own way and his own degree, to enter into possession of our inheritance.

In conclusion. The profound differences between man and man which suggest to some minds that the human race has broken up, under the influence of haphazard breeding, into a multitude of species, and that lineal heredity is therefore the main factor in man's development, and the supreme arbiter of his destiny, really point to a diametrically opposite conclusion. The differences between man and man are caused by human nature—the nature of man as man—striving to realize its vast potentialities, in response to the stimulus of an environment which for each of us is ideally infinite, but actually limited by material conditions and other restrictive influences, and also perpetually reacted upon and modified by the man himself and his fellow-men. In other words, "the many" are generated by the self-realization of "the One"; and "the One"—the fundamental unity and totality of human nature—is at the heart of each individual man.

I have said that another reason why the fatalistic belief in the force of heredity prevails so widely is that pure breeding, whether in a family, a tribe, a nation, a class, or a caste, does undoubtedly safeguard and tend to perpetuate the tradition that dominates the particular environment into which the individual is born. There is a widespread prejudice against marrying into another nation than one's own. There is a still stronger prejudice against marrying into a lower social grade. And the prejudice against marrying into another coloured race is so strong that those who offend against it, especially if they belong to the politically dominant race, are regarded as social outcasts and shunned by their relations and friends. These prejudices are by no means unreasonable. It not unfrequently happens that the children of "mixed marriages" have the failings of both breeds and the virtues of neither. But why? Not because their blood is impure, but because they are born into two distinct traditions, and that those traditions mix badly, if they do not actually refuse to mix. By a tradition I mean the way of looking at life and dealing with life which has grown up among and is now characteristic of a particular race, or a particular community, or a particular class, or even a particular family. Pure breeding ensures the maintenance of such a tradition; and those who are in the tradition and value it are right to object to marrying into a tradition which is antagonistic to or even seriously divergent from their own. But they are wrong to give as their reason for objecting to it that they do not wish to contaminate their blood. What they really mean is that they do not wish to undermine or otherwise impair the tradition in which they have been reared and to which they cling. The notation in which we express ourselves in such cases needs to be revised. When we say that a man comes of a good stock or has good blood in his veins, we mean that he is born into and brought up in a good tradition. When we say that he is well-bred, we mean that, owing to the accident of his birth, he has been, or at least might have been, well brought up. We attribute to "nature" what is really due to "nurture." I have elsewhere referred to the case of the hybrid Eurasian and the pure-bred Jew of the Pale; and as what I said then still seems to me to hold good, I may perhaps be allowed to quote my own words: "It is sometimes said that the Eurasian in Hindostan has the faults of both the races from which he springs. In reality he has the faults of two widely dissimilar environments. For he is in the unhappy position of having a leg in each of two dissevered worlds. If he could be brought up from his birth either as an Englishman or as a Hindoo, all might be well with him. But it is his fate to be brought up both as an Englishman and as a Hindoo, and he is therefore perpetually torn asunder between two great and ancient civilizations which have so long been kept apart that they now refuse to blend. . . ." "The case of the Jew is interesting and to the point. Here, at any rate 'within the Pale,' purity of blood has been strictly maintained, and a social life, based on Pharisaic legalism, has continued unchanged from the time of the Dispersal to the present day. Does it follow that legalism is in the blood of the modern Jew? By no means. What has happened is that the purity of his blood has given him a homogeneous and practically unvarying environment, to the full force of which each individual member of the race is exposed from the moment of his birth. Where there are no marriages, and therefore little or no social intercourse, with outsiders, the same conception of life, the same scheme of life, the same culture, the same civilization, are handed down from generation to generation, and the pressure of their influence on the individual is well-nigh irresistible. But let the Jew emerge from the Pale, and intermarry with the Gentile, and he speedily shuffles off the oppressive burden of the Law." [1]

If these things are so; if the tragedy of the Eurasian is caused, not by two widely different strains of blood meeting in his veins, but by two widely different civilizations meeting in his life; if the legalism of the pure-bred Jew has come down to him as a tradition, and only as a tradition,—fifteen centuries of strict in-breeding having apparently failed to infuse a single atom of it into his blood; if (to take another case) in Paraguay, at the present day, "thanks to a homogeneous environment, we have remarkable homogeneity of character co-existing with almost unparalleled hybridity of race,"—can we resist the inference that the response of human nature—the generic nature of man—to the stimulus of environment is the main factor in the formation of character, and that breeding only counts because, and so far as, it serves to guide and control the formative influences of environment?

[1] *In Defence of What Might Be*, pp. 364–6.

CHAPTER IV

THE THEORY OF STRAIN

FROM the position which I reached at the end of the last chapter I pass on to the conclusion that the theory of "strain," as expounded by Professor Bateson and other naturalists, though it may hold good in an appreciable degree of man's physique, does not hold good of his character. The psychological and sociological implications of the theory of strain are so important that the question of its applicability to the higher levels of human nature deserves the most careful consideration. In his Address to the British Association at Melbourne, Professor Bateson supports his thesis that "of the overwhelmingly greater significance of 'nature' (in human life) there is no longer any possibility of doubt" by an appeal to "the universal experience of the breeder, whether of plants or animals, that strain is absolutely essential, that though bad conditions may easily enough spoil a good strain, yet that under the best of conditions a bad strain will never give a fine result." This argument begs the question which is in dispute. To argue from the facts of plant and animal life to the possibilities of human life is permissible—on two conditions. The thinker must satisfy himself that, as his argument develops, the analogy between the two kinds of life continues to hold good. And he must decline to accept the consequent conclusions until they have been verified in greater or less degree, by observation or experiment, or both. Neither of these conditions has been fulfilled by Professor Bateson. He assumes at the outset that the analogy between the two kinds of life is absolute and final; that it virtually amounts to identity; in other words, that man is an animal and nothing more. And he makes no attempt to verify his conclusion. The question which is really in dispute is this: Does the biological theory of "strain" apply to the higher or more spiritual levels of human nature? If it does, the "universal experience of the breeder" may fairly be appealed to. But until we have satisfied ourselves that it does—until we have satisfied ourselves, for example, that the "lower orders" are, in respect of mentality and character, of an inferior strain to the "upper classes"—the experience of the breeder counts for nothing in this controversy, and Professor Bateson's argument must be ruled out of court.

In order to make his point of view clear Professor Bateson reviews and criticizes a passage in my book *What Is and What Might Be.*[1] In order to make my point of view clear, I will quote his criticism and then reply to it:—

"Having witnessed the success of a great teacher in helping unpromising peasant children to develop their natural powers, he (the author of *What Is and What Might Be*) gives us the following botanical parallel. Assuming that the wild bullace is the origin of domesticated plums, he tells us that by cultivation the bullace can no doubt be improved so as to become a better bullace, but by no means can the bullace be made to bear plums. All this is sound biology; but translating these facts into the human analogy, he declares that the work of the successful teacher shows that with man the facts are otherwise, and that the *average* rustic child, whose normal ideal is 'bullacehood,' can become the rare exception, developing to a stage corresponding with that of the plum. But the naturalist knows exactly where the parallel is at fault. For . . . the bullace is breeding approximately true, whereas the human crop, like jute and

[1] Professor Bateson speaks of my book as "charming though pathetic." I am glad that it charmed so competent a judge. But why does he call it pathetic? Does he think that I am one of the "educationists" whom "faith, not evidence . . . encourages to hope so greatly in the ameliorating conditions of life"? If he does, let me assure him that, on the contrary, it is evidence, not (mere) faith, which has made me an optimist as regards the efficacy of "nurture" in general and education in particular. For many years, if I did not actually believe, I certainly took for granted, that the upper classes were of a superior "strain" to the lower, and I had therefore but little faith in the transforming influence of education. But experience, in "Egeria's" and other schools, convinced me, late in life, that my arrogant assumption was a mere superstition, and that the lower classes were as well able to respond to the stimulus of a vivifying education as the upper.

various cottons, is in a state of polymorphic mixture. The population of many English villages may be compared with the crop which would result from sowing a bushel of kernels gathered mostly from the hedges with an occasional few from the orchard. If anyone asks how there are any plum-kernels in the sample at all, he may find the answer perhaps in spontaneous variation, but more probably in the appearance of a long hidden recession. For the want of that genetic variation, consisting probably, as I have argued, in loss of inhibiting factors, by which the plum arose from the wild form, neither food, nor education, nor hygiene can in any way atone. Many wild plants are half-starved through competition, and transferred to garden soil they grow much bigger; so good conditions might certainly enable the bullace population to develop beyond the stunted physical and mental status they commonly attain, but plums they can never be." What does the last sentence in this paragraph mean? Is Professor Bateson denying my facts, or is he merely denying the possibility of human bullaces being transformed into human plums? I think he is denying my facts. Had I said that *some* of the Utopian bullaces developed into plums, and had I attributed this to "Egeria's" transforming influence, Professor Bateson's explanation of what happened would certainly have been worth considering. But I said then, and I say now with equal emphasis, that before they left "Egeria's" school, all or nearly all the Utopian bullaces had become plums; in other words, that the average child had developed certain plum-like qualities which I enumerated in my book—namely, "activity, versatility, imaginative sympathy, a large and free outlook, self-forgetfulness, charm of manner, joy of heart." [1] When I say this I am stating what I believe to be a fact. Now a fact, or rather the report of a fact, must either be accepted or rejected. If it is accepted, the logical consequences of accepting it must also be accepted. If it is rejected, the rejection must be based on one (or both) of two grounds. The first is that the reporter either misread the evidence of his senses, or, if he spoke from hearsay, was misinformed. The second is that the reported fact is intrinsically quite

[1] That these are plum-like qualities will, I think, be generally admitted.

incredible. Professor Bateson cannot from his own experience deny the fact that I have reported, for he never visited "Egeria's" school. But because his theories fail to account for the fact, he rejects it off-hand, though it is *not* intrinsically incredible, on purely *a priori* grounds. Such a proceeding is unworthy of a scientific mind. I have always understood that when a fact collides with a theory, it is the latter, not the former, that goes to the wall. A witty Frenchman has made fun of the scientists who will not allow that any phenomenon can take place which official science has not authorized Nature to produce. Professor Bateson goes further than this. For he will not allow that human nature can bear any fruit which his biological theories, *based on the study of plants and animals only*, have not authorized it to bear. In taking up this attitude he leans too heavily on the argument from analogy. It is useless for him to tell me that because no amount of culture can enable a bullace-tree to bear plums, therefore the average Utopian child could not have developed the plum-like qualities with which I credited him. I say that he did develop those qualities, and that judicious and sympathetic culture enabled him to do so.

But perhaps Professor Bateson is merely denying in general terms that human bullaces can be transformed into human plums. If so, he is probably right. But if he is, and if my facts hold good, his theory of "strain," so far as it applies to human beings, goes to the wall. I am grateful to Professor Bateson for having compelled me to re-read the passage which he criticized. For I see now that there is a serious flaw in my argument, a flaw which escaped my notice when I composed the passage. I assumed that the rustic inhabitants of Utopia were a "bullace population"; in other words, that they belonged for the most part to an inferior "strain." Whether I really believed this when I wrote my book I cannot say for certain. It is possible that a superstition of which I had but recently, under "Egeria's" influence, begun to divest myself, still lingered in my mind —the superstition that the "lower orders" are by birth and breeding our inferiors in mentality and character. In any case, I wrote as if I was still the victim of that superstition;

and I therefore claimed by implication that "Egeria" had wrought a miracle. Professor Bateson might have reminded me that, as miracles do not happen, if "Egeria's" pupils really reached the plum level, they must have been plums *in posse* from their earliest days. But instead of doing this he assumed, with me, that the bulk of the Utopian children belonged to the bullace breed, and argued from this that they could not and did not develop into plums. My answer to this argument—an answer which I will repeat as often as it is called for—is that plums those children certainly were, and plums of a very high quality,—that the average Utopian child was in fact a better specimen of plumhood than the average product of what we call "good breeding" and "gentle birth." And I can now draw for myself the inference from my own premises which Professor Bateson might have drawn for me (if only to reject it, when drawn),—that neither mentally nor morally are the lower classes inferior *at birth* to the upper; that the average peasant in particular is not a bullace, but a plum—a plum which, owing to the combined influences of poor soil, unfavourable climate, and unskilful culture, has missed its high destiny and fallen below the normal level of plum growth.

How completely Professor Bateson, as an interpreter of human nature, is obsessed by the biological theory of "strain" is shown by the following passages in his Melbourne Address: "Modern statesmanship aims rightly at helping those who have got sown as wildings to come into their proper class; but let not anyone suppose such a policy democratic in its ultimate effects, for no course of action can be more effective in strengthening the upper classes, while weakening the lower."[1] . . . "In all practical schemes for social reform the congenital diversity, the essential polymorphism of all civilized communities must be recognized as a fundamental fact, and reformers should rather direct their efforts to facilitating and rectifying class dis-

[1] The theory which Professor Bateson has expounded must surely have originated in Germany. One can imagine with what gusto the Hohenzollerns and the Prussian Junkers would lay its flattering unction to their souls. One might even conjecture that the professor who elaborated it, if of "bullace" origin, was raised to the "plum" level by royal mandate and made a "von" in recognition of his newly-acquired superior strain.

tinctions, than to any futile attempt to abolish them. . . . The instability of society is due, not to inequality, which is inherent and congenital, but to the fact that in periods of rapid change like the present convection currents are set up such that the elements of the strata get intermixed and the apparent stratification corresponds only roughly with the genetic."

These passages set one thinking. When one remembers by what methods the "upper classes" in this and other countries, and in this and other ages, have gained the upper hand, how largely they have owed their ascendancy to force or to fraud or to a judicious mixture of force and fraud, how much of their reputed ability has been sheer unscrupulousness, how much of their reputed force of character has been ruthless self-assertion,—one begins to wonder what are the qualities, superiority in which differentiates the "high-born" aristocracy from the "low-born" populace. Are they the qualities which Christ pronounced blessed in the Sermon on the Mount? I doubt it. As I turn the pages of history, I find that again and again the ungodly flourished like a green bay-tree,—flourished so triumphantly that he was able to bequeath his ill-gotten prosperity to the third and fourth, and even to the tenth, generation of his descendants. In such a case did the successful scoundrel bequeath his character as well as his position and wealth? According to Professor Bateson he must have done so. But, if he did, there is surely a flaw in his descendants' title to social and political ascendancy.

Professor Bateson has raised an interesting and difficult question. Will he help us to answer it? Are his "upper classes" an aristocracy of physique, of intellect, of morals, of spirituality? That they are "inherently and congenitally" superior in all four directions is a proposition which those who are well acquainted with both classes will laugh to scorn, and which even Professor Bateson will scarcely have the hardihood to maintain. Were the robber knights of the Rhine, are the arrogant barons of East Prussia and the Baltic Provinces "high-born"? Are the Franciscan brothers and sisters, whose ideal of life has always been diametrically opposed to that of knight or baron, "low-born"? The pedigree of a dog or a horse is recorded in certain unmistakable features. In what features, inward or outward, does Nature record the pedigree of the "high-born" or the "low-born" man? This is a point on which Professor Bateson would do well to enlighten us, but on which he prefers to keep silence.

Let us try to answer the question which he has left unanswered. He seems to take for granted that the upper classes in this country—the nobility, gentry, and professional men, let us say—are mostly plums, and that the lower classes—the peasants, miners, and artisans, let us say—are mostly bullaces. Wherein, then, do the upper classes show their inherent and congenital superiority to the lower? That they are richer, better educated, and have more social and political influence goes without saying. But in the first place a man may be rich, well-educated, and influential, and yet be a base-souled villain; and in the second place riches, education, and social and political influence belong to a man's environment rather than to his blood. That the upper classes are of superior physique may perhaps be admitted, though even in this respect the difference between the two classes at birth is comparatively small, the physical superiority of the average adult specimen of the upper classes being largely due to healthier surroundings and better food. That they are superior in mental power is disputable, to say the least. The adult peasant is no doubt less cultured and less intellectual than the adult "gentleman"; but he has been exposed from his birth, both at home and in school, to much less favourable educational influences, and it is to this rather than to any inherited inferiority that his short-comings, cultural and intellectual, are probably due. What the inherent and congenital mentality of the lower classes really is, or how it compares with that of the upper classes, we do not know. What we do know is that the peasant, the miner, and the artisan are born into a cramping and depressing environment, the product of social and economic causes, from which they cannot easily escape, and in which it is as difficult for their mental powers to unfold as for a tree to thrive in an exposed situation or a poor soil. This fact invites imaginative conjecture as to what might be or might have been. The psychology of Gray's *Elegy*, which wisely limits itself to "perhaps" and "may," is, I believe, absolutely sound:

> Perhaps in this neglected spot is laid
> Some heart once pregnant with celestial fire;
> Hands that the rod of empire might have sway'd
> Or waked to ecstasy the living lyre:
>
> But knowledge to their eyes her ample page
> Rich with the spoils of time, did ne'er unroll;
> Chill Penury repressed their noble rage,
> And froze the genial current of the soul.
>
> . . . .
>
> Some village Hampden that with dauntless breast
> The little tyrant of his fields withstood;
> Some mute inglorious Milton here may rest,
> Some Cromwell guiltless of his country's blood.
>
> Th' applause of list'ning senates to command,
> The threats of pain and ruin to despise,
> To scatter plenty o'er a smiling land,
> And read their history in a nation's eyes,
>
> Their lot forbade. . . .

Some such epitaph as this might be written on many a nameless grave in country churchyard or urban cemetery. It was said that in the Napoleonic armies every soldier carried a Field-Marshal's baton in his knapsack; and it is a fact that some of the ablest of Napoleon's lieutenants rose from the ranks. Why? Because in Republican France the superstition of the congenital inferiority of the lower classes had been temporarily swept away by the Revolution, and because the Republican tradition had been inherited by the Empire and respected by the Emperor, whose own genius had raised him from obscurity to supreme power, and who was on the look-out for talent in the armies that he led.[1] In the British Army, where the soldiers fought "under the cold shade of aristocracy," the private who, had he been

[1] "If Louis XVI had continued to reign," says Stendhal, "Danton and Moreau would have been advocates; Pichegru, Massena and Augereau non-commissioned officers; Desaix and Kléber captains; Bonaparte and Carnot lieutenant-colonels or colonels of artillery; Lannes and Murat shop-keepers or kept a post-office; Siéyès would have been a suffragan bishop; and Mirabeau a minor diplomatist."

born in France, might have become a Field-Marshal, would probably have won his stripes, or at best become a subaltern, and gone no further. The constitution of things was against his rising to the height of his deserts. " His lot forbade " his advancement.

The experiment which the Republican War Ministers initiated and which Napoleon carried on is of lasting interest and opens up a wide vista to speculative thought. Professor Bateson will perhaps contend that the Marshals who rose from the ranks were plums which had " got sown as wildings." But no: a Field-Marshal is, *in his own line*, a super-plum, not a plum; and where there is one super-plum there must be thousands and tens of thousands of plums. In the Napoleonic armies, as in the Republican, there was a temporary relaxation of a deadening pressure. If that concession could enable many soldiers, who would otherwise in all probability have lived and died in obscurity, to rise to the very highest grade of all, what might not a general equalizing of conditions do in the way of raising the lower classes to the mental level of the upper? This is a question which the romantic stories of such men as Ney, Murat, Hoche, Lannes, Massena, Augereau and others compel us to ask ourselves. In our attempts to answer it we can, I think, pass beyond the limits of mere conjecture. The " Egeria " of my book was the first to convince me that, under favourable conditions, foremost among which is an attitude of trust and encouragement on the part of the teacher, the village boy or girl can rival the child of the upper classes in all-round mental capacity,—in resourcefulness, in initiative, in versatility, in intellectual power, in literary and artistic taste. Other teachers have since taught me the same lesson. Not long after my discovery of " Utopia," the head master of an elementary school in the East of London showed me some admirable drawings done by his pupils. I asked him what proportion of his pupils could reach that level. He answered: " Had you asked me that question a year ago I would have said '5 per cent,' but now I can say '95 per cent.' " As a teacher of drawing he had recently changed his aims and methods. Had he not done so, he would have continued to take for granted that 95 per cent of his pupils had little or no capacity for drawing. More recently I was shown some thirty or forty poems written by girls in a higher standard elementary school in one of our northern manufacturing towns. The high level of feeling and expression reached in these poems astonished me.[1] The head mistress explained to me that being in need of "copy" for the school magazine, she encouraged the girls to try their hands at writing verse. The girls, who had long had access to a good school library, containing many volumes of poetry, responded with alacrity. The teacher added that "our poetry is only a very small part of our literature scheme,[2] the carrying out of which is to the children pure joy, and these poems are only first attempts." Similar discoveries of latent taste and talent in the average elementary school-child are constantly being made. They point to serious defects in our system or systems of education, which do so much for the child, of whatever social grade, and leave so little to his spontaneous activity, that his mind is still in large measure an unexplored land. If education could be reformed in the direction of setting children free to develop individuality and realize latent capacity, it would, I think, be found that the mental ability

[1] Here is one of the poems :—

LATE OCTOBER

Patter of fitful rain,
Shiver of falling leaves,
And wail of wind which has left behind
The glory of fruit and sheaves.

Mist on the crowning hills,
Mist in the vales below,
And grief in the heart that has seen depart
Its summer of long ago.

A similar and equally successful experiment has been made in one of the lower forms of a Girls' Municipal High School. "Original poetry by children," writes Miss Fletcher, one of the teachers in that school, "is an interesting subject, but space forbids full discussion here. Enough to state that I have experimented independently in this direction, and am amazed and delighted at the result. I believe that most intelligent children of this age have within them, mostly latent, a vein of poetry, simple and rhythmical, and need only the right stimulus to use and delight in the power." Most of Miss Fletcher's pupils would be of "bullace" breed, some being ex-elementary scholars and others the daughters of lower middle-class parents.

[2] This is quite true. The prose efforts of the children are as remarkable as their poems.

of both the upper and the lower classes was much greater than we had imagined it to be. But it would not be found that the mental ability of the upper classes was appreciably greater than that of the lower. Such at least is the conviction which my recent educational experiences and my re-interpretation, in the light which they cast, of former experiences have forced upon my mind.

The idea that the upper classes are by nature morally and spiritually superior to the lower is a dangerous delusion, of which, for their own sakes, those who belong to the upper classes would do well to rid themselves. If the lower classes fill more than their share of our prison cells, the reason is that many of them are born into and reared in criminal surroundings, that they are beset by temptations to dishonesty and other forms of lawlessness to which the upper classes are not exposed, and that, in spite of the desire of our legislators to do justice to all classes, there is still one law for the rich and another for the poor.[1] Criminality is not viciousness. The lower classes may be more criminal than the upper, in the sense of being more frequently convicted of offences against the law, but they are certainly not more vicious.[2] If anything, they are less selfish and less worldly. But this too can easily be explained. The disadvantages of environment are not all on the side of the poor. The rich are exposed to temptations from which the poor are largely, if not wholly, exempt. It was said of old by one who taught with authority that it is easier for a camel to go through the eye of a needle than for a rich man to enter into the Kingdom of Heaven. Did not Christ mean by this that outward prosperity, with its temptations to self-indulgence (a hydra-headed vice), to worldliness (with the perversion

[1] See Judge Parry's book, *The Law and the Poor*, passim.

[2] The upper classes may possibly flatter themselves that they are more continent than the lower. The author of *A Student in Arms* who, as a private, a non-commissioned officer and a commissioned officer in Kitchener's Army, mixed freely with all sorts and conditions of men, disputes this claim. Commenting on the belief that the "lower classes" are "naturally coarser and more animal than the upper classes," he writes: "I want . . . to contradict that belief with all the vehemence of which I am capable. Officers and men necessarily develop different qualities, different forms of expression, different mental attitudes. But I am confident that I speak the truth when I say that essentially and in the eyes of God there is nothing to choose between them."

of ideals which it involves) and to arrogance (with its acceptance as final of an outward standard of value), is ever tending to distract the prosperous from the inward life? Bearing these things in mind, let us hold the scales even between the two classes, and say that on the moral and spiritual planes neither is inherently superior to the other. The present war has proved to demonstration that there are vast reserves of heroism and self-devotion in human nature, and that in this respect the upper classes are not more richly endowed than the lower, nor the lower classes than the upper. One of our officers, writing from the front, says of his men: "I'm not emotional, but . . . since I've been out here in the trenches I've had the water forced into my eyes, not once, but a dozen times, from sheer admiration and respect, by the action of rough rude chaps whom you'd never waste a second glance on in the streets of London, men who, so far from being exceptional, are typical through and through, just the common street average. . . . Under the strain and stress of this savage existence these men show up for what they really are under their rough hides; they are jewel all through . . . and the daily round of their lives is simply full of little acts of self-sacrifice, generosity, and unstudied heroism." And our men at the front have often written in equivalent terms of their officers. The truth is that, in response to the stimulus of this tremendous war, sublime qualities are ever awaking which exist as possibilities in those hidden depths of our nature where distinctions of class and breeding are unknown, and which are therefore, in the real meaning of the phrase, characteristic of man as man. In the Kingdom of Heaven there is no such thing as "strain."

Thus the "inherent and congenital" superiority of the upper to the lower classes, which Professor Bateson seems to postulate, resolves itself, when carefully considered, into a doubtful superiority in physique. When we ask the upper classes to make good their claim to superiority in intellect, in morals, in spirituality, the evidence which they bring forward proves to be wholly inconclusive. On the higher levels of human nature such phrases as *well-born, high-born, well-bred, good birth, good breeding*, and their opposites, have no meaning. Or rather, so far as they have a meaning, they indicate superiority or inferiority in respect of inherited environment, not of breed. The infinitude which is of the essence of human nature is as much the birthright of the peasant or the miner as of the plutocrat or the peer. The biological theory of strain, when applied to human beings, may lend its countenance to the arrogance of those who are born into high places. But that proves nothing except that, like the arrogance which it seems to countenance, the theory, as an interpretation of human nature, is profoundly materialistic at heart. The philosophy of life which resolves psychology into physiology is vitiated by one fundamental fallacy. It ignores the transforming, expanding, sublimating power of consciousness. It ignores the soul.

CHAPTER V

THE ANCESTRY OF THE SOUL

WHAT, then, does a man inherit from his lineal ancestors, near or remote? Is his heritage purely physical? If "Yes" is my answer to this question, I must at once modify it by reminding myself that on this plane of existence and in this life the physical and spiritual sides of man's nature cannot be disjoined. There is a physical side to spirituality just as there is a spiritual side to physique. *Expression*, for example, is a spiritual feature of the outer man, and as such is much more within a man's control than are the physical features which are transmitted to him by his parents and other lineal ancestors. A man cannot, by taking thought or action, alter the shape of his nose, unless indeed by his own folly he exposes it to the ravages of disease; but he can by his manner of living alter and even transform his expression. It is the same, *mutatis mutandis*, with the inner man, the soul. If we think of the soul as *character*, we see that there is a physical side to it, namely, *temperament*. If we think of it as *mentality*, we see that there is a physical side to it, namely, *brain power*. That temperament and brain power, though they seem to belong to the inner man, are in the main inherited (in the narrower sense of the word) is, I think, as certain as that expression, though it seems to belong to the outer man, is not inherited, or is so only in a minor degree.

But temperament and brain power are only the lines or surfaces of contact between the body and the soul. What of the soul itself? Have we any evidence that character, as distinguished from temperament, or that mind, as distinguished from brain power, is transmissible from father to son, or from ancestor to descendant? I think not. Such evidence as seems to be forthcoming is found, when carefully analyzed, to be vitiated, either by lineal heredity having been credited with influences which really emanate from environment, or by temperament having been confused with character, and brain power with mind.

On the other hand there is, I think, positive evidence that the soul does not, or rather cannot, descend from father to son. I have given my reasons for believing that the average man has practically limitless reserves of spiritual and mental vitality, reserves which are not the less real because he may be unable to bring more than a very small part of them into action. In other words, I have given my reasons for thinking that on the higher levels of life our racial inheritance is infinite. If I am right, the question which I have asked is answered. It would be as reasonable to suppose that the Gulf Stream could flow through a drainpipe as that the infinite reserves of mental and spiritual vitality with which each of us is endowed could be transmitted through the medium of a speck of protoplasm.

What, then, is the ancestry of the soul? We are now in a region of pure conjecture. When Professor Bateson tells us that "Shakespeare once existed as a speck of protoplasm no bigger than a pin's head," and that "to this nothing was added that would not equally well have served to build up a baboon or a rat," he is begging a very large question. Because he is an expert at biology he is claiming the right to lay down the law on a matter which is so great and has so many implications that "the soul of the wide world" is alone competent to deal with it. In doing this he is exceeding the warrant of his credentials, high as these doubtless are. It is possible that the statement which he makes so confidently is entirely wrong. It is possible that at a certain stage in the development of the Shakespearean speck of protoplasm, something very important was added to it, namely, the soul of Shakespeare. At any rate, the problem which Professor Bateson solves in this off-hand way infinitely transcends the province of any expert; and therefore, though no one is entitled to dogmatize about it, anyone who will take the trouble to think is free to consider it.

The best way to approach such a problem is to examine the solutions of it that at present hold the field. Of the current solutions of the problem of the soul's origin there are four which deserve attention :

(1) The first is the theory of the *supernatural* creation of the soul.

(2) The second is the theory of the *protoplasmic* origin of the soul.

(3) The third is the theory of *epigenesis*, or the building up of the soul by environmental influences.

(4) The fourth is the theory of *reincarnation*, or the evolution of the soul through a sequence of earth-lives.

(1) According to the first of these theories, each soul in turn is created by the supernatural God and enters the growing organism during its pre-natal life. This theory, which has the sanction of Christian theology, is rigidly predestinarian in tendency ; and as, according to the same theology, the destiny of the individual is either eternal misery or eternal bliss, the theory in question lays a heavy responsibility on him whose creative will is ever peopling and re-peopling the earth. Calvinism has accepted this responsibility on behalf of the Creator ; but the other schools of Christian thought, shrinking from the logical consequences of accepting it, have tried to minimize or to evade it. I will not press this objection to the orthodox theory ; for my own objection to it strikes at its very roots. A theory which takes for granted the dualism of Nature and the Supernatural is conceived, as it seems to me, in error. But this is a point on which I do not propose to enlarge ; for having elsewhere tried to show that our existing disorders and discontents are largely due to our having accepted supernaturalism as a philosophy of the Universe, and worked it out, both in theory and practice, into a philosophy of life, I feel that I need not take pains to disprove this particular application of the fundamental postulate of supernaturalism. And even if I believed in the Supernatural, I should protest, in the name of logical economy, against supernatural causes being invoked to account for natural phenomena while the resources of natural causation were still unexhausted.

(2) I will therefore pass on to the second theory. If the first is spiritually predestinarian, the second is physically fatalistic. In the two sentences which I have quoted from Professor Bateson's Address the protoplasmic theory is set forth with uncompromising directness. I have given my reasons for rejecting this theory. Posing as a reasoned conclusion it resolves itself into the assumption that the "significance" of "nature" (lineal heredity) as a factor in human development is "overwhelmingly greater" than that of "nurture" (environment). This assumption resolves itself into another, namely, that the laws of the plant and animal worlds govern human life, govern it so rigorously that the solution of psychological problems rests with physiology, not with psychology. The positive evidence for the "overwhelmingly greater significance of nature" is not merely inconclusive, but actually admits of being so interpreted as to point in the opposite direction; for again and again we find that traits and tendencies which are supposed to be "inherited" are really due to the racial or generic nature of man, which seems to be infinitely adaptable and resourceful, reacting to the stimulus of an infinitely comprehensive and variable environment. But my chief objection to the protoplasmic theory is that in the act of accounting for the soul it abolishes it. For, in order to pass the soul through the narrow channel of a "speck of protoplasm," it must needs deprive it of its infinitude; and to deprive it of its infinitude is to destroy its identity; for consciousness, which differentiates man from all other living things, is the very principle of infinitude in his life. If the soul is nothing more than a function of the body, the protoplasmic theory of its origin is obviously correct. But in that case the soul is non-existent; and the body, with its powers and functions, is the whole man. If Shakespeare once existed as a speck of protoplasm, and if to this nothing was added that would not equally well have served to build up a baboon or a rat, then the soul of Shakespeare was no more of a reality than the soul of a baboon or a rat.[1] What then? Will this

[1] I mean by this that it belonged to the same order of reality (or unreality). The difference between it and the soul of the baboon or the rat was a difference of degree, not of kind.

physiological solution of the master problem of psychology permanently content the biologist ? No : he is no " vitalist " ; and sooner or later, constrained by the logic of his own conceptions, he will either have to abandon the protoplasmic theory as inadequate or allow a mechanical solution of the same problem to take its place. Life, as the biologist who resolves psychology into physiology conceives it, is bound in the iron fetters of necessity. The constraining forces of heredity, acting through the speck of protoplasm, are irresistible. The biologist will probably admit that a man can modify his environment and to that extent react on his destiny ; but this concession will do nothing to lift the cloud of physical fatalism with which his theory of the soul overshadows man's life. For the power of modifying environment is as much inherent in the speck of protoplasm which will become a man, as any other of its constituent elements ; and when reaction on destiny is itself predestined, it is an illusion to feel that one is free.

(3) The third theory is at once contradictory of and complementary to the second. The basis of it is recognition, *by another school of biologists*, of the fact that " nurture is inconceivably more important than nature." It has been expounded by Dr. Chalmers Mitchell in his instructive book *Evolution and the War*. Dr. Chalmers Mitchell is dealing with the causes of national differentiation ; but his arguments apply with equal force to the causes of individual differentiation. His criticism of Mendelian assumptions is outspoken and direct. He considers that Professor Bateson's " bold pronouncements " in Australia have " opened the flood-gates to dogmatic quackery." And when Professor Bateson tells his audience that " with little hesitation we can now declare that the potentialities and aptitudes, physical as well as mental, sex, colours, powers of work or of invention, liability to diseases, possible duration of life, and the other features by which the members of a mixed population differ from each other, are determined from the moment of fertilization " his critic observes that for the inclusion of " mental potentialities and aptitudes in such a generalization . . . there is no scrap of positive evidence." He adds that " there is nothing but theory to support the

proposition that in the case of man nature 'has an overwhelmingly greater significance' than nurture."

What makes this criticism the more significant is that Dr. Chalmers Mitchell's own standpoint is strictly physiological. It is true that he lays great stress on the part that consciousness and the sense of freedom play in human life; but though he deprecates Bergson's attempt "to associate consciousness and the sense of freedom not merely with human life but with all life," and though he holds that "consciousness and freedom, purpose and intelligence," are not "to be ascribed to lowly animals," he yet believes "with Darwin, that as the body of man has been evolved from the body of animals, so the intellectual, emotional, and moral faculties of man have been evolved from the qualities of animals." Nor does he "shrink from the implications even of the phrase that thought is a secretion of the brain as bile is a secretion of the liver." How, then, has the soul of man, as he reads its history, been evolved? "By the moulding pressure of environment," is his answer to this question. In his opinion "the most important of the moulding forces that produce the differences in nationality are epigenetic, that is to say, they are imposed on the hereditary material and have to be reimposed on each generation." And what is true of the differences in nationality is true of the differences in individuality. "It is after the Miltonoplasm (the germ of the future Milton) has grown into a sentient human being that the factors most potent in shaping the direction, quality, and value of his mental and emotional output come into operation. These factors are in his environment, not in himself: they are products of the 'Kultur' of the nation in which he lives, and they, at least, are created by human will and are subject to human will." So far as "these epigenetic agencies . . . acting on the mind and emotions" are concerned, "the mind and the body of the infant are neutral, clean sheets on which many kinds of writing may be impressed." From these passages I gather that the epigenesists transfer activity from the organism to the environment, and substitute for the physiological conception of the organism reacting to the environment, the more mechanical conception of the environment moulding the organism, moulding its "mind and emotions" as well as its body. But whence does the environment derive its plastic force? The answer to this question is a startling paradox. "The factors most potent in shaping the direction, quality, and value of" a man's "mental and emotional output . . . are created by human will and are subject to human will." How can this be? How can the environment derive its plastic force from the victim of its own plastic pressure? How can a "neutral clean sheet" develop into a "creative will"? To cover a sheet of paper with script will not, as far as I can see, give it the power of creating the writer's pen and ink, not to speak of his right hand, his mind, and his will. Dr. Chalmers Mitchell "asserts as a biological fact, that the moral law is as real and as external to man as the starry vault." If this is so, how can it be said that "its creation and sustenance are the crowning glory of man"? To criticize in detail a theory which entangles itself in such paradoxes would be a waste of time. The objections to it are at once fundamental and obvious. Until Dr. Chalmers Mitchell can explain to us how the transition, in the life of man, from absolute passivity to the highest conceivable form of activity is effected, I must be allowed to hold that the epigenetic, like the protoplasmic theory of the soul, has failed to make good.

(4) When experts flatly contradict one another on matters of vital importance, the amateur instinctively assumes that the truth lies between them, that both are right and both wrong, and that what is needed is a larger and more comprehensive conception, belonging perhaps to a higher level of thought, by which their respective theories will be alternately justified and condemned. The protoplasmic and the epigenetic theories of the soul embody the attempts of scientific experts to solve the central problem of psychology in terms of physiological concepts. So far as I know, these are the only physiological theories of the soul that hold the field; and as they cancel one another, I am driven to conclude that physiology cannot do the work of psychology, that the soul must be accepted on its own evidence, and that all attempts to account for it on physiological grounds must be abandoned as futile.

Now to accept the soul on its own evidence is to accept without reserve the revelation of the growing and deepening light of consciousness. For what is essential in the outgrowth of consciousness is that an inward source of light is bearing witness to itself in the world-revealing rays which it casts, just as the dawning sun reveals the treasures and wonders of earth and in doing so bears witness to itself. That inward source of light is what we call the soul or self. As the soul becomes aware of itself and begins to distinguish between itself and the world which it looks out upon, in the very act of guaranteeing a dependent reality to the latter, it claims intrinsic reality for itself. Recognition of the validity of this claim is the basic assumption of psychology; and if we reject the rival theories of the biologists, we must make this assumption our starting-point in our quest of the true theory of the soul.

Can we do otherwise? If consciousness, with the sense of freedom which accompanies it, is, as Dr. Chalmers Mitchell contends, "the centre from which all science, all philosophy, all emotion, must set out in exploration of the universe and to which they must all return"; if it "transforms all the qualities and faculties acquired by human beings from the animal world and is the foundation of free and intelligent existence"; if it "puts man and the nations he makes above the laws of the unconscious world"; if it "gives man the power of being at once the actor, the spectator, and the critic"; if it "enables him to distinguish between self and not self"; if it "brings with it the sense of responsibility and reality,"—if consciousness is all this, and does all these things, and if all attempts to account for it on physiological grounds are, as Dr. Chalmers Mitchell insists, disastrous failures (his own attempt being tantamount to a confession that the mystery of its origin is impenetrable), what course is open to us but to accept its explanation of itself? Now what consciousness tells us about itself is that its subject, that which is conscious—the soul, as we call it,—is not merely as real as the outward world to which its body or outward self belongs, but has a higher kind of reality which it—the soul—is alone competent to investigate and value.

> There shines no light save its own light to show
> Itself unto itself.

Let us now go back to the protoplasmic and the epigenetic theories, and, assuming that the truth lies between these, let us ask ourselves how far each is right, and how far wrong. The protoplasmists are right when they affirm that the future man is in the human embryo; but they are wrong when they identify the human embryo with the fertilized germ-cell; for in so doing they bring the higher developments of human life under the control of physical necessity, and thereby limit unduly the possibilities of the future man, de-spiritualizing his spiritual life, lowering him to the animal level of existence, and ignoring or at best minimizing his power of transforming himself by reacting to the stimulus of environment. The epigenesists are right when they insist that the "possession of consciousness and the sense of freedom is a vital and overmastering distinction between man and beast"; they are right when they affirm that the possibilities of human development, under the transforming influence of consciousness and in response to the stimulus of environment, are practically boundless, even within the limits of each individual life; they are right when they contend that the differences between man and man, as between nation and nation, are largely environmental, not congenital; but they are wrong when they ascribe quasi-creative activity to the environment and mere passivity and receptivity to the human organism, and they complicate their error and make nonsense of their philosophy when they go on to speak of the environment as the product of man's creative will.

What we need, then, is a theory of the soul, which will hold, with the protoplasmists, that growth is always achieved by reaction to the stimulus of environment, not by passive acceptance of its "moulding" pressure; and yet will hold, with the epigenesists, that in each individual life the possibilities of development, in response to the influence of environment, are infinitely great; a theory which will affirm that each human embryo—the embryo of the future serf not less than that of the future emperor, the embryo of the future fool not less than that of the future philosopher, the embryo of the future felon not less than that of the future saint—is a complex of limitless possibilities, mental, moral, and spiritual, as well as physical; which will affirm, in other words, that the racial or characteristically human element in the new-born infant enormously outweighs the lineal or physically inherited element, and that therefore, instead of being at the mercy of the tendencies which are inherent in his own "blood," each human being is free (apart from the disabilities which may be imposed upon him by the particular environment into which he is born) to range at will through the world which consciousness opens to him, and to develop himself in response to its manifold influences by drawing upon the reserves of potentiality that surge up, when called upon to energize, out of the inexhaustible fountain of his "soul."

Such a theory has long been familiar to the exoteric as well as the esoteric thought of the Far East. According to the doctrine of Reincarnation, the individual soul has not been supernaturally created, has not entered the world in a speck of protoplasm, has not been built up by the moulding pressure of a particular environment, but has descended—from an obscure and infinitely distant source—along the line of its own continuous existence, bringing with it into each new earth-life a heritage bequeathed to it by its own former selves, and leaving behind it at the end of each earth-life the same heritage—but enriched or impoverished by the part that it has played on earth—for transmission to its own future selves. This theory accepts the soul on its own valuation, and, recognizing its potential infinitude, allows it, not years but æons for the work of self-realization, thereby substituting for the idea of the soul being inherited from one's lineal ancestors, the idea of the soul inheriting from itself.

That we may the better discern the trend of this theory, let us contrast it with the protoplasmic, with which, as it happens, it has most in common, but to which it is also most directly opposed. We have seen that on the physical plane of his being a man inherits, lineally, from his own line of ancestors, racially, from the whole human race; his racial inheritance being transmitted to him through the channel of lineal heredity, and modified—stamped with the birth-mark of individuality—in transmission. "It is exactly the same," says the protoplasmist, "on the higher planes of man's being." "It is the same," says the believer in reincarnation, "but with a difference." On the higher, as on the lower planes, the distinction between lineal and racial heredity holds good, and a man's racial inheritance is transmitted to him through the channel of lineal heredity, and modified—stamped with the birth-mark of individuality—in transmission; but on the higher planes a man inherits, racially, not from the human race only, but from the fountain of all soul-life, and lineally, not from his own line of ancestors, but from the line of his own former selves.

There are difficulties in the way of accepting this theory, which I do not seek to minimize. The conception of the soul as super-physical does not readily harmonize with our instinctive assumption that the physical plane is the only plane of *natural* existence, that the world is in itself what it seems to be to our normal perceptive faculties, that the limitations of our bodily senses determine the boundaries of the Universe. But this assumption, with the fatal contraction of the idea of Nature which it involves, is a mere superstition, and, as an argument against the theory of reincarnation, carries no weight. The failure of physiology to do the work of psychology compels us to accept the soul on its own evidence; and when once we have taken this step, we must not shrink from its consequences, however irreconcilable these may be with the unformulated axioms of popular thought.

For my own part, I feel in my heart of hearts that the theory of reincarnation holds the key to the riddle of man's existence; but how the key works I cannot pretend to explain in full. In postulating a plane of being which is at once natural and super-physical, the theory leads us into a world of mystery in which the mind is not at home and cannot expect to find its way. Any attempt that I might make to work out the philosophy of reincarnation would be largely imaginative, and would therefore reflect my own personality and lead at last, in the event of controversy, to the logical *impasse* which Cardinal Newman indicated when he reminded us that where there is no common measure of minds there can be no common measure of arguments. I will therefore content myself with pointing out that the doctrine of reincarnation accepts and even insists upon the fundamental truths which the two biological theories of the soul respectively postulate, but to which, owing to their refusing to entertain the hypothesis of the super-physical, they do less than justice. The first of these is that the future man is in the human embryo, whatever that may be. The second is that consciousness, with the sense of freedom which accompanies it, is the differential feature of the growing man, and that the transforming influence of consciousness on human life is unlimited. If we accept the former conception, while rejecting the hypothesis of the super-physical, we must, with Professor Bateson, identify the human embryo with the fertilized germ-cell; but in that case, if we accept the second conception, we are faced by the difficulty which the theory of epigenesis seeks to evade,—that inasmuch as consciousness is the Protean principle in man's being, the principle of limitless transformation, it cannot itself come under the control of physical necessity, and therefore that the subject of consciousness—that which is becoming aware of itself—cannot pass through the narrow channel of physical generation and lineal heredity. According to the doctrine of reincarnation, the future man, with all his possibilities, up to the last term of ideal perfection, is in the human embryo; but as consciousness is the differential feature of his being, until the subject of consciousness has united itself with his growing body, the human embryo, as distinguished from the embryo of the human body, has not been formed. When that union has taken place, the human embryo—the new-born infant—is ready to start on its career of self-realization; but it is no "neutral clean sheet" waiting for "writing to be impressed" on it by its environment, but a living organism, with limitless reserves of potentiality, which it is ready to realize, not by passive acceptance of the impress of environment, but by active reaction to its stimulus.

Thus the doctrine of reincarnation, while bringing the life of man in its totality under the master law of growth, withdraws the life of the soul from bondage to the laws of physical growth. In other words, it recognizes two kinds of heredity—the heredity of the body, which inherits from the man's lineal ancestors, and the heredity of the soul, which inherits from its own former selves.

This conception throws light on many problems. In particular, it composes the quarrel between heredity and environment, for it enables us to see that there is no such quarrel. When Professor Bateson affirms that "nature . . . . has an overwhelmingly greater significance" than "nurture," he is as wide of the mark as is Dr. Chalmers Mitchell when he affirms that "nurture is inconceivably more important than nature." On the higher, as on the lower, levels of man's being, nature and nurture, heredity and environment, are in very truth the warp and the woof of the tissue of his life. As a controlling factor in human development, heredity counts for no more than environment; and environment counts for no more than heredity. Each in turn counts for everything; but neither counts for anything apart from the other. Each postulates the other Each is complementary to the other. Each measures the other. But only because each is infinite. The nascent soul is a complex of infinite possibilities. It realizes, or begins to realize, these by reacting to the stimulus of an infinitely wide and infinitely changeful environment. Apart from such an environment, its possibilities would remain as dormant as those which are wrapped up in a grain of mummy wheat. If its heredity were physical and limited, its power of reacting to environment would be strictly limited, and the limits of its activity would be strictly predetermined; and we should then have to admit, not that nature counted for more than nurture in the life of the soul, but that necessity counted for everything and freedom for nothing. But in that case there would be no soul. The physical side of man's being would be the only side. When we spoke of the soul, of consciousness, of freedom, of spirituality, we should be cheating ourselves with empty words. The doctrine of reincarnation, by its conception of superphysical heredity, delivers us from these pessimistic conclusions. For it opens down the ages an ample channel for the journeying soul, and so allows it in each successive earth-life to take up anew the task of self-development, ready to measure, with the infinitude of its inherited potentialities, the infinitude of the environing world. In fine, in the doctrine of reincarnation we have the only theory of the origin of the individual man, which, without invoking the Supernatural, safeguards the soul.

It is possible that some persons have attained to certitude in these matters. If there are such persons they are in a more advanced stage of mental and psychical development than I am, and truth, for them, means something wider and deeper, something more absorbing and constraining, than it means for me. For both these reasons they, of all people, would be the last to wish me to accept their teaching until I could see for myself that it was true. For when we are dealing with the master problems of life, the dogmatic attitude, with its implicit assumption that truth is a thing to possess rather than to be possessed by, is symptomatic, not of certitude, but of secret self-distrust. None are so tolerant or so unwilling to proselytize as those who really know. I am not of the brotherhood of those who really know, but I am not wholly blind to my own limitations. And so, speaking as an ordinary man to ordinary men, I repeat what I said at the beginning of this chapter—that when we are considering the origin of the soul we are in a region of pure conjecture, in which anyone with a spirit of adventure is free to theorize, but in which no one may count himself to have apprehended. My spirit of adventure has led me to examine the four theories of the origin of the soul which seem at present to hold the field; and I have now satisfied myself that the most illuminating of these and the least open to destructive criticism is the theory of a reincarnating and self-developing soul or ego, with which the Far East has been familiar for thousands of years.[1] Further than this I have not gone and have no wish to go.

[1] The theory of reincarnation does not solve the problem of the soul's origin. Indeed it is the only one of the four theories which does not pretend to do so. What it does is to throw back the dawn of the soul's life into so dark and remote a past that the problem of the development of the soul takes the place in our minds of the problem of its origin.

CHAPTER VI

THE RANGE OF THE SOUL

THERE is a principle of infinitude in man which we call consciousness. We mean by consciousness the dawn of its own light on the soul. Therefore the real principle of infinitude in man's life is the soul itself. I have tried to prove that each of us has limitless potentialities waiting to be realized, limitless reserves of mental and spiritual vitality waiting to be mobilized. This is one aspect of the infinitude of the soul. Is it possible to advance from this somewhat negative conception of infinitude to a more positive conception ? I think it is.

Let us look at the matter from a somewhat different point of view. Let us start with consciousness of self. In the act of being conscious of my self I am conscious of the permanent and inherent unity of my self, but I am not conscious of its limits. I cannot define its boundaries in any way. I know that it is intimately connected with what I call my body, and that it can make the weal or woe of the body its own. But I also know that it can identify itself with things which seem either to be outside itself or to include itself, and that it can make their weal or woe its own. For example, I can identify myself with my family, with my clan, with my city, with my country, with the whole brotherhood of humanity. I can also identify myself with my school, my university, my profession, my guild or trade union, my political party, my church or religious sect. I can even identify myself with impersonal causes of various kinds, such as the reform of education, the reform of social conditions, the pursuit of beauty or truth. In each of these cases I feel a sense of proprietorship in the community or the cause with which I identify myself. I am proud of its achievements as if they were my own. I take shame to myself for its failures. I sympathize with its troubles and sorrows.

But looking around me I see that some persons have what I may call narrower selves than others, that they do not readily identify themselves with the communities to which they belong, or the causes that might be expected to appeal to them ; that the communal spirit is wanting in them or is only developed so far as it may serve their own selfish ends ; that they are wrapped up in their own bodily well-being and their own material pursuits and possessions. On the other hand, I see that there are many persons whose capacity for losing themselves in communal interests and impersonal causes I can but envy and revere. Again, looking back to my own earlier life I see that the range of my self is much wider now than it was then, that I have more and larger interests, that my power of identifying myself with other persons and other things has gained to an appreciable extent. From these facts I argue that the self varies, as regards the actual range of its life, from person to person, and that it is capable of growing and expanding, of widening the sphere of its sympathies and interests, within the limits of each individual life. And this expansion in the range of the self is not accompanied by any diminution of what I may call the vividness of its consciousness. On the contrary, as the self widens, its consciousness seems to grow more vivid and more alert.

The question now arises : Are there any limits to this process of expansion ? Is there any *a priori* reason why the self—the soul, as we may now call it—should not be able to identify itself with the widest of all communities, whatever that may be ? I know of no such reason. The life of the community is the same, ideally if not actually, for all the members of the community, each of whom can, if he pleases, identify his individual life with the common life. And however wide the community may be, this law holds good. The fact that I am an ardent patriot, that I identify my self—its pains and pleasures, its hopes and fears, its aims and interests—with my country, does not prevent millions of other persons from doing exactly the same. Nor is there any *a priori* reason why each member of the human family should not develop a sense of oneness with all his kind. Now the widest of all communities—wider even than the Kingdom of Man—is the Kingdom of God, the Universe itself. In what relation does each of us stand to this all-embracing unity? The universal life is one and indivisible. We cannot, for example, draw a hard and fast line between the spiritual and the physical life of man, or between the life of man and the lives of other living things. And this universal life, in its undivided totality, ranging between the poles of physical energy and ideal spirituality, and having—one may well believe—inner and innermost lives of its own, is what we mean when we speak of the soul of the Universe. The One Life takes innumerable outward forms; and in each of these cases of self-manifestation it is, as a rule, content to move in a narrow channel, walled in by habit and instinct, untroubled by any message from the infinite sea. But when the One Life enters the channel of man's existence, there comes a profound and far-reaching change. The lesser life begins to be aware—faintly and dimly at first, then by degrees more and more clearly—of its oneness with the larger life. This growing sense of awareness is the dawn of consciousness. Of the transforming influence of consciousness on human life I have already spoken. It reveals to man a universe outside himself, and a universe within himself, and it suggests that these two are ultimately one. Also, since perception of the infinite is of its essence, it tends to raise to infinity all man's powers and tendencies. I have asked if there are any limits to this process of self-expansion, any limitations to the capacity which is inherent in each of us, for going outside himself into a communal life. Consciousness, with its message from the universal to the individual life, is the abiding answer to this question. The expansion of the self will not cease till the individual soul has fully responded to the appeal of the widest of all communities—the universal life.

We now begin to see the meaning, for man, of the process of self-realization or growth. What the oak-tree is to the acorn, that the universal life, the soul of the Universe, is to the human embryo. The purpose of the process of growth is to enable the individual to draw up into himself and convert into himself the infinite life which underlies his own. And the goal of this process is the consciously realized identity of the individual—of each of a billion individuals—with the universal soul. Till that goal has been reached, the process of growth is incomplete, the true self has not been found. When the goal has been reached, the individual has fulfilled his destiny. For, in realizing, fully and finally, his oneness with the universal life, he has entered into complete possession of his racial inheritance, which has expanded, while he was making good his claim to it, to cosmic dimensions; he has grown to the fulness of his predestined stature; and he is at last free to say "I am I."

But is his stature predestined? Is he growing, as other living things are growing, to a predetermined form? I asked myself this question at the beginning of this Part; and since I asked it I have been trying to clear the ground for my answer to it. It is possible that the whole course of cosmic life has been predetermined. It is even conceivable that the whole drama of the Universe, as it unfolds itself for us, is but the self-realization of a seed which has fallen from a parent tree. But if we are to apply the word "predetermined" to such movements as these, we must remind ourselves at the outset that we are using the word in a sense other than that which it ordinarily bears. When we say that a movement which is infinite in all its dimensions has been predetermined, we are obviously subordinating the idea of totality to that of development, and the idea of eternity, which is the temporal aspect of totality, to that of time; and this means that words are failing us, as indeed they are bound to do when we try to bring to the birth conceptions which exceed the compass of our thought.

But what of the individual life? We may well believe that this has its appropriate place in what I have called the drama of the Universe, and we may therefore say, if we please, that it has been predetermined by an infinite will. But here, too, the word "predetermined" will do less than justice to the idea that we are struggling to express. For what is central in the evolution of the individual life is the dawn of consciousness; and consciousness is on the one hand the principle of infinitude in man's being, and is on the other hand accompanied, as it dawns upon us, by the growing sense of freedom, the sense of being able to choose among competing courses of action. Now what is predetermined, in the accepted sense of the word, is both subject to and limited by the stress of what we call necessity; and as the idea of freedom is antithetical to that of necessity, it is clear that to speak of the growth of the individual soul as predetermined is to predicate limitation and subjection to necessity of what is ideally, and therefore essentially, limitless and free.

Let us say, then, in answer to the question which I have asked myself, that, though the general idea of the destiny of the soul being predetermined will always haunt us, the growth of the individual soul is not predetermined, as we, with our experiences of purposing, planning, and executing, understand that word; that on the contrary, as each of us has infinite resources outside himself to draw upon and infinite potentialities within himself to realize, so he is free to use these or to misuse them, and in doing so to help or to hinder the process of his growth. And if his freedom is at first a mere possibility, he can sustain himself with the thought that freedom, like every other human power and prerogative, grows by being exercised; that the nearer he approaches to oneness with the One Life—which, being universal, is presumably self-determined—the freer he becomes from that constraining pressure from without which we call necessity; and that when, if ever, he realizes his sublime destiny, he will have united himself with the fountain-head of all destiny and will therefore have worked out to its last act a drama which, if predetermined in *any* sense of that word, was predetermined by his own ideal self.[1]

[1] This is but a tentative and provisional treatment of one of the greatest of all problems. The problem will be more fully treated in the first chapter of Part IV.

PART III

THE PURPOSE OF GROWTH

CHAPTER I

THE POLARITY OF NATURE

IF we are to win lasting happiness we must make healthy and harmonious growth. All attempts to win happiness by other methods—by the pursuit of pleasure, for example, or riches, or position, or power, or fame—are predestined to end in failure; for the enjoyment of such prizes cannot permanently content us, and happiness is not happiness if there is in it any germ of decay. History teaches us this lesson, and our own experience confirms its teaching. But how is healthy and harmonious growth to be achieved? By the effective realization of potentiality in general, and in particular of those potentialities which are distinctively human. In other words, by our allying ourselves with the central tendencies of our nature. But how are we to find out what are the central tendencies of human nature? By finding out, or trying to find out, what are the central tendencies of cosmic or universal nature—of "Nature," as I will now call it. This is one answer to my question, an answer which is suggested to me by the conclusion which I reached in my last chapter. My study of the problem of the soul has convinced me that the relation between the individual and the universal soul, as between the individual and the universal life, is—ultimately and ideally—one of absolute identity. From this I infer that if I am to interpret Nature I must do so through the medium of my interpretation of myself, and that if I am to interpret myself I must do so through the medium of my interpretation of Nature. Having to choose between these two starting points, I will begin with Nature in order that from my interpretation of her I may return in due course to a new interpretation of myself.

As the being of man comes, or seems to come, under the law of growth, so the being of Nature comes, or seems to come, under the law of evolution,—which is growth "writ large." It follows that if I am to determine the purpose of growth in the human drama, I must first try to determine the purpose of evolution in the cosmic drama.

What is that purpose? From what beginning and towards what goal is the course of evolution taking Nature? And what is happening to Nature as she passes from the source to the goal? Is she preserving or changing her identity? And in what relation do the ideal ends of the process stand to one another? Does the goal say *Yes* or *No* to the source? If the goal is supreme good or supreme reality, what is the source?

Here, as at the outset of every attempt to form a general conception of Nature, we are confronted by the eternal problem of the Two and the One; and if we are to pass on, we must reply to its challenge. If we act otherwise, if we throw a sop to the guardian of the threshold and slip by while it slumbers, it will awake and follow us wherever we go, and throw all our thoughts into confusion. In particular it will follow us, making confusion worse confounded, when we return from Nature to man. If, for example, on the one hand, consciousness, with the sense of freedom which accompanies it, is the differential element in man's being, and, on the other hand, much of man's life is plunged in unconsciousness and is in bondage to necessity, the question arises, In what relation do these opposites stand to one another? Are consciousness and unconsciousness, are freedom and necessity mutually exclusive alternatives? If they are not, what is the relation between them? So, too, when we look at man from other points of view, we see that he has a higher and a lower self, a wider and a narrower self, a spiritual and a material self, a real and an apparent self; that he oscillates between knowledge and ignorance, between happiness and unhappiness, between good and evil. And here, too, we must ask ourselves in what relation do the opposites stand to one another? In each of the given antitheses is the opposition fundamental and absolute? Is the one term nothing more than the negation of the other? It will be dangerous for us to leave these questions unanswered—for what is mere confusion of thought in the sphere of theory may well become confusion of ideals and principles and moral landmarks in the sphere of practical life—and if we cannot now answer them by anticipation, we can at least clear the ground for a serious attempt to deal with them.

Let us try to think the matter out to bed-rock. The movements of human thought are limited, and even controlled, by the exigencies of human speech. We speak in antitheses. Therefore, whether we call ourselves dualists or monists, we are doomed to think antithetically. When I say that we speak in antitheses I mean that our little words, which are also our great words,—the simple, familiar words which sum up whole aspects of Nature's being or indicate whole meridians of Nature's infinite sphere—fall, as a rule, into pairs of opposites. Such opposites are *good* and *evil, right* and *wrong, high* and *low, strong* and *weak, swift* and *slow, light* and *darkness, knowledge* and *ignorance, spirit* and *matter, freedom* and *necessity, Heaven* and *Hell.* The tendency of popular thought is to regard the opposites in each of these antitheses as mutually exclusive alternatives, and to fix an impassable gulf between them. In philosophy this tendency is known as dualism. Now dualism works badly in practice. The fundamental antithesis of Nature and the Supernatural is responsible, as I have tried to show, for many of our misconceptions of the meaning and purpose of life and therefore for many of our follies, failures, and miseries. Dualism also works badly as theory. Its logical fallacies are easily exposed. Expert thinkers criticize it and react against it, and their reaction carries them into the opposite extreme, which we call Monism. Dualism and Monism are the poles between which philosophic thought swings in endless oscillation. Monism emphasizes the fundamental unity of Nature's being and ignores the duality of her aspect. Dualism emphasizes the essential duality of Nature's aspect and ignores the unity of her being. That these antithetical tendencies of thought are both right and both wrong may surely be taken for granted. What is wanted, then, is a larger conception which shall reconcile them by showing that each is a one-sided interpretation of Nature, which needs for its own sake to be limited and supplemented by the other. In other words, we must so think of Nature as to harmonize the duality of her aspect with the unity of her being. We must think of her as two because she is essentially one; as one because she is essentially two.

Along what line of thought are we to work our way to such a conception? We think antithetically because we have no choice but to speak in antitheses. In each of our antitheses each term seems to pass away into infinity. I mean by this that we can follow it in thought in its own direction without ever exhausting its possibilities. I cannot think of intense cold without thinking of intenser cold. I cannot think of intense heat without thinking of intenser heat. Here a question suggests itself which may possibly put us on the track of what we seek. In what relation do the opposing infinities stand to one another? Is each of the opposites infinite only in the direction of its own extreme? And if so, from what line of demarcation or gulf of separation does it start on its adventurous career? Popular thought will answer that antithetical tendencies are infinite in the direction of their own extremes, but finite in the direction of their opposites. Can this contention be sustained? Let us see to what conclusions it commits us. A familiar antithesis is that of *swift* and *slow*. Let us test the popular theory by reference to it. There is no motion so swift but the mind can conceive of a swifter; no motion so slow but it can conceive of a slower. As it passes from swift to swifter, it tends to lose itself in what is infinitely great. As it passes from slow to slower, it tends to lose itself in what is infinitesimal or infinitely little. In either case its horizon recedes perpetually: and if it recoils and returns to its starting point, it does so because it is exhausted, not because it has reached its goal.

This much will, I think, be generally conceded; and I will therefore assume that it is true. But how will the mind act when it moves downward from swift to slow or upward from slow to swift? Will its progress in either direction be arrested by an abrupt change of kind? In other words, is there anything in existence of which swiftness or slowness is absolutely and unconditionally predicable? One's first impulse is to answer, *Yes*; and popular thought (as we have just seen) generally yields to this temptation; but the more steadily we face our problem, the stronger will be the pressure put upon us to answer, *No*. It will perhaps be said that the motion of light is absolutely swift, of a snail absolutely slow. But even to these propositions we must, in the interest of truth, refuse assent. For since there is no motion so swift but we can conceive of a swifter, it must needs be possible to conceive of a swifter motion than that of light; and by comparison with that swifter motion the motion of light is swift no longer, but slow. Here, then, where we seem to be approaching the very extreme of swiftness, we are confronted by the idea of slowness, which seems to have followed its opposite into its remotest stronghold and to be ready to follow it beyond the limits of thought. In like manner, there is no motion so slow but we can conceive of a slower, by comparison with which the slow motion, even if it be that of a snail, may be regarded as swift. And so, when we say that each of the two countertendencies is infinite in the direction of its own extreme, we imply that it is also infinite in the direction of its opposite, the one infinity being, as it were, the counterpart and correlate of the other. This means that the two countertendencies intermix continuously and perpetually, each in turn ranging from its own extreme to that of its opposite. It is true that they vary together in inverse proportion, the one rising or falling as the other falls or rises; but neither is ever met with or can even be conceived in a state of absolute purity, for no effort of thought can free either from some slight alloy of the other. From this point of view we see that what is called the finite is generated by the interfusion of opposite infinities, and that our experiences and our conceptions are made possible by the interaction of counter poles of being which lie beyond the range of our experience and even beyond the horizon of our thought.

Let us now come to close quarters with the popular conception and see what its dualism involves. According to the hypothesis which popular thought instinctively forms and which language seems to sanction, there is a hard and fast line of demarcation between swiftness and slowness, or —to take a more significant example—between *good* and *evil*. I contend that if this were so, and if this example were typical, there would be nothing infinite in Nature except the chasm which rends her asunder. For the difference between good and evil, once it is allowed that these are separate entities, being a complete difference of kind—being in fact equivalent to diametrical opposition—is infinitely greater than any difference of degree in the range of either; so much greater indeed that it tends to dwarf all the latter to zero and to leave us at last with two distinct and virtually homogeneous states or qualities instead of with an infinite variety of shades.

A quasi-concrete example will help me to explain what I mean. Experience has taught men that the tendency of goodness is to generate happiness, and of evil to generate misery. And so, arguing from the facts and laws of this life to the possibilities of the next, they have conceived of two opposite states of future existence—Heaven, in which goodness is eternally and infinitely rewarded, and Hell, in which evil is eternally and infinitely chastised. But between these two they have placed, according to their wont, an impassable abyss, the consequence being that just to fall short of salvation is to be doomed to the hopeless misery of Hell, and that just to escape perdition is to enter—in due season—into the plenitude of heavenly bliss.

Now no one will seriously contend that all the inmates of Heaven are equally holy and happy, or that any of them is as holy and happy as the personal God whom they are supposed to adore. At the same time no one will deny that the difference, in respect of well-being and happiness, between the lowest soul in Heaven and God himself is as nothing compared with the truly appalling difference between what is lowest in Heaven and highest in Hell. But if the difference, within the range of Heaven, between man and God is less and immeasurably less than that between

Heaven and Hell, it is infinite (in the fullest sense of the word) no longer, and Heaven ceases to be illuminated by the light of an unapproachable ideal.

Moreover, though as regards their feelings and surroundings there is an infinite abyss between the lowest of Heaven's inmates and the highest of Hell's, the difference between them in respect of their earthly antecedents is almost infinitesimal, the line of progression from abandoned wickedness to supreme goodness being as a matter of fact continuous; and inasmuch as an infinitesimal difference in causation cannot really produce an infinite difference in effect, our inability to draw a true line of demarcation between the sheep and the goats tends *de facto* (if not *de jure theologico*) to bring both states of after existence within measurable distance of our mortal life, and so to deprive each of the infinity which is commonly regarded as one of its most essential attributes.

Thus we see that, by interposing an impassable gulf between Hell and Heaven, men have, as it were, drained each of these antithetical worlds of its infinity, and transferred the latter quality to the abyss of nothingness which the dualism of their thought has conjured into being.

Something akin to this would happen if the totality of things could be brought under the sway of a single pair of antithetical conceptions. When dualism divides the Universe into the *natural* and the *supernatural* worlds, each of these self-centred spheres of being limits at every turn the expansion of the other, the result being that instead of an infinite and all-inclusive Universe we have an infinite vacuum separating two nominally infinite but really finite worlds. Perhaps it would be nearer to truth to say that both worlds are limited and reduced to finite dimensions by the gulf that separates them: for in order to prevent them from intersecting or otherwise intermingling at any point, the intervening sea of nothingness must flow completely round each of them till at last they become mere islets in its measureless and fathomless flood. It is because dualism tends to produce this unsatisfying result, that the mind is apt to recoil from it and take refuge in monism. In the hope of saving reality from being submerged by the rising tide of non-existence, critical thought tries to get rid of the "estranging main" by proving it to be superfluous; in other words, by cancelling one of the two worlds that it held asunder, and regarding the other as commensurate with the Universe. But the attempt is vain: for the gulf of separation reappears, with the ghost of the dead world lingering on the brink of it, while the surviving world—nature divorced from supernature, matter divorced from spirit, or whatever it may be—instead of expanding till it fills all the realms of being, does but contract the Universe to its own finite dimensions, and, instead of rising to the highest plane of reality, does but degrade the Universe to the level of its own dubious and precarious existence.[1]

Thus it is only by ascribing to Nature continuity of movement that we can safeguard the infinity of her range; and it is only by regarding her as infinite that we can save her (in our thought) from ultimate annihilation, for when once her reality has begun to drain away into any world-dividing abyss of non-existence, a process of shrinkage has begun to which there are no imaginable limits.

From the problem of the relation between antithetical infinities we can now return to the larger problem which divides the dualist from the monist. The conception of continuous movement through an infinite range will, I think, enable us to harmonize the duality of Nature's aspect with the unity of her being. By the light which it casts we see that the opposites into which Nature seems to fall whenever or wherever we look at her, are not distinct and alien principles, not independent entities, not self-centred and self-included worlds, but poles, antithetical and yet correlative, an unbroken stream of existence joining the one to the other, while each in turn is lost in the darkness of infinite distance. From pole to pole there is continuous movement; and movement implies change. Hence the

[1] The pure matter of the materialist is but one degree removed from non-existence. So is the pure spirit of the idealist. The supernatural world is a dreamland. The "Nature" of the naturalist and the supernaturalist is the material world centring in the physical life of man, a world and a life which melt away under the solvent influence of scientific analysis till nothing remains of them but those *primordia rerum* which seem to be on the very confines of nothing.

two are diametrically and infinitely opposed to one another, yet have this much in common that both belong to the same meridian of being. There is no great gulf fixed between them. They are at once infinitely sundered and infinitely united; and they are infinitely sundered just because they are infinitely united. The endless and unbroken chain which unites them is itself the unfathomable abyss which parts them. What separates Heaven and Hell, for example, is not a gulf of nothingness, but the entire diameter of human life. The pure pole at either end is in every case ideal rather than actual. The conception of swiftness (or goodness, or whatever it may be) is one which the mind easily grasps. But our conception of absolute swiftness is at best a mere negation; for all we know about this distant goal is that it lies beyond the range of our experience and even of our imaginative thought, and that the mind which goes in quest of it is doomed to reach on and on without ever approaching it. If, in any given case, we are to have experience of either goal, if we are to deal with it, perceive it, think about it, imagine it, it must actualize itself by entering into combination with its opposite, it must become what it is not in order that it may be what it is. And however near a thing may approach to one or other of its ideal poles, however convenient or even necessary it may be for us to identify it with the one pole and disconnect it from the other—to say, for example, that the movement of light is swift, and the movement of a snail slow—it is none the less in itself a compound product, two-fold in nature and tendency; it has at least some slight alloy of that very influence which it is its function to oppose and deny.

Nature, then, as I think of her, is one because she is two-fold and two-fold because she is one. The unity of her being is the counterpart of her life; for were she as inanimate as certain aspects of her sometimes seem to be, she would be an "aggregate" rather than a "whole." Because she is a whole—and therefore an organic whole—she looks, as all life does, in opposite directions and ranges between two infinitely distant poles; but so entirely are these ideal opposites, unattainable and unimaginable though they be, of the essence of her being, that their eternal and all-pervading interaction may be regarded as the very pulse of her life.

Throughout this preliminary study of a large problem I have taken for granted that neither dualism nor monism is wholly true. This assumption is of course an inference from the very theory of things which it has constrained me to search for and even helped me to frame. My antipathy to dualism forbids me to regard monism and dualism as rival philosophies between which I must make my choice. My antipathy to monism forbids me to assume that either philosophy is absolutely true. Far from being called upon to choose between these apparent alternatives, I feel called upon to reconcile them, to bring them together and fuse them into a higher and wider truth. Both philosophies have much to say for themselves ; but the one unanswerable argument against each is that it is perpetually confronted and held in check by the other.

I have suggested that dualism is a dominant tendency of popular, monism of professional thought. This distinction is possibly correct as far as it goes ; but it does not go far enough. Looking below the surface of things one sees that each of these theories has its anti-pole or necessary counter-theory in the philosophy of the people as well as in that of the schools ; and from this fact one is led to infer that the two counter-tendencies of thought are normal constituents of the human mind. The mind of the thinker, looking at Nature as a whole, refers things either to two principles or to one. As a rule, it finds rest in one principle ; but its choice of one principle is always the outcome of a struggle between two. The ordinary mind, moving along a particular line of thought, sees either the violent contrast of two qualities or the monotony of one. The more conscious side of it is as a rule contented with the dualistic view of things ; but, unknown to itself, it often makes a final and decisive choice between the alternatives that confront it.

I will now continue my attempt to show that the idea of unbroken movement from pole to pole is the higher conception in which these rival attitudes of thought are alternately justified and condemned.

Let us first consider the philosophy of the schools. The theory of things which I have tried to expound holds that Nature at every point and moment in her being looks in two directions, that both as a whole and in each of her many movements she is a process between two poles, and that these are diametrically opposed to one another and infinitely far asunder. It thus takes account of the fact of contrast, without which there is neither colour, nor movement, nor life. So far it is in accord with the basic assumption of dualism. Again, it holds that the two poles of Nature's being, and of each meridian of her being, though as antithetical to one another as light is to darkness, have yet this much in common that they are opposite ends of the one axis on which her infinite sphere revolves, and that within the illimitable limits of our experience they are always interdependent and inseparable. It thus takes account of the fact of unity, without which there is no order in Nature, and if no order then, again, no colour, no movement, no life. Herein it is in accord with the basic assumption of monism. But though it touches each of these great counter-positions of thought, it rests in neither. The moment of its touching the one is the moment of its recoil to the other. It says, with dualism, that there are two principles in Nature, and adds in the same breath, "These are really one." It says, with monism, that there is but one principle, and adds, "This is really two."

In playing this dual part it does but reflect the deeper movement of the mind of man. Though the instincts which carry the mind towards dualism and monism respectively are genuinely natural, the tendency to oscillate between these alternatives is more natural, in the sense of belonging to a yet deeper stratum of our nature. That there are latent forces which make for oscillation is proved by the fact that each philosophy readily transforms itself into the other. Thus, in a dualistic system, if one of the rival principles is regarded as less real than the other, the basic assumption of dualism, by its exclusion of intervening terms between reality and unreality, will, sooner or later, automatically reduce the less real principle to non-existence. On the other hand a monistic system is, as we have already seen, a dualistic system with one of its two terms suppressed; and its ascription of reality to one, and one only, of two rival principles is in itself a proof that the dualistic division of things, and therefore the basic assumption of dualism, has been tacitly accepted.

The instability of the mind in the presence of these opposite conceptions of Nature becomes more clearly perceptible when we turn from the philosophy of the schools to the philosophy of the people. The tendency to see only violent contrasts in Nature is balanced and counteracted by the tendency to ignore all distinctions. More especially is this the case when the ideas that occupy the mind have a practical bearing, as, for example, when men are thinking about good and evil, truth and error, Heaven and Hell. In the eyes of one man these opposites are mutually exclusive alternatives. In the eyes of another the difference between them is either negligible or non-existent. The tendency, half cynical, half indolent, to ignore all distinctions is no doubt much rarer, as a fundamental conception, than the tendency to exaggerate them; but of the two it lies nearer to action, and as it also sometimes becomes a theory, it is well that it should be carefully considered. It is easy to see how it arises. Men are told that the difference between good and evil (let us say) is the difference between black and white; but they see that in point of fact good and evil are everywhere intermingled and shade off imperceptibly into one another; and being thus unable to divide things into the two classes which popular thought and popular speech take for granted, they naturally conclude, in default of the idea of continuity, that there is only one class.

The doctrine of continuous movement from pole to antipole justifies each of these opposite tendencies of popular thought, and condemns each of them just so far as it justifies the other. For it tells us, on the one hand, that gradation in Nature is a process so subtle as to be imperceptible when studied in detail; and it thus accounts for the tendency to ignore distinctions. And it tells us, on the other hand, that accumulated differences of degree amount at last to radical changes of kind; and it thus accounts for the tendency to see only violent contrasts.

The relation in which the two tendencies stand to one another may be looked at from another point of view. We have seen that in philosophy, properly so called, the mind of man oscillates between dualism and monism, finding permanent rest in neither theory and passing readily from the one to the other. We have also seen that the one theory implies the other, postulates it as its counterpart and correlate, and evokes it, as it were, in the course of its own development. It can, I think, be shown that something analogous to this goes on in the region of popular thought. Here, indeed, where we are working for the most part below the level of consciousness, the transition from theory to counter-theory is as a rule practical rather than logical; but even when it is most practical, the process has a logic of its own, which, though it cannot be systematized, admits of being informally set forth.

An example will help me to explain myself, and will at the same time enable us to realize that in this, as in other matters, the connexion between theory and practice is constant and close.

Asceticism and sensualism are typical characteristics of human nature. Each involves a theory, and each has received philosophical exposition. Asceticism is the concrete expression of a philosophy which sunders man into soul and body and regards these as having fundamentally conflicting interests. Feeling called upon to choose between the two, it rightly assigns supremacy to the soul; but the impetus of its preference carries it so far that, instead of being content to subordinate the body to the soul, in the event of a collision between their respective interests and impulses, it tells us that the body, with all that belongs to it, is irredeemably evil, that it ought not to exist, that there is no place for it in an ideal world. From this theory it draws a practical inference. It warns man that his duty is to crush the flesh, to reduce it as far as possible to non-existence, to die to it, to thwart its desires and impulses until they become atrophied by disuse. Thus asceticism starts by affirming two antithetical principles and regarding one of these as more real than the other. So far, well. But since it is blind to the continuity of Nature and therefore ignorant or forgetful of the fact that the mainspring of every living principle is its ceaseless interaction with its opposite, it is driven at last by the logic of its own misconception to refuse recognition to the lower principle, to deny, if not its existence, at least its right to exist. In this way asceticism, as a rule of life, is at variance with asceticism as an abstract principle; but the former is not less false to the laws of human nature than is the latter to the postulates of a true philosophy.

So false to the laws of human nature is asceticism on its practical side, that it always tends to provoke a reaction against itself, and often ends by calling its opposite into vigorous activity. History tells us that to ages of asceticism have succeeded ages of unbridled immorality. After the fastings and penances of the "cowled and tonsured Middle Age," came the Renaissance, with its *réhabilitation de la chair*. After the austerities of Puritanism came the harlotries of the Restoration. Sensualism, like asceticism, has its theoretical side. The latter presupposes a dualistic, the former a monistic conception of Nature. In the world of the sensualist there are no distinctions of kind. Even the primary distinction of good and evil ceases to exist. Whatever is is right. All desires, all impulses, all actions are alike natural and therefore alike lawful. The flesh is as high and holy as the spirit. The claims of the flesh upon us are as just as they are strong. There is nothing to be ashamed of in human nature, nothing to be resisted, nothing to be suppressed. Such a philosophy cannot rest in its original position. The course of nature is against it. Distinctions and contrasts do exist. Body and soul are not on an equality, and it is impossible to act as if they were. Sensualism, having refused precedence to the soul, is compelled to give precedence to the body and finds its natural outcome in abandoned profligacy. It starts by reconciling body and soul, and ends by renewing the feud between them and giving victory to the lower and losing side.

Here, then, we have a transition from monism in theory to dualism in practice, just as in asceticism we have a transition from dualism in theory to monism in practice. The monist, who ignores the law of opposition, becomes a dualist in spite of himself, and to his own undoing. The dualist, who ignores the law of unity, becomes a monist in spite of himself, and to his own undoing. So through our errors and disasters Nature reveals and justifies her purposes and avenges the dishonour of her laws.

In conclusion. There are two great conceptions which bound our thought in opposite directions. We call them monism and dualism respectively. It is in human nature to move towards each of these poles and find rest in neither. In the philosophy of the schools there is a movement from conception to counter conception, through the medium of erroneous theory. In the philosophy of the people there is a similar movement, through the medium of disastrous action. The true theory of things must be the expression and embodiment of this oscillatory movement. It must be for ever touching and for ever recoiling from each of the opposite poles of thought. I claim for the conception of Nature which I have tried to expound—the conception of a fundamental unity which reveals itself in and through continuous change—that it satisfies this condition; that it not merely accepts and registers the tendency of the mind to oscillate between dualism and monism, but is itself in a state of perpetual oscillation between them. And I infer from this (though of course my reasoning is circular) that it is nearer then either of them to the inmost truth of things.

It remains for me to point out that this conception is in harmony with the central tendencies of the present age. This is pre-eminently the age of science; and the culminating theory of modern science is that of evolution. In framing the theory of evolution, science becomes aware of its own dominant aim and purpose. Faith in the continuity of Nature is the secret mainspring of scientific effort; and the desire to establish continuity is an instinct of every scientific mind. The untrained observation of the ordinary man is cognizant of obvious and strongly marked distinctions. Science, while accepting these provisionally, refuses to rest in them. Its function is to analyze, to resolve things into their essential elements, to dissect them into their vital parts. In doing this it finds that things which seem to be disconnected have in reality points of contact, that they spring from common causes, that they are compounded of common substances, that they lose themselves in common results. It understands a thing when it has made clear to itself that the isolation of the thing is, as it has always secretly believed, only on the surface; when it has, further, determined what are the laws or deeper properties which assign the thing its place in the orderly host of natural phenomena, and in virtue of which it is a vital part of a living whole. A latent conviction that "all things are implicated with one another" and that Nature is one, is the potential starting-point of science: and every great scientific discovery has been the outcome of an instinctive effort to substitute one cause for many, and so resolve differences of kind into differences of degree. But though science has always believed that unity and continuity underlie the seeming chaos of Nature, it has but recently become conscious of its faith. In the doctrine of evolution its latent conviction confronts it as a formulated theory. When it applies the idea of evolution to Nature as a whole, it deliberately ascribes to the vast and heterogeneous host of existent things unity of origin and continuity of descent. For the idea of evolution is but an expansion and reinterpretation of the familiar, but profound and mysterious, idea of growth; and to say that a thing grows is to imply that it preserves its unity and self-identity through an infinite series of infinitesimal and wholly imperceptible changes,—a series which carries it at last from pole to anti-pole of its being, from germination (let us say) to maturity, or, again, from birth to the new birth of death.

Thus the master-theory of our age embodies the very conception which mediates, as it seems to me, between dualism and monism,—the conception of Nature as combining in her own being fundamental opposition with essential unity, unceasing change with unbroken continuity. The bearing of this conception on the problem which is the theme of this book will disclose itself as we proceed.

CHAPTER II

THE POLES OF NATURE

NATURE is a process between two opposite poles. From pole to pole stretches the whole diameter of her being. Each pole in turn lies beyond the utmost limits of our thought, its existence being the vanishing point of an infinite "series" rather than a verifiable fact. Within the range of our experience the two are always intermingled. They vary together in inverse proportion. The more (or less) there is of the one, the less (or more) there is of the other. The opposition between them pervades the whole of Nature and takes innumerable forms. Corresponding to these are the many pairs of terms in which language abounds. Each of these antitheses seems to carry us from pole to pole of Nature's being—from infinity to counter-infinity; but its lateral range is as a rule so narrow that in following it out we are confined to a single meridian of her sphere. This means that the antithesis has its counterpart in a particular mental attitude and covers no more of Nature than can be seen from the corresponding point of view. Some antitheses are, however, wider and more comprehensive than others, just as from some points of view more of Nature can be seen than from others. That being so, we must ask ourselves which pair of terms is to be regarded as supreme and all-inclusive, and therefore as best fitted to express the fundamental fact of opposition under its widest and most typical aspect? In other words, by what names are we to designate the absolute poles of existence, the poles in which all meridians may be supposed to meet and blend?

For an answer to this question we must turn to the language of everyday life. What words do ordinary men apply to those supreme counter-tendencies, the interaction of which seems to pervade the length and breadth and depth of the world? It is evident that the words which we are seeking must satisfy certain primary conditions. To begin with, they must be popular, not technical; must stand for what is normal in experience, not for what is temporary or local. In the next place they must be large and vague; there must be as little as possible of what is definite and concrete in the ideas which they tend to call up. Above all, they must be able to open to us infinite vistas, to carry us in a moment beyond the ordinary range of our thought.

Such terms as *good* and *bad*, *true* and *untrue*, *beautiful* and *ugly*, *real* and *unreal*, at once suggest themselves. They satisfy all our conditions. But there is one fatal objection to them. They are *predicative* terms, not *substantive*. I mean by this that if the elusive distinction between things and qualities may be provisionally recognized, these terms are the names of qualities, not of things. The terms that we are in search of must be the names of things, of substantial realities. At any rate they must seem to be so when we first begin to think about them. Where can they be found? If we cannot otherwise solve our problem, let us take Nature as we find her, let us take the world of our experience and follow it backward and forward along the line of our evolution. We shall find that its evolution is a movement from a *material* origin towards a *spiritual* destiny. The path of *analysis*, or *disintegration*, whether its method be static or dynamic, will take us towards those *primordia rerum* out of which the world, as we know it, was built up, and of which it is still composed. These *primordia rerum* are material, in the fullest sense of the word; and the more subtle and penetrative our analysis the more deeply do we plunge into matter. The path of *synthesis*, or *integration*, takes us towards the goal of evolution. As we follow the path, energy changes into life, and life into soul-life, and soul-life becomes more and more spiritual. As the natural movement of our thought impels us to think of what is ultimate in analysis as purely material, so it impels us to think of what is ultimate in synthesis as purely spiritual. At any rate our habitual usage of the words *material* and *spiritual* points to this and no other conclusion.

Is not this, then, the antithesis which we are in search of? I think it is. The popular contrast between *Spirit* and *Matter* seem to me to cover as much of Nature as can possibly reveal itself to human thought; the terms of the antithesis being on the one hand so large and indefinite that the corresponding ideas pass at once, both laterally and lineally, into the "formless infinite,"—and on the other hand so simple and intelligible that anyone can use them without having to explain what he means by them, and anyone can understand from the particular context what they are intended to mean. It may be doubted if there are any words which both appeal to so large an audience and have so wide a range.

When I say that we mean by *matter* what is ultimate in analysis and by *spirit* what is ultimate in synthesis, I have gone as near to defining the terms as it is possible to go. For the rest, they must be left to explain themselves, and to explain each other. One reason why they are indefinable is that their respective meanings are always in motion, never even for an instant quite at rest. The words mean different things to different generations, to different peoples, to different types of mind. Nay, the same person can use them in a thousand different ways, according to the object which he has in view, the matter of his discourse, the line of his thought, and (to speak generally) the exigencies of his context. Another reason why they are undefinable is that the essential meaning of each is bound up with that of its opposite. If we are asked what is meant by spirit, we answer "the antithesis of matter." If, what is meant by matter, "the antithesis of spirit."

Examples of their usage will, however, serve to indicate in what direction their respective meanings naturally tend to move. For the ordinary mind, the world without, the world that is revealed to us by our bodily senses, is material: the world within, the world that is revealed to us by our higher emotions, is spiritual. Animals are spiritual beings as compared with plants. Man is a spiritual being as compared with the other animals. Civilization means, or ought to mean, the outgrowth of spirit, the development of spiritual faculties, the evocation of spiritual wants. The

Englishman of to-day is higher in the scale of spiritual life than the Bushman. The European of to-day, than his prehistoric ancestor. When we eat and drink, when we walk and run, we put forth material energy: when we think and love, when we believe and aspire, we put forth spiritual energy. The love of sensual indulgence is a material motive to action. The love of fame is by comparison a spiritual motive. The love of one's fellow men is spiritual in a far higher degree. The miser devotes his powers to a material, the patriot to a spiritual end. Colour and sound are material, beauty and harmony are spiritual properties of things. Such events as the Battle of Marathon, the death of Socrates, the devotion of Winckelried, the martyrdom of Joan of Arc are on the one hand material phenomena, perceptible by the bodily senses, producing effects which have a narrow circle of disturbance and are measurable (potentially, if not actually) in terms of force transferred or matter displaced. And on the other hand they are spiritual phenomena, making their appeal to reason and emotion, producing effects which have an ever widening and virtually illimitable circle of disturbance, and are for that very reason discernible only by super-physical senses, by trained and ripened experience of human nature, by sympathetic insight into the tangled maze of history, and in general by the "inward eye."

The bearing of this conception on the problem of self-realization has now to be considered. If in the contrast between *matter* and *spirit* we have the highest and most comprehensive of the antitheses that measure the range of Nature,—in the contrast between the *real* and the *unreal* we have the highest and most comprehensive of the antitheses that measure the range of speculative thought. I mean by this that when we try to think about spirit and matter, the first and the last category under which we can marshal our thoughts is that of *reality* (with its opposite). I mean, in other words, that the first and the last question which we have to ask ourselves with regard to the ultimate poles of Nature is: Which is the real or positive pole of existence, and therefore—by right, if not by might—the magnetic pole of our desires and endeavours?

Before we can attempt to answer this question we must bring it within the compass of our everyday life. Regarded as the ideal poles of existence, matter and spirit lie beyond the horizon of our experience and therefore beyond the grasp of our imaginative thought. What we have to decide is, which is the higher reality, which is to be preferred to the other if we are called upon to choose between them. In order to solve this problem, is it necessary for us to fling ourselves into the vortex of the eternal controversy between materialism and idealism? I think not. At any rate, so far as the controversy is metaphysical we shall do well to leave it alone.

"Pure materialism" and "pure idealism" may be allowed to cancel one another. Like all monistic theories of the Universe, they are the outcome of a dualistic movement of thought, a movement which has substituted the false opposition of the real to the *non-existent* for the true opposition of the real to the *unreal*, and which has therefore led us to think of spirit and matter as mutually exclusive alternatives instead of as the poles—opposite and correlative—of a doubly infinite process. Holding, as I do, that spirit is nothing apart from matter, and matter is nothing apart from spirit, I must needs think that each of these rival philosophies has conjured away the Universe and has given us in its stead a metaphysical dream-world, peopled by the shadows of our own theories,—shadows which the reflected glow of our imagination makes visible for a moment on the wall of darkness that bounds our speculative thought.

If our problem is insoluble on the plane of metaphysical speculation, we must, I imagine, come down to a more practical and more popular plane. At first sight it looks as if, on that lower level, the problem was easy to state and equally easy to solve. For those who hold that spirit and matter are both real (each in its own way and degree), the controversy between materialism and idealism resolves itself, as I have already suggested, into a simple question which seems to admit of a simple answer. To say that spirit is to be preferred to and exalted above matter is as much of a truism as to say that light is brighter and more glorious than darkness. The whole evolutionary movement of Nature is marked and measured by the outgrowth of spirit; and in the minds of us who are involved in that movement and whose beings have shaped themselves and are shaping themselves in response to its pressure, there must needs be an instinctive and inalienable prejudice in favour of what is spiritual. The spiritual bias of our deepest desires is at once a clear indication of the direction in which the current of Nature is setting, and an argument in support of idealism which cannot be gainsaid.

So, at least, it seems to me. But the question is not to be so summarily disposed of. We have but to look around us in order to convince ourselves that practical materialism—the choice, in the conduct of one's own life, of the wrong term in the great antithesis—is the source of nearly all the evil and much of the unhappiness in life. And though theoretical and practical materialism are not necessarily conjoined in the same person (the materialist in theory being sometimes a whole-hearted idealist in practice), in logic—the deep logic of natural tendency—they cannot be disjoined. It is well, therefore, that I should try to come to an understanding and a reckoning with theoretical materialism—not the materialism of the metaphysical physicist, which becomes more and more abstract and ineffective, as the *primordia rerum*, eluding the grasp of science, recede further and further into the impalpable—but the materialism which wages war against all our hopes and aspirations, the materialism which chills and darkens life with the shadow of despair and death, the militant materialism of the man of science and the man in the street.

An ill-assorted couple these! So one feels inclined to say. But it is to the collaboration of this ill-assorted couple that we owe the materialistic philosophy which has long dominated human thought. The belief of the man of science that the nearer we are to what is ultimate in analysis the nearer we are to intrinsic reality, has allied itself with the belief of the man in the street that the palpable is the real. And the scientific conception of cause as law or order, merging itself in, or rather confounding itself with, the popular conception of cause as originating force, has generated the confusion between *cause* and *condition* on which most of the arguments for materialism are hinged.

I will try to explain and justify these statements. The primary postulate of popular (as distinguished from metaphysical) materialism is that nothing exists, in the order of Nature, except what is perceptible by man's bodily senses. This postulate is the outcome and expression of an instinctive feeling which is mental rather than emotional, but which is so securely rooted that nothing can dislodge it but a convulsive upheaval of the mind,—the analogue in the sphere of reason of what religious people call "conversion." So firmly convinced is the average man that Nature is co-terminous in all her dimensions with the outward and visible (or material) world, that in order to save the inward and spiritual side of existence from annihilation he has to find an asylum for it in a supplementary world which he calls "the Supernatural." Break down his belief in the Supernatural; convince him that Nature is the "all of being"; and the latent materialism of his intellect will become his accepted creed.

In formulating this creed he will go to the physicist for counsel and guidance. The function of science is to analyze; and a professional prejudice in favour of his own calling tempts the votary of physical science to assume that the path of analysis leads in the direction of reality as well as of scientific truth,—in other words, that what is ultimate in analysis is absolutely real. This assumption is, as we have seen, the basis of "pure materialism," a system of thought which (on the principle of too far East being West) is scarcely distinguishable from its opposite—"pure idealism," and which has nothing in common with the crass materialism of the average man. The ultimate (or penultimate) elements of things which the researches of the physicist have unveiled to his mind are wholly imperceptible by his bodily senses, however much the range of these may be extended by mechanical aids; and as those elements are more real, in the sense of being nearer to the ideal goal of his analytical labours, than the visible phenomena of Nature, he would not hesitate to conjecture, if he had but the full courage of his professional prejudice, that the ultimate basis of existence was an impalpable and therefore (in the popular sense of the word) an immaterial reality. And the further he is carried by his analytical researches into the heart of matter, the more impalpable does the Universe, as it reveals itself to him, become. There was a time when he seriously believed that in resolving matter into "atoms"—the "bricks of the Universe"—he had reached the bedrock of reality. But the discovery of radium awoke him from that comfortable dream. As the "bricks of the Universe" gradually melted away into whirls of energy, he ought to have begun to realize that, even in his sense of the word *reality*, the impalpable is the real. But if on one side of him the physicist is the man of science, on another side he is, what each one of us is, the man in the street, the plain average man. And as he is therefore swayed by the average man's prejudice in favour of the data of the bodily senses, he trusts his own quasi-professional bias in favour of the products of scientific analysis only so far as it gives a general countenance to the popular conviction that the outward and visible world is the whole Universe. He knows from experience that the outward and visible side of Nature is much more amenable to scientific treatment than the inward and spiritual side; and, as a scientific expert, he infers from this what, as an ordinary man, he is already predisposed to believe—namely, that the outward and visible side is the only side. Thus the popular postulate that the visible world is the real world absorbs into itself (in the mind of the physicist) just so much of the scientific postulate that analysis is the only revealer of reality, as it is able to assimilate. In other words, the physicist is not above countenancing the popular belief that the palpable is the real, *so far as this gives support to his own hypothesis that analysis is the only road to reality*, and will even (so much of the average man is there in the average scientist) avert his eyes from the logical consequences of his own hypothesis, *so far as these conflict with the materialism of popular thought*.

There is a similar illogical alliance between popular and scientific prejudices in the arguments by which materialism is supported, as distinguished from the assumption on which it is based. The arguments for materialism are all hinged on a single conception—that of *cause*. Of all conceptions this is the least able to bear the strain of philosophical controversy, with the ceaseless swing and counterswing of thought which it involves. The word *cause* has many meanings and sub-meanings, and is not only apt to suggest different ideas to different minds, but is even ready to take a fresh shade of meaning from every change of context. Such a word can be used with perfect safety so long as there is a tacit understanding between the speaker and his audience as to the sense in which it is to be employed; but it is always liable to stultify the arguments of the man who uses it in the development of a philosophical or quasi-philosophical conception. An iron bridge is blown down by a violent blast of wind. What is the cause of the disaster? The fury of the storm is one answer. The unsoundness of the iron is another. The weight of a passing train. The miscalculations of the engineer. The dishonesty of the contractor. The carelessness of a foreman. Each of these is a possible answer to the question, and each in turn might be accepted as adequate if it happened to respond to what was passing in the mind of the inquirer. The truth is that the meaning of the word *cause* is in the first instance subjective rather than objective, the search for cause being always a search for mental satisfaction, and the cause of a thing having been sufficiently determined whenever the mind finds rest in the account of the thing that is submitted to it.

As our ideas of causation vary from mind to mind, from standpoint to standpoint, and even from context to context, it behoves us to ask ourselves on what principle they are to be classified? It will, I think, be found that they range, for the most part, between two widely divergent conceptions,—the popular conception of cause as originating or producing *force*, and the scientific conception of cause as *law*.

The former has its origin in man's experience of the action of his own will as a causative force. As the action of the will precedes the result which it produces, the idea of priority in time becomes inseparably associated with the conception of cause. Also, as the result, when will is at work, is felt to be subordinate to the cause and to belong to a lower order of things, men instinctively assume that the cause is always higher and more real than the effect, and that the latter is dependent on and even owes its being to the former.

Now when a man looks around him and sees that a given phenomenon A is constantly followed by a given phenomenon B, his first impulse is to assume that a will like his own has been at work. In other words, he personifies the antecedent phenomenon A, and regards B as subordinate to it and dependent on it, as the passive product of its active force. This anthropomorphic tendency, as it is called—a tendency which in bygone ages gave a Naiad to every stream and a Dryad to every tree—recedes as science advances; but the corresponding conception of cause is never wholly eradicated. Ordinary men instinctively assume that the cause is prior in time to the effect, and that it is in some sort higher in the scale of things and more real.

The conception of cause which Science, in her attempt to account for things, has gradually evolved, is entirely different from this. The projection of self into the outward world, which has given us the conception of cause as oringiating or producing force, is foreign to her aims and methods. All outward phenomena are equally real in her eyes; or rather, all outward things are phenomena, the problem of reality being one with which she has no direct concern. Experience has taught her that some phenomena are less palpable than others, and have a proportionately wider range; and this is the only distinction that she recognizes. In her attempts to account for a palpable phenomenon she gradually works her way towards certain impalpable tendencies which underlie it, and the operation of which it duly exemplifies. These impalpable tendencies are known to her as *laws*; and when the relations between a given phenomenon and all the laws that underlie it have been fully determined, the cause of the thing has, for the purpose of science, been fully ascertained. In fine the cause of a phenomenon is the phenomenon itself as fully understood and explained.

But does Science ever really solve the problem of causation? Surely not. Even in her own sense of the word *cause*, her solution of the problem is never more than partial and provisional, for to determine the relation between a given phenomenon and all the laws that underlie it is obviously impossible. But this is by the way. We must look beyond the scientific conception of cause. The search for cause, whatever form it may take, is always a search for mental satisfaction. Does the mind of man rest in the scientific account of the phenomenon? The mind of this or that man, who has a particular object in view, may; but the general mind of man does not. For as soon as Science has explained a phenomenon in terms of the laws that underlie it, the thoughtful mind is sure to ask—and something of anthropomorphism is sure to weave itself into the question—"But what is the cause of those underlying laws?" And when this question has been answered, another of the same character will suggest itself; and so on *ad infinitum*. The truth is that Science, far from solving the problem of cause, puts off the solution of it as long as it possibly can. In the pre-scientific ages a separate cause (in the popular sense of the word) was demanded for each separate phenomenon; but Science has shown us that "each thing is implicated with all," the organization of Nature through her hierarchy of laws being so complete, that to ask the cause of one thing is, in the last resort, to ask the cause of the whole Universe. In fine, Science abandons the search for cause—for *vera causa*—as hopeless, and substitutes for it the work of studying organization and tracing order.

But what will happen when the average man and the scientist come together, perhaps in the same person, and begin to discuss psychological problems from the standpoint of causation? A man receives a blow on the head, and his mind is either permanently or temporarily affected by it. His food disagrees with him, and his temper suffers. In each of these cases the physical or material phenomenon is the cause of the psychical or spiritual. So the scientist will contend: and we must not quarrel with him for doing so. He may even go so far as to say that every psychical state has its exact counterpart in a physical state. Let this be granted, and let it also be granted that there is a point of view from which the scientist is justified in regarding the physical state as the cause of the psychical. Does it follow that the physical state is real and the psychical state illusory? By no means. To draw such an inference is beyond the province of Science; and in point of fact the inference is never drawn by Science as such. But when the average man is told that a certain injury to the brain is almost invariably followed by certain mental symptoms, and that the former phenomenon may therefore be regarded as the cause of the latter, his own conception of cause as originating force—a conception which carries with it the subsidiary notions of reality, superiority, activity, priority in time, and so forth—comes into play, and he jumps to the conclusion that the material phenomenon (the injury to the brain) is the *active* cause, and the spiritual phenomenon (the mental symptoms) the *passive* effect; and when he is told, further, that every spiritual phenomenon—every thought, every emotion, every purpose—has its material counterpart in the brain and nervous system, he naturally passes on to the further conclusion that the material side of man's being is the substance, and the spiritual side the shadow,—a conclusion which is pregnant with all the dogmas of materialism. There is something as it seems to me, of dishonesty (or is it self-deception?) in the attitude of the scientist who uses the word *cause* in one sense and allows his disciple (his "lay" self, perhaps) to use it in another. In any case, an argument which has for its basis a complete confusion of thought is too hollow to deserve careful criticism. The popular or anthropomorphic conception of cause owes its origin to man's secret and apparently inalienable conviction that will is the only originating force. To denounce anthropomorphism in one breath and appeal to the anthropomorphic instinct in the next, is unworthy of a serious thinker.

Socrates in the *Phædo* speaks of the confusion current in his day, between *cause* and *condition*: "It may be said that without bones and muscles and the other parts of the body I cannot execute my purpose. But to say that I do so because of them, and that this is the way in which mind acts, and not from the choice of the best, is a very careless and idle way of speaking. I wonder that they cannot distinguish the cause from the condition, which the many, feeling about in the dark, are always mistaking and misnaming." The distinction which Socrates draws between the cause (τὸ αἴτιον τῷ ὄντι) and the condition (ἐκεῖνο, ἄνευ οὗ τὸ αἴτιον οὐκ ἄν ποτ' εἴη αἴτιον) cannot be too strongly insisted upon, for the tendency to confuse the two still prevails. To say that because I cannot do a kind action without using my brain and my limbs therefore the kind action is done by my brain and my limbs rather than by my self, is equivalent to saying that because a steamship cannot be handled except through the medium of her engines therefore she is controlled and guided by her engines instead of by the mind and will of the officer who is in charge of her. When brain-disorder produces mental derangement, a mechanical explanation of human life is apt to obtrude itself on one's thoughts; but, after all, the inability of the mind (if mind there be) to use the brain when the latter has been seriously injured, no more proves the non-existence of the mind than the unmanageableness of a ship, when her engines have broken down, proves the non-existence of her captain. It is with conditions, not with causes (in the Socratic sense of the word), that scientific investigation is concerned. When will the men of science learn that the conception of cause which is at the root of all controversies as to the reality of spiritual phenomena—a conception, the validity of which (anthropomorphic though it be) is unconsciously taken for granted by the materialist quite as much as by the idealist—is one with which, *as men of science*, they have no concern; that when the word *cause* enters into their treatises, it bears, or ought to bear, an entirely different meaning? Perhaps they will never learn the lesson; for the anthropomorphic instinct is of the inmost essence of human nature, and they will never cease to be men.

The dialectical basis of popular materialism is a perverse confusion between the anthropomorphic and the scientific conception of cause,—conceptions which have nothing in common except that they are at opposite poles of the same meridian of human thought. But the real basis is, as we have already seen, instinctive rather than dialectical. What makes the average man incline, in his speculative moods or moments, to materialism is his latent conviction that nothing exists except what is perceptible by his bodily senses. We have seen that scientific analysis, which, in its quest of ultimate reality, advances further and further into the impalpable, has already undermined this position. But for the final disproof of it we must appeal from the average man's consciousness to his sub-conscious self, from "what he thinks he feels" to "what he feels indeed."

His belief in the intrinsic reality of the palpable is the resultant of three assumptions. The first is that there is a standard of reality. With this assumption we need not quarrel. If there is no standard of reality there is no such thing as reality, and the antithesis of the *real* and the *unreal* (or the *real* and the *apparent*) has no right to exist. That it does exist, that it is a centre round which our disordered thoughts are again and again rallied and reformed, is a sufficient answer to the sneer of the sceptic. A living critic has permitted himself to say that "beauty is as real as beer, but not a whit more real." This is equivalent to saying that the idea of reality is wholly illusory. Nothing is easier and nothing is more futile than to flout human nature in the name of what is miscalled "common-sense."[1] The very cheapness and shallowness of scepticism might well give the sceptic pause. The standard of reality is as real (I cannot help using the word) as the standard of heat in the physical world, or of goodness in the sphere of conduct. That it is less tangible than the latter standard and far less tangible than the former, is nothing to the purpose. All I contend for is that the standard of reality is as real as the idea of reality, which indeed would lose its meaning if phenomenalism and individualism were to dominate human thought. After all, the sceptic can do no more than say that there is no *real* standard of reality, or again that phenomen-

[1] The true "common-sense" of the matter is that beauty is either much more real than beer, or much less real.

alism is a *truer* philosophy (truth being the counterpart of reality) than its rival.

The second assumption is that the standard of reality is subjective (in the generic, not the individualistic sense of the word). This assumption, like the first, is too deeply seated to be open to criticism. In anthropocentricity, rightly understood, we have the only available base of operations for the speculative enterprises of human thought. Man's impressions of things form an environing atmosphere which he cannot, by any effort of thought, outsoar. He may scrutinize his impressions, analyze them, systematize them, but he cannot get beyond them. His very sense of their inadequacy is itself an impression of things—one among many; and though it may modify and even transform the rest, it does not and cannot supersede them. Man's being, with its multifarious powers and faculties, is the cardinal assumption on which his philosophy is always hinged; and his supreme object in thinking is to give satisfaction to some or all of his mental faculties, or, in a word, to himself. Nothing is vainer or more illusive than the attempt to escape from self into a region of objective reality. In conceiving of an "Absolute" we relate it to our own minds; and so self accompanies one even into the inter-stellar darkness of the Unknowable.

It follows that man can no more cease to be anthropocentric in speculation than he can change his identity or abrogate the conditions of his existence. When I climb to a mountain height and survey the surrounding country, I necessarily make myself the centre of the world that is encircled by the horizon, or boundary of *my* vision. And though I know that there are many lands and seas beyond that apparent limit, I must needs think of them as surrounding the world that surrounds and centres in me. As it is on the spatial plane, so it is on the cosmic. Man has no choice but to place himself at the centre of his own environment; and the widest environment with which he can surround himself is his own vision of the Universe. To say that the nature of man is, *for man*, the rule and measure of reality, is to state a self-evident truth.

But it is the whole man, it is the real nature of man (so

far as this can be ascertained), that we must place at the centre of things. It is here, as it seems to me, that popular materialism goes astray. Its third assumption—that man through his bodily senses sees the world as it really is—is not merely gratuitous but demonstrably false. The answer to materialism is that, though in a certain stratum of his consciousness man inclines to a view of things which makes materialism logically inevitable, he is all the time in the depths of his being—at the real headquarters of his life—an incurable idealist. The true standard of reality, besides being personal and subjective, is in a sense ready to one's hand. It is not to this or that side or aspect of human nature that the Universe reveals itself, but to human nature in its totality, to the whole range—potential and actual—of our perceptive faculties. This revelation must be taken as given. Some of our perceptive faculties announce themselves as being higher and stronger than others, as having a clearer vision and a wider and longer range. We must believe that these are what they claim to be, for we have no means of criticizing their pretensions. In other words, we must believe that certain aspects of existence are higher and more real than others. The organization of our perceptive faculties, the arrangement of them according to their several "stations and degrees," is done for us, not by us; for there is no standard save that with which they themselves provide us, by which we can measure their worth.

In arranging themselves in order of dignity and worth, our perceptive faculties solve the problem of reality. They solve it in effect, if not in logic. In accepting the natural order in himself, a man accepts it in the Universe. Idealism, like materialism, begins at home. What a man feels himself to be, that he believes the Universe to be. He does not necessarily argue from himself to the Universe. The macrocosmic belief is no mere inference from the microcosmic. It *is* the microcosmic belief raised to a higher power and operating on a larger scale.

But the transition from the lesser belief to the larger is also logical. And the logic of it is somewhat as follows. When we exercise our perceptive faculties we experience *feelings* of various kinds and degrees. Some of these are of a higher order than others. I mean by this that, in the act of experiencing them, we feel that, by comparison with other feelings, they are pure, lofty, large, magisterial. And I mean that one's sense of the comparative value of the feeling is in every case a vital part of the feeling itself. What are we to infer from this fact ? If feeling is the subjective side of experience, the surface of contact between the organism and its environment,—if, wherever there is feeling, there must needs be something to be felt,—may we not argue that the feelings which are higher than the rest are produced by contact with things which are higher in the scale of being than the ordinary objects of our experience, or, in other words, which are more real ? If, for example, the feeling that is generated by a resplendent sunset or an inspired poem announces itself as being higher than the feeling that is generated by a *pâté de foie gras*, may we not conclude that the sunset and the poem are higher realities than the *pâté*. This conclusion seems to be not merely legitimate, but irresistible. Either we must give up using the word *real*, and in doing so must take upon ourselves the responsibility of cancelling an entire category of human thought, or we must admit that the worth of the feeling measures in every case the degree of reality in the thing that is felt.

But how is the worth of the feeling to be determined ? There is but one answer to this question. We must value our feelings as they value themselves. By what standard do they value themselves ? And how far is it possible for us to work by that standard ? It will, I think, be generally conceded, that our feelings may be classified under two principal heads—*sensation* and *emotion*,[1] and that the feelings which belong to the latter class are of a higher order than those which belong to the former. Now the things that generate sensation in the percipient subject are

[1] For this apparent relapse into dualism the limitations of language are responsible. I speak as if feeling were always either emotional or sensational. I know quite well that (apart from what is purely physical) it is usually both. When I say that a feeling is emotional, I mean that it is predominatingly so. When I say that an emotion is high and puro, I mean that the dross of sensation has been almost wholly refined away.

as a rule palpable and material; and the things that generate emotion are as a rule impalpable and spiritual. When I use the word *impalpable* I am thinking, not of the impalpability which is reached by accepting the palpable, and then analyzing it into its parts and elements, but of the impalpability which is reached by transcending the palpable, by transfiguring it and even in some sort re-creating it. The latter, the spiritual impalpability which is the counterpart of spiritual experience and the object of spiritual desire, is the true antithesis of that material palpability which popular materialism regards as the proof and counterpart of reality.

It can, I think, be shown that emotional feeling is in almost every case the response of the soul to an impalpable —spiritually impalpable—influence. Many, perhaps most, of our emotions are awakened by contact with other human souls. I receive a letter from one who is ten thousand miles away; and, as I read it, I am filled with profound emotion. What is the telepathic influence that has affected me so strongly? Nothing but a message from an impalpable entity—a sister soul. The words of one whom I have never seen—a great teacher or a great poet—bring tears to my eyes. The writer is dead; his body has crumbled into dust; but his soul still speaks to mine, and the emotion that thrills me is my silent answer to his silent voice. We are too often cool and even indifferent in the presence of the living; for, except in rare cases, the veil of what is palpable hangs between us and them. But our intercourse with the mighty dead is always immaterial and always emotional. I read of a deed of heroism; and my heart is fired with unselfish enthusiasm. I meditate on a life of self-sacrifice; and a flood of spiritual aspiration sweeps through the channel of my soul.

Other emotions are kindled by contact with those higher social syntheses which are generated by the evolution of the human spirit. Such emotions are love of one's country, devotion to one's church, disinterested zeal for one's political party. What impalpable entities are these magnets of the heart's desire! What is my country? The land in which I live is a mere symbol. The everflowing tide of its national life is but one of the many aspects of its being. Think of the flood of thoughts, visions, memories, associations; think of the cross-currents of sentiment—love and pride, fear and doubt,—that surge and seethe through the mind at the bare mention of the word *England*, or of the phrase *The British Empire*; and you will realize how immense and how impalpable is the "Mighty Being" which kindles in one's heart the pure emotion of patriotism, how undefinable are its limits, how many are the planes of its life.

Sometimes it happens that strong and enduring emotion is kindled by ideas, such as that of loyalty, of liberty, of feudal devotion, of freedom of conscience, of democratic equality. Here the things that affect us are obviously impalpable. These ideas for which men live and die—what are they? By-products of human thought. Theories steeped in sentiment. Dreams of an over-heated brain. But how vividly, how directly, how lastingly they affect us! Compare the feelings of the man who offers his life for the cause of liberty with the feelings of the man who slakes a parching thirst. The sense of relief from thirst is vivid while it lasts, but it soon vanishes; and when it is gone nothing remains but the consciousness that one's body has been restored to its normal condition. The feeling of devotion which the idea of liberty kindles proclaims itself as high and sacred; and in the act of doing so, in the act of ennobling the soul that it inspires, it tells us that its object, far from being shadowy or illusory, is real in a sense which overshadows all our conventional notions of reality.

There is another class of emotions which may seem to be kindled by material objects. When we listen to beautiful music, when we look at a beautiful scene, our bodily senses are appealed to, and yet our souls are deeply stirred. Are we to infer from this that emotion can be kindled by what is palpable? Not for a moment. I mean by palpable what is perceived by the bodily senses, as such. In a beautiful sonata what is palpable (that is, perceptible by all ears) is so much noise; what is impalpable (that is, perceptible by few persons and therefore not perceptible by the sense of hearing, as such) is the beauty of the music; what is yet more impalpable is the message from the musician's soul.

In a starlit night what is palpable is a vault of darkness studded with points of twinkling light; what is impalpable is the beauty of the scene; what is yet more impalpable is the message of the midnight sky,—the spiritual suggestions of purity, serenity, and majesty that burn (for the soul that can receive them) through the beauty of the midnight, just as beauty burns (for the heart that can discern it) through the starlit darkness of the midnight sky. It is through our ears, but not with our ears only, that we receive the message from the musician's soul. It is through our eyes, but not with our eyes only, that we receive the message of the starlit night. If we received either message with our bodily senses only, all men whose senses were normal would receive it, and all men would be equally and similarly affected by it. The fact that few men are affected by such messages and that those few are affected by them in different degrees shows that they appeal, not to our eyes or ears only, but also to inward and spiritual senses which look through our eyes and hear with our ears, but which, being still in process of evolution, are differently developed in different souls and have but an embryonic existence in nine men out of ten. When we contemplate a scene of surpassing beauty, is not our highest emotion directed towards what is impalpable, immaterial, imperceptible, or perceptible only for fleeting moments—towards what is suggested and symbolized—towards the unattainable, the ideal, the unimaginable,

> The light that never was on sea or land?

May we not even say that what intensifies our emotion on such occasions is our feeling that the real soul of the thing cannot possibly be apprehended? And may it not be that the feeling of being unable to apprehend the real soul of the thing is our very way of apprehending it? It is the endless reaching on of the heart towards what seems to fly before it that makes our emotions (when we are transported by beauty) so poignant and so strong; but it may well be that in our apparently hopeless and even aimless yearning—the quintessential flame of our kindled fire—the hidden soul of things is intimately near to us, its very imperceptibility being the counterpart of its transcendent reality. If this is so, then what is most real in the Cosmos is not that outward, tangible, material side or aspect of it which appeals to our bodily senses, but that inward and spiritual essence of it which constitutes its unity and its life, and which, glowing through and making beautiful the veil of its outward existence, appeals to intuitive senses which are more or less akin to itself.

There are doubtless fire-springs of emotion which lie deeper than any that I have yet indicated. There are moments in our days (if I may regard my own experiences as normal) when we seem to understand all things, when life has no secrets from us, when the meaning of existence is as clear as the fact, the end (the τελος) as inevitable as the process. An inspired passage in a poem or other work of genius may for a moment so entirely change our sense of proportion as to give us a new standard of reality and, in doing so, to transform our experiences of life and nature and reveal to us new aspects of existence. The death-bed of a dear friend may for a moment cancel whatever is physical and instinctive, whatever is unamenable to the healing influence of religious faith or philosophical meditation, in our inborn fear of death. Even the outward world which (as we have just seen), in the act of appealing to our sense of beauty, sends spiritual messages to our hearts, may sometimes send us the most spiritual of all messages—may lift the veil of beauty which sunders the soul of Nature from the soul of man, and initiate us for a timeless moment into the inmost mystery of Nature's life.

May we trust these transcendental experiences? We may because we must. In the moments of which I speak, not only are we conscious of being swayed by feelings which are as strong and vivid as they are new and strange, but we are also conscious that the feelings carry with them high credentials,—trust, complete trust, in the genuineness and significance of the feeling, in the strength and justice of its claims upon us, in its might and in its right to rule our hearts, being in every case an essential part of the feeling itself. And so, though we may be unable to analyze those experiences, or do justice to them even in thought, we can at least feel sure that their objects, though impalpable in every sense of the word, are real (if the quality of the feelings that they kindle counts for anything) in a sense which transcends all our wonted conceptions, and stultifies all our wonted standards, of reality. The impermanence of the feeling—the instantaneousness, the apparent timelessness, of its coming and going—need not disconcert us; for while it lasts it is overwhelmingly strong, and the impression that it leaves, or rather the memory of that impression, is ineffaceable. A lightning flash has pierced our darkness; and we know now—or at any rate we know that we have known—what are the realities that life, in our narrow sense of the word, veils from our sight.

In each of the cases which I have considered, emotional feeling has proved to be generated by the response of the soul to an impalpable influence—impalpable in the sense of transcending the palpable, not of underlying it. The higher the feeling, the more impalpable is the generating influence, and the higher (we must needs believe) is the reality to which it bears witness. From this we may surely conclude that, in spite of the prejudice of man's surface self in favour of the palpable, it belongs to his deeper nature to identify the impalpable—what is ultimate in synthesis—the spiritual, in a word—with the real.

But the final proof that man, though a materialist in theory, is an idealist at heart, lies in the fact that his religious creeds are all dominated by the idea of the Supernatural. In evolving this idea man has provided himself with a materialistic antidote to the poison of materialism. When he consciously magnifies the Supernatural at the expense of Nature, he is unconsciously magnifying the spiritual or impalpable aspect of Nature at the expense of the material. It is because he believes in the supremacy of what is inward and spiritual, and yet cannot present this truth to his consciousness, that he has denaturalized religion in his endeavour to spiritualize it, and, in doing so, has imposed on his life the heavy yoke of priest-craft, has allowed his conscience to become entangled in a network of casuistical rules and ceremonial observances, and his heart (which cannot energize properly except in an atmosphere of spiritual freedom) to enter the prison-cell of a formulated creed. The supernatural world, which his pictorial imagination has called into being and which for him is the highest of all realities, *is* the spiritual world seen through a materialistic medium, presented to thought by the aid of material images, set forth in a materialistic notation, in terms of space and time. An apologist for supernatural religion has said that the supernatural is the real. This is not so; for the supernatural is at best a shadow; but it is the shadow cast by the spiritual, and the spiritual is the real.

I have taken pains to disprove the vulgar assumption that the palpable is the real, for I see clearly that it is the ultimate basis of the materialism which is practical as well as theoretical,—the materialism of popular thought. It is not, however, because it is impalpable that I ascribe reality to spirit, but because it is the product of synthesis, of integration,—in a word, because it is *whole*. If what is spiritual is impalpable, the reason is that wholeness needs for its direct apprehension senses other than those which we speak of as "bodily," that it is the object, not of sight or hearing, but of "contemplation," of "vision," of the "inward eye." It will be understood, then, that whenever I use the word *spirit* (and the words that are akin to it) I have in mind my own definition of it,—I am thinking, not so much of what is impalpable, immaterial, ethereal and the like, as of the principle of wholeness, of organic unity. The idealist, the man who believes that the spiritual is the real, stakes everything—so strong is his bias towards wholeness—on the Universe being in the last resort an organic whole. This, though he may not know it, is the fundamental assumption which determines the whole tenor of his thought.

CHAPTER III

THE DIVINE CIRCLE

THE world, as we know it, is a process between two diametrically opposite and infinitely distant poles. These poles, by whatever names we may please to call them, bound all the movements of our thought and all the flights of our imagination. In what relation does each of them stand to the other, on what I may call the further side of itself, the side which is turned away from us? On the hither side, the side that is turned towards us, the two ceaselessly interact and interpenetrate each other, and, in doing so, generate the world of our experience. When they pass beyond the confines of that world, what happens to them and to the process which they dominate? Are we to think of the Universe—whether its movement be temporal or logical—as emerging from an infinitely distant void of darkness behind us and disappearing into another infinitely distant void of darkness beyond us? No, for in that case the Universe would cease to be universal. With regions of mystery closing in upon it from behind and from before, its infinitude would be limited, and its claim to include all things would no longer hold good. The truth is that the darkness which our thought so readily conjures up represents nothing but our inability to approach either pole. It is on the hither side of each pole, not on the further side, that the wall of night rises up to bar the advance of our thoughts. Beyond its impenetrable barrier the process moves on towards each of its ideal limits; but if its orbit can no longer be traced by our mind, the general character of its movement seems to be determined by a primary necessity of our thought. If the process is really all-inclusive, if it is really commensurate with the Universe, its beginning and its end must coincide. Just as within the range of our experience the opposite tendencies of things are always intermingled, so it is (we must believe) when they pass beyond the range of our experience in the direction of their respective poles. What seems to us to be a straight line, never deviating from its straightness, is really an arc of an infinite circle. In an infinite circle all things must needs be included and all loopholes of escape must needs be closed. The vision of the poet who

> saw Eternity the other night
> Like a great ring of pure and endless light

went to the very heart of reality.

We have seen that in Nature duality of direction is balanced by unity of being. How can this be ? It cannot be, unless the movement of Nature is circular, unless the two poles of her being are one. In this and in no other way are dualism and monism—the two eternal poles of human thought—to be fused into the larger idea that underlies them both. If I stand on the bank of a river and look either up or down stream, I am looking at one and the same moment towards the goal and towards the source of the river ; for every drop of water that passes me is both moving from and moving to the infinite sea. This " circulation of water," as we call it, is symbolical of the cosmic process. An eternal and infinite movement from source to source and from goal to goal—this *is* Nature, this *is* the Universe, and outside this there is nothing.

A strange conclusion this, and one which bears directly on the problem of destiny and duty—the problem of the purpose of growth. We can approach it from another quarter of thought. I have given my reasons for thinking that Spirit and Matter are the master poles of existence. Spirit, according to the definition of the word that I have formulated, is what is ultimate in synthesis ; and it stands to reason that what is finally ultimate (if I may be allowed the pleonasm) is the totality of things regarded as a living whole. The spiritual properties of things are revealed to us by quasi-creative faculties which build things up, in the act of perceiving them, into real, though impalpable, structures, or fuse them into indivisible wholes. These faculties announce themselves as being of a higher order than the bodily senses; and in the act of doing so they tell us that the spiritual aspects of Nature are higher and more real than the material. This law of our nature—a law which we are not competent to over-rule or even ignore—determines the "law" (in the mathematical sense of the word) of our infinite series, the equation to our infinite curve. The path of synthesis, which takes us in the direction of what is spiritual, takes us also in the direction of what is real; and the ideal goal of the movement—the supreme, all-inclusive whole—is on the one hand pure spirit and on the other hand absolute reality. From this conclusion we may draw the further inference (not by any logical process, but by a mere re-arrangement of our thoughts) that pure spirit—the ideal goal of the synthetic movement—is both all-inclusive and absolutely real, in a word, that it is *Everything*.

Let us now see to what ideal goal the path of analysis is predestined to lead us. As we tread this path, as we resolve things into their constituent elements, as we resolve facts into their underlying laws, the life, the beauty, the reality, the very actuality of the Universe seem to fade slowly away; until at last—beyond the atoms or ions of the physicist, or whatever other primordial elements are for the moment to be regarded as ultimate—the pale abstractions of the mathematician (generalizations perhaps from man's sub-conscious and even pre-human experience of the primary elements of things) begin to loom up, like cloud mountains, along the horizon of human thought. It is true that the states of matter which our analysis of the actual leads us to conceive of, if not to believe in, are pure, impalpable, imponderable, ethereal substances which seem to have a quasi-spiritual beauty of their own; but it is a beauty of material, not of form, a beauty which is wholly formless and therefore wholly potential, the very beauty of nothingness, the very splendour of an elusive dream. I speak as an average man, whose starting point, whether he follow the path of analysis or of synthesis, is acceptance of the actual. On either side of the actual lies an impalpable world. The impalpability which synthesis reveals to us appeals to our hearts and seems to be aglow with the flame of life and the sun-like light of intrinsic reality. The impalpability which analysis reveals to us has momentary flashes of light which are suggestive of a far-off glory; but apart from those flashes, which only mock and tantalize our thoughts, it seems to have the darkness and the coldness of interstellar space. When we meditate on these matters we must needs draw our premises from ourselves. The stress and bias of our nature constrain us to believe that the products of synthesis are more real than the products of analysis; and if we allow ourselves to be guided, in our speculative adventures, by this seemingly inalienable prejudice, we shall arrive in due course at the conclusion that what is ultimate in analysis is absolutely void of reality—is, in a word, Nothing. The very function of analysis is to unweave the tissue of Nature, to deprive it of form, to reduce it to a state of pure potentiality; and what is purely potential is of course *actually* null and void.

We have now worked our way to the conception that Spirit, the positive pole of existence, is the pole of Everything, the pole of absolute and all-inclusive being, whereas Matter, the negative pole of existence, is the pole of pure potentiality and therefore of infinite and absolute Nothingness. And yet—and yet—for our minds, through which, if we are to think at all, we must do all our thinking, Everything, when we begin to meditate upon it, is found to be but another name for Nothing. *Omnis determinatio est negatio.* Before we can begin to know a thing we must be able to distinguish it from other things. What cannot be so distinguished is absolutely unknowable, and is therefore, *for our minds,* non-existent. It stands to reason that Everything has no limits, no features, no qualities. There is not a single proposition that we can make about it except that it is not anything; that it is no thing; that it is Nothing. In trying to grasp the totality of things we find that we are embracing a phantom. As our minds move towards pure spirit, they seem to be moving towards absolute reality; when they reach their goal—by a supreme and momentary effort of thought—they find themselves face to face with the hollowest of all abstractions. The light of which they dreamed blinds them so completely that they can see nothing but impenetrable darkness.

What escape is there from this seemingly hopeless *impasse?* There is no escape but that of accepting it and resting in it. Let us arm ourselves with the courage of despair and say boldly that Everything is—Nothing. In saying this we shall have solved our otherwise insoluble problem. For if Everything is indeed Nothing, then the two poles of existence, the positive and the negative, have become one: pure spirit has transformed itself into pure matter; the circuit of being has been completed; the eternal process of creation has been eternally begun. Just as the finite is the meeting ground of Infinity and Zero, so is the world of our experience—the world of finite things—the meeting ground of Everything and Nothing. And just as every movement is both slow and swift, and every altitude is both low and high, so is each thing in the world of our experience both Everything and Nothing—*un tout a l'égard du néant, un néant a l'égard du tout.* But it is not only within the range of our experience that spirit and matter, Everything and Nothing, are inseparable. When we follow spirit out into its lonely purity, we find that it has matter—pure matter, the potentiality of all things which is in itself Nothing—as its eternal counterpart. The same timeless flash of thought which reveals to us Everything reveals Nothing as its other self. But if the relation of pole to pole is, from one point of view, the relation of identity, from another it is the relation of diametrical opposition and infinite aloofness. Absolute swiftness is indistinguishable from absolute slowness, which is absolute rest; but the transition from the latter pole to the former includes and immeasurably overlaps at either end the transition from the speed of a snail to the speed of light. So, though spirit (which is Everything) can become matter (which is Nothing) in a timeless moment, if matter is to transform itself into spirit it must pass through the entire circuit of existence. Stooping into matter (which is perhaps the swoon of its own life) spirit generates and animates the Universe. Emptying itself into Nothing, Everything becomes something, becomes many things, and at last streams back to itself as all things.

I do not allow myself to be imposed upon by this word-play. The conclusions that I have reached have been suggested to me by trains of thought which have evolved themselves in response to the accumulated pressure of experience, and which owe their constraining force to the spontaneousness of their origin and the naturalness of their movement rather than to the cogency of their logic. But I do not allow myself to rest in the dangerously abstract conceptions to which these trains of thought have led me, except so far as they countenance and are countenanced by a profound emotion which seems to be a vital part of my inner life. It is my feeling of "divine homesickness" (to quote Heine's words) which really convinces me that I am returning to the source from which I came; and it is this feeling, struggling to clothe itself in form so that it may present itself to consciousness, which constrains reason to spin theories that shall countenance it, and then weave those theories into a system of thought.

The feeling of "divine homesickness" is the source of much of what is best and purest in the popular belief in God. So far I have said but little about God; and I have had reasons for my reticence. The word *God* has been used so lightly, so recklessly, so familiarly, so dogmatically, so fanatically, so profanely, so hypocritically, and has served as the battle-cry of so many bitter enemies of spiritual freedom and therefore of soul-growth, that I sometimes wish it could be expunged for a while from our vocabulary, and that meantime the ideas of spiritual development, of natural retribution, of the reality of the soul, and of the supremacy of love should be the regents of our inner life. Under the tutelage of those ideas a new conception of God would gradually evolve itself, and at last, when the time had come for it to re-ascend the throne of the human spirit, would reveal itself as the paramount source of their influence and authority.

The current conceptions of God fall for the most part under two heads—Supernaturalism and Physical Pantheism.

The ideas of supreme power and absolute reality are inseparable from the idea of God. So much will be generally conceded. Starting from this latent postulate, supernaturalism conceives God as the Creator of the Universe, and in doing so places him outside Nature and outside human life; while physical pantheism identifies God with the visible Universe, and in doing so places him outside the percipient spirit of man. Both these conceptions (or misconceptions) of God owe their origin to man's over-curious desire to know about God as one knows about a mineral or a plant—to possess God, so to speak, in a formula, instead of being content to be possessed by his life and his love.[1] If we wish to know about a thing, if we wish to think about it, to investigate it, to make statements about it, to write treatises about it, we must be able to separate it from ourselves. It follows that, if we are to think about God, we must begin by separating him from ourselves, we must conceive of him as living a life external to our own. But inasmuch as man is the Alpha and Omega—as well as the centre—of the world of his own experience, it follows further that, in separating God from ourselves, we are also separating him from Nature (as we understand the word). Where, then, does God dwell? Evidently, since Nature is bereft of his presence, in some glorious world above and beyond Nature, which, for lack of a fitter name, we must call supernatural. As our knowledge of Nature extends and our conceptions of Nature widen, the interval between us, who are at the centre of Nature, and God, who is at the centre of the supernatural world, grows greater and greater, until at last the very effort that we make to think about God drives him beyond the utmost confines of our thoughts. Drives him, not merely into exile, but even, in the last resort, into non-existence. For as our conceptions of Nature widen, as each discovery prepares the way for a newer voyage of discovery, as the horizon of the Unknowable recedes further and

[1] It is of course possible to study the genesis of these antithetical creeds from other points of view. In Part I, Chapter II, for example, the evolution of the idea of the supernatural has (pp. 11, 12) been traced back to the inherent dualism of human speech. There is no real discrepancy between the two points of view. Each is valid as a point of view, that is, as affording a partial survey and a provisional explanation of a large and many-sided problem.

further from our vision, the conviction begins to dawn upon us that the Supernatural is but a dreamland, the far-projected shadow of our own ignorance of Nature.

In this way supernaturalism, obeying the unformulated laws of the soul's secret logic, leads at last to the denial of God. The inevitable rebound from this gives us physical pantheism. If the supernatural is a dreamland, God must be brought back from an exile which threatens his very existence with annihilation, and reinstated on the throne of Nature. But as the desire to know about God still dominates our minds, we must take care, even while we restore God to Nature, to separate him from ourselves. What will this involve? It is by projecting himself into Nature, by becoming one with her, by fusing inward and outward into a new and a higher synthesis, that man makes of Nature a living whole. His spirit is creative in its very receptiveness. It constructs the totality of things in the very act of apprehending it. What, then, will be left of Nature if man withdraws himself from her in order that he may fit her for the presence of his knowable God? Nothing but that aspect of Nature which man, by separating himself from it, is able to think about and know about—the material aspect, the despiritualized outward world. Nothing, in other words, but the aggregate of her physical phenomena, the temporal and spatial extension of her being, the mechanical counterpart of her infinite life. The deification of this aspect of Nature gives us the lower pantheism, which should be carefully distinguished from, but is too often confounded with, the higher or spiritual pantheism of mystical thought. The obvious objection to it is that, though it adds an emotional element to popular materialism, it differs from it in no other respect. And the practical refutation of it lies in the fact that the emotional element, being as a rule the product of a theory rather than a faith, is a volatile essence which easily passes away. The general mind of man may rest—for a while—in a materialistic conception of Nature. But the general heart of man, in spite, or perhaps in virtue, of its anthropomorphic tendencies, will always refuse to rest in a materialistic conception of God; and if it should ever abandon the belief in the Supernatural, it would assuredly pass on, in the absence of a radical reinterpretation of Nature, to denial of the Divine.

Supernaturalism and physical pantheism may safely be left to cancel one another. Each in turn is disproved by the fact that, though the other is its necessary correlate and complement, it is also its direct negative. If further proof be needed that both creeds are false just so far as they pretend to be true, it will be found in the fact that supernaturalism is bound by its primary postulate to regard Nature as essentially evil, and that physical pantheism is bound by its primary postulate to regard every detail of Nature as divinely good : and that each of these conclusions (with its endless train of moral consequences) is perpetually refuted by the logic of experience and of common sense. The failure of each creed was in truth pre-determined by the fundamental assumption which generated both. The division of the Universe into " Nature " and " the Supernatural " drains reality away from each of these dissevered worlds. In doing so it undermines the very foundations of religion, for reality—supreme, self-dependent reality—is the first and last attribute of the Godhead.

What lessons are we to learn from the failure of these attempts to solve the greatest of all mysteries ? The first and most obvious lesson is that God is the Unknowable, in the sense that with regard to him every affirmation is a denial, every belief an infidelity, every dogma a blasphemy, every formula an outrage on truth. The old story of Eros and Psyche is eternally true. If we yield to the desire to see our Divine Lover, to know all about the life that embraces and interpenetrates our own, we shall have to pay the penalty of our curiosity—the penalty of driving the Divine Lover into exile. Theology is the true atheism. Agnosticism is the first condition of faith. The Unknown God is life of our life and breath of our breath. The known God is a phantom with which we terrify ourselves in vain. Conceived of as within us—and therefore as unknowable—God is an irradiating light. Conceived of as without us—and therefore as knowable—God is an overwhelming darkness. If we insist on lifting the veil of that darkness we shall find Nothing behind it.

Are we, then, to keep silence about God? Is the word never to pass our lips? No, we may say much about God, but in all that we say we must observe three primary conditions. The first is that whatever we say must be the outcome and expression of spiritual emotion, guided perhaps and systematized by reason, but never losing its emotional character. The second is that whatever we say must admit of being interpreted emotionally and therefore in accordance with the prejudices and personal convictions of its various hearers—prejudices and convictions which our words may modify and even transform, but which we cannot afford to ignore. No proposition about God is even incipiently true which does not carry different meanings to different minds. To develop such a proposition scientifically, to draw formal inferences from it, to fit it into a system, to elaborate it into formulas, is to deprive it of its life, its force, and its meaning, and to change it at last into a string of empty words. The third condition is that whatever we say must be readily translatable into the confession that God is unknown and unknowable. The echo of every creed, of every psalm, of every prayer, must be the cry of the Hebrew prophet "Verily thou art a hidden God."

The next lesson to be learned from the respective failures of supernaturalism and physical pantheism is that if we are to arrive (within the limits prescribed by the above-named conditions) at a conception of God which is true in any sense of the word, we must fuse these anthithetical theories into the larger and deeper idea that underlies them both. Each has its own weakness; but the presence and persistence of each proves that it has also its own strength. The strength of supernaturalism is that in its higher moods it insists on the reality of spirit, that in worshipping God it does homage to the creativeness and omnipotence of spiritual energy, or, in a word, of will. The strength of physical pantheism is that it rescues God from the shadow-world of the Supernatural, and restores (or tries to restore) him to reality, to Nature. The higher creed must be the resultant of these apparently divergent tendencies. It must identify the spiritual God whom it worships with Nature; it must place his creative energy at the very heart of Nature; it must see in the course of Nature the eternal expression of his will, his thought, and his love.

What relation other than that of ideal and ultimate identity can there be between God and the world in which we live ? We are so constituted that we must needs regard the world—Nature from one point of view, the Universe from another—as a cosmos, an organic whole. So vital a part of us is our faith in its ordered unity, that it is this blind, instinctive feeling, struggling to define and express itself, which has been the mainspring of all our efforts—social, political, moral, artistic, scientific—our efforts to organize knowledge, to organize emotion, to organize conduct, to organize life. If this faith is justified—a faith which reflects man's subconscious realization of the essential unity of his own spirit—if the totality of things is at heart a cosmos, not a chaos, in what relation does it stand to that fountain-head of reality which we call God ? Are we to say that God dwells apart from it and controls it from within ? No : for in the first place, if the Universe is, as we must needs believe, infinite on all its planes and in all its dimensions, there is no room for God outside it : it is in itself the All of Being, and apart from it there is nothing. In the second place, if it is a living whole, the spring and centre of its life must be in itself. If God really controls it, he must be at the heart of it, he must animate it from within. In the third place, since God is, *ex hypothesi*, supremely real and alone real (in the full sense of the word), if the Universe were separated from him it would be drained of all reality, and in spite of its palpability, in spite of its being visible, tangible, measurable, ponderable, it would be a world of shadows and dreams.

Or are we to say that God is a part of the Universe, the highest part of it, the part to which all other parts owe allegiance ? No ; for just as the former hypothesis detracts from the infinitude, the vitality, and the reality of Nature, so the latter hypothesis detracts from the supremacy of God. In an organic whole the different parts owe allegiance, in the last resort, to the *whole* rather than to any one of their number ; and their several functions are subordinated, in the last resort, to the function or functions of the whole.

What, then, is left but for us to identify God with the Universe, and to echo the words of the son of Sirach : " We may say much and come short, wherefore in sum he is all ? "

And it is no mere phase or plane of the Universe, infinite though this may be, that we are to identify with God. It is the living whole, the organized totality, the Universe seen as it really is, the Universe seen as God himself sees it. We who live in the midst of the cosmic process cannot see the Universe as it really is. A sense of fundamental blindness is a vital part of every act of sight. But inasmuch as the Universe presents different aspects to our different perceptive faculties, and inasmuch as these faculties arrange themselves (in us who use them) as higher and lower, and constrain us to accept them on their own valuation, we are naturally led to believe that some aspects of Nature are higher and more real than others ; and so, looking up from lower to higher, and from higher to higher still, we arrive at last at the conception of what is ideally highest and therefore supremely real. It is this aspect of the Universe —unknowable, unimaginable, unthinkable, and yet in some sort the inevitable, though unattainable, goal of our speculative thought—it is this final term in our infinite " series," transcending all other terms, and yet summing them up in itself, which we must regard as Divine.

What do we know of this final term ? Nothing, except that it draws our thoughts towards itself with a magnetic force which is all its own. Nothing, except that the path of synthesis, the path of spiritual development, leads us in its direction. The positive pole of existence, pure spirit, the supreme synthesis, the All of Being concentrated in its own quintessential life,—is not this what we mean by God ?

It is in his attempt to account for the existence of the world in which he finds himself that man has evolved the idea of God. He feels that the world, as it reveals itself to him, is not the *causa sui ;* that it owes its existence to some transcendent reality in which it lives and moves and has its being, some paramount power, the withdrawal of which from Nature would cancel the whole phenomenal Universe, yet without subtracting one atom from the sum-total of reality:

> Though earth and sea were gone,
> And suns and universes ceased to be,
> And thou wert left alone,
> Every existence would exist in thee.

Man's premature identification of "Nature" with his own material environment has led him to think of this creative power as above Nature, and to speak of it as supernatural. But as, with the gradual enlargement of his conception of Nature, the Supernatural tends to fade away into non-existence, it becomes necessary for him to reconstruct his idea of creation. The attempt to solve the problem of the world's origin is the final outcome of his instinctive search for cause. We have seen that the popular mind, looking out upon the world which surrounds it, refers all things to the action of a supreme and all-powerful will; and that the scientific mind, surveying the same scene from a different standpoint, refers each thing in turn to the action of Nature, regarded as an all-inclusive whole, operating through a hierarchy of laws. For the solution of the largest of all problems the co-operation of these two conceptions of cause is needed. The creative will must be identified with what is central in the course of Nature; with what is supreme in her hierarchy of laws. Nature must be thought of as the *causa sui*, as the eternal source of her own being, as the author and disposer of her own energies, as the lord and giver of her own life. But we must, I repeat, understand by Nature what is real in Nature, the positive pole of her existence, the final synthesis of her elements, the ideal goal of her movement.

Looking at things from this point of view, we see a new meaning in the problem that confronts us. We see that creation is no definite act in an infinitely distant past, but the eternal correlation of the positive with the negative pole of existence, of pure spirit with pure matter, of pure form with pure potentiality, of Everything with Nothing. In and through this act of correlation—which must needs be, for the positive pole has the negative as its necessary counterpart—the circle of being is eternally begun and eternally completed, and the riddle of existence finds its practical solution, the only solution of which it admits. The vulgar idea of creation as the calling of the Universe into existence out of nothing, is incurably dualistic, and, like every other dualistic hypothesis, tends to reduce both terms in its final formula to zero, or something akin to zero, a phantasmal deity being confronted by a phenomenal world. For this idea we must substitute that of an eternal outflow of being from an aboriginal source—aboriginal, and yet eternal—which we call God. God pours himself away, sends himself as it were into exile; and this emanating energy is ever seeking to return to its home. This twofold movement of flowing forth and returning home constitutes the life of the Universe and—from our point of view—the being of God.

It is worthy of note that the descent of God into matter is the central idea of Christianity, and that the idea was generated by the effort of the human mind to make good the failure of its own earlier thoughts. The creation of the world from without, by the fiat of a supreme will, turned out badly; for the finished product of an all-powerful and all-righteous Creator, which might have been expected to be perfect, proved to be full of imperfection. The story of Creation had therefore to be supplemented by the story of the Fall. And the story of the Fall had to be supplemented by the idea of the Incarnation. For, if the divine failure was to be retrieved, it was needful that God should stoop to the level of fallen Nature and draw her back to himself. Owing to the geocentric character of ancient thought, the redemption of Nature meant no more than the redemption of Humanity; and this was achieved by the birth and death of Christ. The geocentric standpoint is no longer tenable. Creation and redemption are correlative aspects of the same process. The idea of the Incarnation must either widen its scope or become discredited. It is not by descending into the womb of a woman, it is not by becoming flesh, that God redeems a ruined world. It is by descending into Nothing, by charging Nothing, so to speak, with the potentiality of his own perfection, that God creates, sustains, and redeems—or draws back to himself—not a ruined world, but an undeveloped and therefore self-realizing Universe.

If this elusive idea is to be presented to thought it must clothe itself in figurative language. The circulation of water in the physical world has always seemed to me symbolical of the circulation of being in the Cosmos. As the mists that rise from the sea return to the sea in the influx of a multitude of sea-like rivers, so do the forces that emanate from the spirit of God stream back to their source as a multitude of God-like souls. But this simile, though illuminative, and effective up to a certain point, is obviously inadequate ; for in the cosmic drama, which is presumably self-contained and all-inclusive, there is nothing analogous to the part which is played in the physical drama by external influences such as the heat of the sun or the varying temperature of the air.

Can any other simile give us light in our darkness ? One of the difficulties that confront us is that matter seems to have a maximum of *density* which is entirely different from its maximum of *purity ;* and that, therefore, there seem to be two negative poles of existence—one which is diametrically opposite to pure spirit, separated from it by the whole *diameter* of the circle of being, and another—the pure matter, or pure energy, towards which analysis leads us—which is either (according to the direction in which we look) all but identical with pure spirit, or separated from it by the whole *circle* of being. If from one point of view what is ultimate in analysis is antithetical to what is ultimate in synthesis—pure energy to pure spirit—from another point of view the real negation of the latter is that gross, dense, inert state of matter from which we start in our physical researches, and which seems to us to be wholly soulless and even lifeless. How has the latter state been reached and in what relation does it stand to the two extremes that seem to meet ?

At the root of all religion lies the idea that self-sacrifice, leading first to self-loss and then to self-realization, is the supreme law of man's higher life. In feeling its way to this idea, religion has divined one of Nature's deepest secrets and discovered one of her paramount laws. For not only is it true that beyond a certain stage in man's development self-sacrifice is the form which growth necessarily takes, but it may even be said that something akin to self-sacrifice—the giving up of the actual in favour of the ideal—is at the heart of all growth. The highest motive to self-sacrifice, and the only genuine motive, is love—love of a person, love of a community, love of a cause, love of an ideal, love of Nature, love of Man, love of God. The instrument of self-sacrifice is will. The energy of love sets in motion and sustains the energy of will. As religion purifies itself and widens its outlook, the idea of self-sacrifice ascends from man, the worshipper, towards God, the object of his worship, that it may re-descend—with a larger scope and a purer purpose—into the life of man. If man has indeed been made in the image of God, and if the capacity for self-sacrifice is the highest attribute of man, then self-sacrifice—the going out of self in order to find new life—must be of the essence of God. This idea is, I need hardly say, central in Christianity—central both in the teaching and in the life of Christ. His sublime saying, " Whosoever shall seek to save his life shall lose it : but whosoever shall lose his life shall preserve it," dominates all his other maxims. And his own sublime self-sacrifice is his true title-deed to Divinity.

Let us, then, think of God as performing an eternal act of self-sacrifice, as going out of himself in order to find new life, not a new life which is higher than his own, for God is himself ideal perfection, but a life which, beginning as unconscious energy, will at last be raised to the level of his own ; let us think of him as sending forth from himself this emanating energy—radiant and ethereal, but seemingly lifeless—by the propulsive force of his will, and then drawing it back to himself, out of the depths of unconsciousness and seeming nothingness, by the attractive force of his love. Let us now go back to our geometrical simile. Let us again think of the process which we call the Universe as an infinite circle. And on that circle let us take three contiguous points, A (pure spirit—the divine source of being), B (the emanating energy which we have hitherto spoken of as pure matter) and C (the emanating influence of love), B and C being on either side of A ; and let D be the opposite end of the diameter which starts from A. If B, which (with C) is of all points nearest to A, stands for matter at its maximum of purity, D, which is of all points furthest from A, will stand for matter at its maximum of density. The movement from A to B takes place in a timeless moment; but if it is to be continued in its own direction it will have to pass through D—the point at which the divine efflux, once pure and ethereal, will have become most densely material—and then complete the entire circuit before the return to A can be effected. But why should the movement from A to B be continued along the circumference of the circle? Why should it not be tangential rather than peripheral? Partly, no doubt, because the circle, being presumably infinite, has no tangents; but also—the second reason governing and explaining the first—because from the very beginning the movement which is initiated by the propulsive force of will comes under the other aspect of God's being, the attractive force of the divine love, and is thus bent back, as it were, continuously from the tangential course which it might otherwise take. Or we may say, if we please, that as every straight line is the arc of an infinite circle, the movements of the respective energies of will and love, though exactly opposite to one another, must both be circular and both end at last in their eternal source. Or perhaps, more simply, that because efflux and reflux, sending forth and drawing back, are of the essence of the divine life, therefore the cosmic process is an infinite circle, and therefore every straight line, even in space, is the arc of such a circle.

If my thoughts lead me to such paradoxical conclusions as that the divine circle has no geometrical centre but is itself an ever-moving centre, and that the diameter of the circle, instead of being a straight line passing through the geometrical centre, is half the circle, I cannot help myself. My excuse for indulging in these fanciful speculations[1] is

[1] We may, if we please, indulge in speculations which are even more fantastic than this. We may try to construct the cosmic drama with some approach to detail. We may think of the divine effluence as coming forth in a state of ethereal purity and electrical energy, but also of spellbound trance. We may think of it as returning to its eternal source,—not along the path which it has traversed, for the will which expelled it, and went forth with it and in it as *force*, cannot call it back,—but towards the other side of God's being, the side of love. We may think of it, while the first half of the circle is being traversed, as losing its ethereal purity, owing to its ever-increasing distance fron its spiritual source, and sinking, little by

that I am trying to present to my consciousness and, if possible, justify to my reason certain mental feelings of which I cannot rid myself, and which have, I feel sure, a real content. But I know only too well how futile are my similes ; I know well that if there is such a divine efflux and reflux as I have dared to imagine, both processes are eternal rather than temporal, logical (in the deeper sense of the word) rather than actual, the infinite round of existence being, as it were, the very pulse of the divine heart, which lives its life—its own serene, eternal, self-sufficing life—in and through this two-fold process of giving and receiving, of "creating" and "redeeming," or, again, which is *in* itself the eternal efflux of itself from itself and reflux of itself to itself. The attempt to survey from a temporal standpoint a movement which transcends time, the attempt of the part to think about the whole, is a failure in its very inception ; and the similes in which one tries to express the thoughts that such an attempt sets in motion are bound to break down the moment they feel the weight of serious criticism.

The *emotional* interpretation of my thoughts on these

little into the darkness of material density. But as, even from the beginning of things, it has come under the attractive influence of the divine love —the eternal source of life—we may also think of it as waking, little by little, to the light of conscious life. When the turning point of the circle has been reached, the emanating substance has attained to its maximum of density, while in and through its apparently lifeless medium, the soul, which slumbered most deeply—so deeply that it seemed to be non-existent —when its substance was most ethereal, will have waked to consciousness and made an appreciable measure of spiritual growth. From this point onward the development of conscious life is accompanied by the progressive refinement of the substance in which life embodies itself. For as the degree of "spirituality" in the emanating substance varies inversely with the distance of the substance from its eternal source, it is clear that once the turning point of the circle has been reached, matter will begin to regain its lost radiance and purity ; and it is also clear that the life, which had gone far along the path of spiritual development even while its vehicle was becoming more and more densely material, will advance along that path, now that its vehicle has begun to purify itself, with ever-increasing celerity. Words fail us, imagination mocks us when we try to picture to ourselves the glorious destiny of the expanding spirit, which, on the one hand, passes onward from plane to plane of outward being—each new plane being purer, more radiant, and more ethereal than the one which was left behind—and, on the other hand, in its own inward life, climbs higher and higher up the awful heights of thought and sinks deeper and deeper into the fathomless abysses of love. At last the distinction between inward and outward, which had long been tending to efface itself, becomes wholly obliterated, and the spirit, having grown to the fulness of its predestined stature, becomes one with God.

matters is no doubt nearer to truth than the *dialectical.* As an argument for the divine efflux and reflux, the feeling of "divine homesickness" of which I have spoken is worth many theories of the Universe. But there is another interpretation which is still nearer to truth. When the divine emanation, having completed its circle of development, enters in full consciousness into union with the Divine Lover, it returns to its source, not as one spirit, but as an infinity of souls. How or why this "individualization of the infinite" has been accomplished we do not, we cannot know; but that it is being accomplished, that each of us is at once individual and infinite, is a truth which has written itself in living, breathing, moving characters on the scroll of human life. The Divine Spirit, which is one and indivisible, is the true self of each of us; and yet each of us has his own life to live, his own nature to evolve, his own soul to expand. We may, if we please, try to find words for this mystery; we cannot even begin to explain it. The meaning of it is something which each of us must realize in his own existence, must live out—there is no other way to discover it—in and for himself. *I* find *myself* in the midst of the infinite movement of cosmic Nature. The stream of evolution is sweeping *me* onward towards the infinite sea. Therefore the *practical* interpretation of the thoughts and feelings that haunt me is the interpretation that really counts. If the movement of cosmic Nature is indeed a circular movement, from and towards the goal of spiritual perfection, what follows with regard to myself? Destiny, when individualized, reveals itself as duty. If the destiny of Nature is re-union with her divine source, what part am I, a child of Nature, to play in that mighty drama? My being comes under the master law of growth. In the light of the conception of Nature which I have been trying to express, do I not begin to discover—and is it not time for me to begin to realize—in myself, in my way of thinking, feeling, doing, living—*the purpose of growth?*

CHAPTER IV

THE POLES OF KNOWLEDGE

FROM Nature let us return to human nature. What we have found in Nature we may expect to find in human nature—unity of being, duality of direction, continuity of movement, infinity of range. The central fact in human nature is consciousness. The central phenomenon in human life is the dawn of consciousness. The movement which we call the dawn of consciousness is commensurate with the movement which we call development or growth. If these things are so, and if human nature, like Nature, comes under the law of polar opposition, we may safely conjecture that consciousness and unconsciousness are opposite poles of human life.

But this conception is too vague to be helpful. Let us try to limit it. If consciousness and unconsciousness are poles of human life, of what aspect of human life are they *the* poles, of what great " stream of tendency " are they the unknown beginning and the unknown end ? The answer to this question is not far to seek. In life, as we know it, there is an unceasing interplay between *knowledge* and *action*; and there is a point of view from which this interplay seems actually to constitute life. Consciousness (with its opposite) is predicable of both knowledge and action : but that it is primarily predicable of knowledge will, I think, be generally admitted. So intimate indeed is the relation between consciousness and knowledge, that we cannot define the former term except in terms of the latter. The dawn of consciousness, which is characteristic of the life of mankind, and which re-enacts itself in the life of each individual, is the dawn of a new kind of knowledge, a higher kind of knowledge, a kind which differentiates man from all other living things. It follows that only by thinking of consciousness and unconsciousness as the opposite poles of *knowledge*, and studying them as such, can we hope to determine what parts these " mighty opposites " play in the drama of man's life.

When I speak of consciousness and unconsciousness as poles of knowledge I am using language which may seem to savour of paradox. One's first impulse is to assume that knowledge which lies below the threshold of consciousness is not knowledge, and that the phrase " unconscious knowledge " is therefore a contradiction in terms. The only way to meet this criticism is to think, or try to think, the whole matter out. Such matters are best studied in the concrete ; and I will therefore begin with an example. In playing a game of billiards it is desired to produce a certain result. With this end in view, it is necessary that the ball should be hit on a certain spot, with a certain degree of force, with a certain inclination of the cue, and so forth. One of the players, though quite ignorant both of the science and the practice of the game, manages by a kind of instinct so to strike the ball as to produce the desired effect. This correct action on his part implies a certain measure of acquaintance with mechanical laws ; but the man's knowledge, such as it is, has not risen into consciousness ; it is wholly latent and implicit. He could not have told a bystander, even approximately, where or how he intended to hit the ball. Still less could he have told him at what point the ball was to hit the cushion, at what angle it was to leave it, or, in general, by what precise steps it was to reach its goal. So far was his knowledge below the threshold of consciousness, so largely was it confined to the physical side of his nature, that it was only in the instant of outward action that it was in any degree realized and displayed.

There might be another player, ignorant of the theory of the game, but so well acquainted with the practice of it as to have evolved for himself certain rules for playing it, which, though disconnected, unexplained, and seldom consciously referred to, yet enabled him to play with considerable success, and in evolving which he must have acquired, unknown to himself, an intuitive and unscientific knowledge of mechanical laws. In the case which I am considering such a player might be able to tell a bystander with some degree of accuracy where and how the ball was to be struck, and what course it was to take; but he would probably be unable to explain why all this was to be done. And so his knowledge, though of a higher order than that of the first player, would yet fall short by many degrees of the highest form of knowledge; for "*verum scire est per causas scire,*"—to know a thing fully is to throw the light of consciousness far out on all sides of it, to approach it through the laws which it exemplifies and the causes which combine to produce it. A third player might be able to give a scientific explanation of the proposed action. He might be able to bring the case in point under mechanical laws as studied in their bearing on the game, and through these to solve the problem which was involved in the position of the balls. In other words, he might be able to tell us why he did whatever he happened to do. Such a player might not be so skilful or successful as the second or even the first; but his knowledge would be of a higher order and would be more likely to serve for any new conjuncture.

Here, then, are three kinds, or rather degrees, of knowledge. They are degrees in a scale which ranges between the actual and the potential, between the light of consciousness and the darkness of the unconscious life. To know with clear consciousness, to separate one's knowledge from oneself and to present it to one's mind in the form of reasoned conclusions and precise statements, is to realize the ideal of science. From this ideal there is a gradual declension, till at last the distinction between subject and object becomes effaced, and the word knowledge ceases to apply.

Let us look at other examples. A man speaks correctly. That implies knowledge of the rules of grammar. Another man knows the rules and consciously applies them when any difficulty arises. That implies knowledge of the principles of language. A third knows the principles and consciously applies them when there is any doubt as to the rules. Here again we have three degrees of knowledge; and here again the degree of knowledge is measured by the degree of consciousness. Examples of what I may call sub-conscious knowledge, of knowledge which is potential rather than actual, instinctive rather than rational, latent and implicit rather than consciously realized, meet us at every turn. It has often been remarked that people reason correctly who know nothing about logic. They reach right conclusions, not always intuitively, but sometimes by moving along legitimate lines of proof, though they have never so much as heard of the syllogism or given a thought to the methods of induction. Again, it is a matter of everyday experience that children—to say nothing of adults—use words correctly which they could not possibly define or explain: they will even use an abstract noun so accurately as to show that they apprehend its precise shade of meaning; and yet, if asked to explain in terms, however vague and general, what the word meant, they would probably be at a loss for an answer. Those who do understand the meanings of words seldom have recourse to their knowledge when they speak or write. They trust themselves to the guidance of instinct, which works far more rapidly and delicately and often far more surely than reason. "The ear trieth words as the mouth tasteth meat." The poet who invents new and beautiful metres is not always able to account for their melody or even to analyze them into their component feet. The writer of well-balanced sentences cannot always explain on what principle he constructed them or wherein lies the secret of their charm. What abstruse mathematical calculations are made by one who takes aim with a bow! They are made by his eyes and fingers rather than by his head. Similar calculations are made, only more mechanically and also more consciously, by the artillerymen who points a gun.

But I need not multiply instances. I scarcely exaggerate when I say that we unconsciously apprehend the laws of motion and the mechanical properties of matter in every movement of our bodies, the laws of language in every word that we utter, the laws of thought in every inference that we draw, the principles of morality in every whisper of conscience, the facts of the spiritual world in every stir of spiritual emotion.

Recognition of the reality of unconscious (or sub-conscious) knowledge is fatal to that cheap and shallow dualism which assumes that all existent things are either knowable or unknowable, and that there is no intermediate state between knowledge and no knowledge.[1] Nor need we, when we distinguish conscious from unconscious knowledge, fall into the toils of a new dualism. One who believes, as I do, in the unity and continuity of Nature, will expect to find that the outgrowth of knowledge, both in the race and the individual, is on the whole a continuous process, and will protest on *a priori* grounds against the doctrine that from no-knowledge to knowledge—from the darkness of midnight to the light of noonday—there is but a single step. And this expectation and this protest will be confirmed by experience. For, whether we look at the life of the individual or the history of the human race, or survey with the aid of science the ordered gradation of the vegetable and animal worlds, we shall find that the transition from unconsciousness to consciousness is effected not by sudden movements but " by degrees scarce to be perceived." With the dawn of consciousness on the world of life, there is a gradual and indeterminable advance from mere being, through feeling, in the direction of knowing. It follows that knowledge is not, as is commonly supposed, the definable name of a definite mental state. On the contrary, the word

[1] Huxley (the late Professor) says that " the admission of a state of mind intermediate between knowledge and no knowledge is fatal to all clearness of thought." Perhaps it is; but what a circular bit of reasoning this is! Huxley seems to take for granted that we must either think clearly about great matters or not think at all. But that is precisely what is in dispute. If there is no intermediate state between thinking clearly and not thinking at all, then it is certain that there can be no intermediate state between knowledge and no knowledge. To tell those who contend that there are intermediate states between knowledge and no knowledge, that their contention is fatal to all clearness of thought, is (by implication) to ask them to concede what they are busily engaged in denying. For when they say that it is possible to know sub-consciously, they of course imply that it is possible to think darkly and dimly, obscurity of thought being as obviously the counterpart of sub-conscious apprehension as clearness of thought is of conscious knowledge. It is better, as Huxley's opponents contend, to think truly than to think clearly; and as there are matters in which (to quote Joubert's words) " toute précision est erreur," it seems to follow that what is " fatal to clearness of thought " is not necessarily antagonistic to truth. In any case, one who lays great stress on clearness of thought ought to avoid the logical fallacy involved in proving an assumption by means of itself.

can be used in many ways and with many shades of meaning; and of the thing there are many kinds and innumerable degrees. These are degrees in a line which has no clearly marked limit at either end. All we can say of it is that it looks backward towards feeling and instinct and dim unconscious apprehension, and forward towards reason and understanding and that clear, conscious, far-seeing grasp of a subject which is the ideal type of knowledge, and to attain to which in every sphere of its labour is the dream of the human mind.

To this general conclusion there are some important corollaries. The *First* is that *unconscious apprehension is prior in time to conscious knowledge and is at any given moment working in advance of it.* That man acts, feels, and sees before he thinks; that instinct is in the field before reason; that genius works ahead of intelligence; that knowledge must exist before one can become aware of its presence; that perception must prepare the way for inference; that the yarn of experience must be spun before it can be woven,—all these are truths too obvious to need demonstration. Science is pre-eminently the product of consciousness; and every science and every quasi-science had a practical beginning, having gradually shaped itself out of a tentative and experimental handling of its subject-matter, in which its principles were unconsciously apprehended and applied. Thus thought is of older standing than logic; art than aesthetics; literature than literary criticism; morality than ethics; social life than social science. The germs of physical science are to be found in that instinctive knowledge of the laws and properties of external nature which enables the more backward races of mankind (destitute as these are of science) and even the animals and plants, to adapt themselves with much apparent skill and with more or less success to their material environment. Speaking generally, it may be said that the theoretical side of every art, handicraft, sport, and game has been gradually evolved by practice. Men spoke grammar long before they laid down its rules, and wrote verses long before they discovered the laws of prosody. Campaigns were conducted before strategy became a science; and seas were crossed before navigation was taught in schools. The methods of induction were practised by the pioneers of science before Mill formulated its laws. There were reasoners before Aristotle, successful despots before Machiavelli, utilitarians before Bentham, economists before Adam Smith.

As it is in the life of the race, so it is in the life of the individual. We are all learners from the cradle to the grave; and it is in the process of learning, that the superiority of instinct to consciousness, as a pioneer and guide, is most clearly manifest. The child learns the use of his limbs by using them, not by studying anatomy or mechanics. His conscience is developed by intercourse with his equals and superiors, not by the inculcation of moral maxims and principles. He learns to speak his mother tongue by hearing it spoken, and masters it much more speedily and thoroughly than the adult, with his grammars and dictionaries, can master German or French. When one is acquiring a new accomplishment, one begins to act correctly long before one is acquainted wirh a single rule or principle. When one is learning a new science (though here the experience of the race is available for the instruction and guidance of the individual) how little is gained, or rather how much is lost, by beginning with formal propositions, with definitions, rules, and the like! If one wishes to lay a lasting foundation, one must begin with what is concrete. Let the law or principle be first apprehended unconsciously, in and through an instance or series of instances. Then its meaning will be realized. Till then it may be learnt by heart when set forth in a formula, it may be accepted as true, it may even be understood in the moment of demonstration, but it will not be assimilated.

I need not say more in support of this thesis. I am insisting on what is probably self-evident. The common language, and, in spite of many exceptions, especially in the sphere of education, the common practice of mankind confirm what I say. Experience teaches. Practice makes perfect. Example is better than precept. Such maxims as these are on my side. Men habitually act on the assumption that instinct and intuition work in advance of consciousness.

If a boy wants to learn a handicraft, he does not read books about it, he is apprenticed to a master craftsman. If he wants to learn golf, he gets a professional golfer to take him round the links. If he wants to learn medicine or law, he walks a hospital or enters a lawyer's office. If he wants to learn French, or at any rate to master French, he goes to France. All this implies a latent conviction that the unconscious side is, as it were, more deeply seated, more intimately one's own, more near to the realities of Nature, than is the conscious side of one's being.

This leads me to my *Second Corollary*, which is an obvious extension of the first. *As the unconscious side of a man is ever working ahead of his consciousness, it is also ever dealing with higher realities and ever nearer to the truth of things.* I am expressing the same idea in other words when I say that conscious apprehension of a truth implies unconscious apprehension of a higher and wider truth. Thus consciously to discern the solution of a practical problem, is unconsciously to grasp the appropriate theory. Consciously to pass an isolated judgment, is unconsciously to apprehend and apply a principle. Consciously to purpose a noble action, is unconsciously to grasp and cleave to a spiritual idea. But the theory is higher and wider than the problem. The principle is higher and wider than the judgment. The idea is higher and wider than the impulse to action.

The *Third Corollary*, though scarcely more than a re-statement of the second, has a significance which is all its own. To say that the unconscious self is at any given moment dealing with higher realities than those which present themselves to consciousness is to imply that *the true life of man is buried; that the true self is a hidden self; that the higher side of man's being, the side which is in touch with Nature's inner mysteries, lives and works for the most part in the darkness of the unconscious life.* That we may the better realize the significance of this conception, let us consider the phenomenon of *genius*, and examine the attempt that has sometimes been made to interpret it in terms of divine *inspiration*.

We are all familiar with the phenomenon of genius. We call a man a genius when he does work which, besides being excellent of its kind, is of a high order and on a large scale. This is the first thing that strikes us about him ; but, as we shall presently see, the differential property of genius lies deeper than this. Now in bygone times the power of doing or saying wonderful things was regarded as the gift of God. Some one man stood forth among his fellows and spoke words of luminous wisdom or dazzling beauty or burning truth. Those who heard him were penetrated by his influence ; and feeling that his work was far above the ordinary level of human achievement, and being at a loss to account for such pre-eminence, they said he was inspired, breathed into by the Spirit of God. This idea expressed itself in various forms. The *Lawgiver*, the man of super-human wisdom, was either a semi-divine person or one who had direct and special intercourse with Deity. The *Poet*, the embodiment of soaring genius, was regarded as the mouthpiece of Phoebus, as the child of the Muses, as the *vates sacer*. Men spoke of his phrenzy and his divine madness, the "madness which is the special gift of Heaven and the source of the chiefest blessing among men." The *Prophet* prefaced his rebukes and warnings with "Thus saith the Lord" ; and his claim to hold a commission direct from the Eternal was as freely allowed as it was boldly advanced. Something of this faith in inspiration lingers yet. We believe that the writers of the Bible were mouthpieces of the Spirit of God. We believe, in other words, that on the highest and most sacred of all themes those who thought and felt most truly drew their knowledge and power from a supernatural source. And though in theory we reserve the epithet "inspired" for our sacred Scriptures, we find it easy to apply the term to pre-eminent achievements in other fields, especially in those of art and song. This shows that it is natural for man to regard the highest developments of genius as gifts of Heaven rather than as products of earth.

What is there in genius that constrains us to take this view of it ? Socrates—the Socrates of Plato—has answered this question. His search for a man wiser than himself led him at last to the poets, who, he felt sure, would be able to convict him of ignorance. "Accordingly," he tells us, "I took them some of the most elaborate passages in their own writings and asked what was the meaning of them,—thinking that they would teach me something. Will you believe me? I am almost ashamed to confess the truth, but I must say there is hardly a person present who would not have talked better about their poetry than they did themselves. Then I knew, without going further, that not by wisdom do poets write poetry, but by a sort of genius and inspiration. They are like divines or soothsayers who also say many fine things but do not understand the meaning of them." In the *Meno* Socrates speaks of divines and prophets "including the whole tribe of poets" as being "inspired and possessed of God, in which condition they say many grand things, not knowing what they say." This divine possession, or "madness," as he elsewhere calls it, is essential to the true poet. In poetry "the sane man is nowhere at all when he enters into rivalry with the madman." And the proof of this divine madness is that those who are possessed by it "say many grand things, not knowing what they say."

The properties of genius that are dwelt on in these passages—its *blindness* and its *inevitableness*—are the properties that have engendered the current belief in inspiration. When all the natural agencies that mediate between visible effects and ultimate causes appear to be wanting, the mind falls back in its perplexity on the supreme cause of all things, on the operation of God himself. Hence it is, to take an obvious example, that we pray for sunshine and rain. The laws of meteorology are so little understood, and our knowledge of them, such as it is, is confined to so small a circle of *savants*, that ordinary men can see no middle term between the atmospheric phenomena of which they have direct evidence and the ruling or overruling Power in whom they believe. In the same way, when we see that wonderful results are produced by human agency and that those who produce them can give no explanation of their aims and methods, it is but natural that popular thought, which confounds personality with consciousness and therefore draws a sharp distinction between the man of genius himself and the power that seems to constrain him, should identify the latter with the spirit of the supernatural God. Thus the belief in inspiration is found, when analyzed, to rest on the assumption that genius is the product of irresistible forces working below the level of human consciousness.

That this assumption is correct can scarcely be doubted. We know from experience that the man of genius can give no account of what is most eminent and distinctive in his work. He is no critic, in the ordinary sense of the word. The critical faculty, which is predominatingly analytical, rarely co-exists with the creative, and very rarely with the highest developments of the latter. Were the man of genius to reflect on what he did and to ask himself how and why he did it, he would become uncertain of himself when he had most need of assurance. His hand would falter and hesitate and would end by losing its cunning. Poets would often be startled if they could learn what depths of meaning, what niceties of artistic skill had been discovered in their verses. "They said wonderful things, not knowing what they said." Diderot found in some work of David the painter certain excellences of design and effect which the latter, as he confessed, had never intended. "*Quoi,*" cried Diderot, "*c'est à votre insu ; c'est d'instinct que vous avez procédé ainsi . . . c'est encore mieux.*" When Haydn was asked the reason for a harmony he could but answer, "I have done it because it does well": nor could he confute the impertinent critic who found fault with a beautiful passage in one of his works because it violated conventional rules. Ruskin says that great discoveries, such as those of the Thirteenth Century artists in floral ornaments, are "never made philosophically, but instinctively," that is "by the penetrative imagination, acting under the influence of strong affection." The same authority tells us that the Chinese and Hindoos can colour better than we do because "their glorious ignorance of all rules" enables "their pure and true instincts to have play and do their work,—instincts so subtle that the least warping or compression breaks or blunts them."

These examples illustrate a law which is never really violated. Let us take the case of a poet in his season of inspiration. However deeply he may have studied the poetic art, however thorough may be his knowledge of its rules (so far as it has rules), however clear his insight into its principles, however diligently he may apply his mind to the task that he has set himself, the fact remains that the greater part of his work, and all that is best in it, will have to be done by the unconscious side of him—by an originating power whose methods transcend all formulated rules—by a fountain of creative energy directing itself again and again at an object which is known to it rather than to him, and which it attains to perhaps only after repeated failures—by the delicate sympathy of his artistic temperament—by the subtle criticism of his trained and gifted ear. Whatever theories we may hold about genius, we take for granted that it is not self-conscious. Thus we do not ask Shakespeare to give us a coherent philosophy of life. We read his poems. We rightly assume that his philosophy, profound though it be, is no theory; that it is part of his inner nature, and as such is diffused through those creations of his genius in which his inner nature finds its truest expression. We do not ask Phidias to lecture on the laws of plastic art or the deeper laws of form-poetry. We study his sculpture. "Every man of genius," says Lessing, "is a born critic. He has in himself the test of all rules." These words may seem to contradict my statement that the critical faculty seldom co-exists with the creative; but in truth they bear it out. The man of genius is the greatest of all critics in that he is in full possession of the rules of his art—the real, not the conventional rules—rules which criticism, properly so called, can at best but partially discern and imperfectly apply. But both his discernment and his application of them, though full and effective, are for the most part instinctive and blind. He seldom consciously criticizes, and never when he is genuinely inspired. There is no need for him to do so. "He has in himself"—in the "abysmal deeps" of his personality—"the test of all rules." He does not *know* the truth by which his works are permeated. But he does more than know it. He is in permanent contact with it. It is a part of himself. Indeed it is the glory of genius that in this respect it lowers the greatest of men to the level of the least of living creatures. "From a bee," says Ruskin, "to Paul Veronese all master-builders work with this awful, this inspired unconsciousness."

But though unconsciousness is essential to genius, it is by

no means peculiar to it. The least of us is at every moment doing things blindly and unconsciously. The very animals show a knowledge of Nature in all that they do; and yet their whole life seems to be below the level of consciousness (as the word is ordinarily understood). It is not unconsciousness as such, any more than it is success as such, that constitutes the differentia of genius. It is the combination of the two. The man of genius differs from us lesser men in that (in his blindness) he does great and wonderful things while we do small and ordinary things. He differs from us in this, but in no other way. What we do, under the guidance of instinct, does not arrest our attention or constrain us to dwell upon it. His work, on the other hand, forces itself upon our minds. We cannot help gazing at it and wondering what it means and whence it comes. But the riddle is insoluble, and so in our perplexity we have recourse to the direct agency of God. In that we rest, for beyond that there is nothing.

Now we have recourse to the same agency in the case of the lower animals. We say that their instincts are divinely implanted; that the bee is an inspired master-builder; that God teaches the beaver to dam rivers and the bird to build its nest. I have no fault to find with this language; but I wish to fathom its meaning. Instinct, which, according to the current hypothesis, belongs to animals and men of genius, belongs also to ordinary human life, the greater part of which is lived under its direct control. That being so, the theory which attributes the actions of great men and dumb creatures to the inspiration of God, but that of ordinary men to some other source, is plainly untenable; and we must substitute for it the assumption that all instinct comes from God. Furthermore, if we are to reduce genius (in respect of its origin) to the level of animal instinct, we must be prepared to reduce it still lower. If we may not draw a hard and fast line above the bee, there is no reason why we should draw one below it. We say that the honeycomb is made under the direction of God. Shall we not say the same of the rose or of the crystal? Shall we not say that the forces which fashioned these works of art were and are directed by the same power? We do say this, and we say well. But mark what follows. The rose and the crystal are the products of natural forces acting in obedience to natural laws. There is nothing miraculous or supernatural about them. Where, then, does the supernatural element come in ? Not when we pass the boundary line between plant and animal life ; for that boundary line is unstable and undefinable. Not when we pass from brutes to men ; for the hypothesis which we are examining places brutes in the same category with the greatest men. Not when we pass from talent to genius ; for the hypothesis which brings bees into line with creative artists brings ordinary men into line with both. It follows that if we are to regard the movements of inanimate forces and the growth of plants as directed by the God of Nature, we must attribute to the same source the inspiration of the artist and the instinct of the bee. In any case, if we admit that instinct of every kind and grade is divinely inspired, we commit ourselves to the assumption that the God who inspires it is the God of Nature ; for "what is universal is natural," and what is natural and normal cannot also be supernatural and exceptional.

Thus a natural explanation of the phenomenon of genius seems to be forced upon us ; and the form that it takes is the conception of the "buried life," the conception of Nature working below the level of consciousness, yet surely and irresistibly, in the soul of man. It is Nature that is at work, blindly as it seems to us, but inevitably, in the chemical forces of the earth when they form the crystal, in the plant when it puts forth its flower, in the bee when it shapes its cell, in the bird when it builds its nest, in the beaver when it makes its dam. It is the same Power that is at work, scarcely less blindly and scarcely less inevitably, in the artist when he composes and in the poet when he sings. When Nature is at her highest level, is in her sublimest mood, is doing her best and truest work, then her instrument, whoever he may be, is the man of genius. But Nature retains her identity even when she climbs to these unwonted heights. I grant that in passing from the rose or the crystal to the poem or the picture, or again from what is automatic in human action to what is held to be inspired, we are passing from pole to pole of Nature's being. But the movement from pole to pole is continuous: there is no abrupt transition, no catastrophic upheaval, no change of kind.

Now if excellence of result and unconsciousness of method are in equal degrees essential to the work of genius, may we not conjecture that our highest and best work is of necessity unconsciously done? We all admit that the man of genius is, in his inspired moments, nearer to truth than the rest of us. And we all admit that he can give no account of what he says or does. May not these two facts be causally committed? Is it not because he deals with the highest truths and is in direct contact with the sublimest realities, that he fails to understand what he does or what his words mean? Is it not because his ways are so mysterious and his works so wonderful, that he can give no account, even to himself, of either? The objects of his intuition are at once too large to be comprehended, too vague to be defined, too far from his daily life to be reasoned about, too near to his heart to be clearly discerned. But with the search-light of spiritual emotion he penetrates the inner mysteries of Nature, and under the subtle guidance of imaginative sympathy feels his way through a tangled labyrinth of causes and motives, to which conscious thought can never find the clue. Thus it is scarcely a paradox to say that genius works well because it works unconsciously, and works unconsciously because it works well. If this be so, does it not follow that what is best and truest in human nature—its highest intuitions, its largest tendencies, its strongest forces, all that is prophetic in it, all that is clairvoyant (in the spiritual sense of the word)—belongs not to the conscious, but to the buried life?

In comparing instinct with consciousness, we must of course distinguish between the individual and the collective life. It often happens that a man makes profession of high moral principles, and yet, following his own lower instincts, leads an immoral life. In such a case it looks, at first sight, as if theory were in advance of instinct, not instinct of theory. But this is not so. The man's moral (or immoral) instincts are his own, whereas the principles which he professes embody the experience of the race, and are in no sense the products of his own consciousness. In the world at large instinct is in the field before consciousness and works in advance of it; but in the case of the individual, who profits by the experience of the race, this order is often reversed.

But if the comparison between instinct and consciousness is to be made under perfectly favourable conditions, if all disturbing influences are to be excluded, we must broaden the basis of man's life and look at things from a point of view which is at once cosmic and human. When we survey the scientific achievements of mankind and compare them *inter se* in respect of accuracy and certainty, we find (to make a general statement) that it is the outward and visible side of Nature, not the inward and spiritual side, which admits of being consciously known. This fact can easily be accounted for. The students of evolution tell us that Nature worked her own work, followed her own tendencies, obeyed her own laws, fulfilled her own ends, long before she became conscious of what she was doing or made even her earliest effort to interpret the laws and principles of her being. Æons seem to have passed before she outgrew this blind, instinctive life and woke to self-knowledge in the soul of man. The ground which was thus lost to consciousness in "the beginning of things" has never been regained. The rays of light which are shed from the lamp of consciousness fall backward rather than forward. Having entered the soul of man, Nature continues to advance along the path of self-development, leading a spirit-life which, like the life of her earliest days, is for the most part unconscious and instinctive. That this higher life will come under the ken of a higher consciousness, that such a consciousness is being gradually evolved, and that the higher life is being gradually brought under the sway of its light, is what, arguing from analogy, we may well believe. But meanwhile the light of consciousness does not fall, or falls but dimly, on the mighty movement which is going on in the inner life of man; and when it does begin to illuminate that movement, we may guess that new developments of spirit-life are taking place beyond its range. The growth of Nature is marked and measured by the outgrowth of consciousness;

but the outgrowth of consciousness is accompanied, step for step, by the evolution of the buried life, and from first to last the latter leads the way. These considerations seem to point to one significant conclusion. If evolution is, as we must needs believe, an upward movement, the inference is irresistible that the unknown and hidden side of Nature is, in every phrase of her development, her later, her higher, and her more real self. From first to last, what she is is a profounder truth and a more vivid reality than what she knows or believes herself to be.

To my general conception of the range and movement of knowledge there is a *Fourth Corollary* which I will now try to formulate. I have not forgotten, though I may seem to have done so, that consciousness is the very quality which differentiates man from all other living things, and that the dawn of its mysterious light has been commensurate and even coincident with the evolution of the human race. I have said that the unconscious side of man's being is at *any given moment* working ahead of his consciousness and is *at any given moment* conversant with higher realities. The words which I have emphasized are all important. It is possible to regard instinct and intuition as the pioneers in man's onward movement, and yet to hold that conscious knowledge of a truth is a better thing than unconscious knowledge of *the same truth*,—better, because a truth which is consciously realized becomes, or may become, the possession of all men; better, because in the light of consciousness the various implications of the truth and its practical bearings begin to be clearly discerned; better, because in consciously realizing a truth we begin to discover its relations to other truths and so to find a place for it in a system of truth, through which its influence will be indefinitely extended; better, above all, because (as we shall now see) when unconscious has been transmuted into conscious knowledge, a fresh current of unconscious knowledge sets in from those remoter recesses of the buried life which are nearer to reality, to take the place of that which has been consciously realized.

In one respect my language has, I admit, been more or

less misleading. I have hitherto spoken about consciousness as if its sole function were to garner the fruits of the buried life, or (like the administrative officials who follow in the wake of a conquering army) to organize the provinces which instinct and intuition have won from the seeming nothingness of chaos. The time has come for me to remind myself that consciousness has a far deeper meaning than this and a far higher function. We have seen that conscious apprehension of a truth implies unconscious apprehension of a higher and wider truth. But it does more than *imply* unconscious apprehension of a higher and wider truth : it prepares the way for it : it makes it possible. The very fact that a man has become aware of the knowledge that he possesses is a stimulus to further effort on the part of his unconscious self. For it is a tendency of human nature—a master tendency which operates on every plane of man's being—to be dissatisfied with what has been won and to press on towards the unattained. And so the man who consciously apprehends a fact is already, though he may not know it, discontented with the fact as such. He has already begun to ask himself, in some secret recess of his mind : What does the fact mean ? What is its place and purpose in Nature ? What causes have produced it ? What tendencies does it exemplify ? His mind is already beginning, blindly and gropingly, to feel its way towards the law or wider fact in which the isolated phenomenon is grounded and through which it is explained. So, too, when a man becomes aware of an emotional idea which has long ruled his heart, in the very act of bringing it under the control of his consciousness he causes it to draw in from far and near its hidden reserves and supports (that through these it may justify itself to his reason)—to draw these into a region of his subconscious life in which it is possible for them to shape themselves by slow degrees and by a spontaneous process of which he has no cognizance, into new emotional ideas, ready, when their turn comes, to be transmuted by consciousness into new thought. These examples suggest to us that *consciousness, by stimulating the unconscious self into ever fresh activity, plays a leading part in the evolution of the inner life.* They suggest this, and more than this. They suggest that consciousness plays *the* leading part in that great drama. They even suggest that there is a point of view from which consciousness seems to be the only force which can awake the unconscious self from its spell-bound slumber.

When first I spoke about consciousness, I said that it was the supreme transforming influence in man's life. We now begin to guess the secret of its magic power. When water is pumped up from a deep well, fresh supplies of water come in from the underground reservoirs that feed the well, to take the place of what has been drawn to the surface; and so the buried waters, instead of being allowed to stagnate, are kept in constant motion, and their reserves are unceasingly drawn upon. Something analogous to this happens in the buried life of man when its reserves begin to be consciously realized. To believe in the unity of Nature is to believe in the unity of life. Physical energy, physical life, soul life, divine life, all are different, yet all are one,—one infinite reservoir of vital energy. This reservoir of life is at the service of every living thing; but below the human level the organism, controlled as it is by blind instinct and tyrannous habit, is a well from which there is no overflow, and which therefore cannot draw upon and set in motion the hidden source of life. With man it is different. Whether we think of consciousness as causing the overflow, or as being the overflow, matters little. What does matter is that there is a ceaseless overflow from the well of human life. When consciousness awakes, the conscious self becomes aware of things, and, in becoming aware of them, seeks to understand them; for the desire to understand—the desire to relate this thing or that thing to other things and in the last resort to all other things, the desire for more and more light and for more and more experience—is latent in every feeling of awareness. In its effort to understand things, the conscious self draws more things and still more things—inward things as well as outward things—within the ever widening sphere of its awareness; and so, while continually expanding its environment, it sets in ceaseless motion the hidden waters of life.

In his book on *Evolution and The War*, Dr. Chalmers Mitchell writes as follows: "We may agree with Professor

Bergson that unconscious instinct is closer to the heart of life [than conscious action], and that it is the highest espression of the vital force, or we may believe that the replacement of instinct by conscious, responsible, intelligent, experimental action is the fine flower of evolution, but at least we must accept the distinction as fundamental and as obliterating any possibility of useful comparison." In this sentence something of a fallacy lurks, as it seems to me, in the word "or." "Unconscious instinct" may be "closer to the heart of life," and yet the "replacement" of it "by conscious, responsible, intelligent, experimental action" may be "the fine flower of evolution." The controversy between instinct and consciousness is as unreal as the controversy between heredity and environment. The rear-guard of an army has as worthy a part to play as the advance guard. It is the well-being of the army as a whole that matters, not the dignity of this or that part of it. If unconscious knowledge is superior in respect of the reality of its object—if intuition, for example, is in touch with higher realities than reason,—conscious knowledge (which is the basis of "conscious action") is superior in respect of what are commonly regarded as the characteristic attributes of knowledge—certainty, accuracy, clarity, intelligence. To lift unconscious knowledge into the light of consciousness —to awaken consciousness in the depths of the buried life —should therefore be the central purpose of our days.

Let me say in conclusion that if consciousness does nothing more than arouse the unconscious self from its slumber and set its latent activities in motion, it does everything; for it is in and through the buried life that man, if he could only know it, holds intercourse with God. When instinct is transformed into reason, the brute becomes the man. When instinct is transformed into spiritual intuition, the man becomes more than man. It is a great thing to guess the secrets of Nature; but it is a greater thing to commune with her soul.

CHAPTER V

THE POLES OF ACTION

WITH consciousness comes the sense of freedom; and with the sense of freedom comes the sense of responsibility. Antithetical to and correlative with the idea of freedom is that of necessity. As consciousness, in the life of man, seems to be slowly emerging from the depths of unconsciousness, so freedom seems to be slowly extricating itself from the enveloping network of necessity.

To think rationally about freedom is well-nigh impossible. For the function of reason is to discover the all-pervading, all-controlling order in Nature, which it begins (unknown to itself) by postulating; and freedom introduces into human life—the highest plane of Nature that is known to man—an element of apparent disorder, or at any rate of incalculableness, which threatens to stultify all the operations of reason, all its efforts to understand the world. The result is that reason can find no place for freedom in its provisional scheme of things, and is therefore subconsciously prejudiced against it even before it begins to examine its title deeds. Hence the inherent futility of the arguments against —and for—freedom. The history of philosophy tells us that the problem of freedom is at the centre of one of those whirlpools of controversy which are ever changing their scope and their position, but which continue to rotate with unabated energy and which seem as if they would never whirl themselves to rest. The question has been again and again restated, but the answer to it has not been found. Each thinker, in turn, tries to untie the knot, and ends by cutting it. One subtle and insidious fallacy vitiates every argument that has ever been employed in this most barren of logomachies—the assumption that the question is open to discussion. One might as well try to prove or disprove the existence of colour on purely *a priori* grounds as ask, in disregard of the direct testimony of consciousness, whether freedom is or is not a vital attribute of the soul of man. All the arguments for freedom, though they may fill volumes, amount to no more than this: I feel that I am free; therefore I am free. And all the arguments against freedom, though they may fill hundreds of volumes, amount to no more than this: I can find no place for freedom in my theory of things; therefore I am not free.

Can the defender of freedom do more than plead the cogency of the *sense* of freedom? To defend freedom on metaphysical grounds, to pretend to fit it into a reasoned scheme of things, is to play into the hands of the necessitarians (as they call themselves). What really happens in the freewill controversy is that the sense of freedom holds the key to the position against a beleaguering host of theoretical objections. The argumentative defence of freedom should therefore limit itself in the first instance to an attempt to expose the fallacies of the necessitarians. Out of a critical study of their arguments a theory of things may evolve itself which will countenance freedom on dialectical grounds. But to begin by trying to prove that men are free agents is to assume by implication that the question is open to discussion, and in doing so to weaken the authority of the sense of freedom, and therefore to imperil the safety of the beleaguered fortress.

That the question cannot be discussed on its own merits is proved by the fact that in nine cases out of ten the corresponding controversy turns out to be a mere episode in the larger strife between the materialistic and the idealistic tendencies of human thought. The Calvinist and the Mussulman, whose sole concern is for the power and glory of their supernatural God, do indeed regard Man as the victim of a compulsion which is at once spiritual and quasi-mechanical. But, with these exceptions, necessitarianism deprives man of freedom in the interest of material forces and physical laws. For, as a rule, the necessitarian approaches the problem of freedom from the standpoint of physical science. In doing so he necessarily prejudges the question; for physical science finds it needful to deprive the world of freedom (which would introduce utterly indeterminable factors into its problems) before it can even begin its appointed work. But it is not freedom only that physical science finds it needful to withdraw from Nature, or rather from that abstraction which it miscalls Nature, but every spiritual quality. The result of this is that the triumph of necessitarianism is as barren as it is cheap. The aim of the necessitarian is to bind man's will in the chains of mechanical causation; but in the very act of being seized and fettered its victim escapes from his grasp. For the arguments by which he deprives *me* of freedom prove nothing except that *I*—the self, the living soul, the living will (for will is soul on the threshold of action)—have ceased to exist.

Even the determinism (to use a less uncompromising word) which, without actually breaking with the popular psychology, tends to regard every action as the resultant of *motives*, is as destructive of man's personality as the doctrine of human automatism. We do not need determinists to teach us that no man can act except from motives. The question is: Where do these motives come from? From external sources only, or also from the inner life of the man who acts? One knows from experience that every influence which comes or seems to come to a man from without is coloured and otherwise modified by the man's personality. Indeed it is only by entering into quasi-chemical combination with a man's personality that an external influence can transform itself into a motive; and the same motive can transform itself into a thousand different motives by entering into combination with a thousand different minds. The sight of a bottle of brandy is a strong temptation to one man, a matter of indifference to a second, a source of disgust to a third. It follows from these premises that if all motives are, as determinism usually assumes, external to *me*, *I* do not exist. For something of me (so vital is my connexion with my environment) has immingled itself with each of the many motives that govern my conduct; and that something is abstracted from me whenever the motive in question is regarded as wholly external to my will. Therefore, when all my motives have been transformed by determinism into external forces, of which I am the supposed victim, nothing of *me* remains. But if *I* do not exist, it is a waste of time to debate the question of my freedom. My will is an essential part of myself. If I am nothing but a shorthand symbol, my will is obviously non-existent, and as such can neither be bound nor free.

There is one aspect of the problem which the disputants on both sides are apt to lose sight of. As freedom and necessity are antithetical and therefore correlative terms, the vanishing point of either idea must needs be the vanishing point of the other. It follows that if there is no such thing as freedom in Nature, there can be no such thing as necessity. Necessitarianism deludes itself when it claims to have demonstrated the unreality of freedom. What it has really done, if its arguments are as conclusive as it believes them to be, is to cancel an entire category of human thought. But its arguments are inconclusive, in the sense that the more triumphant is their vindication of necessity, the more effectually do they safeguard freedom. For wherever there is necessity there is constraint; and wherever there is constraint there is a constraining power. This power may itself be the victim of a higher necessity, but the chain of effect and efficient cause must lead us at last (ideally, if not actually) to a power which, having nothing beyond or outside it, is self-constrained and therefore free. Thus acceptance of the idea of necessity compels us, sooner or later, to recognise the *a priori* possibility (not to say necessity) of freedom.

Now it is obvious that if the *a priori* possibility of freedom be conceded, Nature, in the cosmic sense of the word, Nature in her totality, is free. For since her limits are presumably illimitable, since her being is presumably the all in all of existence, it is clear that she cannot be controlled by any superior power and that the end of her activities cannot be alien to herself. Though all lesser things be the victims of necessity, she at least is free. She at least is the arbiter of her own destiny, the orderer of her own goings, the lord and giver of her own life. No current stronger than herself bears her along on its waves, for she is herself the master current in which all rivers of energy begin and end, the stream of living waters that moves in an eternal circle from sea to cloud and from cloud to sea.

But when we study the Universe, detail by detail, the freedom that belongs to the whole seems to vanish from our sight. No one would dream of saying that a cloud was free because it moved across the sky; that a stone was free because it rolled down the mountain side; that a flake of snow was free because it floated down to the ground; that a plant was free because it put forth leaf and flower and fruit. Nor need we go far to seek an explanation of what common sense accepts as an obvious fact. For in the first place each detail in the complicated machinery of material existence acts under the stress and pressure of the whole. The proof of this statement rests with physical science, which is ever discovering new links in the chains of causation that bind each thing to all and all things to each. And in the second place the ends for which each particular thing is working lie beyond the scope of its own individual existence. Indeed the ultimate end of its action may be said to coincide with the ultimate end of the Universe. Nor is it only in the lesser details of material nature that necessity reigns supreme. As science advances from effect to cause, and from cause to law, freedom flies before it and finds no rest for her feet. The Dryads have long since left the woods, and the Naiads the streams; and the physical forces that have taken their place are to the full as blind and helpless as are even the least of the phenomena that are supposed to have been produced by their agency and to be governed by their laws. There are no limits to this process. Potentially, if not actually, science is master of the whole material universe. There are islands and continents which it has not yet had time to conquer: yet even on these it has landed and hoisted its flag, the flag of mechanical necessity and physical law.

Where, then, it will be asked, is freedom to be found? I answer "at the heart of the Universe." The true self of Nature, the world seen as it really is, is free. In attaining to the spiritual goal of her movement, in completing the process of self-integration, Nature becomes what she really is. All the terms in the infinite series are then summed up in the final term. All laws, all forces, all phases of development, all planes of being, are gathered up and finally absorbed into the one self-dependent, self-sufficing life. The last semblance of control from without, the last shadow that fate may seem to have cast, has vanished, and the fulness of freedom has been won.

The heart of the Universe, then, is the fountain-head of freedom. The higher self of Nature, the spiritual pole of existence, the supreme synthesis, is free. What follows with regard to man ? In what sense and to what extent is he free ? He is free, with the full freedom of unfettered Nature, so far as he can draw life into himself from the heart of the Universe, so far as he can identify himself with the supreme synthesis, so far as he can live to the spirit, so far as he can live in the infinite and the eternal, so far as he can make the soul or higher self of Nature his own. So far as he can do these things, or rather this one thing—for the one thing has innumerable facets—he is free. So far—but no further. The goal of absolute freedom, as we contemplate it, seems infinitely distant and wholly unattainable ; yet every step that takes us towards it brings its emancipative influence more and more fully into our lives. We are apt to divide things into the bond and the free ; but freedom, like every other natural tendency, is an ideal rather than a possession, a process rather than a fact. The germs of freedom are present in the germs of spirituality, wherever these may be found ; and the degree of freedom is measured by the degree of spirituality, from the first stirrings of mere vitality up to the highest imaginable development of spiritual life. Thus (to take obvious examples) adults are freer agents than children ; men of culture than savages ; human beings than animals ; animals than plants ; plants than machines or stones. If necessity is the law of the world without us, freedom is the law of the inner life of man. Compulsion from within, spiritual compulsion, the compulsion of one's own highest and widest self—*is* freedom.

It is well that we should sometimes remind ourselves that freedom is an ideal rather than a possession, a prize to be won rather than a privilege to be paraded and enjoyed. For it is as easy to overestimate as to underestimate the degree and the range of human freedom. Orthodox Christianity, for example, has always been too ready to assume that the will of man is absolutely and unconditionally free, and that his short-comings are therefore due to perversity rather than to infirmity of will. And there are modern thinkers who seem to share this view. Dr. Schiller, the Oxford philosopher and critic, has recently said that "there is no natural law in progress" and that "we shall never find our way to God unless we realize how entirely free we are to go to the Devil, and how imminent and constant is our danger of going there." Here we have Nature dehumanized and human life denaturalized in order that the freedom of the human will may be duly—or unduly—exalted. If there is no natural tendency towards progress, or *better*ment, in human society, there can be no natural tendency towards *good* in man. Is this really so? Every other living thing is endowed with a natural tendency towards the good, or rather towards the perfection, of its own type or kind. Such a tendency is of the essence of growth. Is man the only exception to this seemingly universal rule? Is his the only life that does not come under the master law of growth? The general tenor of the work on which I am now engaged is my answer to this question. The reason that Dr. Schiller gives for the faith that is in him does not shake the faith that I instinctively oppose to his. Because man is free to go to the Devil, therefore there is no natural tendency towards progress. Acceptance of Dr. Schiller's assumption would not necessarily bind me to ratify his conclusion. But I am doubtful as to the soundness of his assumption. Is man "entirely free to go to the Devil"? In the abstract, perhaps he is. But what of this man or that man? What of the average man? The average man is as little able to go, at will, to the Devil, as to enter, at will, into oneness with God. If anything, he is less able to go to the Devil, for his natural tendency is, as I contend, towards good and therefore towards God. A man must be high in development, must have won a quite exceptional measure of freedom, if he is to qualify for admission to either Heaven or Hell. The average man is no automaton ; but he is, at best, partially, provisionally, and (in the main) potentially free. Inherited tendencies, inherited traditions, compulsorily formed habits, dictated rules of conduct, prescribed ends of action, prejudices of various kinds, his own childhood, his own youth, press in upon him on all sides and seriously restrict his freedom. To suppose that he can at will free himself from the pressure of these influences and go straight to God, or the Devil, as the case may be, is to ignore the teaching of experience. Let a man use such freedom as he possesses, to win more freedom, and let him co-operate, as best he may, with his natural tendency towards good. We can ask him to do as much as this, but we cannot in reason expect him to do more.

Absolute libertarianism (if that is its correct title) is probably as far from the truth of things as is the strict determinism which I have lately criticized. What is needed, as it seems to me, is a theory of freedom which will mediate between these extremes, which will harmonize freedom with natural tendency and natural law, control of one's own destiny with submission to the pressure of the natural forces which are making, in man as in other living things, for development, for growth,—a theory which will tell us that man, unlike other living things, can transform development into self-development, and, though not exempt from the necessity of growing, can himself direct the process of his growth. Such a theory I am trying to think out. In identifying freedom with self-constraint, with spiritual necessity, in regarding it as an ideal to be realized and a prize to be won, I stand (to the best of my belief) midway between the unqualified affirmation of freedom and the point-blank denial of it.

In order to test the worth of my theory and of the claim that I am making on behalf of it, let us confront it with one or two of the difficulties in which any theory of freedom is bound to involve itself, and see how it deals with them.

There is a point of view from which, even in the sphere of moral action, man seems to be under the dominion of irresistible forces and inexorable laws. History is ever teaching us that the ends of human conduct are immeasurably larger than man himself intends or conceives them to be. Again and again, as we study the records of the past, we are forced to confess that men are, as it were, instruments in the hands of some wide and mighty power—the " Providence " of the Christian, the " Destiny " of the Mussulman, the " Nature " of those who can call it by no other name. We aim at this or that immediate object or personal end. Later on either we or those who come after us are able to see that in working for it we were working for ends which we never dreamed of compassing, ends which transcended the range of our desire as far as they transcended the limits of our sight. It sometimes seems as if our impulses, our tendencies, our instincts, desires and passions, our very lusts and propensities to evil, were all being used by Nature for secret purposes of her own. When this feeling takes possession of us, we are tempted to say, with Renan, " Il y à quelque part un grand égoïste qui nous trompe." " Nous sommes exploités." " Quelque chose s'organise à nos dépens ; nous somnes le jouet d'un égoïsme supérieur." At any rate the feeling of helplessness in the hands of Nature is a real feeling ; and the wider our experience and the larger our view of things, the stronger does it tend to become.

But when it leads us to think of our Lord and Master (whoever he may be or whatever we may call him) as a " great egoist " who is exploiting us for purposes of his own, and of ourselves as

> Impotent pieces in the game he plays,

then the spiritual theory of freedom comes to our rescue and provides us with an antidote to our specious but shallow pessimism. For it tells us that, inasmuch as freedom is the counterpart of spirituality both in Nature and in us, we have but to spiritualize ourselves in order to share in Nature's freedom, and to make our destinies coincide, potentially and ideally, with hers. The slave who toils at the bidding of another has no part or lot in the fruits of his labours ; but man, even when he seems to be a passive instrument in the hands of Nature, is toiling for ends which he may, if he pleases, make his own. The sense of helplessness which sometimes overwhelms him is really the sense of the pressure to which the central tendencies of things are subjecting him ; but this despotic pressure is the very source of his freedom, for Nature (so far as she reveals her purpose to him) realizes her own destiny by spiritualizing his life ; and the end for which her central tendencies are working is the evolution of his soul (which is also hers), and its consequent emancipation from the forces that fetter its freedom and impede its growth. That I am clay in the hands of the potter, matters nothing, for it is only in the mould of spiritual freedom that my true self can be shaped. As I expand my being in response to the pressure of Nature's vital forces, I draw those forces little by little within the scope of my own inner life and at last absorb them all into myself.

There are other experiences in the sphere of moral action on which this conception of freedom seems to throw light.

There is one in particular which no one who studies his own feelings can fail to observe. In yielding to a lower impulse—to the passion of anger, for example, or to a fleshly lust—we feel as if we were scarcely free agents. We yield either because we are the slaves of an acquired habit, in which case we are no longer free, or because the impulse comes upon us like a whirlwind and constrains us, as it seems, from without. On the other hand, when we surrender ourselves to the pressure of a higher motive, we feel that we are free ; and the higher the motive, the stronger does our sense of freedom become. I find it difficult to account for these feelings except on the hypothesis that freedom is spiritual necessity, or compulsion from within. The man who does right is constrained by a higher impulse. But the higher impulses belong to the spiritual side of man's nature or, in other words, to the true self : and action that is initiated by one's true self is obviously free. Moreover the ends of righteous action always coincide with the ends of the true self. The man who habitually does right has allied himself with the real or spiritual tendencies of Nature, and in virtue of this high partnership has placed himself (potentially, if not actually) at the centre of the Universe, the point from which all the energies of Nature radiate and to which they all return ; and so he controls the aboriginal sources of his own action and reaps its ultimate results. The bad man, on the other hand, is acted upon from without. The lower impulses which issue in wrong doing belong, either directly or indirectly, to that more animal side of our nature in respect of which we belong to the material universe, and are therefore in bondage—in some sort and some degree—to physical necessity. And the ends towards which they move us are always foreign to our true life and adverse to our higher interests, as is proved by the fact that we curse ourselves for having gained them. Nay, the sources of the motive power that constrains the vicious are not unfrequently external objects which act upon the lower self as a magnet acts upon steel. Thus the drunkard is constrained by the brandy bottle ; the profligate by a seductive face or figure ; the thief or the miser by the glitter of gold.

> How oft the sight of means to do ill deeds
> Makes ill deeds done !

Yet there are times when even the best of men become conscious, perhaps more vividly conscious than the rest of us, of their helplessness in the hands of mightier powers ; and while this feeling lasts they, if not the rest of us, are ready to disown their freedom and glory in their bonds. Religion, speaking as the interpreter of man's spiritual experiences, tells us that when we do right it is not we who do it but God who dwelleth in us. Is this " constraining grace " of God compatible with the freedom of man ? If the vicious are slaves to their own lusts, and the virtuous to the grace of God, are not all of us the bondsmen of necessity ? No, for the pressure of the Divine Will is a source of freedom, not of bondage. In the last resort, indeed, it is the only source of freedom. For to be constrained by God, who, being the spiritual pole of the Universe, dwells in each human soul as its unattainable ideal, is to be constrained by one's best and highest self ; and to be self-constrained (in the deepest sense of the word *self*) is to be free.

The difference between virtue and vice shows itself most clearly in the reaction of conduct on character. By yielding to lower impulses men form bad habits and so forfeit their freedom. By responding to higher impulses they gradually acquire a mastery over the lower self, and so free themselves from the trammels of necessity. In brief, freedom is lost or won by conduct. This fact—for we know from experience that it is a fact—is easily accounted for on the hypothesis that freedom is the counterpart of spirituality. For to be virtuous is to live to the spirit ; and to live to the spirit is both to be and to become free. The vicious man, on the other hand, by degrading his life to the level of its own material subsoil, gradually accustoms himself to the yoke of physical necessity, and in so doing forfeits his birthright and degenerates into a slave.

It follows from these premises that the man who does right without an effort, and therefore without any apparent exercise of volition, is really freer than the man who feels that his will has been in battle and that resistance has been met and overcome. The moral struggle is at heart a struggle against coercion and therefore for freedom : with the gradual acquisition of freedom the tension of the struggle diminishes ; and if freedom should ever be fully and finally won, the struggle would have ceased. Those who do right because they cannot help themselves, because the compulsion from within is overwhelmingly strong, are the freest of men.

Thus there is an intimate connexion between virtue and freedom, and between vice and necessity. Yet nothing short of the total extinction of my freedom can absolve me from responsibility ; and when my freedom has been finally extinguished, I, the self, the ego, shall have ceased to exist, and the question of my responsibility need no longer be discussed. So long as *I* survive, I am potentially free ; and the presence of this germ of freedom suffices to condemn me when I do wrong. When necessity has finally triumphed, nothing will be left for it to coerce. When freedom has finally triumphed, I shall know at last that all the while I—the real I—have been free.

Having tried to justify the conception of freedom as spiritual necessity, by showing that it resolves difficulties and throws light on obscurities in our ethical experiences,

I will now conclude my defence of it by interpreting it in terms of my own instinctive feelings and secret convictions. On one point I have never wavered. I am as free as I feel myself to be. This feeling is its own guarantee; and no argument that draws its premises from a lower level of experience can invalidate it in the court of reason or shake my faith in its authority. But my sense of freedom, though it never sinks to zero, is an exceedingly variable quantity. Sometimes I feel as if my freedom were absolutely unfettered. Sometimes I feel as if I were the plaything of world-wide forces, as helpless—almost—as a straw on a rushing stream. The truth is that the question as to my freedom resolves itself into the question as to the limits of my *self*. If I am nothing but a "conscious automaton," I am obviously the helpless victim of mechanical necessity; but in that case there is no *I* to be victimized. If, on the contrary, I am a spiritual being, a sharer in the inner life of Nature, freedom is my birthright, and the degree of my freedom varies directly with the extent to which I have developed my potencies of spiritual life. In other words, the expansion of my self is accompanied and progressively measured by the expansion of my freedom. It is the movement of the stream of spiritual life through the channel of my being on the way to its own ocean source, that endows me with freedom; and it is the self-same movement that is developing my spirit and making me what I really am. I become free by becoming myself, and I become myself by becoming free. I am not I, in any sense of the word, until I have won some measure of freedom. I am not I, in the true sense of the word, until I have made all the forces that constrain me my own. It follows that the question Am I free? is so far from admitting of a definite and final answer, that it has to receive a fresh statement and a fresh answer and perhaps also an ever changing answer, in the case of each individual man. The terms of the question are always fluid and unstable, and the answer is always moving forward—with the movement of the human spirit—in the direction of its own ideal, the direction of an unqualified and all-embracing "*Yes*."

In the sense of freedom, which is characteristic of man as

man, Nature becomes aware of her own unity and totality and of her consequent exemption from external constraint. In the sense of will-power, which is the counterpart of the sense of freedom, Nature begins to realize that there is a purpose which animates her life. In the sense of freedom, and the accompanying sense of will-power, man becomes aware of his potential oneness with the totality of Nature, and of his partnership with her in the freedom which she enjoys, and—above all—in the purpose which animates her life. That purpose is the realization of potentialities—in a word, growth. The purpose of growth is the realization of spiritual potentialities, or soul-growth; for we mean by spirit what is ultimate in synthesis; and the realization of potentialities is in its essence a synthetic and therefore a spiritual movement, a movement towards organic unity, a movement—in the case of the totality of Nature—towards the finding of the universal soul. When we say that consciousness is dawning on man, we mean, on the one hand, that the universal soul is becoming aware of itself in the individual life, and, on the other hand, that the individual soul is becoming aware of itself in and through its oneness with the universal soul. When we say that the true life of man is "buried," we mean that what is real in the individual life is the life beyond individuality, the life of Nature in her unity and totality, the life of the All. To realize that life, to realize his oneness with the eternal, changeless soul of Nature, to realize that his inmost soul is her soul, that his true self is her self—to realize this supreme truth, not as a formula, nor as a proposition, nor even as the central idea in a system, but as the central fact of his own being—to realize it by living it, by growing into oneness with it, by being embraced by it, by being absorbed into it,—this (if he could but know it) is the ideal end of man's existence and the central purpose of his life.

PART IV

THE PROCESS OF GROWTH

CHAPTER I

GROWTH THROUGH DESIRE

IDEALLY and potentially men is free—free to choose among conflicting ideals, conflicting ideas, conflicting motives, conflicting standards of worth, conflicting courses of action—free, therefore, to direct and control the process of his own growth. But growth, as far as our experience of it goes, is always a movement towards a more or less pre-determined form. The oak-tree is in the acorn. The bird is in the egg. The " baboon " and the " rat," as Professor Bateson reminds us, are in their respective " specks of protoplasm." If these things are so, if growth is indeed the realization of potentiality and therefore the fulfilment of destiny, and if the growth of the human spirit is indeed accompanied by the outgrowth of freedom, with all that freedom implies, we are up against a tremendous practical paradox. By fulfilling his destiny man acquires the power of either aiding or thwarting destiny. By yielding to a relentless pressure—for what pressure is so relentless as that of growth ?—he becomes free either to resist that pressure or to intensify it. By growing, blindly, helplessly, instinctively, he becomes able to direct and control the process of his growth. How can these things be ? How can self-determination be pre-determined ? How can the very stress of necessity set its victim free ?

In the last chapter of the Second Fart of this book I considered this problem, and came to the conclusion—a conclusion which I regarded as tentative and provisional—that though the idea of pre-determination or destiny would always (and rightly) haunt us, the growth of the soul was not pre-determined, in the sense which the word ordinarily bears. But the idea of pre-determination continues to haunt me, for one; and pre-determined in some sense the growth of the soul must needs be,—pre-determined in this sense, if in no other, that as the future oak-tree, with all its typical characteristics, is in the acorn, so the future man, with all his typical characteristics, is in the newborn infant. If this is so, the growing soul is in some sort under the control of destiny; and the question arises, how is the pre-determining pressure of destiny to be reconciled with the sense of freedom—freedom to map out the course of his own life—of which man cannot divest himself, and which seems to gain in strength in proportion as he fulfils his destiny by making healthy and harmonious growth. To this question there is, as far as I can see, but one answer. When I was considering the meaning of growth as the master law of human life, I worked my way to the conviction that in the growth of the individual soul we are witnessing the self-realization, or self-revelation, or self-affirmation (I know not which is the fittest word) of the universal soul; and that the universal soul—the supreme integer, the totality of things in its organic unity—is therefore the true self of each of us. If this conviction is well-founded; if the universal soul, which is absolutely free in the sense of being wholly exempt from external constraint, is indeed the true self of each of us; if it exists as a possibility in each human embryo, just as the forest-like banyan tree (to borrow a pregnant simile from the Upanishads) exists as a possibility in each of its own speck-like seeds,—then the ideas of freedom and pre-determined growth are reconcilable through the paradoxical conception that growth, self-integration, however fully it may be pre-determined, is in its essence a movement towards the achievement of freedom, and therefore that man is pre-destined to become free. And if this is indeed his destiny, then, while he is fulfilling it, he must be winning freedom through his fulfilment of it, and must therefore be free either to thwart it or to ally himself with it. And as, by using his freedom to thwart his destiny, he will gradually forfeit his freedom and become the slave of his own lower desires and impulses—the hereditary enemies of his spiritual growth—so, by using his freedom to co-operate with his destiny, he will win an ever fuller measure of freedom, thereby fitting himself for the work of co-operation, in an ever higher degree. Indeed there is a stage in his development, beyond which his destiny cannot fulfil itself without his active co-operation. Thenceforth, the more effectively he co-operates, the more willing is destiny to hand over to him the duty and responsibility of directing his own growth. At last, in the fulness of time, he will become his own destiny; and pre-determination and self-determination will become one. From this point of view one sees that in man, as in every other living thing, the current of natural tendency is setting towards the goal of perfection, the perfection of the given type, and yet that the individual soul is free—not absolutely, as Dr. Schiller seems to suggest, but within ever varying limits—to go to God or to the Devil, to make or mar itself.

It sometimes happens that ideas which are irreconcilable and even mutually exclusive on the normal levels of experience and thought, admit of being reconciled, and even harmonized into a higher and more comprehensive idea, on that supernormal level which we indicate by the formula "at infinity"; and it certainly seems as if the apparently irreconcilable ideas of freedom and destiny ceased to be irreconcilable when viewed from the standpoint of the ideal and ultimate identity of the individual with the universal soul. Realizing, then, as I do to the full, that the supreme mystery will ever remain mysterious, I must henceforth be content to find rest (such rest as it affords—the rest of eternal motion) in the conception to which the central experiences of my life—the sense of freedom and the sense of pre-destination—as I follow them out in thought, direct my mind, a conception which is a paradox in itself and paradoxical in all its developments,—the conception that to universalize myself, to become one with the soul of all things, is my ideal destiny, and that I can either thwart that high destiny (in the strength of the freedom with which it invests me) and so become the thrall of a lower destiny, or escape for ever from thraldom to destiny by striving to fulfil my own.

Using this paradox,

Which comforts while it mocks,

as my starting point, I have now to ask myself what is to be the process of my growth. Here, as elsewhere, the end must determine the way. If to unite myself with the soul of all things, to become one with the infinite and the eternal, is the ideal end of the process of my growth, it must be my steadfast aim so to direct the process as to live, or at least begin to live, in the infinite and the eternal. What does this mean? It means, for one thing, that, while accepting limitations as inevitable and even salutary, I must resist all limiting influences, *so far as they claim to be final.* This claim, as we know from experience, has to be met and combated again and again. For of the limiting influences which affect the soul, there are few, apart from those which are obviously minor and subsidiary, which do not claim, directly or indirectly, to be final. That this should be so is inevitable. Slowly emerging from a stage of development in which growth, under the guidance of heredity, is blind, instinctive, and compulsory, into a higher stage in which he is called upon to become the free and conscious director of his own growth, it is but natural that man should be held back by the very forces to which he has long been in bondage, from responding to that emancipative appeal. It is but natural, in other words, that spiritual indolence—reluctance to order one's own goings, reluctance to exercise oneself in great matters, reluctance to accept high responsibility, the shrinking back in alarm from the mysterious and the unknown, the clinging to rules, formulas, traditions, conventions, customs, the readiness to obey for the sake of obeying and to conform for the sake of conforming—should be the besetting weakness of the partially emancipated soul.

This resistance, in man's inner being, of the actual to the attractive force of the ideal has its parallel, we may well believe, in other grades of organic life; but in the case of man the tendency has a character and a meaning which are all its own. If man could not consciously resist the expansive forces that are brought to bear on him, he could not consciously co-operate with them. In this, as in other matters, it is consciousness which differentiates him from all other living things. Let us try to think the matter out. The Universe is energy. At the heart of physical energy is the higher energy of life. At the heart of the energy of life is the higher energy of soul-life. Physical energy is one and indivisible. So is physical life. So is soul-life. So is life in its totality, ranging as it does from the pole of unconscious energy to the counter-pole of self-conscious and therefore spiritual life. Life manifests itself in countless outward forms. The One Life is in each of these, inspiring and sustaining it within its narrow limits, ready to answer all its demands, ready to fulfil all its desires, ready to pour itself into the channel of the individual life. There is no life so lowly, but it has the One Life, in its totality, at its service. The ocean is in each of the seas, with all their ramifications, that open out of it. It is in each of the sea-like rivers which its tidal wave ascends. It is in each of the tributary streams, greater and lesser, down to the slenderest rivulet that is fed by the distilled essence from its limitless flood. Nor is it only in the running waters and stored up waters of the earth. It is also in the mists, the clouds, the raindrops, the dews. In fine it is everywhere. Is it not the same with the ocean of life ? But so long as the organism is blind and unconscious, it can draw in from that infinite reservoir no more than will serve to fill the narrow channel, walled in by instinct and habit, by the tradition and the heritage of a thousand generations, in which the current of its life moves. In other words, before consciousness begins to awake, the resistance of the organism to the emancipative forces which are latent in it is virtually[1] absolute. In man the tendency to resist remains ; but, with the dawn of consciousness, the attractive force of the emancipative influences becomes stronger and ever stronger until at last the tendency to resist finds itself confronted by the counter-tendency—the tendency to respond to the call of the infinite and the eternal, to serve under the banner of the ideal, to

[1] Virtually, not literally. It is possible that in every living thing there is an infinite capacity for ulterior development ; but below the human level the consequent movement towards ideal perfection may at best be likened (as has already been suggested) to an infinite " series " which is limited by a finite number.

work for it, to work with it,—and the real drama of man's life begins.

The tendency to resist expansion has behind it the pressure of all the ages since the first stirring of life on earth; and it is only with infinite pains and trouble that the counter tendency is able to assert itself and win its way. Hence the immense, persistent, and self-renewing strength of what I may call the lure of finality,—a lure which is potent, as we all know from experience, in every stage of our development. Hence the alarm—the terror, one might almost say—with which we shrink back from the shadow of the infinite as it begins to steal across our thought,—shrink back from the prospect of endless development, of starting on a journey which will carry us, beyond all familiar horizons, into the heart of the mysterious and the unknown. Hence the secret desire, from which no one is wholly exempt, to find rest, for good and all, in some theory of life, or in some scheme of life, or perhaps in some attitude towards life which is at once a theory and a scheme.

How will the dread of the infinite and the consequent thirst for finality affect the growth of the soul? The soul grows through its activity; but activity is the outcome of desire. Let us begin, then, with desire. The fountain-head of desire is the instinct to live. The character of desire is therefore determined by our conception of life. We begin by desiring the continuance of physical life. Each of us desires to feed the flame of his own life and to pass on the torch of life to the next generation. This is sensual desire. It in itself is natural and necessary. But if we allow ourselves to rest in it, through our inability to rise to a higher conception of life, the quality of our desire will begin to deteriorate. The gratification of sensual desire gives us sensual pleasure, and sensual pleasure may come to be desired for its own sake. This is the first stage in the deterioration of desire. The second stage is to desire over-eagerly the means to the gratification of sensual desire. These means may be summed up under the general head of money or material possessions. The initial reason why material possessions are so much desired is that they enable us to buy all that the body needs. A secondary reason is that they enable us to buy more than the body needs,—comforts, luxuries, and pleasures of various kinds. And the more they give us of these things, the more we ask for. As the means of enjoying life are added to, the standard of living rises. What is luxury to-day may be counted as bare comfort to-morrow, and as less than comfort at a later date. Hence it is that of material possessions, if they are desired as the means to the gratification of selfish desires, there can never be enough to go round. This enhances their value in the eyes of most men, and is a further reason why they are desired. For they become a source of pride to their possessor. They place him high among his fellows. They give him position and distinction. They cause him to be looked up to and envied. And this is not all. They give him opportunities for self-improvement which are denied to his poorer brethren. They give him leisure for serious as well as for frivolous pursuits. They make it possible for him to indulge refined and æsthetic tastes. They bring education, culture, travel, and a general widening of experiences and interests within his reach. Above all, they give him power over his fellow men ; and this, besides ministering to his pride, gives him further opportunities for enriching and otherwise aggrandizing himself at their expense.

Hence it is that in the present stage of man's development the desire for material possessions is of all desires the most widespread and one of the most absorbing. It is also the most fundamentally selfish. For the supreme attraction of material possessions is that they enable a man to grasp and keep for himself a disproportionately large share of what are called "the good things of life." Under the pressure of this sinister desire our social life has become (from one point of view) a chaotic scramble for worldly goods, nation fighting against nation for territorial and commercial aggrandizement, while individuals compete with one another, jostle one another, trample one another down, cheat one another, plunder one another, maltreat and even murder[1] one another in their " fierce race for wealth."

[1] I wonder how many millions of lives, of all ages, have been wantonly sacrificed, in mine and furnace and factory, to the Moloch of commercial greed ?

It is true that this race for wealth has led men to exploit with feverish energy the material resources of the earth, and has thus given them an ever-growing mastery over the physical forces of Nature; but it is probable that had they co-operated for this purpose they would have gone even further in that direction, and it is certain that they would have appreciably raised the general *level* of material well-being; whereas competition, though it has greatly enriched the rich, has in doing so unduly raised the *standard* of well-being, and has therefore impoverished the poor.

And the desire for possessions has done worse things even than these. With the passing of tribal communism and the consequent release of the individual from socialistic pressure, two counter-tendencies of human nature begin to assert themselves,—individualism and idealism, the shrinking back into self, and the going out of self into the ideal and the infinite. The former was at first by far the stronger tendency, the collective selfishness of the tribe having prepared the way for it; and as it found expression for itself in the private ownership of property, so it made that institution the centre of its resistance to the call of the higher and wider self. For a time, indeed, the sentiment of devotion to the community survived as a strong sense of duty to the State; and this sense of duty counteracted the growing individualism of the citizens and held their nascent love of Mammon in check. But as the attractive force of possessions grew with the acquisition of them, their sense of public duty gradually waned, and the love of Mammon became the ruling passion of their lives. Generated as it was by man's growing individualism, this desire for material possessions reacted upon and intensified that contractive tendency. Whatever a man might be doing, whatever cause he might be serving, on however high a plane he might be working, however much he might seem to be co-operating with others, he was ever tending, under the secret influence of this insidious desire, to play for his own hand, to think, first and foremost, of himself. His very idealism, as it began to develop itself, was corrupted and perverted by this subtle poison. Even when he coveted earnestly the best gifts, his desire for them had in it a base alloy of self-interest. If he did good work for his country, he expected to be publicly honoured and rewarded for it. If he achieved "success" in art or letters, he expected money and fame. His desire for ideal truth (if he ever rose to the level of that desire) degenerated into a desire for finality, for certitude, for possession of a formulated creed. His desire for ideal happiness, instead of lifting him on the wings of aspiration, sank to the level of desire for comfort, for luxury, for enjoyment, for repose. Indeed, in far too many cases it merged itself in the desire for possessions (as the source of all those "good things") and strengthened and stimulated the latter in proportion as it de-idealized itself. When the idea of the Universal God began to dawn upon man's consciousness, his instinctive desire to possess what he valued made him dream, if not of monopolizing the Eternal, at least of establishing proprietary rights in his favour and his saving grace. Lastly, when he looked beyond the grave, his individualism clouded his vision. He thought, and was well content to think, of himself as one of a few who were to be saved when the rest of the human race perished everlastingly. Having long been accustomed to see in the secular life a scramble for material possessions, he found it easy to think of the spiritual life as a scramble for the greatest of all possessions —"eternal life."

When the feudal system associated political power, and all that it implied, with the ownership of land, an immense impetus was given to the desire for "property," the effect of which has lasted to this day. As time went on, the feudal baron gave way to the capitalist, and the robber-knight to the company-promoter. But though rapacity changed its methods and its immediate ends, it did not change its purpose. Or, if it did, it changed it for the worse. We have seen that, with the passing of the feudal system, the duties and responsibilities which were inherent in the ownership of property ceased to be obligatory, whereas most of the rights and privileges remained. The result of this was that the desire for possessions became more and more individualistic and selfish, and the pursuit of them more and more absorbing and more and more widely diffused. The consequent externalization of our aims, materialization of our ideals, and debasement of our standards are evils which we now take for granted, so much so indeed that those who denounce them or even deplore them are either laughed at as visionaries or sneered at as hypocrites. And the pity of it is that our philosophy of life completely dominates our philosophy of education, stamping its own fallacies and misconceptions on the system of education which has long passed as orthodox, and through that system—which, being feudal in spirit, is despotic and dogmatic—transmitting from generation to generation the externalism and materialism which are poisoning our souls. Can we wonder that the most selfish of all desires is still in the ascendant, when each generation in turn takes infinite pains to kindle it in the heart of the next ?

I have painted a gloomy picture of the order of things which I find myself. If I have unduly deepened its gloom, the reason is that I have revolted, perhaps too vehemently, against the complacent fatalism which accepts what ought not to be as what must be, and regards as of divine dispensation, as pre-ordained by "the everlasting purpose of God," what is really no more than a particular stage in a great social experiment,—the experiment of permitting private ownership of property in general and of landed property in particular. But the gloom of the picture, however deep it may be, does not move me to despair. Tremendous as is the pressure to which the prevailing misconception of the meaning and value of life subjects each of us, the latent idealism of man's heart stands firm against it. It may need a supreme crisis to call that latent idealism into activity; but it is there, in the depths of man's buried life, waiting for its summons.

When its summons comes, what form will its response take ? I have said that the desire for possessions had its origin in the legitimate desire for the preservation and reproduction of life. If man could have gone on to desire the expansion of life, all would have been well. A few men did. These became the prophets, the torch-bearers of Humanity. But in most men desire took (perhaps inevitably) a wrong turning. The lure of finality was too strong for their undeveloped souls. To desire the expansion of life is to desire what is limitless and therefore, *as a possession*, unattainable. From this the heart of man shrank back as from an adventure which would carry it beyond all its familiar landmarks. Yet, if it continued to desire life, that desire would of inner necessity transform itself into the desire to expand life, to explore its inexhaustible possibilities. What could it do, then, if it was to satisfy its longing for finality, but make the accessories of life, rather than life itself, the object of its desire? It was predestined, one might almost say, to take that turning. But this does not alter the fact that in taking it the desire of man's heart went astray.

How is that mistake to be corrected? The instinct to live is the fountain-head of desire. Let that instinct have its way without let or hindrance. Let it reach on into the infinite and the unknown. Let the idea of life widen its scope till it becomes all-embracing. Then at last the current of desire will run pure and free. The desire for material possessions, by reacting upon and intensifying the selfishness that begat it, has done more than any other influence to thwart the expansive tendencies of man's nature, to arrest the growth of his soul. Let life itself, then, with all its limitless possibilities, become the main object of man's desire,—and material possessions will lose their charm. For the desire for them is, in its essence, a desire for *property* (in the literal sense of the word), for proprietorship, for things which a man can claim as his very own. This desire, which has darkened the world with strife and misery, must give way to the desire for possessions which no man can keep to himself, which each man can share with all,—possessions of which there is enough and more than enough to go round. Such a possession, such a complex of possessions, is life itself,—life in all its infinitude, in all its mystery. The whole sea of life is at the service of each of us. This is the fundamental paradox which confounds the arithmetical notions on which the desire for property is based. The sea of life can give itself freely to all who desire to possess it, can pour itself for ever into each of a million million souls, and yet keep its infinitude unimpaired. The poet of love has told us that

> True love in this differs from gold and clay,
> That to divide is not to take away.[1]

As it is with love, so it is with life. We can draw upon the fountain of life unstintingly and unceasingly, without robbing our neighbour of a single drop of it.

The desire for the fulness of life, then, is the only desire for possession which is inherently unselfish. Indeed it is in itself a desire to become unselfish, to go out of self into an ampler life. If the word *possession* suggests, as it too often does, inclusion in self, or circumscription by self, then the desire to expand life is a desire for something more than possession. It is also, and above all, a desire to be possessed. No man can have proprietary rights in the infinite. Desire to possess life in its fulness is a desire to be lost, to be ravished, to be absorbed. On the higher levels of man's being, activity and passivity in possession are in the last resort the same.

So little indeed of aggressive selfishness is there in the desire to expand life, that in entertaining that desire one is merely laying claim, in one's inmost heart, to what is and has always been one's very own. For the fully expanded, the fully developed self is the real self. It is not until a man has arrived at the maturity of his "true manhood" that he is free to say "I am I." To lose the apparent self is to find the genuine self; and to find the genuine self is to become what one really is.

It follows that the desire to expand life is the only desire which is both self-regarding and unselfish,—in other words, which is both effective and pure. Altruism, in the proper sense of the word, is impossible. The springs of action are, and must ever be, in one's own self. But if the springs of action are to be purified, self must expand till it has been lost and re-found. Egoism will prove to be the truest altruism when, by a life of self-realization through self-surrender, the ego has outgrown—and found—itself.

From whatever point of view we may look at things, we see that the desire to live is better than the desire to possess. The latter desire can seldom be gratified except at the expense of other persons. Therefore it tends to separate

[1] Shelley, *Epipsychidion.*

man from man, and to become a principle of disunion, of disintegration, of disorder, of strife. Whatever else it may do for mankind, it does not work for the general happiness. On the other hand, it is impossible to gratify the desire to expand life, without rendering service, directly or indirectly, to one's fellow men. For we expand life through kindness, through sympathy, through the spirit of comradeship, through unselfish devotion, through love; and the goal of soul-expansion is oneness, in and through the One Life, with all one's kind. Indeed it is only in becoming one with others that a man really finds himself. One of the reasons why it is hard for a rich man to enter into the Kingdom of God is that riches tend to raise a man above his fellows and therefore to separate him from them. The man who stands apart from his kind, however exalted may be his position, however great his power, however strong his will, has fatally contracted the bounds of his own life. Could he but see himself as he really is, he would know that he was a degenerate, and a prisoner, and a slave. And though he has gratified the desire of his heart at the expense of the happiness of others, he has not won happiness for himself. For he had set his heart on what was finite and attainable; and therefore, instead of the joy of pursuit, a joy which is as imperishable as the object of pursuit is unattainable, he has found the disillusionment, the sense of satiety, which is the Nemesis of "success."

The moral of all this is that if the soul is to grow it must desire to grow, it must desire a larger and a fuller life; and that if its growth is to be an adventure into the infinite, it must desire to launch out into the infinite, to explore it, to find its home in it. Nothing less than this must content it; and the desire for this must be the master passion of its life. At present the "mania for owning things" seems to be man's master passion. This mania, in which the resistance of self to all expansive and emancipative influences seems to centre, and the indulgence of which has conspicuously failed to make men happy, must give way to a diviner madness,—to the desires to possess (or be possessed by) the mysterious infinitude of life.

CHAPTER II

GROWTH THROUGH BELIEF

FROM desire let us pass on to activity. There are two great spheres of human activity, *belief* and *conduct*. Let us study our problem as it bears on each of these. I shall be reminded that belief and conduct are not so much two spheres as two aspects—the mental and the moral—of the same sphere; that belief is ever tending to express itself in, and therefore to govern and direct, conduct, and that conduct is ever tending to react upon, and therefore to modify and even transform, belief. I have not forgotten this elementary truth; but I find it convenient, for the better ordering of my thoughts, to begin by separating the two spheres (as I will provisionally call them), so far at least as they will allow me to do so.

In both spheres the dominating influence is the attitude of the soul towards things in general. In the sphere of belief this attitude translates itself into ideas; in the sphere of conduct, into action. One can see at the outset that in both spheres the cult of finality will tend to arrest growth: in the sphere of belief, through dogmatism, to arrest mental growth; in the sphere of conduct, through egoism, to arrest moral growth.

In the sphere of belief the dread of the infinite, by which we are all haunted, gives rise to a cry for authoritative guidance which has echoed through all the ages: "Tell me what to believe, and I will believe it." To this cry for guidance, this heartfelt (though perhaps unavowed) prayer of the alarmed and bewildered soul, we owe all our formulated creeds. And not our creeds only. From "Tell me what to believe, and I will believe it," there is but a step—so easy is the transition from belief to conduct—to "Tell me what to do, and I will do it"; and in response to this appeal our creeds become codes, conventions, customs, and our formulas become rules of life.

But let us begin with the formula and the creed. They have their uses; and we could not get on without them. When ground has been won they help to secure and consolidate a part of it.[1] But they exact a heavy price for their services. For, having secured for the growing soul some measure of progress, they proceed to arrest its growth by imprisonimg it behind their own redoubts and earthworks; and if they could have their way, they would arrest its growth for good and all.

What is their procedure? I have tried to prove that in the "buried" or subconscious life man is in touch with larger realities and in possession (partially and potentially) of profounder truths than those which he consciously deals with. The organ of the "buried life" is intuition, which ranges from the "tact" or direct perception which discovers what is fitting in this case or in that, to the adventurous imagination which is conversant in ways of its own with the ultimate and the universal. As it belongs to the higher intuition to feel and respond to the attraction of the infinite, as it is bound by its charter (one might almost say) to sail in unknown seas, the lover of finality must at all costs reduce it to inaction. Till this has been done he cannot sleep in peace. Posing, then, as the champion of orthodoxy, he forbids his intuition to exercise itself in the great matters which attract and stimulate it, assuring it that the truth about those matters is in the keeping of "authority" and that it is not for it or for him to call the ruling of authority in question. If his intuition allows itself to be intimidated by his veto, it will abdicate its high function, and, becoming gradually atrophied through inaction, will at last cease to energize. This means that the

[1] Only a small part of it. For the pioneers and pathfinders are always in touch with the infinite, and they therefore open up endless vistas to the journeying soul. To these vistas the creed-makers, who are in thrall to the lure of finality, are constitutionally blind; and much of the spirit of the Masters to whom they profess allegiance escapes of inner necessity through the network of their uninspired thoughts. This has always been so, and will always be so, as long as the need for creeds and formulas continues to be felt.

"leader" of the growing soul will wither on its stem, and that the growth of the soul on the mental plane will be brought to a standstill. "Where there is no vision the people perish"; and vision ceases when the inward eye, having been compulsorily blindfolded, at last becomes blind.

If dogmatism says *No* to intuition, it says *No* as peremptorily and as effectively to reason. Indeed it is reason rather than intuition that first comes under its ban. For reason is the organ with which a man consciously, and therefore openly and even defiantly, investigates the great problems that challenge him. In using his reason for this purpose, a man deliberately exercises his right of private judgment; and that right the lover of finality must, for his own peace of mind, disallow. He will therefore try to silence his reason[1] by telling it that the questions which interest it have already been settled by duly constituted authority, and are therefore no longer open to discussion. If reason allows itself to be warned off the field of high thinking, it will retire (as I have already pointed out) to the field of positive science; and, by working exclusively in that field, by confining its activities to the investigation of material phenomena, with regard to which there can be certainty and even (in a sense) finality, it will gradually unfit itself for dealing with matters in which, *pace* the dogmatist, there can be no certainty and no approach to finality. It will unfit itself for high thinking, by ceasing to co-operate, and at last becoming unable to co-operate, with intuition. For it is by reacting on intuition, and through intuition on the "buried life," that reason, as an explorer of fundamental mysteries, does its best work. It sifts,

[1] The antithetical correlate to dogmatism is ultra-docility. Both tendencies are as a rule united in the same person. The three chief embodiments of the dogmatic spirit which History has made known to us are the Jewish Law, the Catholic Church, and the Prussian State. The Pharisee, the typical product of Jewish legalism, was as dogmatic an exponent of the Law as he was a docile student of it. In the Catholic Church authority is dogmatic because it is ostentatiously docile, and the docile are deliberately taught to be dogmatic. Under the Prussian State the officer or official is as servile towards his superiors as he is arrogant towards his underlings, arrogance and servility being the ethical counterparts of dogmatism and ultra-docility. I am therefore justified in assuming that man (in the abstract), as the lover of finality, is both dogmatic and ultra-docile.

arranges, and organizes the data of intuition, not so much in order to arrive inductively at general conclusions (though that may be its avowed purpose) as in order, by convincing intuition of the inadequacy of what it offers, to provoke it to fresh exertion and to a more careful and also more adventurous exercise of its "vision." To quote my own words: "When a man becomes aware of an emotional idea which has long ruled his heart, in the very act of bringing it under the control of his consciousness, he causes it to draw in from far and near its hidden reserves and supports (*that through these it may justify itself to his reason*)—to draw these into a region of his subconscious life in which it is possible for them to shape themselves, by slow degrees and by a spontaneous process of which he has no cognizance, into new emotional ideas, ready, when their turn comes, to be transmuted by consciousness into new thought." It follows that when reason, gagged by authority, ceases to interest itself in first principles, and when the higher intuition is thereby deprived of its stimulating control, stagnation will take the place of activity in those hidden reservoirs of spirituality which are the real head-springs of the ideas that rule the world. In brief, to silence reason is to paralyze the "buried life."

In the *divorce* controversy, of which we have recently heard so much, we have an apt illustration of the paralyzing influence of dogmatism on mentality. The problem in which that controversy centres is complex and intractable in the highest degree. There is no conceivable solution of it which does not bristle with difficulties—economic, social, ethical, spiritual. But to leave things as they are is to perpetuate such glaring evils that those who are interested in the problem are bound at all costs to try to solve it. Great qualities are demanded in those who would embark on such an enterprise,—the power of diagnosing existing evils, the power of calculating the probable effects of proposed remedies, a capacity for evolving and applying large constructive ideas, an ample measure of imagination, insight, and sympathy. Yet the first Anglo-Catholic curate whom you meet will solve the problem off-hand by condemning divorce as such, the ground of his condemnation being a reported saying of our Lord; and if his ecclesiastical superiors will allow him to do so, he will give practical effect to his off-hand solution by refusing to admit to Holy Communion even the most innocent of *divorcés*. The devotion of the Anglo-Catholic curate to his Master is admirable up to a certain point; but it may be doubted if it is wholly disinterested. It is possible that there is woven into it a feeling of gratitude to the Master for having saved his followers the trouble of exercising their mental powers. At any rate the Anglo-Catholic curate and those who think with him are well content to solve their knotty problem by sheltering themselves behind a text which shuts it out from their mental vision, just as the advocates of corporal punishment in the nursery and the school-room have sheltered themselves for many centuries behind the letter of the saying "Spare the rod and spoil the child."[1]

To refuse to think out such a problem as that of divorce is, by implication, to refuse to think out the larger and deeper problems that underlie it. In the spheres of ethics, economics, and politics different concrete problems attract different minds; and each of these problems, if we honestly try to solve it, will force us to meditate on the ultimate issues of life and will therefore give us glimpses of infinitely distant and ever-receding horizons. And he who, through dread of those distant horizons, refuses to think out the particular problem that interests him, subscribing, it may be, to some passing or some party orthodoxy, or, like the Anglo-Catholic curate, deducing a solution from the letter of some Master's teaching, is shirking the burden of exercising himself in the more fundamental problems of life, and is therefore atrophying his higher mental powers and arresting his mental growth.

But it is not only the "orthodox" who succumb to the lure of finality. The desire to go to sleep on a formula is

[1] The persecution of heretics has been defended by Catholic apologists on the ground that St. Paul smote Elymas, the sorcerer, with blindness. Could anything be more puerile? Yet this is a fair sample of the kind of argument with which, when great matters are seriously debated, men who subordinate reason to authority delude themselves and try to delude others.

common to all of us, and it is difficult for even the most adventurous of pioneers to resist it. The soporific formula which the lover of finality is in search of is not necessarily a formulated creed. Any conception of life, any theory of things, in which one rests and beyond which one refuses to look, becomes such a formula. The thinker who has worked out for himself a complete system of thought, if he allows that system to dominate his mind, degrades it to the level of a formula, and falling asleep on it forgets that what first set him thinking was his waking dream of ideal truth. Agnosticism itself may easily become a soporific formula,—a negative dogmatism which has allowed its protest against official orthodoxy to develop into hostility to high thinking as such. I know many men who call themselves agnostics. Some of them are merely incurious and indifferent. The rest are for the most part dogmatic materialists at heart. When dogmatism is in the air, it infects the heretic and the sceptic as well as the "faithful"; and as the basis of nonconformity is usually narrower than that of a dominant creed, it frequently happens that the heretic, being better able to concentrate his self-assertive energies, ends by out-dogmatizing the dogmatists whose teaching he repudiates, and becoming more intolerant than the Inquisitors who once sent his kindred to the stake. But it matters little what creed or system, positive or negative, a man may happen to subscribe to. If his subscription to it is final, if he allows himself to rest in it, if he allows it to come between him and the infinite and the ideal, the ideas that inspire it will sooner or later degenerate into lifeless formulas, and the principles of conduct that it countenances, into mechanical rules. Then his faith will have become a pillow to slumber on, instead of a flag to sail under on a never ending voyage of discovery.

The consequent loss to his inner life will not be merely mental. The veto which he imposes on his own reason and on his own intuition, he imposes, of inner necessity, on the reason and the intuition of each of his fellow men. What is true for him, if finally true, must be true for every man. Dissent makes him distrust himself, dispels his dream of finality, disturbs his slumbrous repose. Hence it is that the cult of finality is ever tending to generate intolerance, the most fruitful and most permanent source of the most anti-human of all passions—hatred. Hatred, the passion which, more than any other, separates a man from his kind, imprisons him in himself, and therefore arrests his soul-expansion or spiritual growth, has many sources and takes many forms. But as a rule it is a shortlived passion, violent rather than intense, and is directed towards a particular person or, at most, a particular party, a particular community, or a particular cause. The hatred that intolerance generates is, on the other hand, a fixed attitude of mind which, if pushed to what I may call its logical conclusion, embraces the greater part of one's fellow men, and is capable of attaining to a maximum of intensity which leaves even the violence of the murderer far behind.[1] And this is not all. Intolerance can do worse than generate hatred. The man who hates his fellow men is not wholly detached from them. He still takes an interest in them, an active though perverted interest, and is therefore not wholly shut up in himself. But the lover of finality who, whether as an individual or as a member of a community, has convinced himself that he has proprietary and quasi-exclusive rights in God's truth and God's favour, is isolated and self-centred in the highest conceivable degree. Even his communal sentiment, if, as is probable, he belongs to a particular religious communion, becomes subordinate to, and may at last be absorbed into, his all-consuming egoism. And the smaller the circle of the "elect," the more complete is the self-absorption of each of its members. It is even possible for the intensity of the "believer's" egoism to deliver him from intolerance, but only by killing in his heart all interest, other than what is purely mundane, in his fellow men. Such cases are probably rare; for, as Pascal has said, "La nature soutient la raison impuissante et l'empêche d'extravaguer jusqu'à ce point la." But the man who can find happiness in the prospect of being "saved" while the bulk of his fellow men perish everlastingly, is by no means a rarity; and the logic of intolerance demands that he should be one of many millions.

[1] In support of this statement I appeal to the history of religious persecutions and wars.

But I am straying beyond the proper limits of this chapter. So difficult is it to draw the line between belief and conduct, that in my attempt to show what havoc the cult of finality works in the sphere of belief, I find myself contending that intolerance, the characteristic defect of the dogmatic believer, by ministering to egoism on a high plane and on a great scale, becomes a demoralizing influence of the first magnitude and therefore works serious havoc in the sphere of conduct. The influence of the cult of finality on conduct will be the theme of a later chapter ; and I will therefore return to the sphere of belief.

In the sphere of belief the cult of finality is the chief cause of arrested mental (and moral) growth. It follows that if growth is to be healthy and vigorous, the lure of finality must be strenuously and steadfastly resisted. No creed, no dogma, no theory of things, no conception of life, no assumption, no prejudice must be allowed to dominate the soul. Even the concrete embodiments of belief, the schemes of life, the traditions, the conventions, the customs, by which social life is regulated, must, on occasion, be challenged and asked for their credentials. Whatever belief the soul may be dominated by, whatever theory or sub-theory of things it may accept as final, is sure to crystallize into a formula ; and the soul that finds rest in a formula has missed, or is in danger of missing, its destiny. The seeker for the health which is happiness must therefore, at whatever cost to his own comfort, keep the growing surfaces of his mind, or at least the unfolding tendrils of its leading shoots, fresh and pliant. If he allows them to become indurated, by ceasing to feed them with the sap that rises from his buried life—the sap of critical, speculative, imaginative thought—they will gradually wither and die, and his mind, though it may develop or over-develop itself in this or that direction, will cease to grow as a harmonious whole.

No lesson is so hard to learn as that of renouncing the desire for finality. No lesson, when learnt, so richly rewards the learner. For it gives him the greatest of all rewards, that of allowing him to approach truth eternally without ever reaching it. In doing this it keeps in constant motion the current of intuitional activity which is ever setting from the dark recesses of his buried self towards his more conscious life. It is through a ceaseless influx from the buried into the conscious life that the process of soul-growth is carried on; and it is only by keeping open the channel of communication, by clearing away the dogmas and other prejudices, personal and impersonal, which are ever tending to accumulate and obstruct it, that such an influx can be maintained. The ideal end of belief is intrinsic truth. The truth of things, which is another name for the inner reality of things, is in each of us; and it will gradually invade us (after the manner of silently rising waters) and enfold us and possess us, if we will but give up our vain dream of possessing it. Not that in giving up that dream we are to cease to desire truth. Nay, it is because we desire truth above all things, desire it more than we desire comfort or peace of mind, that we can be content to wait for it to possess us.

A great faith can co-exist with this seemingly agnostic attitude. A great faith, and a great faith alone, can make it possible,—faith in intrinsic reality, the faith that things are what they are, not what we may have concluded them to be, not what we may believe them to be, not what we may even imagine them to be, the faith that

> The world is what it is for all our dust and din.

The pessimist, the man whose faith is bankrupt, may call himself an agnostic; but he is really a negative dogmatist. The positive or affirmative dogmatist may call himself an optimist; but he is really optimistic only for himself and for those who think with him, be they many or few. His optimism does not embrace more than a fraction of mankind. Still less does it embrace the Universe. The faith which does embrace the Universe, which believes—this is its only dogma—that light, self-kindled and self-sustaining, is at the very heart of the Universe, has no choice but to wed itself to silence. In the presence of the unfathomable mystery of self-dependent reality, speech is an impertinence and may readily become a profanation. "I were but little happy," says one of Shakespeare's characters, "if I could say how much." "I had but little faith," says he whose optimism binds him to silence, "if I could say what I believed and why I believed it."

It might be thought that the higher agnosticism would produce a general paralysis of moral and social activity. But there is no reason why it should do so. Nay, there is a weighty reason why it should not. The man whose mind is open, in the sense of being in touch with the infinite,—open, not from apathetic indifference but from devotion to ideal truth,—will always be exposed to the influence of great ideas; and great ideas do not merely illuminate, but also stimulate and inspire. In social life, though he is keenly interested in the problems that challenge him, and though on the plane of speculation he is the freest of free lances, he will cheerfully obey established rules and regulations, so long as this does not involve him in disloyalty to the great ideas that attract him. In nine cases out of ten he will be well content to be one of the majority. The egoistic desire to be always in an unpopular minority will not appeal to him. Yet he will not stand selfishly aloof from the turmoil of political and economic strife. It will be open to him, as to other men, to choose among conflicting ideals, causes, programmes, parties, and the like; and though he will not believe whole-heartedly in any of these, there is no reason why he should not whole-heartedly prefer this ideal, this cause, this programme, this party to any of its rivals; but his detachment, in his inner life, from the din and dust of the arena will make him charitable and tolerant, and he will always respect the opinions of others and try to see things from their points of view. For—above all—he does not regard truth as the monopoly of any school, or sect, or party, as a prize to possess and be proud of possessing. On the contrary: knowing that, if he will resist the lure of finality, the infinite which is in him will gradually reveal itself to his consciousness, he waits serenely for truth to take possession of him. Serenely, but not passively. If he seems to be passive, especially to those who confound activity with fussiness, the reason is that, as a seeker, he is active on a high plane and on a great scale. "Grow, and you will know," is one of the precepts by which he tries to regulate his life. And this precept is balanced by another: " Know, and you will grow." In other words the activity of the pursuit of knowledge is ever merging itself, in his spirit, in the activity of self-directed growth.

Resistance to the lure of finality is not necessarily confined, as I may have seemed to suggest, to the high levels of imaginative thought. Those who have no turn for high thinking, and who find it necessary, as a basis for action, to profess some formulated creed, if they cannot consciously keep open their communications with the infinite, can at least cultivate the virtue of tolerance. They can at least learn, in the sphere of belief, as in other spheres of human activity, to live and let live. If they will do this, their hold on their own creed, which will not cease to guide and inspire them, will gradually relax its rigidity; and they will come sub-consciously into contact with larger and freer truths than those which they consciously profess their faith in.

For, whatever may be the mental calibre of him who resists the lure of finality, if his resistance does nothing else, it does one thing which includes all other things,—it safeguards or tends to safeguard his spiritual freedom. The source of freedom in a man is, as we have seen, the presence of the infinite in his buried life. The man who resists the lure of finality is living in and living to the infinite, and is therefore both using his freedom and winning an ever fuller measure of it. The lover of finality, on the other hand, in shirking the burden of his own infinitude, shirks the high responsibility of freedom, and, by surrendering himself to direction and dictation, sells himself into captivity, the price that he receives from the buyer being the enjoyment of what he miscalls peace of mind. In my chapter on Freedom and Necessity, I spoke of those opposites as the poles of action. And undoubtedly it is with action that we primarily associate them. But the lines of demarcation which we find it convenient to draw are not necessarily respected by Nature; and freedom to act has its counterpart, in the sphere of belief, in freedom to know. The latter freedom is indeed more than the counterpart of the former: it is a vital part of it. Without freedom to know—

to know right from wrong—freedom to act would be so severely restricted, owing to the ever growing need for precise direction and casuistical decision, that it would at last cease to be. So true is this, that it is freedom to know, rather than freedom to act, of which the lover of finality, when he delivers himself into the keeping of embodied authority, first divests himself. In order to do this, he silences his reason, and, by depriving his intuition of the stimulative criticism of reason, impairs its activity, and so suspends, in part at least, his intercourse with his own buried life. He who would live to the infinite will reverse this procedure. By resisting the lure of finality in the sphere of belief, he will strengthen his intuition—the organ of the buried life—and will thus preserve and develop his freedom to know. And he will reap the reward of his self-restraint, not in the sphere of belief only, but also in the sphere of conduct. For, as he passes from belief to conduct, he will find that freedom to know the real from the unreal becomes freedom to know right from wrong, and that intuition takes the familiar form of *Conscience*.

CHAPTER III

GROWTH THROUGH CONSCIENCE

THE principal link between belief and conduct is *conscience*. A man's beliefs about the larger issues of life dominate, or are supposed to dominate, his conscience; and his conscience regulates, or is supposed to regulate, his conduct.

What is conscience? And how does it work? I will first look at the matter from my own point of view. It frequently happens that one has to choose between conflicting motives to action. In such cases one feels the need of enlightenment. As a motive is always an external or apparently external influence transformed into a spiritual force by passing through a personal medium, the choice between conflicting motives is really a choice between the interests of conflicting selves. By what standard of worth are these interests measured? When the lower self comes into collision with the higher, how am I to know which is the lower self and which the higher? The ideal answer to this question is not far to seek. The distinction between higher and lower is of the essence of my nature, and the higher or more spiritual self announces itself as such whenever I allow it to speak. This voice of the higher self is the voice of conscience. The claim put forward by the spiritual side of one's being—the claim to be the true self, to be the central axis of one's existence, to be the main concern of one's life—a claim which adapts itself to every change of circumstance and therefore takes innumerable forms, yet remains unswervingly true to its final aim—which is again and again dishonoured and rejected, yet never relaxes its hold upon us,—this all-pervading and all-controlling claim, this ceaseless effort of the spiritual germ to assert its hidden presence by realizing its hidden life, is in very truth the light which lighteth every man that cometh into the world. The light is in us, not outside us. The end, the aim, the standard, the measure, the guiding lamp, the warning voice, the accuser, the advocate, the witness, the judge,—all are ours. It is because the spiritual pole of the Universe is in me, not actually but potentially, not as a possession or an achievement but as an ideal to be realized or a life to be evolved, that the light of conscience falls freely on the pathway of my days.

When I say this, I am appealing to the everyday experiences of each of us. Nothing is more certain than that in nearly every case of moral indecision (as distinguished from moral perplexity) we know quite well what choice we ought to make ; and nothing is more certain than that the source of our enlightenment is an inward and spiritual pressure, the stress of an authoritative and self-assertive tendency of our nature, which shows us our road by impelling us towards it, yet in the very act of impelling us invests us with freedom to defy its authority and thwart its will. Again, nothing is more certain than that, in yielding to the inward and spiritual pressure which guides and enlightens us, we rise (or seem to rise) above the plane of mechanical necessity and attain to consciousness of freedom, whereas, if we successfully resist the pressure, we begin to forfeit the very freedom which has made our resistance possible. Thus the seemingly paradoxical theory that spiritual freedom is generated by spiritual compulsion is supported by the normal experiences of Humanity, and holds good of the working of conscience not less than of that of will. The more closely we commune with ourselves in our seasons or moments of moral strife, the more clearly do we see that freedom to know is the very counterpart of freedom to act. It is the ceaseless flow of the real or spiritual tendencies of Nature through the channel of human life that gives us liberty ; and it is the self-same movement that gives us light. That we should be able to resist the pressure of those infinite and eternal forces, that we should be able to choose bondage and darkness rather than freedom and light, seems inexplicable until we remind ourselves that the very pressure which emancipates and enlightens us must needs give us freedom to resist itself.

The anomalies and ambiguities for which conscience is sometimes reproached are easily accounted for when looked at from this point of view. In the infinite stream of spiritual evolution there is a central movement, and there are many side currents and surface eddies. The former represents what is vital and essential, the latter what is temporal or local, in human progress. Of the side currents and surface eddies some are in advance of the central stream; others are more or less abreast of it; others lag behind; others again are backwashes and represent an apparently retrograde movement. The genius of a people is one such current; the spirit of an age is another; a particular creed is a third; a particular social ideal is a fourth. The general movement of the mighty river is in a measure the resultant of the various sub-movements. Some of these it will follow in preference to others. Here or there is one which absolutely determines the line of its advance. But, to speak generally, it utilizes and absorbs into itself each and all of these separate efforts. There is no current, however weak or seemingly ineffectual, from which it has not something to learn or gain. Even the vortices, though apparently stationary, and the backwashes, though apparently retrogressive, are in reality borne forward towards the common goal.

This distinction between the central stream and the side or surface currents, between what is catholic and what is sectarian in Nature, must needs reproduce itself in conscience. Some of the rulings of conscience are universally valid. They embody the judgment of the *orbis terrarum*. They are the distilled essence of human experience, the concentrated wisdom of the nations and the ages. To deny their authority is heresy. To depart from their paths is schism. To fall below the level of the morality which they inculcate is to fall below the normal level of human life. There are other rulings of conscience which belong to an epoch or a people, to a class or a profession, to a phase in social progress or a zone of climate, rather than to the world at large. These rulings are not universally valid, though the ordinary man—the man whose ideas are bounded by the horizon of his circumstances—may be pardoned for assuming that they are. Lastly, there are the decisions of conscience which "private interpretation" has helped to frame. The light which is generated by the spiritual energy of Nature must needs take a colour from every medium through which it passes; and the medium of idiosyncrasy varies from man to man.

That all men should be equally enlightened is indeed as little to be looked for as that all men should be equally free. The stream of human evolution is Nature's effort (or one of her many efforts) to realize her own spiritual ideal; and the advance of the stream towards its goal is marked by the outgrowth of spirituality in the life of man. Wherever there is spirituality there is freedom—freedom to act and freedom to know: but the outgrowth of spirituality takes innumerable forms, passes through innumerable stages, and is measured by an infinite scale; and as no two men are in the same stage of spiritual development, so no two men are equally enlightened or equally free. Potentially, all men are equal, for all men are divine: actually, they differ from one another in every conceivable way. Those controlling forces which I have likened to side currents in the great stream of human progress—the spirit of an age, the genius of a people, a particular creed, a particular social ideal, and the rest—may with equal fitness be likened to refracting media through which the pure light of spirituality has to pass on its way to the individual consciousness, media which on the one hand absorb and reflect the light and on the other hand distort and obscure it. These media are many in number and are in a state of perpetual change and flux. They vary from age to age, from place to place, and from man to man: and within the limits of each individual life they vary from period to period, from circumstance to circumstance, and in the last resort (so potent is the reaction of conduct on character) from deed to deed. When men are agreed as to the end to be pursued, they often differ radically as to the means to be taken, and differences of this sort may easily become "conscientious." The knowledge that is demanded for the solution of a moral problem is not moral only, but also intellectual, in the widest sense of the word; and the differences of idiosyncrasy that refract and otherwise modify the illuminating rays of conscience, belong to every stratum of our being, from the most purely spiritual down to the most grossly material What wonder, then, that I should think right what another man thinks wrong, or that I should condemn to-day what I approved of ten years ago? Perhaps the only thing to wonder at is that conscience does not contradict itself more often and more glaringly than it does.

It is worthy of note that when two men conscientiously differ from or even oppose one another in the sphere of moral action, each is aiming at, and each believes in all sincerity that he is doing, what is right. In other words, the light of conscience, however much it may be refracted or otherwise obscured by the media through which it passes, always reveals itself to those who sincerely desire to see it, as light, as the presence of an ideal. The light that makes its way to my consciousness is probably the purest and strongest light that my inward eye is for the time being able to bear; and if I did not believe in its purity I should perhaps be less ready to accept its guidance.

There are times, however, when my power to discern the light—even the refracted light—that lightens me from within, fails me either wholly or in large measure. Then the problems that confront me seem to be insoluble, and my will is paralyzed by the darkness that envelops my path. These cases of genuine moral perplexity are comparatively rare; but if they are unwisely dealt with, they may easily become numerous, so numerous indeed as at last to invade and overrun the larger part of life. When they occur, conscience is on trial, and the education which it has received—for the use which is made of it is its education, good or bad—is put to a searching test.

How ought conscience to be educated? Let us try to get back to first principles. I am assuming that conscience is the realization in consciousness of an inward pressure and an inward light, and that the source of this pressure and this light is the higher nature, the ideal self, the infinite in man; and I have been trying to show that our experiences of the working of conscience bear out this interpretation of it. But it is possible to look at conscience from other points of view. We teach our children that conscience is the voice of God ; and amid all the variations and fluctuations of our teaching this doctrine stands firm. Even the agnostic poet addresses his deity as one

> whom the hours of mortal, moral strife
> Alone aright reveal.[1]

As is the God, so is his voice ; so is his revelation of himself in the hour of moral strife ; so is the nature of that strife. If we worship an inward God, conscience is a voice from within. If we worship an outward God, conscience, though it may seem to come from within, and though in a sense it does and must come from within, is in the main a voice from without. In our terror of the infinite, in our terror of the unknown depths of our own buried life, in our terror of the "hidden God" whose voice is at first a deep silence and whose light is at first a great darkness, we worship Gods of our own creation—Gods who reveal themselves to chosen instruments, who found Churches, who dictate Scriptures, who deliver Laws. This outward God—for though he takes many forms he is one in spirit and essence—speaks to us through his commissioners and delegates, not through our own hearts. His voice is therefore the voice of the finite, the voice which the seeker for finality loves to hear, and which he listens to so reverently and attentively that at last he can hear no other voice, and mistakes it for the voice of his own inmost soul. When this point has been reached, his conscience has lost the freedom which is the proof of its inwardness, and has become enslaved to outward influences,—to the letter of a law, to the text of a scripture, to priestly direction, to casuistical interpretation. And not to these influences only. For as, with the progress of scientific research and critical thought and the consequent enlargement of our conception of Nature, the idea of the Supernatural loses its hold on us, and the object of our worship, though still an outward deity, becomes gradually secularized and even materialized, conscience shares in its

[1] A. H. Clough, *Qui Laborat orat.*

degradation. The man who worships respectability, for example, may be meticulously conscientious in his loyalty to his quasi-divine ideal.

I have said that for him who worships an outward deity conscience is a voice from without. I mean by this that what is really a voice from within—for the ultimate source of conscience is the inner life—is gradually transformed into a voice from without. Transformed beyond recognition,—despiritualized, mechanicalized, fettered, enslaved. For conscience is another name for intuition—intuition at work is a particular sphere of human activity, the sphere of conduct; and what the cult of finality does to intuition in general, it does to conscience in particular,—it forbids it to discharge its proper function, suspends its characteristic activities, atrophies its higher nerve-centres, arrests its spiritual growth.

Let us return to those cases of moral perplexity, in which, as we have seen, the use that has been made of conscience is put to the test. When such cases occur, the lover of the infinite appeals to principles, the lover of finality to rules. This is the first and most obvious difference between them. But there is another difference which goes deeper than this and has an even wider significance. The two differ from one another as regards the occasions of moral perplexity. The lover of the infinite is seldom perplexed about the details of conduct. In dealing with them he relies on his moral intuition, which, being kept healthy and vigorous by constant exercise, acts so rapidly as not to leave him time for perplexity. It is with regard to the larger issues of life, and therefore to the general courses of conduct, that he is sometimes in grave doubt. On such occasions he appeals to principles, not to rules; and as a principle cannot be interpreted except through the medium of a wider and more magisterial principle, in order to resolve his perplexity as to certain large issues of life, he is led on to deal with larger and still larger issues until he comes at last into the presence of the fundamental mysteries of existence. In thus appealing from principle to principle, he uses his intuition under the stimulating control of his reason, and so receives illumination from the only source which he regards as authoritative,—from the infinite in himself, from the depths of his own buried life.

When the lover of finality is involved in moral perplexity, this process is exactly reversed. It is not with regard to the general courses of conduct that he is troubled—these have been mapped out for him by external authority—but with regard to the details, when, as must sometimes happen, new circumstances arise which the rules or directions on which he relies have not provided for and cannot deal with. As a principle cannot be interpreted except through a wider principle, so a rule, *if it be regarded as intrinsically valid*, cannot be interpreted except by the study of its own wording,—of the letter which killeth ; and such an interpretation gives rise to sub-rules and fresh sub-rules, and therefore to an ever-increasing interest in what is meaningless or trivial. For, as conscience deteriorates and the intuition becomes less and less able to function, the occasions of moral perplexity become, of inner necessity, more numerous, more trivial, and less moral. This tendency has been aptly and abundantly illustrated in the legalism of the Pharisees and in the casuistry of the Catholic Church. When the interpreters of the Jewish Law decided that the difference between keeping food warm for the Sabbath in coarse tow and keeping it warm in flax tow was the difference between right and wrong, and when the conscientious Jew accepted such a decision as binding, legalism was reduced to an obvious absurdity,—obvious to the least enlightened of onlookers, obvious to all except to those who were immersed in such trivialities,—and the quest of finality was fittingly rewarded by the descent of the soul into the lowest depths of the infinitesimal.[1] That such a decision should have been seriously given and seriously accepted, that it should not have been instantly laughed out of court, shows that in the doctor of the law and his disciples conscience had died out into ultra-scrupulous conscientiousness, and that the intuition had ceased to work.

[1] The quest of finality is, after all, the quest of what is intrinsically unattainable. No man can find permanent rest in the finite. Our choice lies, though we may not know it, between the infinite proper and the inverted infinite, which we call the infinitesimal. If we will not struggle upwards to the former, we shall have to sink to the level of the latter.

When the moral intuition ceases to work, the lower self finds its opportunity. The degradation of reason which necessarily follows when, divorced from intuition, it is used to elaborate rules of conduct into sub-rules, makes it all too ready to pander to those baser desires and passions which are ever waiting to assert themselves, and which are naturally most active and insurgent when the sense of moral proportion has been lost. In the development of an external morality, a time is sure to come when the votary of the law will devote his ingenuity to keeping the letter of it, while evading or violating the spirit, and when casuistry—whether professionally or privately practised—will become the art of inventing excuses for wrong-doing. It is said that predatory financiers in the United States and elsewhere have lawyers in their pay, whose business it is to enable them to cheat and rob on a large scale without actually transgressing the letter of the law. When conscience, in its dread of the infinite, becomes enslaved to external authority, there is a danger, to say the least, of the lower self playing the part of the predatory financier, and reason the part of the unscrupulous lawyer. It is a danger to which we are all exposed; and the surest safeguard against it is to keep the moral intuition alert and vigorous by exercising it freely—even at the cost of communing, or striving to commune, with the infinite—in regard to the weightier problems of conduct and the larger issues of life.

For, if the wrong way to educate conscience is to fetter it with rules and enslave it to detailed direction, the right way is to allow it to function freely. This means, in the first place, that there must be no limit to the sphere of its activity. I have said that conscience mediates between belief and conduct. If it is to function properly in matters of conduct, it must be allowed to exercise itself freely in matters of belief. For, when it deals with cases of moral perplexity, it works by secret and subconscious methods of its own. What those methods are we cannot say with certainty or precision. But we may be pretty sure that if conscience is healthy and vigorous, it will solve the given problems by applying—instinctively and therefore swiftly and unerringly—principles to rules, and ideas to principles.

For this to be possible, the soul, of which conscience, like mind and will, is a vital aspect, must be in touch with what is ultimate and innermost, and must therefore have successfully resisted, and must still be successfully resisting, the lure of finality. It follows that if conscience is to guide us aright in small as well as in great matters, we must cling tenaciously to the right of private judgment, in great as well as in small matters, recognizing that each of us must use the channel of his own individuality in order to escape from bondage to individualism and egoism, that freedom to know is as sacred a heritage as freedom to act, and that the supreme authority to which conscience owes allegiance is the ultimate source of its own enlightenment—the infinite in man.

This is one aspect of the education of conscience. There is another which is of almost equal importance. If conscience is to function properly in cases of moral perplexity, we must always and unhesitatingly obey its intuitive decisions. For if we disobey them, we shall probably try to find reasons for rejecting them, and in doing so we shall interfere with the secret subconscious methods by which conscience solves the problems that confront it ; and, in interfering with them, we shall tend to derange and disorganize them, with the inevitable result that we shall either paralyze conscience by making it unhealthily self-conscious, or sophisticate and pervert it. The old paradox that if we would know the will of God we must do it, is the expression of a profound and vital truth. The very constitution of our being tells us so much about our duty and destiny that, if we will but follow its implicit guidance, it will not fail to tell us more and more. The theory of life that is incarnate in each of us resolves itself into a single precept : "Turn towards the light that is in you." This precept is as easy to understand as it is hard to obey. Obey it, begin by obeying it, and you will learn what it means and to what goal it will eventually lead you. Set your face in the right direction, look towards the magnetic pole of your being,—the pole that permanently attracts those desires and instincts which you feel to be higher than the rest. Do this, and you have already entered the path of duty. Keep on doing this, and every moral problem will solve itself as you proceed. It is the desire for ideal good, the desire to live to and for and in the infinite, which makes you ask for enlightenment; but the desire will itself enlighten you if you will but yield yourself to its guidance, for the man who desires strongly has already in some sort discerned his goal.

It will perhaps be contended that the sense of duty is an essential element in conscience, and that the sense of duty is the sense of obligation towards what is outside oneself. That there is a vital connexion between conscience and duty goes without saying; but it is through the medium of spiritual freedom, not of bondage to external authority, that the connexion is maintained. When the interests and inclinations of the lower self collide with those of the higher, the latter (as we have seen) asserts itself to be higher by making us *feel* that its desires and impulses are superior to those of the lower self, superior in ideal worth if not in actual strength, superior in ideal worth and therefore, in spite of all appearances to the contrary, superior also in actual strength. This is a two-fold feeling. On the one hand there is the feeling of being warned and directed and guided. When this feeling predominates, we say that we are obeying the voice of conscience. On the other hand there is the sense of latent compulsion, the feeling that pressure is being put upon us by an inward and spiritual power. When this feeling predominates, we say that we are acting from a sense of duty.

The truth is that freedom (of both kinds) and duty are absolutely inseparable. Freedom, divorced from duty, is not freedom, but lawless and aimless licence. Duty, divorced from freedom, is not duty, but the despotism of material force. The sense of duty, like the sense of freedom, is a sense of inward and spiritual pressure, combined with a sense of exemption from external control. When we use the word *freedom*, we dwell on the sense of exemption rather than on the sense of pressure. When we use the word *duty*, we dwell on the sense of pressure rather than on the sense of exemption. But neither sense can exist apart from the other: or rather each sense is of the very essence of the other. When I say that I have a sense of duty, I mean that I am conscious of a claim being made upon me, a lawful claim which I cannot resist by any but violent or quasi-material means,—a claim the very enforcement of which is a source of spiritual freedom, in that it disdains to enforce itself by any but spiritual means, and so leaves me free (the paradox is unavoidable) either by resisting it to forfeit freedom, or by meeting it to win freedom, the very freedom by which alone it can be met. And I am conscious, further, that the claim upon me is made by myself, by what is highest and most real in *me*. My sense of duty is the sense of pressure put upon me by the infinite in me, by my own ideal self. The sense of pressure is present because the attraction of the infinite is a real *force*. The sense of freedom is present because the ideal self is the real *I* and because action which is initiated by *me*, the real *me*, is necessarily free. Indeed I am never really free except when I yield to the pressure of my ideal self; for in yielding to that pressure I allow the true self to energize; and then for a moment it is *I*, the real I, wholly self-constrained and therefore wholly free, who act.

Freedom, Conscience, Duty,—it matters little which of these names we use when we try to find words for that singular experience, that feeling of being at once coerced and free (the coercion being the very source of the freedom) which is the central feature of man's moral nature. The experience must be taken as given. To construct it *a priori* is as impossible as to disprove it on *a priori* grounds. Arguments against it which are drawn from lower levels of experience fall to the ground when confronted by a feeling whose very presence in our hearts is a call to us to lift our thoughts and our theories on to higher levels of experience, and to widen the whole horizon of our minds. If we wish to account for the feeling, we must ask it to help us to construct a theory of things in which a fitting place will be found for it. Whether we are conscious of its help or not matters little. That a sense of compulsion should have a sense of freedom as its other self is inexplicable except on one hypothesis, namely, that the forces which constrain my inner life—unlike the material forces which act upon me from without—are my own, in the sense of belonging to what is real, though perhaps as yet unrealized, in *me*. The latent pressure of this hypothesis on my thoughts was no doubt the chief factor in the evolution of that paramount theory of things which I have been trying to expound, and in the light of which I can now see a meaning in the central paradox of man's inner life. The Universe, as it seems to me, is an infinite process from and to the ideal goal of spiritual perfection. The life of man is one of the channels through which the ocean river of cosmic energy takes its appointed course. This stream of Nature's central forces through the life of man in the direction of a goal which is hers and his—hers in that it is the real or positive pole of her being and therefore the magnetic pole of all her desires and efforts, his in that it dwells in every man as an infinitely distant yet ever present ideal—this flow of spiritual energy reveals itself as Freedom, whenever the pressure that it exerts is realized as originating in man's own ideal (and therefore real) self; as Conscience, whenever the pressure is realized as guidance and stimulus from within; as Duty, whenever the pressure is realized as the advancement and enforcement by a high authority of an incontrovertible claim. In other words, that compulsion from within which reveals itself to me, now as a sense of moral obligation, now as a warning, a guiding, and an inspiring voice, is the only source of the only freedom which is worth dying—and living—for, the freedom which is the counterpart of life.

CHAPTER IV

GROWTH THROUGH CONDUCT

A. The Aim

THE pressure of the central tendencies of Nature (in and through their efforts to realize themselves) on the individual life and personality generates the sense of duty, with all that duty implies. The being of Nature is an eternal struggle, and that struggle re-enacts itself in each of us. There is, however, a change, as we pass from the larger to the lesser stage,—a change from destiny to duty, from *is* to *ought,* from might to right. By generating the sense of duty, Nature makes each of us, in the region of "free conscious action," the instrument of her will. The tendency that is winning presents itself to consciousness as the tendency that ought to win. When we say that we ought to do so and so, we mean that we are biased in favour of such and such a course of action, that our sympathies are enlisted in behalf of such and such a cause. And it is by setting up in our minds a bias in its own favour, by enlisting our sympathies in its own behalf, that the tendency which is winning ensures its ultimate triumph and proves its inherent strength.

Destiny determines duty. The real tendencies of Nature are the well-springs of the ideal. The flow of the stream of cosmic energy through the channels of the human soul gives a central aim and purpose to each individual life. To become conscious of this central aim and purpose is wisdom : to co-operate with it is goodness. Let us ask ourselves what it is.

When we say that destiny determines duty we have given our first answer to this question. Just as what I do believe in the secret recesses of my heart coincides with what I ought to believe, so what I am doing (what is being done in me, for me, and through me) in the depths of my buried life coincides with what I ought to do. The real movement of Nature, the movement towards her own ideal, which is carried on in me and in each of my fellow men, not merely determines but may even be said to constitute the central aim and purpose of my life.

I have given my reasons for thinking that the real movement of Nature is a spiritual movement and that the ideal of Nature is pure spirituality. If this is so, the duty of man is to spiritualize himself, to aim at spiritual perfection. This is the goal towards which we are all being carried, with or without the consent of our foresight and our will. It is for us to decide whether we shall swim with or against the current of our destiny, a current which is strong enough to sweep us towards its own goal even when we seem to be stemming its waters. To swim with it, to co-operate with the forces that are making for the evolution of our spiritual nature, is, for obvious reasons, our wisdom, our duty, and (in the truest sense of the word) our happiness.

But what do we mean by spiritual perfection ? It is well that we should ask ourselves this question. In the idea of spirituality there are many pitfalls. Associations cling to the word which are ever tending to narrow, degrade, and emasculate our interpretation of it. Let us, then, get rid of these by going back to what is elementary and abstract in our usage of it. We have seen that the path of synthesis takes us in the direction of what is spiritual, and the path of analysis in the direction of what is material; and we have inferred from this that pure spirit—the spiritual pole of existence—is the supreme and all-inclusive reality, the last term in Nature's infinite "series," and the term in which all other terms are at once transcended and summed up. We have seen, in other words, that the idea of spirituality is the resultant of two fundamental conceptions. For we may think of the last term in the cosmic series as transcending all the other terms, as rising (in the loneliness of its perfection) above their lower and grosser levels of existence—in a word, as being absolutely *pure*. Or we may think of it as summing up all the other terms, as absorbing them into itself, as being the principle of unity in their multiplicity and diversity—in a word, as being absolutely *whole*. These two conceptions—purity and wholeness, spirituality proper (as, in deference to popular usage, we may perhaps call it) and all-embracing reality—are the divergent sub-ideas, of which the central idea of spirituality (in the widest and deepest sense of the word) is the resultant. It is in the highest degree important (as we shall presently see) that each of these conceptions should at all times balance, limit, and support the other.

This interpretation of the word *spiritual* throws a penetrating light on the problem which we are trying to solve. To spiritualize his being is the first and last duty of man; and to spiritualize one's being is something more than to refine and purify it; it is also, and above all, to universalize it, to expand it till it becomes commensurate with the highest and widest of all communities, till it becomes one with the totality of things, one with the world-soul, one with God It is towards the light of this infinitely distant ideal that man does and must set his face.

This conclusion, which my mind, in its speculative orbit, has already touched, but to which it now returns, with a clearer consciousness of the part that it has to play and a fuller realization of its meaning, is something more than a quasi-logical inference from metaphysical premises. The deepest experiences of the soul bear it out. The desire for re-union with God is the central feature of that mystical (spiritually mystical) element in religion, which dogmatism, with its instinctive antipathy to whatever is natural, spontaneous, and spiritual, has always either frowned upon or ignored, but which has been the very life and soul of every living creed. "To become one spirit with God" is the master desire of the Christian mystic, whatever may be the church or sect to which he happens to belong; and though this fervent dream far transcends the normal scope of Christian thought and feeling, the significant fact remains that the cardinal doctrine of Christianity is the expression in a quasi-concrete form of the idea that the soul of man is potentially commensurate and even identical with the soul of God. In the Far East the desire for re-union with God is more widely diffused and more openly professed than in

Christendom, and has a more pantheistic flavour, manifesting itself for the most part as a longing for re-absorption into the living Whole. Whatever form the desire may take, it is sure to be scoffed at by " common sense " and radically misinterpreted by popular thought. The idea that underlies it is so essentially inward and spiritual that the mind which thinks (as most minds do) in pictures and images, must needs turn it into nonsense before it has begun to criticize it. Even Tennyson, one of the most imaginative of poets, was not imaginative enough to do justice to this grandly mystical idea. For him, as for most of us, absorption into the living Whole implied the loss of consciousness and the destruction of personality.[1] In reality it implies the exact opposite of each of these. It implies a development—an expansion and illumination—of consciousness, which carries it far beyond the horizon of our thought ; and it implies the finding of the real self, which is impersonal indeed, but only in the sense that it is the very fountain-head of personality.

It is because popular thought separates God from Nature and from Man, that it regards re-union with the divine as intrinsically impossible ; and it is because it identifies the Cosmos with the visible universe that it shrinks from a destiny which it regards as but one degree removed from annihilation. It is not until the Cosmos has been first spiritualized and then deified, that the inward meaning of the desire for re-union with it can disclose itself to human thought. I am, *quâ* body, a part of the material universe, but in no sense one with it. On the contrary, all of it that is outside my body is a vast "Not-myself" ; my consciousness severs me from it. Inclusion in a whole is an entirely different thing from oneness with it. If I am but a drop in the wide ocean of being, my life is distinct both from the lives of all other drops and from the life of the ocean as a whole. We must dismiss from our minds all mathematical and mechanical notions and all material

[1] That each, who seems a separate whole,
Should move his rounds, and fusing all
The skirts of self again, shall fall
Remerging in the general soul,

Is faith as vague as all unsweet !
In Memoriam.

images when we ponder on the spiritual mystery of re-absorption into the divine life. If I am to become one with the Universe, I must become one with it *quâ* soul. I must expand my being till it becomes identical and commensurate with the essence of all things. I must absorb the divine soul into mine as truly as my soul is absorbed into the divine. I must make the All-consciousness my own.

An infinitely distant goal this, and one which, though eternally approachable, is also eternally unattainable. Yet nothing less than this can content me as the ideal end of my existence. And it is only in making this goal the ideal end of my existence that I can see a meaning in that cosmic circle of being in which I have already professed my faith. As each wave of effluent life completes its infinite movement, it streams back to its divine source, not as a mere refluent wave of vital energy, but as a host of godlike souls. This is the fundamental miracle of existence, that the One life becomes Many, and in the fulness of time (or of eternity) lifts each of the many lives to the unimaginable level of its own purity and perfection.

If, then, the spirit of man is to fulfil its destiny, it must labour unceasingly to widen the sphere of its vision, to enlarge the scope of its energies, to develop all its powers, to deepen all its depths, to exalt all its heights, so that at last, "at infinity," it may be able to share in the divine consciousness, and to merge its being—to lose itself and to find itself—in the divine life.

What is the way to this ideal end? The time has come for us to prepare for a descent into the sphere of practical life, of conduct. We have studied the problem of growth in the sphere of belief. We are now in the borderland between belief and conduct. We have come to the confines of that borderland, and we must be prepared to leave it. When I ask how the process of soul-growth is to be carried on, I am thinking, now and henceforth, of growth through conduct.

We have seen that the end of the process of soul-growth is spiritual perfection,—another name for which is union or re-union with God; and we have also seen that the idea of spirituality is the resultant of two fundamental conceptions, "spirituality proper" (by which we mean absolute immateriality or transcendent purity) and "all-embracing reality." Here we have two distinct ways of thinking about God, the spiritual pole of the Universe; and it is well that we should think about God, when we are about to pass from belief to conduct, for duty to man, which is so large an element in conduct, is regulated, in the last resort, by one's conception of duty to God.

The two ways of thinking about God are really one, in the sense that neither discloses its true meaning until it has merged itself in the other; but we shall find it convenient, at any rate in the first instance, to regard them as two. We will begin, then, by giving two rival answers to the question which we have asked ourselves; and when we have set forth each answer and exposed its inadequacy, we shall perhaps be able to bring the two together and fuse them into a higher truth.

Let us first think of God as pure spirituality, in the narrower sense of the latter word. If God is pure spirituality, and if union with God is man's destiny, it stands to reason that it is man's duty to lead a purely spiritual life. How is this to be done? As a matter of fact each of us is at any given moment leading many lives—the animal life, the domestic life, the social life, the business life, the professional life, the artistic life, the literary life, the scientific life, the political life, and so forth. Each of these lives is so varied and complex and has so many sub-lives dependent on it that the environment, even of the average man, seethes and surges with the cross currents of a thousand aims, interests, pursuits, and pleasures. That being so, a new question arises: Are not these lives and sub-lives, these aims, interests, pursuits, and pleasures so many hindrances to and distractions from the true Godward life, the life of "pure spirituality"? Ought not one to turn one's back on these lower and lesser lives, to renounce them, to die to them? In fine, is not the path that leads through self-denial to inward and spiritual aspiration and effort the only way of safety for the soul that seeks to be "saved"?

A logical process, which is vital rather than formal, and which is based, in part at least, on the popular confusion between spirituality and immateriality, has led many men to answer " yes " to this question. The ascetic ideal has a strong, though intermittent, fascination for the human spirit ; and the corresponding life, the life of holiness or saintliness, the life which holds itself aloof from "the world," has won for itself, from men who do not attempt to lead it, a degree of almost superstitious reverence which no student of human nature can afford to ignore.

Yet the inadequacy of the ascetic ideal is too patent to need demonstration. The form which asceticism takes is, as a rule, that of monasticism, the withdrawal of the ascetic into a communal life which keeps him entirely aloof from the world. In India the wandering ascetic takes the place of the monk. And where Puritanism survives, the ascetic, though otherwise withdrawn from the world, is allowed to live the lives of domesticity and " business " and is not expected to mortify his flesh. Were the monastic ideal widely and consistently pursued, the secular activity of what we call the civilized world would be almost entirely suspended, and the life of man on earth would come to an abrupt end. But, apart from these practical objections to what is undoubtedly the most popular form of asceticism, it is easy to see that, even as an ideal for the individual soul, the ascetic life is fatally defective, that in spite of its consuming zeal for spirituality, its spiritual merits are small. Each of the many lives which ordinary men are doomed to lead and content to lead has its counterpart in an environing " world." Thus there is the world of the senses, the world of the domestic affections, the social world, the professional world, the world of business, of art, of letters, of knowledge, of public action. If each of the corresponding lives is to be renounced by the man who is seeking after God, does it not follow that each of these worlds is destitute of God's presence ? Where, then, is God to be found ? In the " abysmal deeps " of one's own soul ? But what is left of the soul when self after self (for each environing world centres in a separate self) has been cast aside as a mere "body of death" ? What will be the issue of this process, of this progressive denaturalizing of the spiritual world and despiritualizing of Nature? Will not God at last be driven away from the world which he animates and sustains,—driven beyond the horizon of human experience, beyond the "flaming walls" of the environing Universe? Will not the God whom the "saint" seeks after prove to be the visionary ruler of a phantom world? And what shall we say of the life that is devoted to the pursuit of this illusion? Can the powers of the soul grow to maturity in a vacuum? Is it "goodness" to be destitute of human sympathy, to have stifled natural affection, to let one's talents and energies rust in disuse, to be blind to the wonder and glory and beauty of Nature, to be insensible to the magic of art and song, to be indifferent to the progress of knowledge and the evolution of thought? If these negative virtues, each of which tends in its own way to restrict the scope of man's life and to narrow or rather to mutilate his soul,—if these constitute "saintliness," and if soul-expansion is the ideal end of human action, can we say that the saint—be he a Trappist monk, a sanctimonious Puritan, or an Oriental ascetic—is leading the ideal life?

Let us now ask ourselves what form the growth of the soul is likely to take in the life of one who thinks of God, not as pure spirituality, but as all-inclusive reality, as all-sustaining energy, as the All of Being, as the living Whole. For such a mind the goal of soul-growth—oneness with God—seems to be comparatively easy of access. It is the destiny of each of us to live many lives, to have his being in many worlds, to adjust the respective aims and claims of many selves. One has but to live each of these many lives freely and fully (so the pantheist instinctively argues) in order to find the God whose presence illuminates each of these many worlds, and in finding him to realize the divine potencies of one's own many-sided self. The merits of this pantheistic conception of life must not be made light of; and the sweeping condemnation which holiness is apt to pass on the resultant manner of living must be regarded as the outcome of a narrow mind and an unsympathetic heart. The atmosphere of freedom with which the soul that has a large outlook on life surrounds itself is eminently favourable to growth; and the tolerance, the good-humour, the breadth of sympathy, the far-reaching interest in things, which the life of vivid and varied experience tends to generate, are probably quite as near to the true centre of gravity of human life, to the " Kingdom of God," as are the purity, austerity, and singleness of heart of the ascetic saint.

Quite as near—but no nearer. The defects of the life that is based on self-indulgence (even in the widest sense of the word) are as real and as fatal to soul-expansion as are the defects of the life that is based on ascetic self-denial. The man who sees God in each of the many worlds that surround him, and who, having ceased to conceive of God as a spiritual ideal, has lost his standard of comparison, will tend to regard all the worlds, all the spheres of activity, as equally divine, and will end by losing sight of the primary distinction between higher and lower, between real and unreal, between right and wrong. That such a conception of life is fatal to the pursuit of an ideal, fatal to self-culture, fatal to soul-growth ; that it tends to unweave the fabric of man's higher life and transform the cosmos which his spirit is slowly evolving into a formless chaos ; that it tends to degrade the divine from the highest summit of the soul's aspiring dreams to the lowest level of the actual,—is a self-evident truth which I need not take pains to demonstrate.

But the more directly practical consequences of the pantheistic hypothesis are so grave and their ulterior tendency is so disastrous, that I must be allowed to try to forecast them. When the distinction between right and wrong is deliberately ignored, a view of life begins to prevail which is at first simply non-moral, but gradually, under the stress of subtle spiritual forces, becomes immoral and even defiantly anti-moral. The attempt of the pantheist to live freely and fully in each of the many worlds that surround him—to live as freely and as fully in this world as in that —is foredoomed to failure, for the obvious reason that the various worlds are more or less in competition with one another, and therefore will not allow him to divide himself impartially among them. Whatever view of life we may take, we must admit that, as a matter of plain experience, we are again and again called upon to choose between conflicting motives to action. In such crises the soul that regards all courses of action as equally right will be apt, in the absence of a guiding principle, to yield to the pressure of momentary desires and impulses, the strength of which, when the counter-influence of a moral ideal has been withdrawn, may well become irresistible. If every desire and every impulse is divine, the grosser desires and baser impulses have as strong claims upon us as those which come from higher and purer sources. Let this be admitted ; and the grosser desires and baser impulses will speedily develop an energy so cyclonic as to sweep away all moral restraints and in the end to obliterate all moral landmarks. The practical value of principle in the region of conduct lies in this, that it opposes a constant and permanent resistance to the short-lived violence of lust and passion, and so sustains the soul until the tempests that assail it have worn themselves out and died away. In the life that is wholly destitute of principle there is a serious danger lest might, the mere quasi-physical might of the passing desire or impulse, should become the sole measure of right. Were this to happen, a new principle of action, a perverted and anti-moral principle, would have been introduced into human life. It may be doubted if any life can be carried on for long without the support and guidance of principles. If moral principles are openly disavowed, the very absence of principle—the conscious acceptance of the impulse of the moment as authoritative—will itself become a principle of action, a demoralizing principle which will disorganize human life and make at last for the degeneration, the living death of the soul. The man who has got to regard good and evil as virtually interchangeable terms will sooner or later pass beyond the point of perfect neutrality—a point at which no one can rest for more than a moment—and restore the distinction between good and evil, but in an inverted form. The spiritual influences which denounce and resist the aggressive claims of lust and passion and selfishness will become the object, not of the tolerance which his philosophy ought to extend to them, but of his active antipathy. Having begun by saying that evil (or what passes for such) is no worse than good, and good no better than evil, he will go on to say : " Evil, be thou my good."

As each of these one-sided conceptions of life has proved a practical failure, we must now bring them together in order that they may combine their respective merits and correct each other's defects. We have deduced our ethics from our theology. The former having failed to satisfy us, we must go back to the latter and endeavour to purify the springs of action at their fountain head. We must begin by reminding ourselves that the seemingly divergent conceptions of God which we have found it convenient to regard as two are virtually and essentially one, that neither of them is what it really is or means what it really means, so long as it is divorced from the other. Pure spirituality and all-embracing reality are one and the same thing. The actual world of which we have experience may possibly be a mere phase or aspect—one among many—of the actual Universe. But, whatever may be its limits or dimensions, "it is our all"; and to seek God apart from it or beyond it is to reduce both it and him to non-existence. It is not by emptying the actual world of its substance that we arrive at spirituality. It is by informing the actual world with all that is truly substantial (in the proper sense of the word) —with life, with soul, with unity, with reality. The actual, divorced from the spiritual, is a chaos of "jarring atoms"; an infinity of virtual nothingness. The spiritual, divorced from the actual, is a pure illusion, a mere figment of speculative thought. The imaginative mind is apt to think of pure spirit as either an empty metaphysical abstraction or a highly volatilized cosmic essence. It is neither of these: it is the most concrete, the most substantial of all realities. The spiritual is the life, the soul, the unity, the totality of the actual. If it is not this, it is null and void. We must seek for it in the actual, or give up our quest. But in seeking for it in the actual, in pursuing it through all the details of life as a realizable though infinitely distant ideal, we gradually transform the actual into the real. The synthetic processes which are evolving the spirituality or vital unity of Nature, are making the actual what it really is. The intuitive faculties which discern the spirituality of Nature reveal the actual as it really is. In the supreme synthesis which men call God, the actual—the all-embracing totality of things—becomes (we must needs believe) both purely spiritual and absolutely real.

If this conception of God is to find appropriate expression in the sphere of moral action, the two theories of life which we have set forth and criticized must be combined by some quasi-chemical process into a new theory of life, larger, saner, and more harmonious than either of its component parts. The ideal of spiritual purity and perfection must be steadily pursued; this is the beginning of wisdom and of virtue. But it must be pursued through the environing medium of the actual. In this way and in no other can we give substance and reality, meaning and purpose, to what would otherwise be the vainest and most illusive of quests. We must count nothing in Nature as common or unclean. The worlds that surround us are all illuminated, *each in its own manner and degree*, by the light of God's presence. We must therefore try to live freely and fully in each and all of these, as freely and as fully as is compatible with the due recognition of their respective degrees of dignity and worth. But if we wish to arrange them in their natural order, we must apply to them, each and all, the one infallible test with which Nature has equipped us. Whether we consciously pursue an ideal or not, we must, if we wish to live wisely and well, again and again make our choice between conflicting motives. In these seasons of inward strife we must either have recourse to our dream of spiritual perfection and subordinate all motives to this one paramount aim, or we must allow might—the might of each momentary impulse—to become the measure of right. Our more immediate motives, however many and various they may be, will all, in the last resort, come under the control of one or other of these competing principles of action. Thirst for the ideal is, whether we realize its influence or not, the suzerain motive of our lives. This "master-presence," this haunting vision of spiritual perfection, will itself (if we allow it to have its will) arrange, by reference to itself—arrange in order of natural worth and intrinsic reality—the various lives that we lead, the various worlds that environ us, the various desires, aims, and interests that compete for our favour, the various motives to action among which we are called upon to choose. Armed with the clue of faith in the ideal, the soul can find its way through all the mazes of the actual. Deprived of this master clue, it has no sense of scale and no standard of value; and in its attempts to order its goings, it will infallibly lose itself in what has become, for it, the most bewildering of labyrinths.

To the question "How is soul-growth to be achieved?" we can now answer "By the pursuit of the ideal—the ideal of spiritual perfection—in and through a vivid and varied life in the actual."

The thesis of this book is that happiness is the concomitant of "healthy and harmonious growth." The conclusion which I have just reached throws light on the part which the word "harmonious" plays in this formula. The growth of a thing is always carried on in all the "dimensions" of the world to which the thing belongs. In this outward and visible world from which all our similes are drawn, there are three spatial dimensions; but when we talk about the growth of material things, we find it convenient to let two of these dimensions coalesce into one. A tree, for example, which, in virtue of its majesty and beauty, may be regarded as a fit symbol of the growing or expanding soul, is said to grow in two dimensions only,—upwardness and outwardness, height and girth. In the tree that grows naturally, healthily, and under the most favourable conditions, there is (or, at any rate, there may be supposed to be) a perfect harmony between the two modes of growth. When trees are planted close together, their upward growth is fostered at the expense of their outward. When trees are "pollarded," their outward growth is fostered at the expense of their upward. The mast-like growth of the former type is as far removed from the symmetry and beauty of a harmoniously developed tree as is the bush-like growth of the latter. It is the same with the soul. The healthy soul is one which grows strongly upward and strongly outward, and maintains, on the whole and in the long run, a progressive balance between the two modes of growth. This balance is of the very essence of the soul's life and health. Each mode of growth must be carried on, not only for its own sake, but also for the sake of the other. Unless the soul grows steadily upward, its outward growth, besides being unsymmetrical and otherwise unlovely, will neither be varied nor full. The ideal, and the ideal alone, gives to the various lives that man leads their proper values; and unless each life has its proper value assigned to it, unless each branch takes its due direction and grows with its due degree of strength and luxuriance, it will impede or be impeded by the growth of other branches, its output of twigs and leaves will be either excessive or defective, and the general lateral growth of the tree will be confused, inharmonious, and unproductive. So, too, unless the growth of the tree in girth—a growth which carries branch-growth with it—is duly proportioned to its growth in height, the tree will not ascend in safety, except while it remains in the cloistered shade of its woodland life. Transplanted into the open—and sooner or later every soul must breathe the air of spiritual freedom or give up the business of growing—the soul that has made no branch-growth, except at the top of its stem, where branch-growth produces top-heaviness, will probably fall a victim to one of the many storms that are waiting to assail it; its morbidly narrow idealism will expose it to reactionary influences which may well level it to the very ground; and it is even possible that in the end its loss of an ideal will be as complete as its pursuit of an ideal was fanatical and uncharitable. The soul that combines outward with upward growth will ascend at last to higher levels of spirituality than the soul that thinks of nothing but ascending, and neglects, after each fresh upward effort, to widen the basis of its growth. In the soul that is growing symmetrically and productively, the steadfast ascent towards the ideal, towards what is at once central and supreme, is carried on quite as much through the lateral development of the branches—each developing itself in due subordination to and in due harmony with the growth of the whole tree—as in the vertical development of the stem. The maintenance of a balance between the two modes of growth is quite as important as the maintenance in each dimension of a vigorous habit of growth. Indeed, without the maintenance of the balance, vigorous growth in either dimension is impossible.

Soul-expansion, then, or soul-growth, is a continuous

movement of the soul in the two dimensions of upwardness, or inward and spiritual aspiration, and outwardness, or many-sided interest and sympathy. Each mode of growth should be as vigorous and as persistent as is compatible with the vigour and the persistence of the other; and it is by duly and permanently maintaining the balance between the two modes of growth, that the full development and final triumph of each is assured.

CHAPTER V

GROWTH THROUGH CONDUCT

B. The Way

IT is in the sphere of Conduct that ordinary men—men who are unintellectual and unimaginative, men who have no turn for high thinking or cosmic feeling—make or unmake their souls. For such persons the battle that is being waged in the sphere of belief is of vital interest, but chiefly because in that sphere and in the course of that battle *ideas* are formed and transformed, and because ideas, through their control, first of belief and then of conduct, rule the world. But it is not to the ordinary man only that the sphere of conduct offers the choice between life and death. For the more exceptional man, the man who has a turn for high thinking and cosmic feeling, the sphere of conduct has a twofold interest and a twofold meaning. Through the reaction of his conduct on his character the thinker, as we may call him—and after all there is something of the thinker in each of us—makes or unmakes his own soul; and through the reaction of his conduct on his whole attitude towards life, and therefore on his ideas, he helps to make or unmake the soul of others.

In the sphere of conduct the desire for finality which is generated by our instinctive dread of the infinite, takes the deadliest of all forms. If it is bad for a man to find rest in a formula, or a rule, it is far worse for him—it is death itself, or at least the beginning of death—to find rest in his own undeveloped self. The man who finds, or tries to find, rest in his own self, whatever form his cult of finality may take, is an egoist; and egoism is the beginning and end of immorality. That the conception of the meaning and purpose of life for which I am pleading is borne out by the collective experience of mankind, seems to be proved by one significant fact. If we examine our unwritten codes of moral law, we shall find that in each and all of them whatever is accounted evil—be it a desire, an act, a quality, or a habit—tends either to contract the soul or (at best) to arrest its growth.

Let us start with the ordinary self and ask ourselves how its various vices and moral weaknesses react upon it. Let us first consider those which are commonly regarded as the lowest and grossest,—incontinence, intemperance (in food and drink), indulgence in drugs, uncontrollable anger, the lust of cruelty, and the like. All these "war against the soul." In other words, they tend to degrade it to the level of its own animal plane of existence. This they do in two ways. They set up in the soul affinities for material ends and objects, and so drag it back into the mire (for mire it is until it has been transfigured and spiritualized) out of which it is ever struggling to emerge. And they bind the soul in the iron chains of immutable habit, thereby depriving it of freedom, which, as we have seen, is the very counterpart of spirituality and therefore one of the vital conditions of spiritual development. Thus they not merely hinder the soul from growing but they actually reverse the process of its growth,—contract it, degrade it, unweave the fabric of its higher self.

Next to these carnal vices come the moral failings which are generated by petty egoism,—vanity, self-conceit, self-importance, self-will, envy, jealousy, malice, slander, and other forms of uncharitableness. By petty egoism I mean that attitude towards life which reflects the reluctance of the soul to meet the demands that self-development makes on its energy and devotion, and its consequent attempt to find a substitute for self-development in self-assertion. When a man loves himself (as it is but right that he should do) and yet will not take the trouble to earn self-love by self-development, he must needs try to persuade himself that his actual, undeveloped, self-centred self is worthy of a sentiment which is really his initial response to the call of the ideal self. With this end in view, he must, if possible, get others to think well of him, or at least to think much of him, and so provide him with an antidote to his own secret self-distrust. He must try to bulk large in the eyes of his neighbours, to impose himself upon them, to assert himself against them, to bend them to his will, to exalt himself at their expense, to get himself talked about, to make himself envied, applauded, followed, imitated. The sphere of his influence may be a very narrow one, but it will probably be large enough for his purpose. If he can but be the centre of a circle, it matters little how small that circle is. In his desire to push himself to the centre, or to what he conceives to be the centre, he necessarily disregards the rights and interests, the feelings and susceptibilities of others, and so sets up a habit of selfishness which at last becomes his second nature. But the real source of his moral failings lies deeper than men suspect. From first to last his life is based on self-deception. When his secret doubts have at last been silenced, when his secret self-distrust has been removed, when he has convinced himself that his ordinary self is worthy of the high esteem in which he desires to hold it, worthy of the love which really belongs to his ideal self,—then the process of soul-growth has been arrested, and degeneration of his moral tissue has set in.

There is a third group of vices which is the outcome of egoism working more boldly, more aggressively, and on a larger scale. The desires for wealth, for power, for position, for fame, lead men to practise every kind of injustice and unkindness towards their fellow-men, to oppress them, cheat them, rob them, ruin them. And these desires are all generated by the effort to aggrandize the ordinary self instead of expanding it, to enrich it with the accessories of life instead of with life itself. The soul in which covetousness and ambition—vices which have ever deluged the world with blood and darkened it with misery—flourish most vigorously is one in which self-love, though strong and insatiable, has been entirely divorced from spiritual aspiration. The effect of these vices on the soul that harbours them is, on the one hand, to destroy its sense of proportion and its standard of reality, and at last to materialize and externalize its whole outlook on life,—and, on the other hand, to make it more and more self-centred, till at last it is drawn by an irresistible current into the bottomless vortex of its own ever-narrowing self. Consciously, we condemn these anti-social vices because of the ruin and woe that they work among men. Unconsciously, we condemn them because they harden, debase, contract, and warp the soul.

There are other evil tendencies which are compatible with a comparatively high degree of spiritual development. It is possible to be proof against all the solicitations of sensual desire, to rise superior to every form of petty egoism, to despise wealth and power and fame, to have successfully practised self-control and self-culture, and yet to be possessed by demons of pride and hatred. In these vices resistance to the centripetal tendencies of Nature starts from a far higher level than in any other: for that very reason it is stronger, more effective, and more injurious to the soul that practises it. The last, the highest, the most spiritual, the most deadly of all forms of iniquity—pride, and the hatred which pride engenders—are the products of an intense and far-seeing individualism; the fruits of a soul in which dread of the infinite has changed into abhorrence of the infinite, and which is therefore ready to spiritualize itself in order that it may meet with their own weapons the spiritual influences which it fears and detests,—ready to go far along the road of self-expansion in order that it may strengthen itself to resist the higher expansive forces which must sooner or later be brought to bear upon it, in order that by setting these at defiance it may separate itself—in the madness of its self-exaltation—separate itself fully, finally, and irretrievably, from the soul of the Universe, from the spirit of God. A wise instinct has led men to think of the master spirit of evil, the "Prince of Darkness," as possessed by the most egoistic, the most centrifugal of all passions,—as the very personification of *pride*.[1]

[1] The genesis of spiritual egoism may be studied from a somewhat different point of view. When the desire for absolute freedom allies itself with revolt against the haunting claim of the infinite, the resultant way of living will be egoistic in the fullest and deepest sense of the word. For if the universe is a living whole, the only way for each of us to integrate himself (and so win freedom) without disintegrating it, is to become one with it, to merge his being in the infinitude of its life. He who thinks to win freedom, not by growing into oneness with the living whole, but by becoming a living whole on his own account, by integrating himself independently of the supreme integer, by separating himself from the cosmic life and finding the fulness of life in a little world of his own, has renounced his high birth-

In each of the four types of evil living which I have briefly described the dominating motive is the desire for finality, the desire to find lasting rest in the undeveloped or partially developed self, in defiance of the demand for self-realization which the inward ideal, the infinite in man, is ever making, and, until its voice has been finally silenced, will never cease to make.

In the first life, the life of self-indulgence, or *animal egoism*, distraction from the haunting claims of the inward ideal is sought in sensual pleasures of various kinds. That such distraction should have to be sought shows that the inward ideal is pressing for recognition, and that its claim has not been rejected and is not yet wholly ignored.

In the second life, the life of self-assertion, or *petty egoism*, the claim of the inward ideal is not deliberately rejected, but, partly from spiritual indolence, partly from lack of imagination, it is persistently ignored. No attempt is made to develop self. No serious attempt is made to lift self above the average level of human achievement. Ambition, even of the worldly type, is wanting. So far as an attempt is made to magnify self, it usually takes the negative form of belittling other persons and depreciating their work. Such as the self is, undeveloped and undistinguished, with its petty aims and interests and its narrow sphere of activity,—recognition and acceptance are demanded for it; and to secure these, by whatever means and at whatever cost to others, is the central purpose of what is in effect, if not in intent, an essentially selfish life.

In the third life, the life of self-aggrandizement, or *aggressive egoism*, the claim of the inward ideal is more or less consciously rejected, and outward ideals are adopted in its place. Wealth, power, position, fame are regarded as ends in themselves and are pursued ruthlessly and unscrupulously, in entire disregard of the feelings and interests

right to the act of laying claim to it prematurely, and has become a disintegrative and morbific influence in the body politic of the great world to which, in spite of himself, he still belongs. Separatism, spiritual egoism, when it is deliberately adopted as a scheme of life, is the sin of sins, the malady of maladies, the equivalent, in the pathology of the soul, of the disease of rebellious and therefore malignant growth which we call cancer, in the pathology of the body. And the end of it is not freedom, but imprisonment in an ever narrowing self.

of others. To achieve greatness, not by becoming great—by "growing in wisdom and stature"—but by seeming to be great, by energizing on a great scale, by being the centre of a great circle of disturbance, by wielding power over many men, is the summit of the soul's ambition. In such a life success, as the world interprets the word, is the proof and measure of reality; the shadow of power—power over others—is preferred to the substance of power—power over self; and the pomp and glitter of life are mistaken for life itself.

In the fourth life, the life of self-development for self's sake, the life of *spiritual egoism,* the inward ideal seems to be consciously accepted, but it is pursued for the sake of self, not for the sake of liberation from self. This distinction is all-important. Self-development, when the stress is laid on *development,* is the one unfailing antidote to selfishness. Self-development, when the stress is laid on *self,* is selfishness raised to the highest imaginable power. In the life of spiritual egoism, the inward ideal is pursued up to a certain point, but only in order that the rebellious soul may learn (taught by its enemy) how best to resist and defy it.[1]

There are two features, then, which all vices, all bad habits, all forms of moral evil have in common,—two features which are really one. They are all generated (if we go back to their fountain head) by the desire to find rest in the actual self, whatever that may happen to be,—to find shelter in it from the pursuing shadow of the infinite, to find release in it from the hateful necessity of growing in mind and spirit, of realizing an inward ideal in one's own character and one's own life. And they all tend, in their various ways, to arrest, if not to reverse, the process of soul-growth.

There is an obvious moral to these reflections: *Be good, if you would be happy.* Be wise, also, if you can. But in any

[1] There is no reason why all these lives should not be lived by the same person. I have found it convenient to separate them, but I know well how ready they are to intermingle their respective influences; and I doubt if there are many men who have not at one time or another felt the attractive force of each kind of life. The attractive force of the third and the fourth lives may be rarely felt, and may be evanescent when it is felt. Yet most men know from personal experience the meaning of the words *ambition* and *covetousness;* and there are few men who have not had their moments (if not their seasons) of *spiritual pride.*

case, and above all, be good. There are few men who can, even if they will, be wise. But there are few who cannot, if they will, be good. Be good—but why? Because growth makes for happiness, and goodness makes for growth. Am I then bidding men be good for selfish reasons? No, but for the most unselfish of all. For the growth that makes for happiness is never-ending growth, growth that reaches on and on into the infinite, growth that makes men outgrow self, and escape from self, and forget self.

How then, is goodness—moral goodness, virtue, righteousness, right conduct—call it what you will—to be achieved? By resisting the lure of finality, by refusing to rest in self, by trying to escape from self. This is an obvious answer to my question. Let us see how it bears on each of the four vicious lives. In the life of self-indulgence, the lure of finality takes the form of the lure of the senses, and escape from self means escape from the animal self, from bondage to the flesh. How is this escape to be effected? Mainly by the exercise of *self-control*. Other influences, such as the cultivation of sympathy and the enlargement of the sphere of interest, will count for something, in some cases for much. But the supreme emancipative influence, and the one which can never be dispensed with, is self-control. For the life of self-indulgence is not necessarily anti-social. In some of the most odious and demoralizing of sensual vices the vicious man is the only sufferer. It is true that systematic self-indulgence unfits a man for social service. And it is true that if the sensualist finds it necessary to sacrifice the well-being of others to the gratification of his own desires, he will do so with but little compunction. But it is also true that in his general attitude towards his fellow-men he is not consciously or even subconsciously selfish. He does not wish to assert himself against his neighbour, or to dominate him, or to aggrandize himself at his expense. Still less does he wish to stand aloof from him. As often as not he is by nature friendly and good-natured, and in some of his failings he finds that the sense of companionship enhances his pleasure. What he does wish is to indulge his own desires and passions, at whatever cost to his own well-being or (if it must be so) to the well-being of others.

The self-control that keeps the animal in man in its place, reacts on and strengthens the will; and a strong will is an essential element in a strong character. But a strong character is not necessarily a good character; and a strong will may be used for purposes of evil as well as of good. Let us go on to the second type of life—a type with which we are all familiar—the life of petty egoism, the life of him who, succumbing to the lure of finality, tries to find rest, for good and all, in his ordinary, average, everyday, superficial self,—undeveloped, unexpended, unaggrandized, unadorned. Unlike the life of self-indulgence, the life of petty egoism is necessarily selfish, in the sense of being anti-social in tendency,—instinctively rather than deliberately selfish, but selfish to the very core. Its selfishness is, however, restricted, in aim and in scope, by want of character, by weakness of will. The obvious antidote to petty egoism is the cultivation of *sympathy*, of the power of going out of self into other selves and other lives. Here sympathy takes its place by the side of self-control as one of the great emancipative influences in man's life. And it is well that it should do so. For if selfishness, unalloyed or insufficiently alloyed with sympathy, were to unite itself with force of character, the life of petty egoism would automatically expand into the life of aggressive egoism, of self-aggrandizement, the difference between the two lives being that in the latter there is not only greater mental power and a larger outlook on life, but also, and above all, a stronger will.

In the life of self-aggrandizement, as in the life of self-assertion, the antidote to the poison of selfishness is the cultivation of sympathy. But as the will is stronger and the whole scope of life is wider, a fuller measure and perhaps a higher kind of sympathy will be needed if the poison is to cease to work. Let us pause for a moment and see where we stand. In the sphere of conduct there are two great factors in self-development,—self-control, which enables a man to subdue the animal in him and in general to master the lower self, and sympathy, which enables a man to escape from "self" by the widest and most open of all channels, by the overflow of his life into the lives of others. That we should keep the balance between the two factors, that progress in each should be met by progress in the other, is essential if "growth in grace" is to be duly maintained. In particular, the stronger the will, the greater the force of sympathy that will be needed in order that the selfishness which, when allied with will-power, tends to become ruthless and aggressive, may be disarmed.

What the loss of the balance between the two factors may mean, the fourth type of life, the life of spiritual egoism, will bring home to us with convincing force. Neither in the life of self-assertion nor in the life of self-aggrandizement is the capacity for sympathy wholly wanting. The fact that both lives are anti-social, in their respective degrees, shows that those who lead them take some interest in social life. The petty egoist has his cliques and coteries; he takes sides in quarrels; he plays off his friends against his enemies. The more adventurous egoist has his allies—partners in his schemes of self-aggrandizement—and his followers. This means that the spirit of comradeship has not died out of either heart. But spiritual pride completely isolates a man from his kind. Nay, it does worse than isolate him. No man can balance himself for more than an instant on the knife edge of absolute indifference. In our general attitude toward mankind, we must choose between sympathy and antipathy. And our choice, when once made, will carry us very far. We have seen that in spiritual egoism dread of the infinite has become hatred of the infinite. But to hate the infinite is to hate the ideal element in man. It is to hate the divine spirit which is the true self of each of us. It is to hate mankind in the act of hating God. The choice between sympathy and antipathy becomes at last the choice between love and hate. To live the life of spiritual egoism in its fulness presupposes exceptional powers and exceptional experiences, and is therefore given to few men. But many men have felt the sinister fascination of spiritual pride. The temptation is one to which men of strong character and great intellectual power are peculiarly exposed. When self-development has been carried, through the practice of self-control, to the high level of complete self-mastery, one stands at the parting of two infinite ways. If the balance between self-control and sympathy has been lost—and to lose it at all is to run the risk of losing it completely—the man who is high in development is a devil in the making. If the balance has been maintained, he is an angel in the making, a saint (in the larger sense of the word), an initiate into the high purposes of God. For on the level which he has reached there is only one way in which the maintenance of the balance can be provided for : *Sympathy must expand into all-embracing love.*

Let us now follow, in the sphere of conduct, the career of one who seeks happiness through soul-growth. He has set out, as will gradually be revealed to him, on the greatest of all adventures. Happiness, as he understands the word, is the sense of well-being. Well-being, as he understands the word, is another name for healthy and harmonious growth. The way of growth is the realization of infinite potentiality. The end of growth is oneness with the infinite and the divine. The way of growth is therefore the way of out-growth, of endless self-surrender, of endless emancipation from self. Realizing this—if not consciously, then in some secret recess of his soul—he will also realize that in the sphere of conduct, as of belief, his arch-enemy, whatever may be the stage of his development, is his own actual self. For his actual self shrinks from the prospect of never-ending development, of having to realize an unattainable ideal, of having to reach on and on into the infinite ; and it therefore longs for finality, for rest in its own achievements and attainments,

> for a repose which ever is the same.

But this longing, which will repeat itself again and again, must be met and combated as often as it invades his soul. For if he yields to its pressure he will find that arrested growth is incipient death.

He will need guidance in this great adventure ; and guidance will be freely given to him. Of guidance from without he will have enough and to spare,—law (written and unwritten), tradition, custom, public opinion, the pressure of social and ethical ideals, parental or quasi-parental advice, priestly direction, and so forth. But if he is to make a right use of guidance from without, he must have guidance from within. And guidance from within will also be at his service. The ideal which he is seeking to realize is in himself, in his buried, subconscious life; and if he will but turn towards its light, though at first it will scarcely be discernible, it will not fail to illuminate his path. But the inward ideal—the infinite, the universal element in his being—is the same for all men; and he will therefore need guidance into the path by which he, such as he is, is to be led into the broad highway which all will have to tread. That guidance too is at his service. His own individuality mediates between his actual and his ideal self; and if he will be true to it, it will give him the guidance that he needs, for it is itself the path that he is seeking. But he will be true to it, not because he owes allegiance to his individual self, but because he owes allegiance to his ideal or universal self. For by the individuality of a man we mean the channel of communication between his buried and his conscious life; we mean the pathway from the actual self to the high-road that leads to the ideal; we mean the way of escape from "self" which Nature, he being what he is, has marked out for him. If our adventurer will be true to his individuality, if he will resist the lure of finality, the desire of his undeveloped self for authoritative direction and detailed instruction from without, his path, as he follows it, will lead him at last into the life beyond individuality; just as the river which follows its own channel to the sea ends at last by merging its individuality in a life which is infinitely wider and deeper than its own.

As a theory of life, the life of the senses will not long detain him. The sensualist mistakes pleasure for happiness—a fundamental mistake for which he is doomed to pay dear. Pleasure is generated by the gratification of a particular desire, by the well-being—apparent, or at best temporary—of a particular nerve-centre or group of nerve-centres. Happiness is generated by the well-being of the whole man. But the whole man is the real self; and the real self has yet to be realized, and will not be realized until life in and to the infinite has begun. The difference between sensual pleasure and true happiness, is, therefore, the difference between what is temporary and even momentary, and what is eternal; between what is finite—verging in some cases towards the infinitesimal—and what is infinite. Whatever may be the actual attraction of a life of "pleasure" for our adventurer, its ideal attraction is virtually negligible. But its actual attraction for him may be strong, and in any case—whatever form it may take and whatever force it may exert—he will have to hold it in check. How is this to be done? Not by mortifying the flesh, but by dominating it. Self-mortification would upset the balance of his nature and disturb the harmony of its growth. The flesh is the vehicle of the spirit, and therefore its servant and instrument, not its hereditary enemy. He will allow the flesh to have its way so long as its desires do not conflict with the interests of his higher self. When they do, he will resist its impulses, he will place an armed guard in charge of it. In other words, he will steer a middle course between self-indulgence and self-mortification by practising self-control.

With his spiritual nerves and sinews braced by this discipline, he will face the more subtle and complex temptations of social life. Here the desire for finality makes for egoism, for petty egoism when the character is relatively weak, for aggressive, adventurous egoism when the character is strong. The seeker for happiness will find deliverance from egoism in responding to the call of the infinite. No one who has given his heart to the infinite, will mistake the semblance of reality—whatever may be the weight of opinion that vouches for its genuineness—for reality itself. And with the sense of reality will come the sense of proportion, the power of appraising at their proper value conflicting ideals and competing courses of action. In the life of petty egoism what a man is reputed to be is his chief concern. In the life of aggressive egoism achievements and possessions—the means to the acquisition of power—are his chief concern. When they are brought to the touchstone of the inward ideal, the touchstone of intrinsic reality, the hollowness of these outward ideals is at once exposed. It is not what a man is reputed to be that matters, but what he is in himself. The reputed self is neither actual nor real.

What a man has made of himself is at least an actuality, and therefore matters much. What he might make of himself, what he has it in him to become, matters more, for in the last resort it is the central reality of his existence. So, too, achievements and possessions, however great they may be, are always finite and measurable, and are therefore convicted of unreality when exposed to the searchlight of the infinite; and power over others is but the shadow of the reality of power,—power over the limitless reserves of vitality which are locked up in oneself. With his heart set on the infinite, the voyager will pass in safety through the ill-charted seas of social life, with their ever-changing shoals and currents; and as the false ideals of social life lose their power over him, his sympathetic instincts will spontaneously increase their activity—for the basic element in sympathy is the sense of oneness with the one all-embracing life—and will balance and, if necessary, hold in check the increasing force of will which reflects the discipline of his self-control.

It is well that he should give those instincts free play. His perils are not yet over. The very steadfastness of his purpose, as he reaches on into the infinite, by causing a disproportionate development of his will-power, may yet prove his undoing. The consciousness of having dared much, and endured much, and achieved much, and the consequent sense of power, may tempt him to concentrate his interest in himself, and may to that extent isolate him from his fellow-men. Were this to come to pass, were the balance between self-control and sympathy to be lost, he would be exposed to the deadliest of all dangers. For why has he followed the path of self-development? Why has he resisted the lure of finality? Why has he braved the perils of the mysterious and the unknown? Is it for the sake of self or for the sake of emancipation from self? This is the question of questions. The answer that he gives to it will decide his destiny. If he is over insistent on *self*-development, on making *his own self* one with the infinite, it is possible that he may succumb to the last allurement of his finite self in the very act of flattering himself that he has finally triumphed over it. It is possible that, having escaped a thousand perils, he may suffer shipwreck in sight of his goal.

But if he has indeed given his heart to the infinite, all will be well with him; for in and through his ever-growing love of the Divine Lover—the soul of his soul, and the soul of all soul-life—his sympathy with his fellow-men, which has probably been partial and fitful, will expand into all-embracing sympathy, and his all-embracing sympathy will be transfigured into all-embracing love.

When that goal has been reached, when self-development has lost itself, and found itself, in self-surrender, when the fulness of self-mastery has wedded itself to the fulness of love, life in the infinite will at last have begun. Till then there can be no haven for the seeker after happiness, no rest for his growing soul. Then there will be rest indeed, but rest in the infinite, the rest of eternal unrest. What that rest, the "peace which passeth all understanding," may mean, he will not know till he has entered into it.[1]

Before I close this chapter let me say a word to those who are wavering, in the sphere of conduct, between desire for the greatest of all adventures and desire for finality,—for mental and spiritual repose. The latter desire will never be fulfilled. A man may possibly find rest in a belief, in a theory, in a formula. He may never find rest in *self*. If we are to live we must work; and if we are to work we must serve; for work which is not service is the activity of a

[1] There is one aspect of the moral struggle which I have ignored in this chapter, not because I undervalue it or have forgotten it, but because it is, as it happens, the central theme of this book. The desire for finality in the sphere of conduct, the desire to find rest in the undeveloped, unexpanded self, leads, as we have seen, to every kind of self-seeking and self-indulgence, and therefore to every kind of wrong-doing. But what is most deadly in the desire is that it perverts a man's very effort to do right, that it takes advantage of his very conscientiousness to lead him astray. For the man who wishes to do right and yet shrinks, in his timidity and self-distrust, from the exercise of spiritual initiative, will go to external authority for instruction and guidance, and, where these are forthcoming, will ask for them in ever fuller measure, till he will end by selling himself into slavery and accepting his bonds as the purchase money of his soul. That this attempt to be "saved" by mechanical obedience, by response to pressure from without, makes for spiritual death, that it demoralizes the sinner and even tends to devitalize the saint, is an obvious inference from the assumption which dominates the whole course of my thoughts—the assumption that life is the reward of growth, and that growth is response to pressure from within.

lunatic or an idiot, not of a rational man. But whom or what are we to serve? Our choice lies, in the last resort, between serving self and serving the Universe. And the higher we climb, the more fateful will be our choice and the deadlier the consequences of mischoice. We have to choose between two exacting taskmasters. The more we give, the more will each of them demand. But if they are exacting in their demands, they are generous, according to their respective capacities, in their rewards. For each of them will give itself, and nothing less than itself, to its devotee. The Universe will give itself to him who lives for it. In other words, it will place all the infinitude of life at his disposal. Therefore the more faithfully he serves his Divine Master, the wider will be the scope and the more vivid the play of his life. And "self" will give itself, with equal liberality, to the man who is self-centred and self-indulgent. But, in response to each act of self-concentration or self-indulgence, self will shrink a little, like the magic skin in Balzac's famous allegory. And to this process of shrinking there is no limit. "When a man begins to live for self he narrows his horizon steadily, till at last the fierce inward driving leaves him but the space of a pin's head to dwell in."[1] Our choice, then, is not between toil and rest. Toilers we are and must ever be. Our choice is between the toil that liberates and the toil that enslaves. If we will not take the trouble to expand life, we shall have to labour assiduously to contract it.

[1] *Light on the Path*, by M. C.

CHAPTER VI

EARLY GROWTH

THE early stages of growth are by far the most important. "Well begun is half done." A good—or a bad—start in life is half the battle of life,—half-way towards victory or half-way towards defeat. It is more than half the battle. It is nearly the whole of it. What men or women are when they have "finished their education" that they will continue to be, in all essential features, to the end of their days. There are many exceptions to this rule; but in spite of the exceptions the rule holds good. The moral to it has been drawn for us by a master hand. In a passage in the *Laws* which deserves to be far better known than it is, Plato, when considering the various offices of State, gives priority, *hors concours*, to the Directorship of Education on the ground that "whatever the creature, be it plant or animal, wild or tame, if its earliest growth makes a good start, that is by far the most important stage towards the happy consummation of the excellence of which its nature is capable." For more than twenty centuries these wise words—prophetic in their wisdom—have fallen on deaf ears. The time has come for us to weigh them, if not to lay them to heart. In the world of plant life early growth, except so far as it is directed by man for purposes of his own, is under the control of two factors, "nature" (heredity) and environment. It is the same in the lower grades of animal life. But in the higher grades a new factor comes into play, or rather a new influence is introduced into environment—the influence of "nurture," in the form of parental care and control. Nature, working through inherited instinct, is still the predominant influence in fostering growth. But the higher the grade of life, the more does nurture count for. And in the case of man nurture counts for so much as to place him in a class by himself.

For this there are many reasons. I will content myself with naming five. The first is that of all young creatures the human infant is by far the most helpless and dependent. The second is that the period of helplessness and dependence lasts longer in its case than in that of any other living thing. The third is that the child, as a conscious being, can receive and obey orders,[1] so that those who have charge of him can direct the activities, physical, mental, and moral, by which he develops himself, and can therefore control the actual process of his growth. The fourth is that the child, as a conscious being, and therefore as a potentially free agent, can through his own action, whether that action be spontaneous or authoritatively directed, either accelerate or retard his own growth, and that the retarding of growth can be carried so far as to arrest or even reverse the process. The fifth is that, on all the planes of his being above the physical, the child has unlimited reserves of potentiality waiting to be developed.

Hence the enormous importance of education. During what is pre-eminently the period of growth, the period in which the future man is, as a rule, either made or marred, the period in which character and mentality, being tender, sappy, and pliable, are ready to receive decisive bents,—during all the years of infancy, childhood, and adolescence, the educator (the parent, the nurse, the teacher, the guardian) is a providence to the growing child, a good or a bad providence, as the case may be. His opportunities are boundless, but they are opportunities for evil as well as for good. Consider what they are. He has control of the child's environment, in general. In particular, he has control of the child's supply of food,—food of all kinds, food for the body, food for the mind, for the heart, for the soul. He can give or withhold stimulus,—the magnetic, personal influence which is so favourable to soul-growth. The child, being ignorant and comparatively helpless, seems to be waiting for direction and instruction, and he can give these in un-

[1] The horse, the dog, and the elephant can do the same, but not to anything like the same extent.

stinted measure. Through his command of the child's activities he can control the very process of his growth, for what the child does, in obedience to orders, must needs react on what he is ; and he can even enter in some sort as a transforming influence into the laboratory of the child's inner life. And as the child's reserves of potentiality are limitless, the range of his transforming influence is correspondingly wide.

With such opportunities awaiting him, the educator, if he is wise and sympathetic, may well become the guardian angel of the child's expanding life. But he is much more likely to become its evil genius. The temptations to misuse his opportunities will be almost irresistible. It is a mistake to suppose that direction and instruction are intrinsically good influences in the child's life. It would be nearer the truth to say that they are intrinsically bad influences. Direction may easily take the place of self-direction ; and instruction may easily stifle the desire for and sterilize the pursuit of knowledge. The teacher who directs for the sake of directing or instructs for the sake of instructing, is doing for the child what the latter ought to be doing for himself ; he is therefore repressing the spontaneous activity which is of the essence of growth, and he is atrophying faculty by relieving the child from the necessity of using it. And the chances are that the direction which he gives so freely will be to a large extent *mis*-direction. For what does he know of the real nature of his pupil ? When we say that the child's reserves of potentiality are infinite, we imply that his inner nature is mysterious, unfathomable, unknown. Yet if the educator is to order the child's goings wisely and profitably, he must have sounded those depths and penetrated those mysteries, and must have acquired an illuminating, if not a searching, knowledge of the nature with which he has to deal. But what likelihood is there of his acquiring such knowledge so long as he prevents the child's nature from revealing itself, so long as he takes for granted that the child is to become (or rather to be made) a mere replica of himself ? The education that is all direction and instruction perpetuates the ignorance on which it is based. In other words, it is a vicious circle, from which the educator, until he changes his aims and his methods, will not be able to escape.

Let us ask ourselves what education might do, and then see what it usually does. The wise teacher will base his system of education on whole-hearted trust in the child's unrealized possibilities, and on partial distrust of himself. He will assume at the outset that the child has an instinctive desire—not the less genuine because it is largely subconscious—for self-development, for knowledge, for social order. He will give him as favourable an environment as possible. He will give him (as far as lies in his power) abundant and varied food. He will give him stimulus—if he can. He will give him guidance, sparingly, and judiciously,—the guidance that attracts, not the guidance that compels. He will give him instruction, when he thinks it will profit him. And he will give him disciplinary direction, when he feels that he cannot do otherwise. But he will do his best to encourage self-discipline and self-instruction; for he will know that the former is the real moulder of character, and the latter, the real fountain-head of knowledge. For the rest, he will keep discreetly in the background, leaving the work of education in the main to the spontaneous energies of the child's unfolding nature, and waiting patiently for that nature to reveal itself—to reveal itself, first as expanding life for the child, then as guiding light for the child and for himself.

But if he will do these things, he will be one in a thousand. The atmosphere that the teacher breathes is charged with hostile influences, which he finds it hard to resist, even if he wishes to do so. The whole existing constitution of things is against him. The feudal system is dead. Feudalism is slowly dying. But the influence of a dominant idea outlives by many generations the systems and institutions in which it embodied itself; and it is therefore no matter for wonder that our general outlook on life is still predominatingly feudal, and that the social organization of what we call the civilized world is still feudal in spirit. The basic idea of feudalism was—and is—distrust of human nature, and the consequent assumption that men must, for their own sakes, be socialized and moralized by external authority, that well-being must be imposed upon them from without, instead of being evolved by them from within. The last stronghold of feudalism, the last refuge of irresponsible authority, is the school. The reasons for this are obvious. The child is helpless and dependent and is, therefore, on the one hand in need of care and control, and on the other hand unable to defy the authority of the teacher, however arbitrary and despotic it may be. The teacher is himself the victim of feudal pressure; and it is but natural that he should seek to pass it on. The lust for dominion, from which no one is wholly exempt, and which throve with special vigour in the soil of feudalism, still lingers in his heart. It is infinitely easier to coerce the child than to inspire him, to discipline him than to help him to discipline himself, to instruct him than to stimulate his desire for knowledge, to order his goings for him than to give him freedom for self-development. In the world which surrounds the teacher, and for which he is expected to prepare the child, outward ideals are still in the ascendant, success is still measured by outward standards, outward ends of action are still set before men from their earliest to their latest years. So long as this is so, the production of material and therefore measurable results by coercive and quasi-mechanical methods will be the aim of all but a small minority of teachers.

The features of the orthodox type of education are familiar to most of us. The basis of it is distrust of the child, balanced by inordinate self-confidence on the part of the teacher. The child is congenitally naughty and stupid, as well as ignorant. As he is naughty, he must be forcibly drilled and disciplined into the semblance of good conduct. As he is ignorant and stupid, as his mental stomach is empty and his mental digestion weak, he must be forcibly dieted on peptonized rations of information. Distrust of the child both presupposes and perpetuates ignorance of his nature. No attempt is made to explore its unknown depths, to help him to realize an inward ideal, to seek light and guidance from within. Outward ideals (if one may call them so) are set before him, outward standards of value, outward ends of action. No attempt is made to discover his latent capacities; and if these do not obtrude themselves on the notice of the teacher, if they do not openly demand the means of expression, it is assumed that they do not exist. No attempt is made to consult his desires, his tastes, his inclinations. His business is to produce certain outward results at the bidding and under the direction of his teacher. As ends of action, these results do not (in all probability) appeal to him; and he must therefore be alternately bullied and bribed into producing them. His baser fears must be appealed to by the threat of punishment. His baser desires, by the promise of material rewards. The results which he is expected to produce are visible, measurable, ponderable. His progress in producing them can therefore be accurately tested and appraised. The process of testing is known as examination; and the verdict of the examiner is the final end of action for both the teacher and the child. In working for the examination the child enters—and is intended to enter—into competition with his class-mates, whom he henceforth regards as his rivals and possible enemies. This appeal to his competitive instinct, supplementing the threat of punishment and the offer of reward, takes the place of the appeal to his disinterested desire for knowledge—to his instinctive desire to overcome difficulties, to solve problems, to gain power, to develop faculty—to his more deeply seated, because more vital and essential, desire for beauty, for truth, for ideal good—to his sense of duty—to his love of his teacher and his school.

In such an atmosphere the sense of reality—of intrinsic reality—is deadened, if not wholly lost. The feeling that "I am what I am" gives way, in the subconscious mind of the child, to the feeling that "I am what I am reputed to be"; the feeling that things are what they are, to the feeling that they are what they are said to be. "Will it pay?" takes the place of "Is it what I am seeking? Is it true?" "Will it satisfy the teacher (or the examiner)?" takes the place of "Does it satisfy my desire for knowledge?" "What is my place in class?" takes the place of "What progress have I really made?" The child is living in a world of make-believe, and he bears himself accordingly. The teacher is equally out of touch with reality. Indeed, it is because the teacher, through his distrust and consequent ignorance of the child's nature, has lost touch with reality, that the child, his victim, is in the same plight. The teacher assumes, as a matter of course, that he knows how the various subjects ought to be taught. How does he teach them? If I cannot say for certain how he teaches them to-day, I can say, with some approach to certainty, how he taught them in a not very remote yesterday—a yesterday which, if I am not wholly misinformed, still largely dominates to-day. Was the subject *Reading?* The child began by learning the names of the letters in the alphabet, and was then launched on a course of a-b, *ab.* Was it *Writing?* The child filled whole copybooks with strokes and pot-hooks and hangers before he was allowed to form a single letter. Was it *Arithmetic?* He began with rules and tables and abstract numbers. Was it *Geography?* He began with definitions, and went on to lists of capes and bays, of countries and towns. Was it *Languages?* He began with declensions, conjugations and vocabularies? Was it *Drawing?* He began by drawing straight lines, followed by arbitrary arrangements of straight lines, and went on to simple curves, followed by arbitrary arrangements of curves. Was it *Woodwork?* He spent weeks in planing and weeks in chiselling before he was allowed to do any constructive work. Was it *Religion?* He committed to memory the Church Catechisms, an assortment of texts and hymns, and the names and dates of the Kings of Israel and Judah. I doubt if there was a single subject in which the teacher did not invert the natural order of things, the order which he would have followed if he had studied the child's nature so far as to acquire an elementary knowledge of its laws and tendencies.[1] That those ways of teaching were repugnant

[1] As masterpieces of bureaucratic imbecility, the syllabuses issued by the Education Department for use in Elementary Schools in the late seventies and early eighties of the past century, deserve to be carefully studied. It will be found that in each subject there was one cast-iron scheme which was binding on all the schools in England and Wales; and that in almost every case provision was made for the subject to be taught upside down. The teachers had no voice in the matter. They had to work by the syllabus, whether they approved of it or not,—to work for a yearly examination, on the results of which depended their success in their profession and the financial prosperity of their schools. That Govern-

to the child, that he hated his lessons, that he got through his tasks reluctantly and perfunctorily, in no way disquieted the teacher, or shook his confidence in himself. So complete was his severance from reality, that the child's instinctive protest against the methods of educational orthodoxy was regarded as a proof, not of the unsoundness of those methods, but of the inherent naughtiness and rebelliousness of the child.

It will be said that things are better to-day than they were in that dismal yesterday. Perhaps they are ; but so far as first principles are concerned, there has been no appreciable change. Let us return, then, from the past tense to the present. What is happening to the child who is passing through the educational mill ? Many things are happening to him. The first—and the last—is that *his individuality is being systematically starved and stifled.* His teachers do not think of him as an individual. They think of him as a unit in a class, one of twenty or thirty (or more) children who are all doing the same work at the same time and are all supposed to be in the same stage of mental development. Independent action on his part is strictly forbidden. Independent thought is discouraged, and even—in the most vital of all matters—authoritatively proscribed. Little or no scope is allowed him for the exercise of initiative, of judgment, of self-reliance. No attempt is made to discover his tastes or his aptitudes, and the idea of providing for the satisfaction of them is foreign to the whole scheme of his education. The last thing that his teachers contemplate is that he should be himself, that he should become what he has it in him to be. The consequent loss to his inner life is incalculable. For his individuality is his appointed way of escape from "self" ; and the suppression of individuality means a general narrowing of life and a general stunting of growth. It is true that if all goes well with him, he will, in

ment officials, sitting in their rooms at Whitehall—men of academic distinction, no doubt, but who had no experience of teaching and had not even a bowing acquaintance with psychology—should have thought themselves competent to determine in detail how all the subjects were to be taught in all the "standards" of all the schools in the country, shows how dense was the fog of unreality and illusion in which education was wrapped in those days. Since then the fog has lightened somewhat and has perhaps begun to lift, but it still overhangs the land.

the fulness of time, pass beyond individuality; but he will do so by outgrowing it under its own guidance, not by suppressing it. To suppress individuality, to force the growing child into a given mould, to compel him to conform to a given pattern, is to imprison him, so far as he is living his own life—(for conformity to a pattern is a mechanical, not a vital process)—in his own petty, ordinary, unexpanded self.

The suppression of his individuality has many aspects. The deadening of his intuition is one of them. The more you do for a child in the way of directing his conduct, instructing his mind, and regulating his beliefs and opinions, the less need is there for him to exercise that great, many-sided perceptive faculty by which each of us, in the absence of specific guidance, steers his way through the perplexities and complexities of life—the faculty for evolving senses and sub-senses in response to the stimulating pressure of an ever-changing environment—a faculty, the generic name of which is intuition, but which has many sub-names, such as discernment, discretion, sense of propriety, taste, tact, conscience, the power of divination, insight, genius. This protean faculty is the organ of the buried life; and the autocratic education, which, in its zeal for machinery, leaves little or no room for it to be exercised, obstructs, if it does not actually close, the channel between the buried and the conscious life, and to that extent cuts the child off from his true base of operations, from the vast reserves of potentiality which are stored up in his inmost self.

His reasoning powers are equally and similarly blighted. From his earliest days his instinctive desire to understand the how and why of things is ruthlessly repressed. When he enters the schoolroom and begins to receive formal instruction, he is not allowed to see a meaning in anything that he is required to do. Blind faith is demanded from him, and the strain on his faith is made as severe as possible. Curiosity as to the use and purpose of what he is doing is an indiscretion which must not be repeated. Whatever may be the subject taught, he has to begin, as we have seen, with what is dry, formal, and abstract—names, dates, tables, lists, rules, declensions, conjugations, mechanical exercises, and the like—with what to him is meaningless, and repulsive because it is meaningless. Conclusions are presented to him for committal to memory, which he might, with a little encouragement and guidance, have worked out for himself; facts, which he might have been led to anticipate; rules, which he might have been helped to discover. The result is that his work becomes drudgery—(for monotonous work which is done under compulsion and in which one cannot see a meaning, is drudgery in the fullest sense of the word)—and his intelligence remains undeveloped through not being allowed to come into play.

His will is weakened by the over-strict discipline which allows but little room for it to be exercised. When mechanical obedience is systematically exacted, action tends to become automatic and machinery tends to take the place of life. Predetermination on the part of the teacher, when carried to excess, is incompatible with the outgrowth of self-determination on the part of the child. When freedom to choose is limited to the choice between obedience and disobedience, and when the chief motive to obedience is the fear of pains and penalties, opportunity for the exercise of will-power, for the practice of self-control, for the acquisition of mastery over self, can scarcely be said to exist. It used to be believed—and the belief is by no means extinct—that the will of the child was congenitally "perverse," and that the duty of the teacher was to "break" it. But the remedy for perversity (if the child happens to be afflicted with that very rare malady) is to train the will judiciously and sympathetically, not to break it. A broken will is seldom met with at the present day; but weak, vacillating wills are at least as numerous as they ever were. And if he whose will is broken has lost command of the helm of his own life, he whose will has been weakened by over-discipline and over-direction holds that helm with an uncertain purpose and an unsteady hand.

He is being forcibly desocialized. His teachers, who, in their ignorance of his real needs and legitimate desires, have made his school life as dull and repulsive as possible, finding that they cannot otherwise interest him in his work or rouse him to exertion, have made a base appeal to his competitive instinct, and have even gone so far as to compel him—by their system of marks, prizes, and (so-called) orders of merit—to enter into rivalry with his class-mates, thereby encouraging vanity, jealousy, selfishness, and individualism, and discouraging sympathy, the spirit of comradeship, and the spirit of co-operation. They would probably defend themselves, if their action was criticized, by an appeal to "common sense." But the common sense of the matter, if they only knew it, is that they do not understand children and will not take the trouble to study them. Experience has proved that the child is by nature a social being, with a marked capacity for evolving social order, and that if he is given fair play his competitive instinct will be readily swamped by a rising tide of good fellowship and good will. In Montessori classes, for example, where children of quite tender years are provided with suitable occupation and given freedom for self-development, and where the attitude of the teacher is one of trust and encouragement,—in spite of the complete absence of what I may call police-supervision, anti-social action, such as quarrelling or petty larceny, is almost entirely unknown. In the happy atmosphere which they are allowed to breathe the children speedily learn for themselves the great lesson of *give and take, live and let live ;* and a social life, based on sympathy, goodwill, mutual concession, and willingness to co-operate, spontaneously comes into being. Where such a life exists, the children regard one another as comrades, not as rivals, and if any attempt were made to introduce the spirit of competition into the school they would strongly resent it. If it is a mistake to make a child work against the grain of his mental nature, it is worse than a mistake—it is a sin against the Holy Spirit—to try to correct that mistake by compelling him to work against the grain of his moral nature. Of all the wrongs that education does to the child, perhaps the worst is that of making him an individualist and an egoist against his will.

His vitality is being forcibly lowered. Nothing is so depressing as to have to work against the grain in an atmosphere of repression, suspicion, and mistrust. Nothing is so vitalizing as to be allowed to work with the grain in an atmosphere of freedom, with the sense of being believed in and trusted to do one's best. What sunshine is to the growing plant, trust is to the growing child—the trust that is the outcome of sympathy and understanding, the trust that looks for the best and therefore appeals to what is best in child or man, the trust that sets the spirit free. The education which is dominated by distrust, which assumes at the outset that the child is a potential rebel and criminal, by lowering spiritual vitality, exposes the soul to the inroads of various forms of moral evil—there being in this respect a complete analogy between plant life and human life—and so goes far towards justifying the underestimate of human nature on which it is based. The most demoralizing of all influences, the most provocative of moral infection, is that of lowered vitality. The most moralizing of all influences, the most protective against moral infection, is that of healthy and harmonious growth.

There is no inward ideal to inspire and guide him. Or rather, there is an inward ideal, but he is not allowed to look to it for inspiration and guidance. He has to look for inspiration and guidance to the existing order of things as embodied in his parents and teachers. The actual, the traditional, the conventional, supported and (if need be) enforced by authority, comes between him and the ideal of his inmost heart. "Make me your model," says the parent or the teacher, "and do what I tell you, and all will be well." If progress, whether collective or individual, is the outcome of the effort to realize an unattainable ideal, what hope is there of progress (towards "true manhood") for the individual who, as a child, is compelled to model himself on an obviously imperfect pattern? And what hope is there of progress, other than material, for the race so long as each generation in turn insists on stamping itself, with all its defects and limitations, on its successor?

Such is the type of education which has long been accounted orthodox in this and other Western countries. It seems to have been framed for the express purpose of strangling growth and sterilizing life. Is that the intention of those who administer it? Probably not. Yet if it were, they would be true to the logic of the idea which dominates it. That idea is, as we have seen, distrust of human nature. The two great streams of feudal tendency meet in the nursery and the schoolroom,—secular feudalism, with the distrust of human nature which has been generated by the contempt of those in authority for the poor, the helpless, and the ignorant, and spiritual feudalism, with the distrust of human nature which has resulted from the ascendancy, in its philosophy, of the doctrine of original sin.

I am told that men no longer believe in original sin. If this were so, the arch of Christian theology would have lost its keystone. For if there has been no Fall, there is no need for a Redeemer. And in that case, what becomes of the Christian scheme of salvation, in which the figure of the Redeemer is surely central and supreme? But the doctrine of original sin has by no means passed away. To say that it has is an Anglican libel on Christendom. The Anglican "intellectual" seems to think that what he has ceased to believe is not worth believing, and that doctrines which he has disowned may therefore be accounted dead. He is welcome to his own interpretation of Christian teaching, but he must not imagine that all Christians are as free and easy in their beliefs as he is. If he would study a Roman Catholic Manual of Theology or attend a course of Calvinistic sermons, he would find that the doctrine of original sin was still very much alive.

But let us assume, for argument's sake, that the doctrine, though neither dead nor dying, has begun to fall into disrepute. What then? Has it not dominated the popular theology and the popular philosophy of the West for more than a thousand years? And if it died to-morrow, might not its influence be expected to survive for a thousand more? The feudal system passed away some centuries ago; but the sinister influence of a system which associated political power and responsibility with the tenure of land and which therefore led the ruling classes to despise and oppress the landless and unenfranchised masses, still permeates our social and political institutions and affects our whole outlook on life. And if there is any sphere of human activity in which the doctrine of original sin, were it proscribed elsewhere, might be expected to find a safe asylum, the sphere is that of education; for it is through the medium of education that the present stamps itself on, and therefore perpetuates itself in, the future; and until education has been completely transformed, it will continue to be, what it has long been, the most conservative, not to say reactionary, of all the influences that mould our social life.

Whatever, then, may be happening to the doctrine of original sin as a theory, we should expect to find that it was still a potent practical force. And that it certainly is. Allying itself with feudal contempt for the mass of mankind, it has ever generated and still continues to generate an immense underestimate of human character and capacity, which has found expression in our educational systems, and which is confirmed, from one generation to another, by our educational experiences. I think I have somewhere told the story of two Californian ladies who, having spent some weeks in Montessori classes, where the children were allowed to be their natural selves, when asked what general impressions they had carried away from them, replied that what had impressed them most was the discovery, which came as a shock to their preconceived notions, that children are by nature intelligent and good. By assuming, under the influence of the doctrine of original sin, that children are by nature stupid and naughty, and by handling them accordingly, education of the orthodox type has precluded itself from discovering that they are really intelligent and good. Hence its tendency to perpetuate and intensify the underestimate of human character and capacity which has done so much to paralyze the higher activities of the West. *Possunt quia posse videntur*. Self-confidence gives power. If it does so, if it braces the will and nerves the arm, self-distrust may be expected to do the opposite—to relax the will and unnerve the arm. That little or no progress, other than material and *cultural* (in the German sense of the word), has been made in Christendom since the days of the Roman Empire, is largely due to the fact that man has distrusted his own nature, has thought to be "saved" by supernatural means, and has kept his workaday life—the life of the natural man—down to the low level of his self-distrust.

That there is an irreconcilable feud between the doctrine of original sin and the doctrine of salvation through growth, goes without saying. If man is shapen in iniquity, if his nature is congenitally depraved, what can growth along the lines of his nature do for him but ensure his perdition? A poisonous seed will develop into a poisonous plant, and the more luxuriantly it grows the greater will be its capacity for evil. When growth means progress in corruption, it is the duty of those who control growth to arrest so deadly a process. Under the shadow of distrust of human nature what was bound to happen has happened. Education was bound to become supernaturalized, externalized, mechanicalized. Salvation through mechanical obedience was bound to take the place of salvation through vital obedience, through self-development, through growth. That these things have happened, that education is what we know it to be, shows that the doctrine of man's congenital depravity has a practical logic of its own which is still at work.

What, then, shall we who believe in human nature do to give effect to our faith? If salvation, if the well-being that leads to happiness, is to be achieved by growth, education must be transformed beyond recognition. Instead of allowing it to strangle growth by suppressing freedom, we must henceforth consider how best it can give freedom for growth. Such a change will not be accomplished in a day, or a year, or even in a generation. For we are involved in a vicious circle, a false ideal of life having generated a false ideal of education, which, when embodied in a system, tends to react upon and stereotype the false ideal of life; and the process of reforming education through a radical change in our ideal of life, and of reforming our way of living through a radical change in our ideal of education, will inevitably be painful and slow. But whatever may be our difficulty as to ways and means, our aim must always be revolutionary. We must aim at nothing less than the complete de-feudalizing of education—the complete emancipation of the child from hurtful pressure, the pressure that strangles growth.

Where and how are we to break into our vicious circle? We must, I think, begin by recognizing that the ultimate source of authority is not the will of the teacher, not the will of the State, not even the will of human society, but the will to live of the unfolding spirit of the child. Let this fundamental truth be grasped, and reforms which embody it will follow of their own accord and in their own good time. Instead of basing our whole educational system on profound distrust of the child's nature, we shall gradually learn to base it on faith in the inherent sanity of the great forces which are at work in his expanding life, in the limitlessness of his unrealized reserves of capacity, and in the general orientation of his nature towards good. We shall then relax the rigour of a discipline which takes for granted that the child is a potential rebel and criminal, and which therefore does its best to crush his spirit and mechanicalize his life. And we shall relax the rigidity and formality of a system of instruction which takes for granted that the child is as stupid and helpless as he is ignorant, and which, by forcibly cramming him with pellets of information, does its best to starve his desire to win knowledge for himself. And in general we shall relax the dogmatic and dictatorial attitude which reflects our secret conviction that the mind of the child is at best a blank page waiting to be written on, and that his character is at best unkneaded clay.[1]

If we will make the experiment of giving freedom to the child, and persevere in it in spite of inevitable mistakes and failures, results will follow in due season which will surprise us. Relieved from the deadly pressure which was paralyzing his natural activities and therefore either arresting or destroying his expansive tendencies, free at last to obey the laws of his own being rather than the arbitrary commands of his teacher, the child will begin to make healthy and harmonious growth; and his consequent sense of well-being will be realized by him as that fine flower of happiness which we call *joy*. In the atmosphere of joy his deeper nature will begin to reveal itself,—his sympathy with other persons and other forms of life, his power of respond-

[1] We have already begun to do these things, but we do not know why we do them, and we are therefore doing them gropingly, falteringly, and spasmodically, and in the face of obstacles which a clearer perception of why we are doing them would help to remove. Our attempts to reform our educational methods will not be effective until we have begun to revolutionize our educational aims.

ing to the attractive force of beauty, his desire for knowledge, transforming itself, as it is gratified, into disinterested devotion to truth. And with the consequent heightening of his vitality there will come to him—for our "circle" is now the reverse of "vicious"—a fuller measure and a purer quality of joy.

There I must leave him. He has entered "the Path," and the way is open to his unattainable goal. And though the Path, besides being infinitely long and arduous, is all too easy to lose, he will not lose it if he will accept the guidance that has been and will be given to him. The light of joy is the light of his own inward ideal; and if he will trust himself to it he will not go far astray.

PART V

THE FRUITS OF GROWTH

CHAPTER I

PHYSICAL WELL-BEING[1]

MENTAL growth, æsthetic growth, moral growth, spiritual growth,—each of these is an adventure into the infinite. Physical growth is not. The limits of physical growth are, in each individual case, strictly predetermined. I mean by this that each of us has it in him, at birth, to attain to a certain measure of physical perfection. That measure of physical perfection is not only a limit which he will never overpass, but also a goal which he will never reach ; for in order to reach it he will need what he cannot hope to have—a perfectly favourable environment throughout the whole of the ascending curve of his life, and a perfectly favourable reaction of his soul on his body. But the fact that physical perfection is a goal which will never be reached does not make it the less individual and finite, finite because limits are set to it which may not be overpassed, individual because those limits vary from man to man. In other words, physical perfection, though an unattainable goal, is not, like spiritual perfection, an unrealizable ideal. For the true ideal is always universal and infinite—universal, because it is infinite, the same for all men because its infinitude dwarfs to nothing all the actual differences between man and man.

It follows, with regard to physical well-being, that the

[1] Each of these aspects of man's well-being might well claim a whole volume—not to say many volumes—for itself. I have done no more than try to prove, in each case, that well-being is the reward, direct or indirect, of soul-growth.

question to be considered is not how far will a man's growth carry him into the infinite, but how near will it take him to his own predestined goal? This is equivalent to asking what hindrances will there be to his physical development and how are those hindrances to be overcome?

The hindrances to physical development fall under six principal heads:

1. Inherited disability.
2. Pre-natal injury.
3. Unfavourable environment.
4. Self-inflicted injury.
5. Neglect of physical culture.
6. Excessive regard for one's own health.

1. *Inherited disability*, and 2. *Pre-natal injury*.

These stand apart from the rest in that they take us back into the region of pre-natal destiny. Strictly speaking, then, they fall outside the scope of my inquiry; but so large a part is assigned to them, especially to the first, in popular estimation, that I cannot well afford to ignore them. It is now generally admitted that inherited physical disability counts for much less than was at one time believed. Even in the lowest grades of social life the new-born baby, in the absence of pre-natal injury, is as a rule fairly strong and healthy and of normal weight.[1] Much of what used to be attributed to unfortunate heredity is now seen to be due to unfavourable environment, especially in the early years of childhood. It is, however, probable that, with improved social conditions and with cleaner and healthier living on the part of the parents of the rising generation, there would be a gradual rise in the average level of inherited physique. At any rate it is a significant fact that the disease which scourges sexual immorality, and for which moral progress would therefore be the surest remedy, is the disease which, more than any other, transits its baneful influence from parent to child.

Pre-natal injury, if not purely accidental, is the result either of unfavourable social conditions or of avoidable parental neglect. If, for example, the mother is seriously

[1] See *Health and the State*, by Dr. W. A. Brend.

under-fed, especially during the period of gestation, the physique of the baby will probably suffer ; and a drunken mother may well inflict serious, if not irreparable, injury on her unborn child.

On the whole, then, it may be said that though the prenatal history of the normal child, even in the poorest home, is by no means unfavourable, any considerable rise in the general level of moral and social well-being would probably reflect itself in an appreciable improvement in the physique of the new-born infant.

3. *Unfavourable environment.*

Environmental hindrances to physical well-being may be classified as follows :

i. Underfeeding and improper feeding.
ii. Insanitary surroundings, such as overcrowded dwellings, defective drainage, defective water supply, insufficient light, and impure air.
iii. Insanitary occupations.
iv. Unfavourable conditions, such as lack of opportunity for recreative games and exercises, drab and monotonous surroundings (including monotonous occupation) with their temptations to drink and other forms of spurious excitement,—and the like.
v. Parental neglect, whether due to poverty, to ignorance, or to demoralization.
vi. Repressive education. The education which is given to the masses, besides being unduly sedentary and often carried on under insanitary conditions, is (as we have seen) vitiated by the current confusion between drill and discipline and between dogmatic direction and instruction, and it therefore tends, through the cramping pressure which it exerts, to arrest growth and lower vitality on all the planes of the child's being.

These hindrances to physical well-being are nearly all under communal control ; and until our communal life is based on co-operation rather than competition, on self-sacrifice rather than self-seeking, they will not be removed or even appreciably lessened. But moral growth on the part of the individual will lead to the gradual substitution of spiritual for material ends and inward for outward standards, and through this to a general raising of social ideals and of the whole tone of social life ; and this will have a favourable reaction on our environment and therefore on our physical development. Such a far-reaching measure of social reform as I have in mind will be slow in coming ; but it is permissible to dream that it will come.

4. *Self-inflicted injuries.*

Of the various hindrances to physical well-being these are the most serious and (with the possible exception of environmental hindrances) the most common. We may classify them under four chief heads :

i. Overeating.
ii. The drink habit.
iii. The drug habit.
iv. Sexual incontinence.

Of all these forms of self-indulgence it may truly be said :

> The gods are just, and of our pleasant vices
> Make instruments to scourge us.

Each of them is responsible for many diseases, and in general for much physical suffering and deterioration. What is common to all of them is that they are forms of self-indulgence ; in other words that they are due partly to pleasure being mistaken for happiness, partly to want of self-control. The temptations to self-indulgence which beset us are attributable, in part at least, to unfavourable social conditions ; but the inability to resist such temptations is a moral weakness, and is not to be remedied except by moral growth, which, if carried far enough, will both raise man's standard of happiness and strengthen his vacillating will.

5. *Neglect of physical culture.*

Physical culture has played a prominent part in the life of certain peoples, notably the Ancient Greeks ; and it still plays a prominent part in the life of certain "Savage" tribes. It is an aspect of self-development to which the conditions of life in highly civilized, and, above all, in highly industrialized countries, are distinctly adverse; and it should therefore be the aim of the legislator, the social reformer, and the educationist to make due provision for it. The means of physical culture are athletic games, open-air sports, and systematic physical training. The lack of opportunities for athletic games and open-air sports is largely due to defective social arrangements; and the neglect of physical training is the result of many causes, educational, social, and moral.

6. *Excessive concern for one's own bodily health.*

This is a fruitful source of worry and anxiety and therefore of physical derangement. In extreme cases it may even amount to monomania. The antidote to it is serenity of soul; and serenity of soul—the sense of being in harmony with the general purposes and tendencies of the Universe—is not to be attained except through "growth in grace."

We see, then, that all the avoidable hindrances to physical well-being are, in respect of their origin, either social or moral; and as social reform is, on the whole and in the long run, the outcome of moral progress, of the transformation of our ideals and the raising of our standards, we may say without exaggeration that physical well-being is ultimately dependent on moral well-being, that health of body is a by-product of health of soul.

But it is not only by removing hindrances to physical well-being that health of soul promotes health of body. The vitalizing influence of spiritual joy makes itself felt on all the levels of man's life. And as that influence can triumph over physical disabilities when these exist, so, when physical disabilities are absent, it can make the consequent sense of well-being an element in its own vital energy. For if health of soul makes for health of body, health of body can, in its turn and in its own way, react upon and minister to health of soul. But its own way is in the main a negative way. When physical health is perfect a man can forget his body; and the sense of physical well-being can therefore lose itself in that sense of general well-being which is realized by him who experiences it as happiness.

When I speak of "salvation through growth," I am thinking of the growth which is an adventure into the infinite, the growth of the soul. The growth of the body, which is at best a movement towards a finite goal, is not an essential aspect of the growth of the soul. It is possible, as many a watcher by a sick-bed will tell you, for the flame of soul-life to burn most brightly when the flame of corporeal life is burning low, or even flickering towards extinction. Nevertheless, when we take a broad view of things, we see that the growth of the soul, if healthy and harmonious, makes the best possible provision (through its control of the influences, moral and social, that affect our physical well-being) for the growth and therefore for the well-being of the body. Live to the spirit, which is the supreme synthesis, and therefore the inward harmony, of all the parts, all the powers, all the aspects of man's being,—live to the spirit for the sake of the spirit, and you will find that, without intending to do so, you are taking thought, in the most effectual way possible—taking thought both as an individual and as a member of a community—for the welfare of the flesh.

But what of physical beauty, the beauty of human form and face? Is this an essential element in physical well-being? I have no ready-made answer to this question. The standard of physical beauty varies from people to people and from age to age. But through all its variations there seem to be two more or less constant elements in human beauty—constant in the sense that no age and no people is insensible to them—the evanescent charm of physical health and the more durable charm of facial expression. And, as it happens, both these elements—the latter directly, the former indirectly—come under the control of the "inner man." Therefore I cannot but think that if life were less selfish and less sordid than it is, if men were less absorbed in material interests and pursuits, if they had more time and more leisure to "possess their souls," if they could open and keep open their hearts to the vivifying influences of earth and sky, of art and song, of great thoughts and great causes, there might be a general rise in the level of human beauty, due to the gradual diffusion of the reflected glow of a spiritual light, and it might become possible for "beauty born," not "of murmuring sound" only but of many beautiful things and even of the totality of beautiful things, to "pass into the face." For what differentiates physical beauty from the other aspects of physical well-being is that there is a spiritual element in it, which may be a mere possibility, but which admits of indefinite expansion if favourable influences are brought to bear on it. The growth of the soul, as we have seen, makes for physical well-being by removing hindrances to the due development of the body. But its action on physical beauty is of a different character. In response to its subtle stimulus physical beauty ceases to be merely physical: the spiritual element in it begins to reveal itself, and at last becomes symbolical of the soul's well-being and transfigures the whole outer man.

CHAPTER II

MENTAL WELL-BEING

THE growth of the body is a movement towards a finite and predestined, though unattainable goal. The growth of the soul is a veritable adventure into the infinite. So is each of its vital aspects. For the unconscious aim of the growing soul is to grow into oneness with Supreme Reality, to realize the Ideal of all ideals; and Supreme Reality reveals itself in many ways, and in each of these revelations announces itself as the ideal end of desire and effort.

Thus it appeals to the soul, through the medium of its *imaginative reason*, as the final end of its mental activity, of its disinterested desire to perceive, to understand, to know,—and in doing so reveals itself, in the last resort, as Ideal Truth.

Again, it appeals to the soul, through its *sensuous imagination*, as the object of sense-born, but self-refining and self-transcending desire,—and in doing so reveals itself, in the last resort, as Ideal Beauty.

Once more, it appeals to the soul through its *conscience*, through its desire to order its own goings aright, to make the right choice among conflicting motives to conduct,—and in doing so reveals itself, in the last resort, as the supreme end of human action, as Ideal Good.

Lastly, it appeals to the soul through no intervening medium, *as soul to soul*, as the Universal to the individual soul,—and in doing so reveals itself, in the last resort, as Love.

Here are four aspects of the self-revelation of the Divine through the self-realization of the soul. Let us first think of the growth of the soul as *mental*, as a movement towards

Ideal Truth. The fruits of growth, in this sphere of the soul's activity, may be summed up under the general head of mental well-being; and mental well-being may be defined as nearness to ideal truth. What does this mean? In our attempt to determine its meaning, we are faced at the outset by a practical paradox. The surest proof of nearness to ideal truth is consciousness of being far from that unattainable goal. In other words, mental well-being has its counterpart, not in a state of certitude, but in an endless quest. The desire for ideal truth, if we duly stress the word *ideal*, is not a desire for possession. For it is of the essence of an ideal always to elude the grasp of the pursuer and so to lure him on into the mysterious and the unknown. If we could attain to possession of ideal truth we should have lost our prize in the act of winning it. The dogmatist, the lover of finality, the man who "counts himself to have apprehended" in great matters, has actually turned his back on the goal which he believes himself to have reached. We must therefore convince ourselves at the outset that desire for possession of the truth of things is incompatible with desire for ideal truth; and that if we are to find happiness in the satisfaction of the latter desire we must make renunciation of the former our starting-point in our great adventure. But if desire for ideal truth does not mean desire for possession of the truth of things, what does it mean? This question, as it seems to me, answers itself. Desire for ideal truth means desire to be possessed by the truth of things, to be possessed by it in its own good season —to be enfolded by it, interpenetrated by it, inspired by it —and meanwhile, as a preparation for that act of initiation, to make oneself worthy to entertain so divine a guest.

How is this to be done? In the first place—and in the last place—by resisting the lure of finality, by refusing to rest in any theory of the Universe or any formulated scheme of life; in other words, by renouncing self in the sphere of high thinking, by emptying the mind of its cherished convictions, so that it may be filled, in the fulness of time, by the spirit of truth. But will this act or effort of renunciation bring happiness? It will certainly not bring comfort. On this point we must make our minds quite clear. But it will bring happiness. For, in the first place, to attain to fluidity of belief and to keep belief fluid, demands a great and sustained mental effort ; and such an effort, involving as it does the constant exercise of all our higher mental powers, will necessarily make for mental growth and therefore for mental well-being. I have elsewhere said that if the pursuit of truth is to be effective, reason and intuition must co-operate and the balance between the two must be maintained. Divorced from the other, each of these sovereign faculties makes for dogmatism, for the acceptance of what is relatively and provisionally as absolutely and finally true. The man who, on the mental plane, identifies himself with his reason, will allow his own arguments to impose on his mind unduly, and, in the absence of the undermining protests of intuition, will invest his own logically reasoned conclusions with the weight and authority of scientific truth. In like manner the man who, on the mental plane, identifies himself with his intuition, will allow the subconscious working of his mind to control his whole speculative outlook, and, in the absence of the searching criticism of reason, will invest his own intuitive convictions with the weight and authority of inspired truth. These are extreme cases, but they are typical of two great tendencies of popular thought. The true centre of thought is perhaps equidistant from both extremes. The mere intellectual is as far from the truth of things as the mere visionary. In each case a subtle form of self-love has paralyzed the harmonious working of the mental powers, and has caused the mind of the teacher to succumb to the lure of finality and find repose in the possession of a formula or a catchword, instead of in the prosecution of an endless quest.

If the lure of finality is to be successfully resisted, if conviction, instead of crystallizing into dogmatism, is to remain fluid and mobile and evolutionary, if the mind is to keep open its communications with the infinite, the balance between reason and intuition must, at whatever cost, be duly maintained. The conclusions of reason must be reviewed and criticized by the intuitive judgment, by the mind unconsciously applying its own unformulated principles. And the decisions of intuition must be reviewed and criticized by the rational judgment, by the mind consciously, or subconsciously, applying its own formulated or semi-formulated rules. But the maintenance of the balance must be dynamic, so to speak, not static; oscillatory, not quiescent. The attempt to maintain it will involve the assiduous exercise of all our mental powers; and the reward of this will be all-round mental progress. But progress, as we know from experience—whether in the life of the individual or of the race—is never equable or regular. At one time there is excess in this direction; at another time, in that. Indeed the effort to correct such inequalities, to restore the balance as often as it is lost, is one of the chief causes of progress. And, however much we may try to maintain the balance between reason and intuition, it is certain that we shall never attain to complete equilibrium. At one time reason will be in excess, at another time intuition. But if the maintenance of the balance is our chief concern, the excess will be duly felt as such, and will therefore, in the natural course of things, begin to correct itself. When reason is in excess, the consequent sense of disharmony will stimulate the intuitional side of the mind to renewed activity; and when intuition is in excess, the consequent sense of disharmony will stimulate the rational side of the mind to renewed activity. And so the attempt to maintain the balance, which will again and again be restored and again and again lost, will necessarily react upon our mental development, sustaining it from season to season and distributing it, as it were, over the whole surface of the expanding mind.

In other words, the attempt to deliver the mind from the fundamental fallacy of dogmatism (the dogmatic diathesis being the outcome and the evidence of one-sided mental development) by maintaining the balance between reason and intuition, will, if faithfully gone about, result in healthy and harmonious mental growth. And in such growth we shall find the true solution—or rather we shall provide for the true solution—of the master problem of existence. In our present state of mental development we are not equal to the task of solving that problem; and it is well that we should recognize this fact. We may, if we please—we may, because we must—amuse ourselves by trying to guess the riddle which is behind all riddles; and the attempt to do so, if we will but reject every guess as wide of the mark and keep on guessing, will not be wasted, for it will react, as we have just seen, on our general mental development. But for the right answer to the riddle we must wait, and be content to wait, till our minds are equal to the task of guessing it, till we have grown to the requisite mental stature. The supreme problems of thought will be solved, not so much by any conscious attempt to solve them (as one solves problems in mathematics or chemistry) as by the actual growth of the mind, in response to which the problems will perhaps re-state themselves and point the way to their own solution. Or rather, by the actual growth of the soul. When the mind becomes equal to the task of solving those great problems, it will find that it has outgrown itself and merged its life and its growth in the general life and the general growth of the soul. For it is by the waking of consciousness in the hidden depths of our buried life that the growth of the soul has been and is being effected. The dawn of consciousness has already wrought miracles. But it is possible that these are as nothing compared with the miracles which it has yet to work. It is possible that there are whole aspects of Nature's being, whole realms of existence, which are waiting for us to discover them through the evocation of appropriate senses,—waiting, in other words, for consciousness to awake in the corresponding strata of our souls. To accelerate the dawn of consciousness, to work unceasingly for the deepening and diffusion of its light, is a task into which we must throw all our powers, including those which we speak of collectively as mental. Including those, but going far beyond them. The waking of consciousness is a process of which mental progress is one aspect, and one only. The precept "Grow and you will know" does not stand alone. There are other precepts which are at least equally significant, and equally imperative in their claims. We shall come to some of these when we are considering other aspects of soul-growth. Meanwhile, as we are now considering the mental aspect, let us receive the precept "Grow and you will know" and lay it to heart.

Grow and you will know, and while you are growing possess your soul in patience, and wait for the fuller revelation of the dawning light of truth.

Wait in patience: and patience will become serenity, and serenity will become hope and faith and joy. With healthy and harmonious growth will come the sense of well-being which we call happiness. This is one reason why the attempt to keep belief fluid and prevent it from crystallizing into dogma must needs bring happiness to those who make it and sustain it. But there is another reason. Or rather, the one reason—for there is only one—may be looked at from another point of view. The path through faith and hope is not the only path from serenity to joy. There is another path—through tolerance, through charity, through sympathy, through love. It is in following this path that agnosticism, in the true sense of the word, finds its fullest reward. He who knows that he does not and cannot know will look with an impartial eye on all attempts and all pretensions to know. Though he will subscribe to no creed, he will sympathize, in varying degrees, with all creeds; and as he has no system of his own to uphold and propagate, it will not be possible for any rival system to disturb his peace of mind. He will say *Amen* in his heart to Emily Brontë's daring challenge to "orthodoxy":

> Vain are the thousand creeds
> That move men's hearts: unutterably vain;
> Worthless as withered weeds,
> Or vilest froth amid the boundless main,
> To waken doubt in one
> Holding so fast by thine infinity. . . .

But in his attitude towards the "thousand creeds" he will pass beyond the limit of mere defiance. Realizing, as he does, that "we are all seekers still," he will regard the dogmatist as a fellow-seeker who, having mistaken a particular aspect of truth for truth itself, has broken off abruptly in the middle of his search, and the dogmatism of whose dogmas is their chief defect. A large, all-embracing tolerance, which will bear with everything in the sphere of belief except aggressive intolerance, will gradually take possession of his mind and heart; and the charity which is the active principle in tolerance will be ready to expand, in due season, first into sympathy and then into love.

That fluidity of belief, by giving free play to the sympathetic instincts, makes for happiness—for inward peace in the soul of the agnostic believer and for peace and good-will in the world at large—is suggested, to say the least, by the plain fact that dogmatism, crystallization of belief, is one of the most fruitful of all sources of unhappiness,—of bitterness in the soul of the "orthodox" believer, and of strife and misery in the world at large. On this point the teaching of history is conclusive. The *odium theologicum* is proverbial. The most cruel of all wars are those which have been waged in the name of religion. And the story of religious persecution is the blackest chapter in the history of mankind. And the misery which dogmatism has caused —the evil passions which it has awakened, the suffering, the desolation which it has let loose—does but reflect the unhappiness which darkens the heart of the dogmatist. What is the explanation of this paradox? Why should he who professes to have found inward peace in the teaching of "authority" be fiercely intolerant of those who do not share his beliefs? Because, though he may not know it, he has not found inward peace. I do not wish to suggest that dogmatism is necessarily intolerant. There are many professing dogmatists who are indifferentists at heart. There are others—we may still reckon them by millions—who, having drunk in their faith with their mother's milk, take it for granted as they take air or light for granted, and are scarcely aware that there is any faith but their own. But whenever the spirit of curiosity, of inquiry, of free criticism awakes from its intermittent slumber, when things which have long been taken for granted begin to be called in question, dogmatism, like every other tendency of human thought, must needs become self-conscious. And the self-conscious dogmatist proves to be a sceptic at heart. For now he *realizes*, if he never did so before, that there are other faiths than his own. "The thousand creeds that sway men's hearts," or, rather, the nine hundred and ninety-nine which are not his, *do* waken doubt in some dark, remote recess of his sub-conscious mind. His very zeal for "the faith "—his readiness to take up arms against its opponents, to persecute heresy, to outlaw dissent, his rancorous vehemence in controversy, his reckless use of such opprobrious epithets as *atheist* and *infidel*—is symptomatic, not of "indefectible certitude" but of mental uneasiness, of secret self-distrust. He who "protests too much," if he is not consciously trying to deceive others, is unconsciously trying to deceive himself.

Those who really know, and who know that they really know, are of all men the most tolerant. Ignorance may move them to pity; but doubt, dissent, denial, far from moving them to anger, do not so much as ruffle their peace of mind. What chemist would think of being angry because an established chemical formula was called in question? What physicist would wish to confute the lunatic who tried to prove that the earth was flat? It is in the borderland of Science, it is where doubt and uncertainty still linger, that we have anger, rancour, vehemence in assertion, heat in argument, hatred of dissent. The tragedy of dogmatism is that the dogmatist, in his dread of the mysterious and the unknown, has sold his birth-right—freedom—to "authority" for mental repose, and that the purchase money has not been paid, and can never be paid, in full.

If the attempt to close the mind, on the higher levels of thought, is so fruitful a source of unhappiness and unrest, may we not conjecture that the open mind, which is the proof and the reward of mental growth, will bring happiness and inward peace? The aspects of the soul are many, but the soul itself is one; and growth of mind, on the higher levels of thought, is also—in some sort and some measure—growth of imagination, growth of conscience, growth of the higher emotions, growth of the whole inner man. The reason why fluidity of belief must sooner or later bring happiness to the believer is that to keep an open mind about great matters, not from indifference but from devotion to ideal truth, is to keep an open heart, and that an open heart is at peace with itself and with all the world. The all-embracing tolerance which is the counterpart of faith in ideal truth, will develop of inner necessity into all-embracing sympathy; and all-embracing sympathy will develop of inner necessity into all-embracing love. As the open mind is waiting to be possessed by truth, so the open heart is waiting to be possessed by love.

Need I add that the well-being which rewards mental activity on the highest levels of thought, will make its presence felt on all the lower levels, down to the lowest level of all,—down to that quasi-physical side of mentality which we call brain-power or brain-efficiency? All our mental powers have to co-operate in the quest of ideal truth; and the man who makes that quest the main purpose of his life, who, in prosecuting it, is alternately adventurous and critical, imaginative and logical, will allow none of his mental powers to become atrophied through disuse, but will keep them all active and alert; and, in the absence of injury through disease or accident, the efficiency of his brain will have to keep pace with the growing efficiency of his mind. And he will find that on every level of thought the chief hindrance to the pursuit of truth is the self-love which resists the emancipative processes of growth. Whatever matter may be under discussion, it is self-love, the obstinate clinging to one's own theories, one's own assumptions, one's own points of view, one's own habits of thought, which militates against the disinterested pursuit of truth, warping the powers, misdirecting the energies, and vitiating the arguments of the disputants, substituting jealous rivalry for fraternal co-operation, and subordinating the desire to arrive at the true solution of a problem to the desire to score points in a duel of words. The history of every science tells us that scientific progress has again and again been retarded—for years, for generations, even for centuries—by petty self-love, self-love manifesting itself either as jealousy of superior talent, or as a selfish conservatism which regards criticism of what is orthodox and established as an attack on its own vested interests, and resents every attempt at reform as a personal affront.

On every level of thought the one precept holds good: *Grow and you will know*. Subdue self-love, and you will at once foster your own mental growth and accelerate the advent, first of positive, then of ideal truth. Grow, through mental self-discipline and moral self-mastery, and in the fulness of time—or of eternity—you will solve all problems, either by working them out to their respective solutions or by allowing them to solve themselves in your inner life. On the lower levels you will possess knowledge and be happy in possessing it. On the higher levels you will become worthy to be possessed by ideal truth ; and while you are waiting, in the serenity of faith, for that divine consummation, you will perhaps be too happy to realize your own happiness.

CHAPTER III

ÆSTHETIC WELL-BEING

As it is the consummation of mental well-being to be possessed by ideal truth, so it is the consummation of æsthetic well-being to be possessed by ideal beauty. When supreme reality reveals itself to the soul through the medium of the bodily senses, when it presents itself as the object of sensuous or semi-sensuous desire, we get beauty. The pursuit of truth is at first active and aggressive, a desire to possess, and enjoy and make use of possession; but, as the pursuit develops, as it enlarges its scope, as its object draws the pursuer on beyond the limits of any dream of possession, the desire to possess gradually transforms itself into the desire to be possessed. In the pursuit of beauty this order is to some extent reversed. The response to the appeal of beauty is at first passive and receptive, an opening of the heart to the influx of a semi-sensuous delight, a desire to be flooded with pleasurable sensation, a desire to enjoy for the mere sake of enjoyment. But the luxury of passive enjoyment will not permanently content the heart. Under the stress of its own intensity the desire to enjoy will become active and aggressive. For, as a man's perception of beauty grows deeper and clearer, he will find that if he is to continue to deepen and clarify it, he must try to express it; he will find, in other words, that if he is to continue to enjoy, he must make progress in enjoying, and that if he is to make progress in enjoying, he must try to create.

The relation between perception and expression is a theme on which I have already written; and as I find that since I wrote I have not changed my point of view, I will ask leave to quote my own words (with a few trifling alterations):

"Perception and expression are not two faculties, but one. Each is the very counterpart and correlate, each is the very life and soul, of the other. When perception is real, living, informed with personal feeling, it must needs find for itself the outlet of expression. When expression is real, living, informed with personal feeling, perception—one's own perception of things—must needs be behind it. More than that, the perceptive faculties grow through the interpretation which expression gives them, and make but little growth in any other way. And the expressive faculties grow by interpreting perception, and make but little growth in any other way.[1] The artist, for example, who tries to draw what he sees (and feels) is training his power of observation, not less than his power of expression. As he passes and repasses between the object of his perception and his representation of it, there is a continuous gain both to his vision and to his technique. The more faithfully he tries to render his impression of the object, the more does that impression gain in truth and strength; and in proportion as the impression becomes truer and stronger, so does the rendering of it become more masterly and more correct. So, again, if a man tries to set forth in writing his views about some difficult problem—social, political, metaphysical, or whatever it may be—the very effort that he makes to express himself clearly and coherently will tend to bring order into the chaos and light into the darkness of his mind, to widen his outlook on his subject, to deepen his insight into it, to bring new aspects of it within the reach of his conscious thought. And here, as in the case of the artist who tries to draw what he sees, the reaction of expression on perception will be met and matched by the reaction of perception on expression. Even in so abstract and impersonal a subject as mathematics the reaction of expression on perception will be strong and salutary. The student who wishes to master a difficult piece of bookwork should try to write it out in his own words; in the effort to set it out concisely and lucidly he will gradually perfect his apprehension of it. Were he to solve a difficult problem, he would

[1] When I say this I am of course straining to the utmost the respective meanings of the words *perception* and *expression*.

probably regard his grasp of the solution as insecure and incomplete until he had succeeded in making it intelligible to the mind of another. When perception is deeply tinged with emotion, as when one sees what is beautiful, or admires what is noble, the attempt to express it in language, action, or art, seems to be dictated by some inner necessity of one's nature. The meaning of this is that the perception itself imperatively demands expression in order that, in and through the struggle of the artistic consciousness to do full justice to it, it may gradually realize its hidden potentialities, discover its inner meaning and find its true self."[1]

If the general principle that perception and expression act and react on each other, each helping forward the evolution of the other, applies to every side or aspect of man's life, it applies more particularly to the æsthetic side, to the cult and quest of beauty. In the spontaneous attempt to deepen and clarify the perception of beauty by finding suitable expression for it, the cult of beauty becomes a quest and an adventure, and Art—creative art—begins. Begins —and ends (though of course it has no ending) ; for it is in the attempt to attain to vision by revealing it, that Art finds its final as well as its initial meaning.

There are many media of artistic expression ; and therefore, though Art is one, there are many arts. Each of these has its own subdivisions and its own sub-arts. But these are matters which I need not discuss.

If the secret of mental well-being may be set forth in the precept : *Grow and you will know*, the secret of æsthetic well-being may be set forth in the precept : *Grow and you will see*. That the growth of the soul is the pathway to ideal beauty seems to follow from the fact that all the hindrances to æsthetic well-being, to the perception and expression of beauty, fall under the head of arrested soul-growth. Grow and you will see (and hear) ; and the more clairvoyant (and clairaudient) you become, the more your vision (and your hearing) grows in clearness and penetrative power, the more urgent will be its demand for expression. Why, then, is the demand so seldom made, and why is the response to it so often ineffective ? Chiefly, I think, because of the para-

[1] *What Is All Which Might Be*, pp. 84–86.

lyzing influence of education. It will be said that artistic genius is rare. No doubt it is. But artistic capacity is by no means rare. On the contrary, as we are just beginning to discover, it is part of the inheritance of every normal child. It has taken us a long time to make this discovery. That young children delight in drawing and colouring, in modelling, in dancing to music, that they have a keen sense of colour, of form, of rhythm, are obvious facts. What have we made of these facts ? They might have suggested to us that the artistic instinct, which must needs have artistic capacity as its counterpart, does at least exist as a possibility in every human being, that it is one of the "clouds of glory" through which the life of each of us dawns on earth. But, while duly recognizing the artistic leanings of young children, we have been content to believe that, except in rare cases, artistic capacity does not and cannot survive childhood, our reason for this belief being that the child's interest in art and his desire to express himself in art cease, as a rule, at an early age. We have not asked ourselves why this fate should befall them. We have taken for granted that somehow or other they go out like the flame of a candle in a draught. Had we paused to reflect we might have reminded ourselves that, apart from accident, a natural instinct, like the flame of a candle, does not die out except for lack of appropriate food.

We are now, as I have said, beginning to discover that, if it is duly fed and fostered, the artistic capacity of the normal child will persist and develop and bear fruit in due season. The indications that this is so are as yet few ; but they are significant. We owe them to the faith and enterprise of certain gifted teachers. In the school in "Utopia" which I have described elsewhere, the children, under sympathetic guidance and in response to the stimulus of freedom, took to brush drawing, to folk songs, and to morris dances as ducklings take to the water, and produced results which surprised all who visited the school. What made their achievements the more remarkable was that "Utopia" is a rural village in a county inhabited by what is supposed to be a slow-witted and unmusical people. I have already told the story of the teacher of drawing who, having changed his aims and methods in the direction of giving his pupils freedom for self-expression, found that 95 per cent of them could reach a level which had previously been reached by only 5 per cent. A great pioneer, whose work is being carried on by a band of trained teachers, has made a similar discovery in the sphere of music. He and his followers have proved to demonstration that musical capacity is far more widely diffused than we had imagined and has far greater possibilities. They have even proved that musical composition is a natural mode of self-expression, which children will use freely if they are allowed and encouraged to do so. And what is true of music is true, as certain pioneers are beginning to discover, of poets. The Headmaster of a Grammar School for Boys, the Head Mistress of a Higher Standard Elementary School for Girls, and an Assistant in a Municipal Secondary School for Girls have convinced themselves that children "have within them, mostly latent, a vein of poetry, simple and rhythmical, and need only right stimulus to use and delight in their powers"; and the work of their pupils (if I may judge from specimens which I have seen) should carry the same conviction to all unprejudiced inquirers.

Similar discoveries are constantly being made. The conclusion to which they point is that, however rare artistic genius may be—and it is possibly less rare than we are apt to imagine—artistic capacity is part of our normal equipment. And if artistic capacity could be given fair play, if the earlier stirrings of æsthetic sensibility could be allowed to express themselves, on the one hand opportunities would be given to artistic genius to reveal and assert itself, and on the other hand the general level of artistic achievement—the plateau from which the great peaks soar skyward—would be appreciably raised.

But why does artistic capacity so seldom come to maturity? Why is it so systematically repressed in early life? Because psychology and education act and react on one another, for good or for evil; and because at present, owing to each of them being in its infancy, their reciprocal action is harmful to both, education being based on ignorance of human nature and tending to perpetuate that ignorance by preventing human nature from revealing itself. The result of this is, as regards the culture of artistic capacity, that education, having utilitarian ends in view and being ready to assume, on the authority of a shallow popular psychology, that the artistic instinct is an altogether exceptional gift, denies to that instinct opportunities for development and so blights it before it has begun to unfold.

But though repressive education is the most serious of all hindrances to æsthetic well-being, it is not the only hindrance. If it represses, and therefore atrophies, artistic capacity in childhood and adolescence, the environment of the adult tends to deaden what is the counterpart of artistic capacity,—æsthetic sensibility. The materialism and externalism of modern life, which are at once the evidences and the causes of arrested soul-growth, are ever tending, especially in a highly industrialized country like ours, to surround us with ugly sights and ugly sounds. Every factory is an eyesore, a vast amorphous block of brick or masonry, pierced with innumerable windows, with a giant chimney belching forth black clouds of almost solid smoke. And our mines and metal-works, with their unsightly dumps and slag-heaps, and their intervening spaces wasted and scarred and blasted by our ruthless industry, are even more repulsive. What can be more depressing than the dingy, monotonous, sordid suburbs of our busy towns? What more distressing than the noises of its factories, its metal-works, and its streets? In such regions, the dwellers in which are numbered by millions and will presently be numbered by tens of millions, Man, as a builder, instead of trying to adorn the surface of the earth, seems to be doing his best to deface it. If men are sensitive, as they surely are, to their everyday surroundings, how can æsthetic sensibility be expected to thrive amid such sights and such sounds as these?

But it is not only by surrounding us with what is mean and ugly that modern commercialism and industrialism wage war against the cult of the beautiful. It is also by preoccupying our minds with selfish ambitions and sordid cares. When travel in mountainous regions was difficult and dangerous the grandeur of mountain scenery was lost on the traveller. A wonder-world was waiting to be discovered, but it was not for him to explore it.

> The sleep that is among the lonely hills

was a terror to him, not an inspiration. His mind was so preoccupied with the risks and discomforts of his journey that he had no eye and no thought for the more spiritual aspects of his surroundings. In like manner, and for a like reason, when the rich are devoting their time and their energy to making themselves richer, when the poor are working long hours in mill or mine or foundry either for the bare means of subsistence or for a modest rise in the scale of comfort, the doors of the soul are perforce closed to the appeal of what is beautiful. Men are living their lives on another and a lower plane. Their minds are absorbed by other desires and other interests. If they have leisure to enjoy themselves, they need the distraction of coarser and more palpable pleasures. Can we wonder that when beauty, whether of nature or art, whispers its message, there is no receiver in the soul to vibrate in response to it? Can we wonder that in many, perhaps in most hearts, the æsthetic sense, and with it the artistic instinct, is dormant, if not dead?

And if, as sometimes happens, the artistic instinct is strong enough to resist the numbing pressure of education, and to hold its own against the rivalry of "business," with its thousand cares and interests, and of the pleasures in which busy men find distraction and relaxation, will the path to æsthetic well-being lie open to the artistic soul? Perhaps it will; but new dangers will beset it. Self-love, the deadly enemy of self-growth, wearing a new form as often as occasion may require, will haunt it from day to day. Again and again a wayside inn will tempt the traveller to make it his home and give up his adventure into the infinite. The thirst for popularity, for notoriety, for "success" and the prizes that reward success, professional jealousy and spite, readiness to repeat the shibboleths of the various schools, and to allow the corresponding theories to limit outlook and distort vision,—these influences and such as these will stand in the way of devotion to art for the sake of art, and will make it difficult for the artist to prepare his soul for its high destiny,—for being possessed, in the fulness of time, by the ideal of which he dreams. Above all, he will be tempted to rest in his own achievements, to be satisfied with the progress that he has made, to work by his own formulas, to repeat himself in this and other ways,—if he is popular, to accept the " voice of the people " as the " voice of God,"—if he is unpopular, to console himself with the reflection that " it is always lonely on the heights." Should he succumb to this temptation, the balance between perception and expression would become *static*, and his adventure into the infinite would come to an abrupt and ignominious end. For the function of art is to interpret the feeling which beauty kindles in the heart that is open to its influence, to interpret this feeling by trying to express it, and—through the oft-repeated failure of that attempt—to reveal to the feeling its own depths and its own subtleties, and so to awaken the profounder and more spiritual emotion, of which it is, as it were, the first intimation, the first stirring into life. The artist who is satisfied with his work has lost touch with his own infinitude, and has therefore forfeited the licence under which he works.

For all these maladies there is one remedy, against all these temptations there is one shield—soul-growth. As vigorous growth, by producing strength and elasticity of fibre, enables a plant to beat off the pests that are ready to assail it, so, if free play can be given to the expansive forces and tendencies that are latent in the artistic soul, the surest of all antidotes will be found for the protean poison of self-love.

Grow and you will see. Grow and you will hear. What will you not see? What will you not hear? Who can impose limits on the clairvoyant and clairaudient soul? One of the vital characteristics of the great artist is his *impartiality*,—his catholicity of taste, his freedom from professional jealousy, his disinterested delight in beauty, his readiness to admire artistry (by whatever hand it may have been produced), his sympathetic interest in his fellow-men and all their ways and works (even in those which as a moralist or a social reformer he might condemn), his power of seeing beauty in the "altogetherness" of things which in detail are sordid and ugly. And this impartiality, like the tolerance of the agnostic believer, far from being merely negative and passive, admits of endless expansion and development. Indeed, if it is allowed to have its own way, it will be carried at last by its own natural momentum into what is really the highest form of activity, into that all-embracing receptivity which is, in the true sense of the word, creative. For to see things in their totality, and therefore in their ordered beauty (whether the vision embody itself in outward form or not), is an essentially artistic achievement. And the artist whose synthetic and abstractive genius enables him to build up trivial and commonplace and even unlovely details into beautiful wholes—in other words, whose perception is itself creative—is qualifying himself for the highest of all artistic achievements (in which receptivity and creativeness become one) for the achievement of beholding, unblinded, the splendour[1] of the living Whole, of discerning the ordered beauty and vibrating to the innermost rhythm of the Universe. "He who has been instructed thus far in the things of love, and who has learned to see the beautiful in due order and succession, when he comes towards the end will suddenly perceive a nature of wondrous beauty (and this, Socrates, is the final cause of all our former toils) . . . beauty only, absolute, simple, and everlasting, which without diminution and without increase, or any change, is imparted to the ever-growing and perishing beauties of all other things. He who under the influence of true love rising upward from them begins to see that beauty, is not far from the end."[2]

Is this the Beatific Vision? If it is not, it is very near to it. The Beatific Vision is, I imagine, the revelation of the "unbeholden essence" of all things to the spiritual senses in their totality, to the soul acting as its own medium and its own organ of perception. But if that revelation is reserved for those who have climbed to the higher planes of being, it is possible for us to have foretastes of it, through the æsthetic senses, while we are still in the flesh. To some of us the foretaste comes through the medium of music.

[1] The outward splendour. The inward splendour shines for itself alone. "You will enter the light but you will never touch the flame."

[2] Plato, *Symposium*. Diotima is speaking to Socrates.

To others through the medium of poetry. To others, again, it is a direct message from what we call the outward world. Nor need one be an artist, in any technical sense of the word, in order to experience it. All that one needs is a certain measure of æsthetic sensibility and a soul which can withdraw for a season from the business and the tumult of the world.[1] "To speak for myself [who am no artist]—the early summer morning always bears me a message, of the genuineness and authoritativeness of which I cannot, while the impression lasts, entertain the faintest doubt. New cosmic forces seem to reveal themselves, forces whose serenity and majesty belong to some other world than ours; the all-pervading stillness and freshness and purity seem to herald the advent of some transcendent power; while the sense of being alone with 'Nature' cancels for the moment all those distracting influences which ordinarily restrict our outlook and cloud our skies. The resultant feeling is one which, for obvious reasons, I cannot even attempt to express in words. But, as the cold flush of dawn steals along the hilltops, and as the mists rise up from the river meadows, I feel—nay, *I know*, with an assurance which transcends all conviction—that the greatest of all problems has been solved for me, not by being worked out to a solution, but by being 'utterly abolished and destroyed.'"[2] In such an experience the soul attains, if only for a moment, to æsthetic well-being, to nearness to ideal beauty. The moment is fugitive, but it takes the soul out of time into eternity, and it is therefore a possession for ever.

[1] The expression which is the counterpart of perception and which fosters æsthetic sensibility does not *necessarily* take the form of artistic creation. A man may commune with himself as well as with others; and in trying to express what he has seen or heard, he may be prevented by the very intensity and subtlety of his feeling from doing justice to it in any outward form. A great poet has told us that there are many poets "sown by Nature" who have "the vision and the faculty divine," yet want "the accomplishment of verse"; and what is true of poetry is true of art in general. But this does not alter the fact that for nine men out of ten æsthetic sensibility finds (or should find) its counterpart in artistic expression, and that each of these tendencies develops itself through its reaction to the stimulus of the other.

[2] I wrote these words many years ago in a book which went out of print and has not been reprinted. My excuse for repeating them is that the book is dead and forgotten, and that I do not think I could find fitter words for the experience which I was trying to describe, an experience which is still mine in the sense that it has woven itself into my inmost life.

CHAPTER IV

MORAL WELL-BEING

IDEAL truth is a particular aspect of the Absolute Ideal, the Divine Life. So is ideal beauty. To be possessed by ideal truth, to be possessed by ideal beauty,—each of these is a sublimely high destiny. But there is a higher,—to be possessed by the Divine Life itself. The path to that goal is the path of *Conduct,* in the fullest, widest, and deepest sense of the word. And this path is, as it happens, open to all men. But are not all paths to the Ideal open to all men ? In theory they are ; and in a perfectly ordered communal life they would be. But actually, things being what they are, education being what it is, the conditions of our social and economic life being what they are, the paths to ideal truth and ideal beauty are open to very few. And if they are ever to be thrown open to all men, the path of conduct must be followed till it leads, through the transformation of character, to the spiritualization of our aims and the corresponding transvaluation of our values, and therefore to far-reaching social and economic reforms. Things being what they are, opportunities for mental and æsthetic development are denied to most of us. But we all have dealings, daily and hourly, with our fellow-men ; and in those dealings we have opportunities for conquering self or being conquered by self, for expanding life or contracting it, for finding our souls or losing them.

This is one reason why conduct is, as has been said, "three-fourths of life." But there is another. In the quest of ideal truth, as in the quest of ideal beauty, a man is trying to find something which is, in a sense, outside of and beyond himself. In the quest of ideal good, in following the path which leads to oneness with the Divine Life, he is trying to find his own true self, to become what he is meant to be. In order to attain to mental well-being he must follow the precept, "Grow, and you will *know*." In order to attain to æsthetic well-being he must follow the precept "Grow, and you will *see*." In order to attain to moral well-being he must follow the precept "Grow, and you will *become*." He can, in a sense, distinguish between himself and the object, even the ideal object, of his knowledge. He can, in a sense, distinguish between himself and the object, even the ideal object, of his vision. But in no sense can he distinguish between himself and what he is destined to become.

As by mental well-being we mean nearness to ideal truth, as by æsthetic well-being we mean nearness to ideal beauty, so by moral well-being we mean nearness to ideal good. The end of moral action, in this case or in that, is what the actor deems to be *good;* and the supreme end of moral action is therefore ideal good. Now the end which moral action, *as such,* does in point of fact serve, is that of establishing the higher self of the actor at the expense of the lower, the wider self at the expense of the narrower; and the ideal end of this process of raising the plane and widening the scope of life is the universalizing of the individual life, the merging of the individual soul—through its expansion, not through its annulment—in the infinite soul, in the soul of the Universe. In other words, ideal good—the final end of moral action—may be defined as oneness with Supreme Reality, with the Divine Life. And the path to this goal is the path of self-losing and self-finding, the path of dying to the lower self and living to the higher self.

The language which I am using is unavoidably dualistic. But I do not wish to suggest that there are only two selves, the lower and the higher, and that to die to one of these is to live to the other. Any self, however high or wide it may be, which claims finality, which invites us to rest in it, to identify ourselves with it, to regard its interests as the supreme end of aspiration and effort, is a lower self. The self of the patriot is a lower self, if he allows the frontiers of his country to determine the limits of his moral obligation and adopts an anti-human attitude towards the rest of his fellow-men. The self of the religious devotee is a lower self, if his zeal for his own religion makes him intolerant of all others. And the self of the philanthropist is a lower self, if he cannot find a more than human ideal for Humanity, if he cannot look beyond the Kingdom of Man to the Kingdom of God. Each of these enthusiasts is degrading what ought to be a higher self, by resting in it, by investing it with finality. The swiftness with which light moves baffles imagination. Yet if light were to claim to have attained to absolute swiftness, it would, in making that claim, convict itself of being relatively slow. In like manner, the higher self—the highest conceivable self—would be self-degraded, if it claimed to be the highest of all. The obligation which our infinitude lays upon us is a heavy one. If we would lighten it, we must advance to meet it. If we try to evade it, it will crush us into the dust from which we came.

He who would find the higher self must die to the lower self,—die to it, not once only, but again and again. But he must die to it by living to it, and living through it, and living beyond it, not by saying No to it at the outset. It is not until the lower self claims to be final and tries to detain him and make him forget his goal, that it reveals itself as lower, and that he must therefore say No to it. In other words, though self-denial will have to be practised again and again, the path to ideal good is in the main a path, not of self-denial but of self-development or self-realization. The ideal self is the true self; and it is therefore ours in promise and potency, ours as a possibility, ours as a seed to bring to maturity, from our very earliest days.

But there are pitfalls, as we all know, in the word *self*, as in every word which has a wide range of meaning. And there are corresponding pitfalls in every word in which *self* is a prefix. In particular, the word *self-realization* readily lends itself to misinterpretation. So readily, indeed, that until we have convinced ourselves that the self is a process, not a result, that the true self is an ideal, not a possession, the gospel of self-realization is a dangerous gospel to preach and to hear. The author of *A Student in Arms* tells us that at Oxford, in his undergraduate days, there was a craze for "self-realization." Let us see what the word suggested to the undergraduate mind. "In those days," says our author, "the great feature of those of us who tried to be 'in the forefront of modern thought' was their riotous egotism, their anarchical insistence on the claims of the individual at the expense even of law, order, society, and convention. 'Self-realization' was considered to be the primary duty of every man and woman. The wife who left her husband and children and home, because of her passion for another man, was a heroine, braving the hypocritical judgment of society to assert the claims of the individual soul. The woman who refused to abandon all for love's sake was not only a coward but a criminal, guilty of the deadly sin of sacrificing her soul, committing it to prison where it would languish and never bloom to its full perfection. The man who was bound to uncongenial drudgery by the chains of an early marriage or aged parents dependent on him, was the victim of a tragedy which drew tears from our eyes. The woman who neglected her home because she needed a 'wider sphere' in which to develop her personality, was a champion of women's rights, a pioneer of enlightenment. And on the other hand the people who went on making the best of uncongenial drudgery or in any way subjected their individualities to what old-fashioned people called the sense of duty, were in our eyes contemptible poltroons. It was the same in politics and religion. To be loyal to a party or a Church was to stand self-confessed a fool and a hypocrite. Self-realization, that was, in our eyes, the whole duty of man." Self-realization *is* the whole duty of man. So far the Oxford undergraduate of that day was in the right. But in his interpretation of the idea of self-realization he paid a poor compliment to his *self*. He identified his real self with his individuality, with that which differentiated his from all other selves; and he therefore meant by self-realization the cult of individuality for its own sake, the assertion and establishment of the individual, as against the communal (not to speak of the universal) self,—in the last resort, the apotheosis of selfishness in morals and anarchism in social life. But self-realization really means the use of individuality in order to pass beyond individuality, in order to transcend self.

Let us come to an understanding with ourselves on this vital point. A man's individuality—I cannot say this too often or too emphatically—is his own appointed way of escape from "self." If he will not use it for that purpose, it will become a prison to him—a prison within a prison—instead of an outlet into the open. There are other ways of escaping, or seeming to escape, from self. There is the way of blindly submitting to direction and instruction, and, in general, of yielding to pressure from without. This way, which has many side-ways, does but substitute one bondage for another. In delivering a man from anti-social individualism, it enslaves him to conventionality and custom; it mechanicalizes and devitalizes his life. And too often it leaves him in the prison of self in which it found him, having made escape from it impossible by introducing into it an asphyxiating atmosphere of make-believe, of hypocrisy and cant. The path of individuality, on the other hand, will lead us into the open air,—but only on one condition. We must follow it, not for its own sake, but for the sake of the open air to which it leads. If we follow it for its own sake, because it is easy or pleasant or interesting or otherwise attractive, if we make it an end in itself, then, when it begins to ascend and become arduous, we shall probably turn out of it into what will seem to be a continuation of it but will really be an alluring bypath; and that bypath, winding back and down hill, will lead us at last into the lowest dungeon of the prison from which we believed ourselves to have escaped.

So far indeed is individualism, the cult of individuality for its own sake, from being the true counterpart of self-realization, that the only way to realize *self* (in the full meaning of the word) is to refuse to *rest* in any self, however high or wide it may be, or however strong may be its claim to our devotion. In morals, as in every other sphere of the soul's activity, the lure of finality is our deadly enemy. The temptations with which it assails us may be looked at from two points of view. On the one hand, it tempts us to rest in a lower self, a self which is lower (however high it may happen to be) because it claims to be final; and it renews this temptation again and again. On the other hand, it tempts us to work for outward and finite ends, and for those only, instead of for the one end which is inward and infinite. These outward ends fall under the two general heads of *pleasure* and *success*. The range of pleasure is from what is most coarse and most sensual to what is most subtle and most refined. The range of success is from what is most sordid to what is most exalted, and from pettiness to grandeur of scale. But, however refined may be our pleasure, however exalted may be the level, however grand the scale of our success, if we invest either of these ends of action with finality, it will imprison us in our lower self; and then the only hope of escape for us will be that, when pursuit has become attainment and attainment possession, the prizes which lured us on with the promise of enduring happiness will turn to the dust of decay in our hands.

> Things won are done: joy's soul lies in the doing.

If we would keep on "doing" we must aim at the unattainable, we must find our highest pleasure in the growing pains of our higher self, and our best success in our failure to realize our infinite possibilities. Then "joy's soul" may perhaps be ours.

On the plane of conduct, as on all other planes, the growth of the soul is effected by the maintenance of what I have called a dynamic or progressive balance between the expansive and the contractive tendencies of our nature, between the *diastolē* and the *systolē* of the spiritual heart. On the mental plane, intuition, with its haunting vision of the infinite, is the expansive tendency; reason is the judicial, the critical, and therefore the contractive tendency. On the æsthetic plane, perception is expansive; expression—which is ever seeking to impose on perception the limitation of form—is contractive. On the moral plane, the expansive tendencies may be summed up under the general head of sympathy; the contractive, under the general head of self-control. In each of these cases the function of the limiting or contractive faculty (if I may use that word "without prejudice") is to strengthen and deepen the expansive faculty's capacity for expansion. This it does, partly by helping it to hold and consolidate whatever ground it may have won, partly—and chiefly—by throwing it back upon itself (through its criticism, direct or indirect), by compelling it to reconsider its aims and ways, and, as the result of such reconsideration, to bring fresh reserves of potentiality into action. And the balance between the two tendencies or forces or faculties (or whatever else we may please to call them) is, I repeat, a progressive balance—a balance which is again and again lost and again and again restored.

How the maintenance of a progressive balance between sympathy and self-control makes for moral growth is a theme on which I have already written and to which I need not now return.[1] The outcome of moral growth is the continuous expansion of the soul or self; and when this process has been carried so far that feeling has become fellow-feeling, and fellow-feeling has become all-embracing, the soul has attained to moral well-being and the end of the first stage in the path of conduct is in sight. He who has found his true self has made the joys and the sorrows, the successes and the failures, the glory and the shame of all his fellow-men his own. He feels what they feel because his life, by the force of its own natural expansion, by the actual widening of its spiritual horizon, has become one with theirs. Nor is it only with his fellow-man that he has this sense of oneness. He feels that all life is akin to him; and in the overflow of his sympathies he even passes beyond the limits—if there are any limits—of life.

In the all-embracing sympathy of the man who lives to his higher self we have the equivalent, on the moral plane, of the all-embracing tolerance of the thinker and the all-embracing impartiality and receptivity of the artist. But the tolerance of the thinker and the impartiality of the artist lose themselves at last in all-embracing sympathy, and are great (from one point of view) because they have it in them to do so. Therefore, as ends of human development, mental well-being and æsthetic well-being are in a sense subordinate to moral well-being. Yet even moral well-being, all-embracing sympathy, is not an end in itself. Or, rather, if it is to become an end in itself, it must pursue its adventure into the infinite. It must renew itself again

[1] See Part IV, Chapter V.

and again by finding practical expression for itself on an ever-widening scale. And it must move towards its ideal consummation by losing itself in all-embracing love. In other words, if moral well-being is to become an end in itself, it must on the one hand realize itself in *social well-being,* and on the other hand transform itself into *spiritual well-being.*

A brief summary of the contents of this chapter and its two predecessors may not be out of place. It is by the maintenance of a progressive balance between reason and intuition, that intuition becomes all-penetrative and therefore all-tolerant,[1] and that the intuition of truth develops into the vision of ideal truth. It is by the maintenance of a progressive balance between the expression and the perception of beauty, that perception becomes impartially receptive, or, in a word, creative, and that the perception of beauty develops into the vision of ideal beauty. In like manner, it is by the maintenance of a progressive balance between self-control and sympathy, that sympathy becomes all-embracing, and yet strengthens rather than weakens itself by its limitless diffusion, and that the soul finds, in oneness with all its kindred, the ideal good of which it dreams. As tolerance and impartiality are particular forms of sympathy, ideal truth and ideal beauty, as ends of human activity, are, to that extent, subordinate to ideal good. But, for the rest of their dominions, they own fealty to a yet diviner overlord. And even ideal good, oneness through sympathy with all kindred things, though an end in itself, is not the τέλος τελειόαττον, the complete and final end, of existence. If it is to attain to that consummation, if it is to attain to oneness with Supreme Reality, with the Divine Life, sympathy must transform itself into love.

[1] *Cf.* "Tout comprendre c'est tout pardonner."

CHAPTER V

SOCIAL WELL-BEING

IF social reform is to have a permanent foundation it must be based on moral progress. Otherwise our social structures, however skilfully they may have been devised, will prove to have been built on shifting sand. Moral progress is marked by the suppression of self through the expansion of self and the consequent outgrowth of sympathy. Sympathy, the sense of oneness with others which results from the gradual widening of one's spiritual horizon, is the ideal basis of social life. The actual basis is, as a rule, self-interest. From time immemorial men have banded themselves together for purposes of mutual help and protection and—as regards their neighbours—for purposes of aggression and defence. But here, as elsewhere, it is through the triumph of the ideal over the actual that progress has been and will be made.

In a well-ordered tribe the devotion of the individual to the community was complete. The social ideal of "each for all and all for each" was fully realized, and a high level of morality was reached.[1] But, to speak generally, the

[1] As tribalism is dying I speak of it in the past tense; but it is by no means dead: and when the conditions are favourable its characteristic virtues still survive. Mr. Homer Lane, the eminent psychologist and social reformer, has told me that in an Indian (North American) village in which he lived for some months, he found a higher level of morality than he had met with elsewhere. A magistrate in Pondoland has spoken to me in almost equally laudatory tones of the morals of his *protégés*. The Santals, an aboriginal people in the uplands of Bengal, seem to have all the primitive virtues. Many of them are now working as coolies in Mesopotamia. An Indian Subahdar who was in charge of one of their groups said to Mr. Edmund Candler, the War Correspondent: "There is no fighting, quarrelling, thieving, lying among them, Sahib. If you leave anything on the ground they won't pick it up. No trouble with womenfolk. No gambling. No tricks of deceit." A British officer in the company who knew them in their own country told Mr. Candler the same tale: "They are the straightest people I have ever struck. We raised them in

frontiers of the tribe determined the limits of morality. Beyond those frontiers, apart from such rudimentary conceptions of inter-tribal morality as self-interest might have dictated to the warring tribes, there was little or no sense of moral obligation. A man might be just, upright, and kindly in his dealings with his fellow-tribesmen and might be capable of prodigies of heroism and self-sacrifice on behalf of the common weal, and yet be a monster of cruelty and treachery in his dealings with the enemies, actual or possible, of his tribe. The explanation of this practical paradox is simple. The moral outlook of the tribesman was bounded by the needs and demands of the community to which he belonged. If cruelty and treachery to "foreigners" served, or might seem to serve, the interests of his own community, they were virtues in his eyes, not vices.

With the gradual supersession of tribal, first by civic, then by national life, society became more and more complex, and the basis of morality was completely transformed. The progressive expansion of the supreme political unit, and the corresponding expansion of the individual's range of activity called into being a multitude of sub-communities; and conflicting claims on a man's loyalty and devotion began to make themselves felt. One result of this was that the complete absorption of the individual into the collective life of the community, which was characteristic of tribal times, gradually passed away. When a man numbered his fellow-citizens by millions instead of hundreds, and when he belonged to a dozen communities instead of to one, his sense of communal obligation necessarily lost in intensiveness

the district, paid them a month's wages in advance, and told them to find their way to the nearest railway station, a journey of two or three days. They all turned up but one. They are very honest, law-abiding folk. They leave their money lying about in their tents, and it is quite safe. They have no police in their villages, the headman settles all their troubles. There's no humbug about them (as workers) . . . and they are extraordinarily patient and willing." Why are these primitive peoples so virtuous? Because, I imagine, the simple and stable conditions in which they live give full play to the natural goodness of human nature. The fact that we, with our vaunted civilization, fall so far short of them in virtue, suggests to my mind that much of human viciousness is due to the difficulty which men find in adapting themselves to a highly complex and ever changing environment. If you gave the North American Indians, the Pondos, and the Santals a new environment which was more complex and less stable than their own, it is probable that the strain on their character would be too great for them, and that their morals would go to pieces.

what it gained in extension. On the one hand, the individual began to look beyond the limits of the nation, with its millions of citizens, in the direction of Humanity, with its hundreds of millions; and the idea of a pan-human community, and of an even wider community which transcended the limits of experience—the Kingdom of God—began to shape itself in his mind. On the other hand, in the general confusion which the growing complexity of social life brought with it, he began to be thrown back on his own individual aims and interests; and, instead of being cared for by a quasi-socialistic government, he began to find it needful, in part at least, to shift for himself. In other words, idealism and universalism in one direction, and individualism in another, began to compete with and overshadow the communal devotion which had hitherto dominated his life.

The difficulty of adapting himself to an environment which became more and more complex and more and more unstable, the difficulty of steering his course through a sea which abounded in cross currents that were ever changing their direction, and in shallows and sand-banks that were ever changing their position, gave rise, in man's life, to a succession of problems moral, social, and political, which have hitherto defied solution. For thousands of years we have been experimenting with various types of governments and various forms of social organization, each of which has had its own moral ideals and standards; and not a single experiment has been permanently successful. The experiment which concerns us most, the feudal experiment—of irresponsible government by a privileged and propertied minority—has proved a failure; and in the awful war which is now devastating the civilized world, we are witnessing the dying convulsions of the feudal order of things, an order which has long determined, and still largely determines, our political, our social, and even (in no small measure) our moral outlook on life.

What will be the next stage in our social development? "The world," says the President of the United States, "must be made safe for democracy"; and the feeling that government must henceforth be based on the will of the people is in the air. In the horrors of the present war we are reaping the natural fruits of irresponsible government; and whatever changes may be in store for us, a permanent reversion to an order of things which the logic of events is discrediting with such terrible emphasis, is in the highest degree improbable. The masses are beginning to awake from the drugged slumber of the feudal ages, to look around them, to think, to speak, to organize themselves for collective action. For this incipient change there are many reasons. The spirit of man, by the force of its own natural expansion, is straining to breaking-point the fetters in which "authority" had so long bound it. For growth, if it is to be real, must come from within and cannot be superimposed from without. If man is to fulfil his destiny he must have freedom to develop himself; and experience is teaching him that without political freedom spiritual freedom will be incomplete. He must learn to govern himself, to control his lower nature, if his higher nature is to be free to evolve itself; and he must learn to govern himself politically and socially, as well as morally, if his moral self-government is to reach the level of self-mastery. It is not so much a privilege which the masses are agitating for as the right to take up a responsibility which they can no longer evade.

This is an aspect of the problem of government which such critics of democracy as the gifted author of *Le culte de l'incompetence*[1] are apt to ignore. The democratic sentiment is, in its essence, an instinctive protest against the deadening effect of a repressive regime. Other and baser feelings mingle themselves with this, and both colour it and are coloured by it. But because this instinctive protest—itself the outcome of man's secret desire for and effort towards self-realization—is at the heart of the sentiment, the cause of democracy, though its past be one of grotesque and pathetic failure, is certain of ultimate victory. In all the excesses and follies of democracy, in all its envies and jealousies and rancours, in all its meanness and pettiness, in all its baseness and sordidness, in all its ignobility and vulgarity, there is one thing which Demos, whose very delirium has a sanity of its own, is subconsciously struggling to

[1] M. Emile Faguet.

say: "If you will insist on closing in upon me with commands and prohibitions and directions; if you will insist on telling me what I am to think, to believe, to aim at, to desire, to do; if you will insist on regulating my life in all its details; if you will insist on doing for me things which I ought to learn to do for myself,—you will make it impossible for me to develop my own powers and faculties, you will arrest my growth and suffocate my life. Stand aside, then, and let me have access to the air, and the sunshine, and give me freedom to breathe, to live, and to grow."

Here is one reason why the tide is setting towards democracy. It is a reason which has always been and will always be operative. But it is now being reinforced by another reason which is, in a special sense, characteristic of the present age. Applied science, though it puts terrible weapons in the hands of a tyrant, is in the long run the deadly enemy of tyranny. For it enables tyranny to become so oppressive that men must either make an end of it or allow it to strangle their souls. The discoveries and inventions of the past and present centuries are producing social changes which tend to make government more and more highly organized and therefore more and more inquisitorial. The improvements in the means of transport, which have already gone far, and, now that the air has been mastered, will go much further, have made for the more effective centralization of authority, which can now stretch out its arms to the furthest limits of the world, and can also concern itself with details which formerly escaped its supervision. And though this progressive centralization is necessarily balanced by progressive decentralization, new nerve-centres evolving themselves as the main nerve-centre gains in extent and complexity, the decentralization of authority, by bringing it nearer to the daily life of each of its subjects, makes it more rather than less inquisitorial. And if it is inevitable that authority should become more and more inquisitorial, it is also desirable. For, thanks to the achievements of applied science, especially in the fields of engineering, of sanitation, and of the prevention and treatment of disease, authority, whether central or local, can now do far more for the well-being of the citizen than was possible in pre-scientific and pre-"industrial" days. But the more authority does for the citizen, the greater is the amount of direction, whether positive or prohibitive, with which it will restrict his action, and the more it will tend to encroach on his freedom. The compulsory notification of infectious diseases, the compulsory segregation of infected persons, the compulsory education of children and (as is now proposed) of adolescents, and compulsory military service, are cases in point; and there are many other indications that even the Englishman's home is no longer an impregnable castle, and that official interference with family life is likely to increase as time goes on. And it is vain for the individualist to kick against these pricks. In a highly organized community where each is implicated with all and all with each, the influence of the individual, for good or for evil, on the well-being of his neighbour is more subtle and pervasive and operates on a larger scale than in a community which has a simpler and looser social organization; and the control of the individual by the State or the sub-state must therefore go far beyond the collection of taxes and the punishment of crime. That being so, it is imperative that if the State is not to encroach unduly on the spiritual freedom of its citizens, the ultimate source of authority should be the will of the people rather than of an autocrat or a ruling caste. When men were lightly governed, the existence of a central despotism was compatible with a large measure of spiritual freedom for the individual—freedom to be himself and to live his own life. But when, as now, government is necessarily, and rightly, inquisitorial, if it is also irresponsible, the pressure of the State on the individual may well develop, as it has done in Prussianized Germany, into a soul-destroying tyranny to which History has no parallel.

For this reason, if for no other, the advent of democracy may be foretold and welcomed. But though democracy has been coming for many generations, it has so far failed to arrive. I mean by this that, though we have the form of democracy in many countries, we are still far from the spirit of it. And in the absence of the spirit, the machinery of democratic government is all too easily captured by unscrupulous adventurers of various kinds,—piratical capitalists, self-seeking demagogues, professional wire-pullers, and the like. But why are we still far from the true spirit of democracy? Because we are still in the grip of feudalism. We are trying to graft democratic institutions on the stem of the feudal tradition; and our democratic aims and efforts are consequently blighted and perverted by the poisonous sap of our social life, the very sap which is supposed to feed and sustain them. A tradition which has been firmly established for centuries, and which is deeply rooted as well as widely spread, outlives by many generations its own apparent decease. The feudal lord, to whom the rest of the community looked up for authoritative direction and guidance, yielding to the temptations to which his commanding position exposed him, set an example of selfishness, rapacity, and arrogance, which was only too loyally followed, the result being that not individuals only, but also whole classes and whole nations, became infected with the virus of his characteristic vices.

Hence the tears that we are shedding now. The feudal lord is still, though we may not know it, our model. The individualism and materialism with which he inoculated us pervert every attempt that is made to purify government and reform society, vitiating public life with selfish ambitions and therefore with intrigue, chicanery, and corruption, infecting manners with a snobbishness which alternates between cringing servility and vulgar self-assertion, and causing a general scramble for power and possessions, in which the individual either fights for his own hand or combines with others for purposes of aggression or defence, in which class is arrayed against class, and nation (as in the present war) against nation. What hope is there for democracy so long as the feudal spirit—the desire for property as the basis of power and position and privilege, and therefore of freedom to enjoy "the good things of life"—is in the ascendant, and infects all the social strata down to and including the unpropertied masses, into whose hands authority, by a force akin to that of gravitation, is gradually passing?

There is one hope and one only for democracy—"a new

creature." We must be born again. Our ethical ideals must be reconstructed. The pursuit of ends which are outward and material, and therefore finite, must be subordinated to the pursuit of the end—the one end—which is inward and spiritual and therefore infinite. Self-development, as the central purpose of life, must take the place of self-aggrandizement. Self-surrender (as the first condition of self-development) must take the place of self-seeking and self-assertion. Devotion to the common weal will then be rebuilt on another and a more lasting foundation. As against the tyranny of the tribal consciousness, individualism has come to stay. But it will have to be transformed beyond recognition by being subordinated to a higher and remoter end. The complete absorption of the individual into the community, involving as it does the narrowing of his spiritual horizon and the circumscription of his expanding life by the tyranny of the State, is no longer either possible or desirable. A new kind of communal devotion, based on the suppression of selfishness by idealism, of the lower by the higher self, will come into being. A man will serve whatever cause or causes may seem to be worth serving because he has already devoted himself to the greatest of all causes. And he will live and die for his country because he is also a citizen of another country—the Kingdom of God.

Then the socialistic dream of "each for all, and all for each" will begin to be realized; and the economic problems which have so long pressed for and defied solution will begin to solve themselves. Till then the dream will remain a dream. And when it begins to be realized, we shall find that it is—what it was not and could not be in tribal days—a self-transcending ideal, an ideal which spontaneously and progressively widens the sphere of its own authority and influence. Until it has been transfigured by devotion to an infinite ideal, devotion to a community, a tradition, or a cause has an element of selfishness at the heart of it which will sooner or later warp the character of the devotee. The tribesman, as we have seen, might be a model of virtue, according to the standard set him by the tribal tradition, and yet be ruthless and treacherous in his dealings with the other tribes. And the French nobleman of pre-Revolution days might be unswervingly true to his own aristocratic traditions, might be the soul of loyalty and honour, a devoted husband, a loving father, a faithful friend, and yet be so inhuman in his attitude towards the bulk of his fellow-countrymen that he could find no better name for them than *canaille*, a name which was charged with contempt and antipathy and aloofness. When we return to the lost ideal of " each for all and all for each," we shall find that if it is to be a possession for ever the word *all* will have to widen its meaning till it carries us at last beyond the furthest horizon of human thought. And we shall find that if that ideal is to regulate the relation between the individual and the community, it will also have to regulate the relation between the lesser and the larger community, till at last loyalty becomes religion, and all communities, from the least to the largest, claim devotion from their members because they themselves are members of a yet larger community and live for it and in it and through it, giving it unstinted service and receiving from it the quickening current of life.

This is indeed an infinitely distant goal. But, for that very reason, its claim upon us is irresistibly strong. And, infinitely distant though it be, it is towards its " high, white star " that the social reformer, if he would do anything of lasting value, must set his face. If he cannot dream of a pan-human community, of a brotherhood of the nations, the reforms that he may carry out within the limits of his own community will have in them, from their very inception, the germs of decay. The saying that

> It takes the ideal to blow a hair's-breadth off
> The dust of the actual

is a daring paradox, but it is also a profound and inspiring truth.

If men will grow in grace they will solve the problem of living happily together. And if they will learn to live happily together they will remove the most serious of all hindrances to growth in grace. The action (for good or for evil) of morals on politics is necessarily and accurately balanced by the reaction (for good or for evil) of politics on morals. It is through his unceasing effort to adapt himself to an environment which his own reactivity is ever modifying, that a man grows—in mind and spirit—grows healthily or unhealthily, vigorously or feebly, harmoniously or inharmoniously, well or ill. And his politico-social action is one of the chief means at his disposal for moulding and controlling, for giving form and character to his environment. History has fully proved that a social tradition which is clearly defined and has the weight of ages behind it may easily determine a man's whole moral outlook on life. The tribal and the feudal traditions are cases in point. We have seen that the goal of moral growth, at any rate from one point of view, is the outgrowth of all-embracing sympathy. In tribal times the community, by claiming for itself the whole of man's devotion and service, made the outgrowth of all-embracing sympathy impossible and therefore arrested moral growth. In feudal times, when a small minority could pride themselves on the possession of power and privilege and property and look down from that artificial pedestal on the mass of their fellow-citizens, despising them for the very disabilities which their own privileged position had imposed on them, thinking of them as the dust beneath their feet, speaking of them as a mob, a rabble, a *canaille*,—when the greed and selfishness of the ruling classes descended, by force of example, from stratum to stratum of society,—when fellow-feeling was almost wholly subordinate to caste-feeling, while the looseness of the social order was all the while encouraging an individualistic scramble for possessions, as the source of all that seemed to make life worth living,—what place was there—what place is there (for feudal influences still dominate our lives)—for the all-embracing sympathy which alone can humanize and moralize mankind? But I need not take pains to prove that politics react on morals as surely and as strongly as morals act (and react) on politics. The ultimate reason why "the world must be made safe for democracy" is that as irresponsible authority, by fostering materialism and egoism in high places, demoralizes first the rulers and then the ruled, so, by withholding freedom for self-development, it demoralizes first the ruled and then the rulers. It is not only in order to remedy injustice, to appease legitimate discontent, to diffuse comfort and material well-being, that we must work for political and social reform. It is also, and above all, in order to raise the moral standard, in order to foster the growth of the soul.

I am speculating somewhat largely. But there are two practical corollaries to my conclusions. The first is that if democracy, in the true sense of the word, is to come, Demos must submit to discipline,—not the discipline of mechanical drill, but the discipline of organized comradeship. He must obey the leaders whom he himself has chosen and obey the laws which he himself has made. If he will not do this, if he will allow individualism and egoism—ill weeds that grew apace in the soil and air of feudalism—to seduce him from loyalty to the community and to those who administer its affairs, democracy will degenerate into mob-rule, and mob-rule into anarchy, and the consequent demand for a "saviour of society" will re-establish irresponsible authority in high places, and throw back, perhaps for centuries, the cause of freedom and growth and life.

The second corollary is that if democracy is to come, we must be ready, each and all, to shoulder the burden which its coming will lay upon us. No man is entitled to stand aside from public life.[1] To do so is a refinement of selfishness. In countries which are nominally democratic, it is customary for men of honour and refinement and culture to renounce politics on account of the jobbery, the corruption, the trickery, the intrigue, the sordid aims, the nefarious practices which seem to be of its essence, and with which,

[1] Not even the youngest child. If society is to be reformed, the reformation of it must be begun in the nursery and the schoolroom. The social instinct which is latent in every child must be allowed and encouraged to unfold itself. In the feudalized type of education which still prevails in this and other countries the child is compulsorily desocialized (see Part IV, Chapter VI), and the child is father to the man. This is a matter on which I have already written, perhaps too often and perhaps (though I doubt if that is possible) too strongly. My excuse is that the social aspect of education is of supreme importance and that hitherto it has been almost entirely ignored. What is needed for the transformation of society is the transformation of the individual,—in other words, "a new creature"; and if the new creature does not come to the birth, or begin to come to the birth, in childhood, the chances are that he will never be born.

as they say, they do not wish to soil themselves. In taking up this quasi-monastic attitude they are doing their best to perpetuate and intensify the very evils which they see and deplore. They are allowing political power, with all its social and ethical implications, to fall into the hands of men who will make the worst possible use of it. They are encouraging the unscrupulous financier, the needy adventurer, the ambitious schemer, the professional demagogue, to exploit their fellow-citizens for base and selfish purposes of their own.[1] And their desire to keep themselves clean from the soilure of "the world" is, though they may not know it, as futile as it is immoral. It is immoral, because the sense of separateness, which is the very negation of sympathy, is the strongest of all hindrances to moral progress, to the expansion, through sympathy, of the growing soul. It is futile, because we *are* inextricably bound one with another, each with each and each with all, and are therefore doomed to be infected, sooner or later, with the very evil which our own fastidious aloofness, by selfishly shrinking from it, has helped to create. "The sin and the shame of the world are your sin and shame, for you are a part of it; your karma is inextricably interwoven with the great karma: and before you can attain knowledge you must have passed through all places, foul and clean alike. Therefore remember that the soiled garment you shrink from touching may have been yours yesterday, may be yours to-morrow. And if you turn with horror from it, when it is flung upon your shoulders, it will cling the more closely to you. The self-righteous man makes for himself a bed of mire."[2]

The philosophy of self-righteousness and social aloofness is vitiated by a fundamental misconception of human nature, the very misconception which it is the purpose of social and political reform to correct. The real basis of

[1] In the United States, where *Pecca fortiter* is an honoured maxim, it seems to be customary for unscrupulous capitalists and their legal and political henchmen to capture the machinery of democratic government—or at any rate *local* government—and use it for base and selfish purposes of their own, plundering and murdering their fellow-men without compunction, under cover of the letter of the law. See the works of Winston Churchill, Upton Sinclair, and other American novelists of the social reform school, *passim*.

[2] *Light on the Path*, by M. C.

democracy is the latent infinitude of man. Actually unequal in a thousand different ways, we are potentially equal because the unrealized possibilities, even of the least of us, are limitless. Freedom to realize those possibilities must therefore be the foundation of our political life. When that foundation has been securely laid, it will be possible for the sense of equality, and therefore of fraternity, to become the ruling principle of our social life. For freedom is the first condition of moral progress ; and the higher we raise our moral standard, the keener will be our sense of our shortcomings, or, in other words, of our unrealized possibilities, and the stronger will be our sense of oneness—through the infinitude which is common to all of us—with our fellow-man. When faith in human nature is strong enough to generate faith in the efficacy of freedom ; when the vision of the infinite in man is strong enough to generate the sense of all pervading equality ; when sympathy, the product and the proof of moral growth, is strong enough and large enough to generate the sense of all-embracing comradeship,—then we shall have the democratic spirit ; and without the democratic spirit no democratic institution can serve its purpose or endure. But faith in human nature, the sense of our own infinitude, and the expansion of sympathy are all bye-products of the growth of the soul. Therefore, if we would reform society we must first reform our own lives. And if we would purify politics we must first purify our own hearts. The Kingdom of Heaven is a community as well as an inward state. But if we would realize it as a community we must also realize it as an inward state.

CHAPTER VI

SPIRITUAL WELL-BEING

WE mean by mental well-being nearness to ideal truth. We mean by æsthetic well-being nearness to ideal beauty. We mean by moral well-being nearness to ideal good. What do we mean by spiritual well-being? I will answer this question, tentatively and provisionally, by saying that spiritual well-being is nearness to Ideal Reality. But what do we mean by ideal reality? Words necessarily fail us when we try to express the largest and deepest of all truths. Let me say, then, "with stammering lips," that I (for one) mean by ideal reality what is absolutely and intrinsically real; I mean self-existent, self-dependent, self-centred, self-contained reality: I mean the ideal of all ideals, the ideal synthesis of ideal truth, ideal beauty, ideal good; I mean the totality of things envisaged in their organic unity; I mean the living Whole, the All of Being, the Soul of the Universe; I mean, in a word, God. Nearness to God is spiritual well-being. Oneness with God is the last term in spiritual well-being, and therefore the last term in the ascending "series" of human happiness.

What then do we mean by God? We have identified ideal reality with God. Are we now to identify God with ideal reality? Must we be content to move to and fro between these two terms, defining each as the other? Is there no way of escape from this *impasse?* Let us see if we can find one.

On the mental plane God reveals himself as ideal truth. On the æsthetic plane, as ideal beauty. On the moral plane, as ideal good. On the mental plane the divine appeal is made to that blend of intuition and reason, of the heart and the head, which has been called "imaginative reason." On the æsthetic plane, to that blend of the heart and the senses which we call the sensuous imagination. On the moral plane, to that blend of the heart and the will which we call conscience. In each of these cases a particular aspect of the divine nature reveals itself to a particular side of human nature, to a particular organ of cognition, to a particular vehicle of consciousness. A luminous veil hangs between the two natures, a veil which belongs, as it were, to both. On the spiritual plane this veil of separation begins to fade away. What is uttermost and innermost begins to reveal itself, not as ideal truth, not as ideal beauty, not as ideal good, but in its own essential nature,—for this is what we mean by ideal reality. And it makes its appeal, not to any one organ of cognition, not to any one side of man's being, but to the soul of man in its totality, to the soul acting as its own organ of cognition, acting through its whole "apperceptive mass." In other words, God, as such, reveals himself to man, as such. The "Oversoul" reveals itself to the soul.

Can we get behind this conception? Perhaps we can. But let us first ask ourselves what are the distinctive signs of spiritual well-being. There is one sign which cannot be mistaken,—*inward peace*. By inward peace, I mean the peace which is the counterpart, not of repose in finality but of repose in the infinite. Repose in finality is a sleep, from which one must sooner or later awake if it is not to deepen into the sleep of death. Repose in the infinite is the very fulness of life. The man who has found inward peace has attained to equilibrium, not to stagnation. The scale of his activities is so great that the noise and turmoil of what is usually counted as life no longer disturb him. Now and henceforth he

> looks on tempests and is never shaken.

"No array of terms can say how entirely at peace I am about God and about death." So speaks the poet of cosmic optimism. If we cannot echo his words and add a fervent *Amen* to them, we are still far from the Kingdom of God.

But how few of us are at peace about God and about death! Ideally, trust in God is of the very essence of religious faith. Actually, religious faith is seldom strong enough to rise to the level of reposeful trust. The man who is consciously religious is, as a rule, tortured with distrust of the Deity whom he worships. He thinks of him as a God of wrath, as an exacting creditor, as a vindictive tyrant, as one who demands much and is extreme to mark what is done amiss. He thinks of himself as a debtor who cannot meet his obligations, as an offender who has incurred the extremest of all penalties, as a brand to be snatched, if possible, from the burning. He tries to find out on what terms God will cancel the debt which he, the debtor, cannot pay, will remit the penalty which he, the offender, has incurred. With this end in view, he studies his sacred Scriptures; he consults professional advisers of various kinds,—doctors of the law, priests, casuistical experts, and the like. He wonders if he has succeeded in propitiating God and averting his vengeful anger. He hopes for the best, but continues to fear the worst.

Or, if he does trust God, his faith in him is racial, national, sectarian, not cosmic, not even human. He trusts him as the God of Israel, as the God of Christendom, as the God of Islam, not as the God of the Universe. He trusts him because the religious community to which he belongs enjoys the special favour of God. He trusts him because he himself is a Catholic, a Presbyterian, a Plymouth Brother. He cannot bring himself to trust him because God is the Father of all men and because he himself is a man.

The truth is that the selfishness of the undeveloped man, his longing for finality, his desire for possession, follow him into the sphere of religious belief and practice. The God whom he worships is *his* God—the God of his church, of his sect, of his nation, of his tribe. He is the friend of his friends, the enemy of his enemies. Through the institution or community to which he belongs he has proprietary rights in God, he enjoys a monopoly of his favour. In the Religious Wars of the sixteenth and seventeenth centuries the God of the Catholics was on one battle front, the God of the Protestants on the other. To-day the Mussulman slaughters the Armenian, the Jew, the Greek, *ad majorem Dei gloriam*; and the German Emperor is confident of victory because "the Lord of Creation above is an unconditional and avowed ally on whom [the German people] can absolutely rely."

It is because the God whom he worships is *his* God that the "orthodox" believer is so seldom at peace about him. We are never wholly at peace about the things that we possess. Our title to them may be insecure. They may be taken away from us. They may deteriorate with time. They may disappoint our expectations. We may cease to care for them. They may fail us in various ways. The man who prides himself on his orthodoxy, who flatters himself that his God is the true God, has all the time a haunting sense of insecurity. The fact that other persons worship other Gods seems to invalidate in some degree the claim of his own God to absolute supremacy; and the very fanaticism and intolerance with which he tries to make good that claim bear witness to the doubt and distrust which, unknown to him, are corroding his heart.

If selfishness is the beginning and end of immorality, if it contracts the mind and the heart and arrests the growth of the soul, what limit will there be to its influence for evil when the form that it takes is the desire to appropriate God? The answer to this question rests with the history of religion in all countries, and especially in those which acknowledge the overlordship of the "jealous God" whom Israel revealed to mankind. That it should have been possible, that it should still be possible, for men to commit the foulest crimes against their fellow-men, and yet to believe, in all sincerity, that by doing so they were serving and pleasing God, proves to demonstration that the desire to appropriate God, by sanctifying selfishness, tends to raise it to the highest imaginable power, to so high a power, indeed, that at last the worship of God becomes the worship of the Devil. And if we mean by the worship of the Devil the apotheosis of selfishness, then I am by no means sure that it is not a further stage in Devil-worship to believe, as many virtuous and respectable persons have done, and still do, that only a remnant of the human race will be "saved," and that it is the whole duty of each of us to strive by every means in his power to gain admission into that exclusive circle.

In the jealous desire to appropriate the favour of the jealous God, the cult of finality, which is man's besetting weakness, reaches the last term of its malignant activity. Shrinking from the too great adventure of expanding into the infinite, through the realization of his own limitless possibilities, man tries, by establishing proprietary rights in God, to contract the infinite within the limits of his own unexpanded self. Of all the demoralizing influences which man is fated to introduce into his own life, this audacious attempt to delimit the infinite is the most demoralizing; and because its range is as wide as that of life, and because it admits of endless transformation, it goes far towards guiding and controlling the rest.

The antidote to the desire for possession is the desire to be possessed. No man can be at peace about God who is taking part in the scramble for possession of him. And only those who are at peace about God have attained to spiritual well-being. He who would find God must wait to be possessed by him. If he will not do this, his quest will be in vain. And while he is waiting for that supreme consummation, he must try to make himself worthy to welcome the divinest of all guests. How is this to be done? By practising self-surrender, by learning to lose self. But the self-surrender must be of a different kind from what is usually practised. The disinterested seeker for ideal truth learns to master self in a particular field of its activity; he learns to suppress a particular inclination—the desire for fixity and finality in the sphere of ultimate belief. But though, in suppressing that desire, he completely masters self, he does not master the whole of self. His effort will probably react, in greater or less degree, on his whole character; but it will not lead to the last term of self-surrender. Fluidity of belief can co-exist with æsthetic insensibility and even with moral selfishness. But if a man would be possessed by God, his surrender of self must be complete in both senses of the word. *The whole of self must be wholly surrendered.*

Now we have a special name for such total self-surrender. We call it *love.* The essence of love is entire loss of the entire self. Herein it differs from sympathy. The man who has attained to all-embracing sympathy lives in the lives of others. But he also lives in his own life, being able in some sort to enter into the life of his neighbour through the very vividness of his own. The man who loves his fellow-men (in the fullest sense of the word *love*) has lost his own life, but has found it again in the lives of others. In the passion of personal love—of man for woman, of woman for man—the loss of self, while the passion lasts, is complete. The very purpose of the passion, from one point of view, is to reveal love (with all its infinite possibilities) to man, to tell him how far self-loss can go and what it really means.

> Learn by a mortal yearning to ascend,
> Seeking a higher object. Love was given,
> Encouraged, sanctioned, chiefly for that end,
> For this the passion to excess was driven,
> That self might be annulled : her bondage prove
> The fetters of a dream, opposed to love.

But the passion, as a passion, as an ecstasy, as utter loss of self, is necessarily short-lived. And there is no direct path from it to all-embracing love. As a revelation and an inspiration, it has done and will do its work. But the path to all-embracing love lies through all-embracing sympathy.

In other words, spiritual well-being is the crown and consummation of moral well-being. It is easy to make light of morality ; but though we may and must transfigure it, we cannot otherwise transcend it. Nietzsche, the prophet of anarchism, dreamed of passing " beyond good and evil." He might as well have dreamed of passing beyond life and death. We mean by moral good what makes for union ; and we mean by moral evil what makes for disunion. This is the fundamental difference between the two ; and it is a difference which holds good even on the highest imaginable level of existence. The ideal consummation of moral good is love ; and love is the supreme principle of unity, of integration, in Nature. The ideal consummation of moral evil is hate ; and hate is the supreme principle of disunion, of disintegration, in Nature. Love is stronger than hate, good is stronger than evil, because union is strength and disunion is weakness. An army of devils, even if each of them had a master mind and a master will, would always be vanquished by an army of angels, because the former, disintegrated by the centrifugal force of hate, would become a disorganized host of self-seeking individualists, whereas the latter would be automatically disciplined and organized by love. It is love which makes the totality of things a cosmos, a universe, a living whole. But it is from moral good that we must advance to the spiritual good which is its consummation; it is from sympathy that we must advance to love, and it is from love of man that we must advance to love of God. "If a man loveth not his brother whom he hath seen, how can he love God whom he hath not seen?" This is not to say that love of man is commensurate with love of God. The two loves are in a sense incommensurable. But when a man has learned to love his fellow-men, he will find that his love is spontaneously transcending its own limits and widening out into cosmic love, into love of God. And then he will learn that love of God, love of the infinite which is in man—and not in man only—was all the while at the heart of the sympathy with others which widened in due season into all-embracing sympathy, and was then transfigured, first into love of man, and last into love of God. Then he will be ready to receive the Divine Lover: and he will know that his love of God is something more than the response of his soul to the love of God for him; that in some mysterious sense it *is* that divine love; that, in the last resort, God is both the Lover and the Beloved; in fine, that God is Love,

> no more, since more can never be
> Than just love.

When he has learned this lesson, he will have attained to the fullest measure of spiritual well-being, for he will have found his true self in oneness with God.

CHAPTER VII

BEYOND WELL-BEING

LOVE is the consummation of spiritual well-being. When I say this I come near to saying all that need be said. For spiritual well-being—the well-being of the spirit of man, of the soul in its unity and totality—is the consummation, not of moral well-being only but of well-being in general and of each of its many aspects. It follows that every movement towards well-being, so far at least as it is an adventure into the infinite, finds its fulfilment in love. Even the thirst for knowledge, the satisfaction of which is mental well-being, may slake itself at the fountain of love. For the supreme object of knowledge is Supreme Reality; and we mean by Supreme Reality the unity of the Universe, the synthesis of all things in God. To attain to knowledge of God is therefore to attain to the summit of mental well-being. But how is this to be done? To think worthily about God is beyond our power. To know about God, as the physicist knows about air or water, is so infinitely impossible that to aspire to such knowledge is to profane the Divine. If we are to know God we must become one with him. There is no other pathway to our goal. Knowledge, in the ordinary sense of the word, implies a distinction between subject and object, which is provisional, not final, and which breaks down completely when we lean upon it with the full weight of our thought. The ideal of knowledge is oneness with the thing known. I know the soul of a friend, not by dissecting it with a scalpel or studying it under a microscope, but in and through the sympathy which draws our souls together and makes mine in some sort one with his. In like manner I know the Cosmos or totality of things, not by means of scientific investigation or philosophical reflection, but by becoming one with what is real in it, by touching the spiritual pole of its being, in other words, by losing myself in love of God. When I so lose myself, my mind is possessed with ideal truth.

And not with ideal truth only. What is ideal truth for the mind is ideal beauty for the heart. The gratification of æsthetic sensibility constitutes æsthetic well-being. But if æsthetic sensibility is to be fully gratified—in the sense of realizing that it can never be gratified—it must learn to transcend itself, it must become an ardour, a passion, a pursuit. When the appeal of Supreme Reality to the sensuous imagination draws forth the response of disinterested delight; when vision becomes revelation; when the æsthete becomes the artist, and the artist becomes creative, in and through his desire to tell others what he has seen and felt,—then æsthetic well-being loses itself in spiritual well-being because it has already lost itself in love.

The development of moral into spiritual well-being has already been traced. The secret of that inevitable development is that love is the apotheosis of sympathy, and therefore the fulfilling of the moral law. In transforming itself into spiritual well-being through the medium of love, moral well-being prepares the way for the advent of the social Kingdom of Heaven by providing for social life the only foundation which is both firm and sure. The truth of this statement is, I think, self-evident. If love could become the master law of man's being, all social problems would spontaneously solve themselves.

Along whatever road, then, we may travel in quest of well-being, we find that the goal, the ideal goal, of that road is love. In attaining to that goal do we pass beyond well-being? I cannot help asking this question; but I know not how to begin to answer it.

Beyond well-being. What do these words mean? Is there a beyond? If there is no beyond, well-being is not well-being, for it cannot transcend itself. If there is a beyond, it is a higher development of well-being, and therefore it is no beyond.

Spiritual well-being is the summit and perfection of all well-being. The consummation of spiritual well-being is therefore the summit and perfection of happiness. The man who has found his true self in oneness with God has grown to the fulness of his ideal stature. He has carried the process of growing to the last term of its ascending series, and has therefore won the prize of supreme happiness, the prize which he set out to win. So one feels impelled to conclude. But may one rest in this conclusion ? Is not the last term in the process of soul-growth infinity ? Has not the adventure into the infinite ended in the adventurer losing himself —and finding himself—*in* the infinite ? And if so, has not well-being been carried so far that it has at last transcended itself ? When a man has lost himself in love of God, will not the ideas of well-being and happiness have retired of their own accord into the background ?

More than forty years ago, when Moody and Sankey, the American evangelists, came to this country, a friend of mine who had come under their influence was in great trouble about his soul. He feared lest he should be " lost " and wondered how he was to be " saved." When he had confided his trouble to me, I tried to console him by saying : " What does it matter whether you or I are lost so long as it is well with God ? " There our dialogue ended. My protest fell on deaf ears. I cannot tell how I came to utter it. I had no theory of things in those days which countenanced, or came anyway near to countenancing, the complete self-effacement that I advocated. I had never heard of Brother Lawrence, the Carmelite Monk of the seventeenth century, who liberated his soul from the haunting fear of being damned, by saying to himself : " Whatever becomes of me, *whether I be lost or saved,* I will always continue to act purely for the love of God." I can only suppose that my words surged up of their own accord from some occult depth of my subconscious self. But I think there was a deep truth at the heart of them. In Clough's familiar lines :

> It fortifies my soul to know
> That though I perish, truth is so ;
> That howsoe'er I stray and range,
> Thou art the same and dost not change.
> I steadier step when I recall
> That, if I slip, thou dost not fall.

The same truth is expressed in other words. In the saying of the Chinese sage, " Never will I enter into final peace alone, but always and everywhere will I suffer and strive until all enter with me," it is expressed in another notation. My words were, I imagine, an instinctive protest against the religious individualism with which Israel's attempt to monopolize the God of the Universe has filled the Western world. If the scramble for material possessions demoralizes all who take part in it, what word will describe the deadening influence of the scramble for "salvation" which goes on in the name of religion? The least that one can say of it is that it despiritualizes the spirit of man. Until a man can say with his whole heart: "I am content to be a transient flicker of God's eternal flame. I am content to be nothing so long as God is everything"; until a man can say to God, "Thy will be done, even though it be to my own undoing," the surrender of the individual to the universal soul is not complete.

A man will readily sacrifice his physical life in order to save the lives of others. Men who have earned the bliss of Nirvana will renounce it (so Buddhist sages tell us) in order that they may return to earth and help their fellow-men. Is there any reason why a man should not be willing to be "lost," if by making this last sacrifice he could help others to be "saved"? It is easier to ask this question than to answer it. Such an extremity of self-surrender as I have in mind is at once imaginable and unimaginable. A man might conceivably devote himself to "perdition" for the benefit of other souls. But his effort to achieve perdition (if I may use such a phrase) would of necessity defeat itself. For his sublime self-sacrifice would be the last term in the process of self-losing; and the more completely a man loses himself, the more completely will he be possessed by God. And to be possessed by God is to be saved, in a sense which goes far beyond all that we have ever meant or could ever mean by salvation. Therefore the more a man tries to kill out the desire for happiness, the happier he will be. When Brother Lawrence gave up thinking about his own salvation and made up his mind always "to act purely for the love of God," he thenceforth "passed his life in perfect liberty and continual joy." Life, as we live it, is a succession of practical paradoxes. The last and the greatest of these is that the ideas of well-being and happiness are ever urging us to pass beyond their own limits, and yet, when we try to do so, insist on following us wherever we go. This paradox opposes a barrier to my thoughts which they can neither face nor turn. They must therefore be content to accept defeat.

I will now set forth in a few sentences the main argument of this book. I have been trying to discover the secret of happiness. I have assumed that happiness is definable as the sense of well-being. My meditations have convinced me that the way to well-being is the way of soul-growth ; that the way of soul-growth is the way of self-surrender (since, in the course of growth, self has again and again to be outgrown and left behind) ; that complete loss of self (the counterpart of the complete finding of self) is therefore the perfection of well-being ; and that the sense of such well-being is perfect happiness. This, as it seems to me, is the conclusion of the whole matter. But is it the final conclusion ? Is the pursuit of happiness compatible with complete loss of self ? Is not the idea of happiness the last vestige of that love of self which must be effaced before the loss of self can become complete ? Such questions flash from time to time upon one's mental vision. The answer to them, if indeed they will tarry for an answer, is, as we have just seen, a baffling paradox. If it is true that the desire for happiness must be renounced for the loss of self to be complete, it is equally true that in complete loss of self man finds his highest happiness. This means that for the present, at any rate, we cannot transcend even in imagination the ever-receding limits of the world of thought and action which comes under the control of the idea of happiness. But will it always be so ? Is the idea to be accepted as final ? Perhaps not. Perhaps the day will come when man will have climbed high enough to see beyond even its immense horizon. And perhaps, when that day comes, a graver and grander conception of destiny will begin to ascend, like a new constellation, from the dark underworld of his buried life.